The Morning Chronicle's

LABOUR AND THE POOR

Volume VIII

THE MINING AND MANUFACTURING
DISTRICTS OF WALES

The Morning Chronicle's

LABOUR AND THE POOR

VOLUME VIII

THE MINING AND MANUFACTURING DISTRICTS OF WALES

FROM OUR
SPECIAL CORRESPONDENT

Edited By
Rebecca Watts & Kevin Booth

Ditto Books
www.dittobooks.co.uk

First Published by Ditto Books 2020

© Ditto Books 2020

A catalogue record for this book is available
from the British Library

ISBN 978-1-913515-08-9 (hardback)
ISBN 978-1-913515-18-8 (paperback)

Cover Image:
Nant Y Glo (Monmouthshire)
From "The History of Wales"
Bernard Bolingbroke Woodward
Published 1853
Image courtesy of The British Library

"*Thieves, prostitutes, vagrants, the idle, the reckless, and the dissolute, here live in a miserable companionship. This neighbourhood formed the main scene of our inquiries; and what I that day saw of misery, degradation, and suffering, I shall remember to the end of my life.*"

Contents

List of Illustrations

List of Illustrations

From "The Book of South Wales, the Wye, and the Coast"
Samuel Carter Hall
Published 1861
Courtesy of The British Library

"Thieves, prostitutes, vagrants, the idle, the reckless, and the dissolute, here live in a miserable companionship. This neighbourhood formed the main scene of our inquiries; and what I that day saw of misery, degradation, and suffering, I shall remember to the end of my life."

Preface

This work attempts to be a faithful reproduction of the "Labour and the Poor" letters as printed in *The Morning Chronicle*. Only obvious typographical errors and omissions have been corrected. Variations in the spelling and hyphenation of words have largely been retained. We hope any such inconsistencies prove to be of some historical interest to the reader.

As much as possible we have tried to recreate the original layout and styling of the text and all factual tables have been reproduced as closely to the originals as possible with only minimal alterations made where necessary to improve readability in the e-book format.

Not all letters were titled. Where missing we have added titles to the Table of Contents to assist navigation and explanation of content. The letters themselves are as per the originals.

A handful of illustrations have been added to each volume. These did not appear in the original text but hopefully provide added interest.

R. W.
K. B.

Introduction

In 1849 a leading London-based newspaper, *The Morning Chronicle*, undertook an investigation into the working and living conditions of the poor throughout England and Wales in the hope that their findings might lead to much needed change.

The reputed catalyst for their "Labour and the Poor" series was an article written by Henry Mayhew recording a journey into Bermondsey, one of the most deprived districts of London, which was printed in September 1849. Following this it was proposed that an in-depth investigation be carried out and "Special Correspondents", the investigators, were selected and distributed around the country. The first article or "Letter" appeared on the 18th of October 1849 and the series would run for almost 2 years and 222 letters.

The well-known and respected writers and journalists recruited for the task included Henry Mayhew who was assigned to the Metropolitan districts, Angus Bethune Reach to the Manufacturing districts, Alexander Mackay and Shirley Brooks to the Rural districts and Charles Mackay to investigate the cities of Birmingham and Liverpool. The author of the letters from Wales is as yet unknown.

The "Labour and the Poor" letters were extremely popular at the time, being widely read throughout the nation and even abroad. The revelations in them caused quite a stir amongst the middle and upper classes of Victorian society. *Letters to the Editor* poured in with donations for specific cases of distress that appeared in the letters and also for the general alleviation of the suffering of the poor. A special fund was set up by *The Morning Chronicle* to collect and distribute these donations.

These *Letters to the Editor* have been included in this series, predominantly in the Metropolitan district volumes whose letters elicited the majority of responses. They provide a unique window into the thoughts and sentiments of the Victorian readership as they react to the incredible accounts of misery and desperation being unveiled.

The Morning Chronicle's extraordinary and unsurpassed "Labour and the Poor" investigation provides an unparalleled insight into the people of the period, their living and working conditions, their feelings, their language, their sufferings and their struggles for survival amidst the poverty and destitution of 19th century Britain. An investigation of such magnitude had never before been attempted and the undertaking was truly of epic proportions. Its impact at the time was profound. Its historical importance today is without question.

Map of The Coal Field of South Wales

LABOUR AND THE POOR.

THE MINING AND MANUFACTURING DISTRICTS OF SOUTH WALES.

[FROM OUR SPECIAL CORRESPONDENT.]

MERTHYR TYDFIL.

LETTER I.

Charged with the duty of reporting upon the condition of the labouring classes and the poor throughout the Principality of Wales, I direct my attention, in the first instance, to the great iron-works and collieries of South Wales—because these occupy by far the most important and interesting division of the country, as regards the purposes of my inquiry, and also because, as will be seen in the course of my Letters, they stand most in need of an early investigation.

In order to convey to the reader a clear and just comprehension of the economy of the mining and manufacturing systems, as at present working in South Wales—without which he cannot fairly judge of the relative position, and the reciprocal claims and duties, of the workman and his employer—it is first necessary to give some account of the vast tract of mineral deposits which affords a field for the labour of the one, the capital of the other, and, under a proper state of things, the profit of both. This done, I shall commence my inquiries with Merthyr, the metropolis of the iron works, which affords the best opportunity for witnessing the conduct and deportment of the master and the workman, and for noting the advantages and benefits, the hardships, vices, and imperfections, which characterize the operation of the mining and manufacturing systems as long settled in these populous districts. The general plan which I intend to follow will develop itself in due course; at present it is enough to say, that I shall take the various points for observation in the order in which they naturally present themselves to a person engaged in such an inquiry, who seeks only for material and pertinent facts.

The tract of country popularly known as "the Mineral Basin of South Wales," extends from Pontypool in Monmouthshire on the east side, through Glamorganshire, running, with its southern edge, by Risca below Caerphilly, through Pentyrch on the river Taff, by Llanharry, north of the towns of Cowbridge and Bridgend—passing under the waters of Swansea Bay, by Taibach near Aberavon—appearing again between Swansea and the Mumbles—and, after crossing the peninsula of Gower, running by Llanelly and Kidwelly in Carmarthenshire, and shaping its course for St. Bride's Bay, which forms its western extremity. To the north it stretches away through the Gwendraeth Valley, by Llandebie, Hirwain, Merthyr, Bute, Sirhowy, Nantyglo, and so round to Pontypool. Its *mean* length, for the purposes of calculation, may be laid at seventy miles, and its average breadth at twenty—which gives an area of fourteen hundred square miles. Throughout this vast space, above a thick bed of carboniferous limestone, the numerous strata of coal and iron-stone are deposited. Intervening between the limestone and the ironstone measures, lies a stratum of millstone grit—another called the Farewell Rock—and a third of sandstone so hard and durable as to be used in the construction of the smelting furnaces. Upon this repose the whole of the iron and coal measures. These rocks "crop out," as it is termed, at the edges of the coal-field, and indicate, by their appearance, its limits. In many places the coal comes actually to the surface. From the surface coal descends at an angle, which is called its dip, towards a point, which is not, however, the centre of the basin. On the north side, the angle of inclination is seldom more than ten degrees; but on the south the dip is rarely under thirty-five, and frequently it is as much as forty degrees; consequently the minerals are workable to greater advantage, and at smaller expense, on the north than on the south side of the field. The deepest part of the basin is in the neighbourhood of Neath, a little to the west of its centre; the lowest strata are there nearly 700 fathoms below the outcrops of some of the superior strata in the more hilly districts. At a depth so prodigious, it is obvious that mines could not be worked with profit. But a fortunate circumstance has rendered a vast breadth of this part of the coal-field easily available, where otherwise it would have been unserviceable. Nearly along the deepest part there occurred at some remote period a convulsion of nature, which, running east to west, has uplifted the rocky strata with the superposed minerals to the surface, dividing the great basin into what are called the north and south troughs. This friendly help to the miner, called by Conybeare "the anticlinal axis, or elevated line of division," enters the basin near Moidart, crossing the Ebbw river, the Sirhowy, by Velin Vach, and the valley of the Taff at Newbridge—passing through Blaen Ogwr, Cwm Garw, Maesteg, Cwm Avon, on to Baglan—and running out of the coal measures, near Swansea. Within the range of this line of elevation the coal strata have been thrown up and divided into masses, north and south, which slope away gable-shaped, like the roof of a house. The dip caused by this subterrene disturbance to the respective troughs on either side, is at an angle of from 10 to 20 degrees throughout the greater part of the coalfield eastward of Cwm Avon; and the minerals are as easily worked as at the outcrop on the northern edge of the basin.

The perpendicular depth of the iron and coal strata is, according to De la Beche, 11,000 in the northern, and 8,000 feet in the southern trough—making a difference of 3,000 feet between the two outcrops. Disposed at irregular distances within these limits lie the several strata of coal and iron. Lowest and most valuable of these are the iron-stone measures, comprising the "black pins" ore and the "white ash" coal; next in ascending order come the Pennant measures, which contain the black-band iron-stone, beds of fire clay, and the "brown ash" coals; lastly, and nearest to the surface, are the Mynyddyslwyn measures, which yield the "red ash" coals. It is the produce of this series which has been so extensively exported from Newport during the past century. Each of these groups contains several veins of coal, varying in thickness from one to ten feet. Twelve of the veins run from three to ten feet thick, making an average of 72 feet, and the remainder from one foot to three feet, so that we have 95 feet as the average thickness of the beds of coal under the surface of 1,400 square miles—a quantity which, taking our annual consumption at 20,000,000 of tons, would supply our demands (assuming the whole to be workable) for two thousand years. A cubic yard of coal weighs about a ton, and a cubic yard of stacked iron-stone, of the ordinary quality, about 35 cwt.

It remains to speak of the iron-stone. This valuable mineral is found below the coal-measures, and interstratified amongst them. It varies in thickness from an inch to ten inches; it presents various appearances, but generally is a dark-coloured, compact, and heavy stone. It is of two kinds—argillaceous or clay, and carboniferous or blackband ironstone. Carbonic acid, alumina, and silica are the substances which chiefly compose the former—carbonic acid, alumina, silica, and bitumen, the latter. We shall see, hereafter, when I come to treat of the process of smelting and manufacturing iron, the interesting mode in which the workman, ignorant of chemistry, and following only the sure guides of practice and experience, disengages the metal from the carbonic acid, the flint, and alum, with which it is incorporated. The average yield of Welsh iron-stone, according to the analysis of Dufresnoy and Berthier is—usual ore, 31.4; rich ore, 42.0 per cent.; the same calcined stands 44.7 and 60.0. The abundance and richness of this invaluable mineral in the Welsh coal-field are testified by Mr. Moses, a well-known mining-engineer, in a very useful little book, written with the purpose of giving his peculiar views of the geology of the Welsh mineral basin to the scientific world. He says:—

"In the district between the river Taff and Swansea bay there has been found, by actual workings in those places some distance apart, a thickness of upwards of 100 inches of ironstone in 100 yards depth of ground, yielding on an average 35 per cent. of iron. There is to be observed in these lower rakes of ironstone a *pin*, which is designated by the miners *tobacco pin*, from its resemblance to a roll of twisted tobacco. In the Merthyr district, and along the north and east outcrop, it accompanies the *rough pin* between the second and third vein of coal, in ascending order in the coal strata. On the south outcrop it is met with between two seams of coal, identical in position with those it intervenes on the north crop, and known as the two *Criburs*. We also find in this series nodules of ironstone, comprising compartments with the impressions of plants, and sometimes leaves, as it were, around which argillaceous matter and carbonate of iron have been collected, forming, in many instances, balls of ironstone from six to eighteen inches in diameter. Perhaps the most interesting nodule of ironstone to be met with in this series is that which presents when broken an oval-shaped cavity of from two to three inches in diameter. In the invert dome of this we have repeatedly observed a crystal of wonderful brilliancy, many of which were little inferior in lustre to a sudrass, a Sulbampoor diamond of the fourth class. It is rather a remarkable circumstance that diamonds of the first water are occasionally found imbedded in iron ores in South America, occupying a drusy cavity in much the same manner as the crystal met with in the ironstone nodule just mentioned."

I was shown some of these crystals a few days ago—they were of hexagonal form, varying in size from that of a small peppercorn to that of a large pea. Some were as pellucid as clear water—one in particular, a small one, showed the prismatic colours like the diamond, sparkling most brilliantly. They were collected by an ironmaster named Wayne, as the best he had met with. There are few miners who have not some taste for natural history; many possess specimens of these crystals. The miner's cabinet is his cupboard, where he keeps these little curiosities in a wine glass or a tobacco-box.

The approach to the mineral district of South Wales lies on all sides, except the north, over richly cultivated flats and fertile slopes; but when you reach the point where the limestone appears, upon which the iron and coal repose as above stated, suddenly the face of the landscape changes—and there rise before you lofty barriers of rocky mountains, nearly destitute of cultivation, whose storm-blanched summits and heather-clad declivities afford sustenance only to the heathcote and a few small sheep—all is dreariness and sterility. But the value of every acre of this land is immense. Mr. Moses states, in the book I have referred to, that he "is acquainted with landed property in the mineral basin of South Wales which at the present time is considered to be worth upwards of £100,000, and which could have been purchased fifty years since for less than £1,000." I was myself shown, by Mr. Joseph, of Plymouth works, on the side of the mountain facing the new forge at Duffryn, a small farm of fifty acres, which, as the deeds of conveyance show, was sold in the reign of Charles II. for £27; at present the lease of the minerals only, the surface being let separately, brings in upwards of £1,000 a year to the fortunate proprietor. This is but one of several striking instances of the increased value of property which have been pointed out to me.

It is for the most part in the valleys which convey the waters from the mountains southward to the sea, that the iron works are situated. Here they are surrounded with the materials they consume, for which there is an easy descent; while they at the same time have a facility of outlet for the manufactured iron to the port where it is shipped. The brawling and impetuous currents, during the course of ages, have worn deep hollows, laying bare, and in frequent instances dividing, the strata of minerals which the ground contains, so as to enable the miner to work by "levels"—that is to say by galleries driven horizontally into the body of the mountain. But in by far the greater number of instances the mines are worked by pits, and by the use of contrivances which in their proper place will be described.

There exist but scanty and imperfect materials for a history of the rise and progress of the coal-trade in South Wales. Indeed I may say, once for all, that the information to be gleaned from books regarding the iron as well as the coal trade in the Principality is very scanty, often conflicting, always ill-arranged, and generally insufficient. Mr. Porter,

though he gives several tables and much information relative to the
north country collieries, is silent respecting the Welsh. However, I
will do the best in my power to give an idea of the extent of the export
trade; and when, hereafter, I write upon the iron works, I shall show,
as far as I can, the rate of consumption in the manufacture of iron.

The ports of Newport and Cardiff are the principal points of outlet
for the Welsh coals. Within the past ten years the export has been
largely extended, owing in a great degree to the favour in which the
Welsh coals are held for steam purposes. Now that a scientific inquiry
by two of our most eminent geologists, at the instance of Parliament,
has established their superiority over all others for the use of the steam
navy, there can be no doubt that the demand, and consequently the
trade, will be greatly augmented. Immense quantities of coal are sent
by sea to Somersetshire, Devonshire, and Cornwall—while on the
land side the counties of Cardigan, Brecon, Radnor, and Hereford, are
mainly supplied from the Welsh coalfields. The following will show
the increase of the coal trade at the ports of Newport and Cardiff
from the year 1829 to 1843, both inclusive:—

		Tons.
1829...Coals sent to the ports of Newport and Cardiff		573,491
1839...Ditto	ditto	730,130
1843...Ditto	ditto	943,080

I have been unable to obtain returns for both ports subsequent
to 1843, but by a statement furnished to me by Mr. Forrest, of the
quantity of coals sent down the Glamorganshire Canal to the port of
Cardiff in 1848, the amount was then 436,981 tons. It would seem that
the rate of increase in the export of coal during the above interval of 15
years has been much greater at the port of Cardiff than at Newport.
Between 1829 and 1843 the increase at the port of Cardiff was not
less than 269,379 tons, while at Newport it was only 100,165 tons.
This may in part be accounted for by the superior accommodation
now afforded to shipping in the magnificent sea docks at Cardiff, as
compared with that of Newport. The increase calculated up to last
year, as regards Cardiff, was from 83,729, which was the quantity in
1829, to 436,981, making a total increase of 353,252 tons in the export
of 1848, as compared with that of 1829. Large shipments of coal are
also made from the ports of Swansea, Neath, and Porthcawl, of which
I can obtain no account; but the quantity shipped in the various Welsh

ports of the Bristol Channel may safely be set down at 2,000,000 tons a year.

I have said that a Government Commission had been charged with the duty of inquiring what coals are best suited for the purposes of the steam navy. This task was confided to Sir Henry de la Beche and Dr. Lyon Playfair, whose second report (just published) is now before me. The "calorific value" of Welsh coals, as compared with the Lancashire and Newcastle coals, is shown as follows:—

Welsh Coals . . . . 102·52
Newcastle . . . . 93·82
Lancashire . . . . 89·68

Their relative "economic value," as tested by the number of pounds of water evaporated by equal given quantities of coal, stands thus:—

Welsh Coals . . . . 29·87
Lancashire . . . . 25·93
Newcastle . . . . 25·78

I should here explain that in making this table I took the aggregate of the highest three numbers given as the result of the experiments on the several varieties of coal—thinking it a fairer mode of showing their relative worth than simply to select the return set against the best colliery of each of those great divisions of our coal-fields. It may be useful to the public to learn that the five Welsh collieries whose coals stand highest in value in the above cited report are—

Thomas's Merthyr.
Nixon's Merthyr.
Hill's Plymouth Work, Merthyr.
Aberdare Company's, Merthyr.
Gadly's nine-feet seam, Merthyr.

By this statement it will be seen that the best steam coals existing in this country are found in the immediate neighbourhood of Merthyr.

On the subject of iron smelting, and the quantity of coals consumed in the process, we are more fully informed, though the returns for the whole of the Principality have not been brought down later than 1840. In that year there were made in South Wales 505,000 tons of iron, in the smelting of which there were used 1,436,000 tons of coal, being something less than three tons of coal for every ton of iron produced; whilst in Staffordshire there were made 427,650 tons of iron at a consumption of 1,665,000 tons of coal. It is interesting to observe by this comparison how the comparatively limited experiments made under the superintendence of De la Beche and Playfair, as to the value of coals for rough purposes, are corroborated by the practical results of working on a stupendous scale, as in the iron works. The higher calorific value of the Welsh coal could not be more satisfactorily shown than by the number of tons used in smelting given quantities of iron in South Wales, compared with Staffordshire, as contrasted in the above statement. In fact, the Staffordshire coals appear not to have been admitted to the competition for the supply of the steam navy. The balance in favour of quantity and cost of production is largely in favour of Wales. It may be interesting to observe in this place, that the united produce of the ironworks in England and Wales is 1,155,400 tons a year. Of this, the share contributed by South and North Wales is 531,500—that by Staffordshire, 427,650 tons. Adding these amounts together, and subtracting the product from the total made in England and Wales, it will be found that the quantity made in Wales and Staffordshire comes within 196,250 tons of the total smelted in the remaining iron districts. The value and importance of the Welsh coal-fields, and the desirableness of perfecting their economy and further developing their immense resources, are, I think, abundantly shown by the facts and figures above given.

It is a happy coincidence, and worthy of remark, that the iron ore, the limestone, and the coal, each being a necessary element in the manufacture of iron, are found together, being raised from the same pits. With these may be enumerated the red sand-stone and peculiar clay from which the fire-bricks are made, for lining the furnaces, no other materials being capable of enduring the intense heat employed without fracture or fusion. It might have been that the ore, like that of copper, was to be found nowhere but at a distance from the fuel necessary for smelting it; in which case, as all our manufactures repose on our iron and coal, the expense of smelting being greater by the cost of transport than it now is, our productive industry would have been proportionally obstructed, and the national wealth would have been far less than it is at present.

A short sketch of the history and statistics of the iron trade, as it illustrates the advance of one of the most important and thriving branches of our manufactures, will hardly be considered out of place. In the year 1740, when charcoal was the only fuel used for the purpose of smelting iron, there were in England and Wales 59 furnaces, of which the annual produce was 17,350 tons. At that time the consumption so far exceeded the home manufacture, that it was computed that England imported annually 20,000 tons of foreign iron, of which 15,000 tons were from Sweden, and the remainder from Russia. For this we paid, mostly in money, £150,000. Petitions were presented to Parliament about that time, in which it was stated, as a reason why pig-iron from the American colonies ought to be admitted to the British market, that we "could not increase the quantity of bar iron we made, by reason of our woods being so far exhausted as to have greatly enhanced the price of cord-wood; but were we to import more pig-iron from America, and make less of it at home, we should be able, with the same quantity of wood we now consume, to make more bar iron at home."* About 1750, owing to the scarcity of wood, pit-coal came into use for smelting; but the imperfect method of "blasting," which operation was then performed by rude bellows, seldom permitted the produce of each furnace to exceed ten tons weekly, while in summer it fell below seven. In 1788 the number of tons made in England, Wales, and Scotland, had increased to 68,300, of which quantity 55,200 were smelted with coke, and the remainder with charcoal. At that time the number of furnaces had risen to 85. From that period, owing to the improvements in the steam-engine, and the substitution of cylinders for bellows in blasting, the advance was rapid. In 1796 there were in England, Wales, and Scotland, 121 furnaces, producing yearly 124,879 tons. The increase in 1806 was to 173 furnaces, yielding 258,206 tons; there were then in existence 233 furnaces, of which 60 were out of blast. In 1823 there were at work in Great Britain 259 furnaces, producing 442,066 tons. In seven years from 1823, the furnaces increased upwards of 100, about one-third of the total number. This differs, indeed, from a statement of Sir John Guest before a Parliamentary Committee, to the effect that the manufacture remained nearly stationary between 1823 and 1831, when it again advanced. But, according to the returns, there were at work in 1830 not fewer than 360 furnaces in England, Wales, and Scotland, the make from which was 678,418 tons—showing an increase of 101 in the number of furnaces, and of 236,351 tons of manufactured iron during the interval between 1823 and 1830. The quantity of iron made in 1836 was estimated at 1,200,000 tons. In 1840, as appears by a statement drawn

---

* Scrivener, p.171.

up by an iron-master named Jessop, there were in this country 402 furnaces in blast, of which 162 used the last improvement—hot-blast. The annual make of these furnaces was then 1,396,400 tons. Since that year no data, comprehending the whole of Great Britain, are furnished, by which the advance may be estimated; but, taking into consideration the impetus given to the trade by the vast extension of railways at home and abroad, during the past four years, it may safely be computed at one-third. Through the kindness of Mr. Robert Crawshay, and the obliging assistance of Mr. Forrest, of Navigation-house, Cardiff, I am enabled to show the increase which has taken place between 1840 and the present time, in eight of the ironworks, of which five are among the most important in the Principality. In the year 1840 there were conveyed down the Glamorganshire canal to Cardiff, the place of export, the following quantities of iron from the several works, as under:—

W. Crawshay	35,507
Pen-y-Darran Iron Company	16,130
Plymouth Forge Company	12,922
Aberdare Iron Company	10,327
Gadly's ditto	1,345
Brown, Lenox, and Co.	2,476
Taff Vale Iron Company	4,902
R. Blakemore (now Booker and Co.)	3,175
Tons	86,784

In the year ending the 31st December, 1848, there were carried down the same canal to the place of export from the above works the subjoined quantities:—

W. Crawshay	67,498
Pen-y-Darran Iron Company	21,180
Plymouth Forge Company	25,692
Aberdare Iron Company	19,652
Gadly's Iron Company	297
Brown, Lenox, and Co.	1,499
Taff Vale Iron Company	13,694
T. W. Booker and Co.	5,500
Tons	155,012

By these particulars it appears that the increase in the make of iron at the above works in the year 1848, as compared with the quantity they produced in 1840, is not less than 68,228 tons, being something more than 75 per cent.; and this notwithstanding the fact that the interval from 1841 to 1844 was one of great depression in the iron trade. I am sorry that I cannot render this account complete by the addition of the "make" of the Dowlais Iron Company, which is conveyed to the port of Cardiff by the Taff Vale Railway—since, up to the time of writing, I have not been favoured with the returns.

The total increase during the century extending from 1740 to 1840 appears to have been from 59 to 402 furnaces, and from 17,350 to 1,396,400 tons of manufactured iron—an advance which strikingly evidences the vast extension of our productive industry in this most important staple of commerce, and the proportionate enlargement of the national wealth.

I have already stated that the amount contributed by South Wales to the above total of the iron made in Great Britain in the year 1840, was 505,000 tons; and that the probable increase since that time may be estimated at a third. But were the markets propitious, the capabilities of this rich mineral basin are such as would admit of an indefinite extension in the working. At present there are miles along its southern and northern edges which offer numerous sites and abundant material for iron-works where none at present exist. This, however, is not a time for multiplying the works. The unsettled state of the Continent during the past two years, and the embarrassments of the railway companies, have greatly depressed the trade, and reduced wages. I have been unable to procure or construct a table of the fluctuations in the price of labour during the past ten years, but I shall give as much information hereafter as I can gather upon this point. In the meantime, the following statement, showing the export of manufactured iron during ten years up to 1843, from the ports of Cardiff and Newport, which are the great outlets for the produce of the South Wales iron-works, will also give, by the expansion or contraction of the "make," some idea of the fluctuations in the price of the labour, which in general advances or declines with the demand for iron:—

Number of tons of iron sent from the iron works of South Wales, to Cardiff and Newport, from 1834 to 1843 both inclusive:—

	Tons.		Tons.
In 1834	239,528	In 1839	307,584
1835	273,928	1840	326,442
1836	273,726	1841	260,380
1837	266,910	1842	310,420
1838	297,359	1843	324,688

Remembering the sensation created several years ago by the appli-cation of the "hot-blast" (which is air heated to a very high tempera-ture previously to its being used for blasting) to the smelting of iron, and the results that were then predicted in the event of its general adoption, I looked with some curiosity for the working of it when I came into this neighbourhood. To my surprise I nowhere found this greatly-vaunted improvement in operation. The chief recommenda-tion claimed for the hot-blast was the saving of fuel; but that which was a great consideration in Scotland, where the system was first tried, is of small account in Wales. In the former country there were re-quired 8 tons of the weak coke there made to smelt, with the cold-blast, one ton of iron; and it is stated that the same end has been ef-fected with hot-blast of a temperature sufficient to fuse lead, and with only 2¼ tons of raw coal, which undoubtedly is a vast improvement. In Wales, the coal being very strong, very abundant, and therefore cheap, there is not the same inducement for adopting this process; independently of which there exists amongst the iron-masters a prej-udice against it, founded on a belief that it does not produce such tough and serviceable iron. These circumstances sufficiently account for the adherence of the Welsh iron-masters to the old and long-tried system.

It is impossible to estimate with anything like accuracy the amount of capital embarked in the iron and coal trade throughout the Principality. The books which ought to afford such information are, on this point, as indeed on many others that require elucidation, totally silent. Could it be ascertained, the amount would astonish those who, not having seen the ironworks and collieries, have but a feeble idea of their magnitude, and of the resources necessary to work them. The large fortunes acquired by the established ironmas-ters tempted, more particularly within the last fifteen years, many capitalists to embark in the iron trade; and various public companies have also been established with this purpose; but an instance of complete success I cannot now call to mind, whilst of failures I could name several. In truth, whatever be the amount of capital to work with, a new establishment must be years before it can pay. The building of furnaces, smelting-houses, refineries, forges, mills, and engine-houses, and the erection of large and costly machinery, are by no means the heaviest items of expenditure; there is the lease and royalty in the minerals, and above all the heavy charges of sinking pits, driving levels, erecting steam-pumps, and whimsies, with the various other items attendant upon the under-ground workings. Without a sufficient number of pits open, it is in vain the endeavour to make works pay. There is, indeed, an observation common in the Principality, founded, as such remarks generally are, upon experience, that "fools open pits and works, but wise men step in and work them." And this, I believe, is really the case.

The number of persons of both sexes engaged in the iron works and collieries of Wales, are stated in the last census returns as under:—

Persons engaged in mining coal in Wales . 13,801
      ,,   ,,   in mining iron 1,522
      ,,   ,,   · in the manufacture of iron 3,966

Total 19,289

Such is the official return for 1841, but it was obviously much below the mark even then; in proof of which I may observe that at that time, when women were not prohibited by law from working in the mines, the number is stated to have been only 182—whereas, in three out of the four great iron works *at Merthyr only*, now that women are excluded from underground labour, there are at present employed, as the returns supplied to me show, no less than 545 in and about the works; an increase, in the face of a reason for a decrease, which cannot be accounted for by the extension of the trade. There are now employed in the works at Merthyr and Dowlais, under and above ground, about 20,000 hands.

The labour of these classes, from the highest to the lowest, is of the heaviest kind: often it is highly dangerous. To "win" and "get" the minerals at prodigious depths in the bowels of the earth, surrounded by a sulphurous and explosive atmosphere, and subject to accidents which no human sagacity can foresee nor any precaution avert; to convey the rough treasures to the surface; to break, cleanse, and calcine, to smelt, refine, and manufacture them—are the duties of the workman. For the successful accomplishment of these tasks, the requirements are— physical courage, strength, and endurance, and, above all, a fair degree of practical skill; these qualities are combined in him. Although capital is the motive power, it is upon the rude virtues of the workman that the entire system of the manufacture of iron practically relies. If our coal and iron form the substantial basis of our national opulence and power, he by whose skill and labour those minerals are produced ought at least to be well clothed and well fed, to have the means afforded him of educating and advancing his children, and of providing for his old age out of the produce of his labour whilst he is capable of work. It is my duty to inquire and ascertain if opportunity for all this is afforded him by the remuneration which he receives at the present time; and to show, as far as I may be able, the relation subsisting in these districts between the price of labour and the profits of capital. It is an arduous undertaking. I enter upon it with diffidence, but will perform it to the best of my power, without favour or affection to any party.

In no other part of the mineral district of South Wales are the peculiar characteristics of the population engaged in mining and the manufacture of iron so strikingly developed as at Merthyr; nor is there any other place which affords so favourable a point for observing the merits and defects of what may be comprehensively termed the economy of the iron works. I have, therefore, come to Merthyr, and I propose going in the first place, as a stranger would, over the town itself, noting its appearance particularly in regard to its sanitary condition, as this more immediately and powerfully affects the labouring classes and the poor than any other question—wages, perhaps, excepted.

The town of Merthyr Tydfil is situated amidst lofty mountains at the upper end of a narrow valley where the Morlais unites its waters with the Taff. Extending from Plymouth Works, on the main river, it follows the course of the Taff on the left up to Cyfarthfa; branching off at an intermediate point on the right, it skirts the precipitous valley of the Morlais up to Dowlais. It is a town of modern date; for, though a village known in Welsh history as the scene of the murder of a Christian Princess, Tydfil, by a party of Saxon pagans about the eighth century, it was not until some eighty years ago, when the attention of an enterprizing man named Bacon was directed to the coal and iron mines in this neighbourhood, that it began to enlarge. So light was the value at that time set upon property in this district, that Mr. Bacon obtained a ninety-nine years' lease of a tract eight miles in length and four in breadth, for a reserved rent of £200 per annum. In 1783, after having acquired immense wealth, he disposed of the remainder of his interest in leases, the greatest portion to Mr. Crawshay, the grandfather of the present owner of Cyfarthfa works, and the remainder to Mr. Hill, whose descendant now holds the Plymouth works. At different periods the works at Dowlais and Pen-y-Darran were established, and the town, from time to time, was enlarged, co-extensively with the advance and prosperity of the iron-trade. In 1796, there were in Merthyr, including Dowlais, nine furnaces; at present, there are forty-four. The length of the town, from the turnpike near Plymouth works to the extremity of Dowlais, is two miles and a half. The population, at the census of 1841, was 34,977, but is now above 40,000. The number of inhabited houses, in the census return, is 6,413; at the present time the overseer's rate-book shows the number rateable to the relief of the poor as 7,500. The ascent from the banks of the Taff to Dowlais is continuous, and in some places steep, so as to afford every facility for sewerage and for cleansing the streets. The situation of the town is favourable for health, being open, airy, and well exposed to the sun; the lower part stands at an elevation of 500 feet above the sea docks at Cardiff, as shown by the locks in the Glamorganshire Canal, which conveys immense quantities of the iron and coal from hence to the sea. Dowlais rises about 500 feet above the lowest point of Merthyr, so that, if height has anything to do with salubrity, Dowlais, standing 1,000 feet above the sea, would be (presuming no counteracting influences at work) a healthy place. There is, then, no cause, arising from local position or climate, why Merthyr should be an unhealthy town, yet beyond question it is unhealthy. The prevailing disease is fever, from which the town is never free. During the visitation of the cholera, in the months of July, September, and October—an event which has a gloomy prominence in the memory of the inhabitants—there were attacked 3,624 persons, of whom 1,524 died; this gives a per centage of one person attacked in every twelve, and one death in every twenty-eight of the entire population. I made this calculation from the papers, with the kind assistance of Mr. Frank James, the superintendent registrar; therefore, startling as the facts appear, they may be relied on. When it is remembered that this awful destruction of human life occurred almost entirely amongst the labouring classes, the amount of destitution and suffering entailed by the loss of parents, may be in some degree imagined. The number of orphaned children thrown upon the parish for support by this fearful visitation, was 462, of whom 51 had lost both father and mother; the number of widows left to the charge of the parish was 182. Besides these many children who have lost their parents now provide for themselves in the works, and many no doubt have wandered away in search of a better home elsewhere. It is pertinent to this part of my subject to show that, whatever it may be, there is something prejudicial to infant life in Merthyr. During seven years extending to 1847 inclusive, there died yearly, of children under five years of age in Merthyr Tydfil parish, not fewer than 607. In the same period the births were annually 1,636—this from carefully abstracted manuscript returns. The official statement of the registrar-general also shows that the mortality here is very high among children. In the unions comprising Cardiff, Bridgend, and Neath, on the southern border of the mineral basin, and containing some extensive iron and copper works, there were 1,601 births during the year 1846, and of deaths under five years, 412; while in the same year in Merthyr union, which comprises several agricultural parishes, the births were 1,381, which, it will be seen, is less than in the unions abovenamed; and the deaths under five were 496—a proportion greatly unfavourable to infant life in the Merthyr Union as compared with the others. It is clear, then, that there must exist in Merthyr some active causes prejudicial to human life; and as, whatever these may be, they cannot but tend to the unhappiness and physical depression of the poor, it becomes a legitimate subject for inquiry in their place, whether they may not be ascertained and the evil cured.

The first impression of a stranger who visits Merthyr is, that it is a town of workmen's houses. The shops are not numerous, considering the population; I should say they do not constitute more than a fifteenth part of the entire town. The professional men are not more numerous than the absolute requirements of the place demand, and there are scarcely any local gentry, so that houses of a good class are extremely rare. The style of building is of the rudest and least commodious kind, and is one cause of the low state of health above alluded to. It strikes the observer when in the lower town (still called "the village" by old people) that the houses have been formed from a low and rude model. There still exist several of the original houses, mere hovels of stone, having no upper storey, and covered with thatch, the eaves of which may be touched with the hand. On this type the builders have improved, by the addition of a loft above the ground-floor, and in many instances by a division of the dwelling into four rooms; but, as if alarmed at the innovation, they have done this timidly and scantily, for the houses are still very low and ill-ventilated. The better class of tradesmen have advanced a little, raising their houses to a second floor, but in a narrow spirit, for the upper rooms cannot but be inconveniently low. A tradesman named James, who had lived in Manchester, but is opening business here, is building a house in the High-street, on the same scale as good houses in English towns; and though not lofty, as compared with houses in London, it overtops the adjoining tradesmen's houses, even more than the latter overtop the cottages of the labourers. It is to be hoped this model will be serviceable, and that builders here will improve by the example. The main streets have a road sound at bottom, which is all the praise that can be awarded them, for they are rarely cleansed. It is, however, in the streets and courts which branch off on the right and left, that the filthy state of the town is most apparent. There is not a public sewer or drain throughout the town of Merthyr—a place, be it remembered, having upwards of 40,000 inhabitants. In a newly-erected street there is indeed a drain, made by a private individual, of about a hundred yards long, but I am aware of no other in the town, though the slope of the ground offers every facility for cheap and effective sewerage and cleansing. The houses, those of the tradesmen excepted, have no privies, nor any receptacle whatsoever for house-refuse, nor have they, except in a few instances, any outlet behind. The consequences, as regards public decency and health, are absolutely shocking. In the district between High-street and the river in Pen-y-darran, and particularly in Dowlais, where, though the highest part of the town, cholera raged with the most deadly malignity, the heaps of putrefying and fermenting refuse are as astonishing as they are poisonous. In one of the close courts here, consisting of four houses, a woman told me there were deaths from cholera in three; and matters would have been worse, no doubt, if the medical men had not immediately cleared every house where a death occurred, sending the inhabitants to the temporary refuges erected on the surrounding hills. There is not a wall, a heap of scoria from the works, or a vacant spot of ground, that is not covered with abominations. The banks of the Taff form one vast and continuous mass of rubbish. The courts, and often the middle of the streets, are obstructed with heaps of ashes, ordure, the refuse of vegetables, and the clotted hay of which the Irish and some of the Welsh make their beds. Upon this is thrown all the slops of the houses—the consequence being that there is set up in these masses of rubbish a fermentation which disengages gas of a kind equally pungent to the smell and injurious to animal life. The roadways of the streets, especially in the quarters Dowlais and Pen-y-darran, are in rainy weather absolutely impassable; they are a mass of festering black mud, into which the wheels of the carts which carry coal to the houses sink deeply. Crossings are here and there made—not by the commissioners of light and paving, for there are none—not by the parish, for the roads have never been surrendered to their custody in proper repair, consequently the parish is not compellable to keep them up—not by the iron-masters, whose houses form the streets, but by the inhabitants themselves, who, for their own convenience in crossing these stinking and poisonous sloughs, have here and there, in an irregular manner, placed stones in the mud, to facilitate their transit. No wonder, with such a state of things, that disease is rife and life precarious. Looking at a gigantic heap of this refuse, stretching along the bank of the river, I was forcibly reminded of those mounds of rubbish which travellers describe as existing in Cairo and other cities of the East, and to which is attributed much of the severity of the plague. As regards results the parallel is complete, though the magnitude of the evil is, perhaps, greatest in the East. But, bad as this is at present, it is vastly better than it was before the cholera visited the town. Conscious of the frightful state of the streets and courts, and alarmed at the approach of the pestilence, the parish authorities made strenuous exertions to purify the town. Upwards of two hundred notices were served on various persons for the removal of nuisances. Many abominations were removed at the expense of the parish—amongst these was a heap of refuse that had been accumulating for fifty years by the tram-road side, which contained by measurement 500 cubic yards, and cost £15 for its removal. This I had from official authority. The next, and a still more serious, evil is the scarcity of water—that necessary element for comfort, cleanliness, and health. Carefully examining every quarter of the town, I found but three pumps and one shallow draw-well, which, being without apparatus for raising water, I conclude was of no service. In Dowlais and Pen-y-darran there are a few "spouts" fed by landsprings, from the mountain above, which afford streams insufficient in quantity and of uncertain supply. To these the women and children resort in crowds, often waiting hours before their turn comes round. In summer, when the drought cuts off the water, the sufferings of the people are very severe; women then wait the night through, in order to get in their turn a pailful of this indispensable element. This, though strange, is literally the fact. This evil is felt the more acutely, because the occupation of the colliers and miners is of so filthy a nature that they are compelled to wash themselves all over at their return from their day's work, for which purpose a large quantity of water is, in this large town, daily required. Everywhere great complaints were made to me of the privations and inconvenience this circumstance occasions. One woman said, "My husband earns eleven shillings a week, and I would give one out of it for plenty of water." In the lower town, the supply is scarcely better. A woman in a wretched court informed me that they had to fetch water for domestic purposes from the other side of the Taff, which was done by wading the river, but when there was flood, they had to go round for it by the iron bridge, a distance of a mile. Almost directly afterwards, having wandered to the side of the Taff, I saw girls of from ten to fourteen years of age, wading the river, which reached above their knees, bearing on their heads small barrels, or in their hands large tin jugs, some going to, and others returning from, the well which my informant had alluded to. This scarcity of water was pointed out to me by the Rev. Mr. Campbell as the most crying grievance the people have to endure; and I am convinced it is. Yet water is abundant in the mountains above, and the traveller who, on his way to the town, passes fine reservoirs kept up apparently regardless of expense, and with extreme care, might suppose that at least the houses, if not the streets, would be well supplied. But the water in these reservoirs, and the copious streams of the rivers Taff and Morlais, are absorbed entirely in the works. The iron-masters have a long-vested and absolute right in them, and the only question affecting them in this particular is whether, knowing the condition of the town, they ought not to have assisted the inhabitants in procuring a supply from a quarter which would not affect their own interests. There is a point in the mountains not far from the town where water might be obtained from a rivulet called Taff Vachan; the ravines below it, which are nevertheless much higher than the town, might at small expense be dammed up so as to form natural reservoirs, from which a supply of pure and good water might be had at a comparatively trifling expense. But in this place the working classes and the poor are almost entirely unrepresented; they are from their circumstances and position utterly helpless as regards the improvement of the town, and although they have the sympathy of the clergy, professional men, and tradesmen, amongst whom exists a great degree of public spirit, hitherto nothing has been done. The rest of this evil is to be found in the want of a central authority—a corporation, or at least commissioners under a local act, by whom the administration of the affairs of the town may be conducted. Though coal is to be had for almost nothing, there is not a single public lamp in Merthyr; the consequences as regards crime and public decency in a manufacturing town of forty thousand inhabitants may be well imagined. There exists, indeed, a gas company which supplies the tradesmen and such persons as care to consume gas. Formerly the town was lit by the Commissioners of Roads from the turnpike funds, but the reduction of the number of toll-gates, which took place at the period of the "Rebecca Riots," so narrowed their income as to necessitate the giving up of the public lights. Since then the town has remained unlit as it is at present.

Such, then, is the sanitary condition and outward appearance of the town of Merthyr; in my next, having in the interim visited the works, I shall describe the various processes in the manufacture of iron, the condition of the workmen, as I find them in their labour; after which I shall give my attention to the collieries, and in due course visit the cottages, and consider the question of wages, education, crime, and pauperism, with such incidental subjects as may appear to deserve remark.

LABOUR AND THE POOR.

---◆---

THE MINING AND MANUFACTURING DISTRICTS OF SOUTH WALES.

[FROM OUR SPECIAL CORRESPONDENT.]

MERTHYR TYDFIL.

LETTER II.

The town of Merthyr is seen to the greatest advantage by night. Conscious of this, and aware that by day its appearance is none of the best, the inhabitants proudly ask the stranger if he has viewed it from the surrounding heights after nightfall? Should he answer in the negative, they tell him he has not seen Merthyr. The traveller, crossing the vast and dreary mountains which enclose the town, and without hedge or tree to guide him, lamenting the darkness of the night, suddenly, to his admiration, sees the low-hanging clouds divide, and a broad flash of light reflected on the winding track-way before him. He looks up; the very sky seems on fire—changing from deep red to brightest yellow, as the vistas vary. As yet he is miles from the town; there is not an object visible to break the black outline of the mountains; the solitude and desolation are complete; but the light, which he knows to be that of the furnaces at Merthyr, cheers and befriends him, and he pricks on with fresh impulse for the place of his destination.

Arrived within sight of the town, the scene is grand and imposing. In the valley on which he enters there are scattered, at various distances, the extensive works which have converted a secluded and almost untenanted district amongst the mountains into a centre of active business—a field of enterprise for the capitalist, and of employment for a swarming population. There is, at least, one point of view from which all the works comprised generally under the name "Merthyr" are visible. On the right the lofty blast-furnaces of Cyfarthfa and Ynys-fach project upwards huge volumes of crimson flame; below these, and yielding a yellow light, the tall chimneys of the refineries, and of the puddling and the balling-furnaces, severally glow

with fire, and add to the splendour of the scene. Further down the
defile are the furnaces and forges of Plymouth works; on the left,
in the narrow and precipitous valley of the Morlais, those of Pen-y-
darran; above, glowing brilliantly, stands the vast circle of furnaces at
Dowlais; higher still, and perched as it were in the very clouds, are the
fiery domes of Ivor. Long lines of yellow flame, stretching along the
hills behind and beside the works, mark the "coke-pits" where the bituminous coal is prepared for the furnaces. From the fork of the river,
where stands the ancient church with its massive square-built tower,
the town stretches up the hill to Dowlais—its outlines dimly traceable
against the embankment of cinders on the other side of the ravine.
The overhanging mountains are black as ink, and the clouds, which
settled upon their ridges at sunset, now roll down, catching the light
in their skirts and refracting it with rosy hues, as they hurry towards
the sea. The sky over the valley is of narrow extent; but, as the drifting
rack divides, affording a glimpse of the firmament, the very stars look
pale by contrast with the fires which burn below. The scene powerfully affects the imagination, for it has vastness, suggestiveness, and
mystery. Dante might have borrowed hints from it—Martin alone
could paint it.

Entering the outskirts of the town by the Brecon-road, the extensive works of Cyfarthfa are upon your right hand; on the left, seated in
a park backed by plantations, stands Cyfarthfa Castle, the residence
of Mr. Crawshay, who is the sole proprietor of these works. Impelled
by curiosity, you turn aside and visit them. Crossing the Taff, which
in winter is an impetuous mountain torrent, though dry during the
greater part of the year—its waters being then diverted to supply the
requirements of the works—and entering the area occupied by the furnaces, mills, and forges, the famed spectacle of iron works by night
stands before you. At a height of fifty feet from the ground the huge
funnels of the blast furnaces appear, at equal distances, through a platform of solid masonry, sending forth their wavy lines of lurid fire.
Ever and anon the men who feed them, flitting from point to point,
are seen in relief, small and black, against the flames. Below, at the
furnace-holes, jets of flame gush out, and there run thin streams of
fluid metal from the taps down the casting floor, with a light so intense that the eye cannot endure it. The lofty chimneys of the refineries, and of the puddling and balling furnaces, glow with fire. Through
the circular openings above, in the masonry, and between the arches
and buttresses of the forges, a hundred rays of brilliant light stream

out, joining or intersecting each other with a curious effect. Huge volumes of luminous steam float upwards to the clouds. The men—as in a seeming atmosphere of flame they run nimbly here and there—appear small as pigmies, by contrast with the lofty buildings in which they work. Yet amidst this seeming confusion, all is order and method; and it is impossible to regard the scene without a sense of admiration that beings apparently so insignificant can control and regulate at their will such vast bodies of an element so powerful and destructive as fire. Those objects, with the varied sounds which fall upon the ear—the roaring of "the blast," the loud hissing of steam-engines, the hum of heavy machinery in rapid motion, the clanking of heavy bars, the rattling of the trams, the shouting of the halliers, and others engaged in piling, loading, and removing the manufactured iron—produce on the mind impressions which no language can adequately describe. I once heard the visual part of this scene likened to a cathedral on fire: though striking, it was, as regards the variety of the colours and the intensity of the light, if not in respect of extent and magnificence, a poor comparison.

Resuming your course to the town, you pass the head of the Glamorganshire Canal, one of the earliest constructed, upon which, previously to the formation of the Taff Vale Railway, the iron manufactured in this neighbourhood, and the coal hence exported, were conveyed to the sea-docks at Cardiff. This canal is navigable for barges of twenty-four tons; it has a fall of upwards of 500 feet, distributed over forty locks, and in some places it is carried along the face of mountains 300 feet above the level of the river. So much has the trade in iron and coal increased, that, notwithstanding the formation of the Taff Vale Railway, the traffic is so great as still to return the shareholders a handsome per centage. A large number of hands are employed in working this canal, but their circumstances, owing to the general low rate of wages in the district, are necessarily poor.

Entering the town, you observe a large throng of people moving lazily along the middle of the street; for the pavements, where such exist, are so narrow, and the trap-doors so rickety, that walking on them is neither safe nor convenient. I am told that by this peculiarity of taking the middle of the road the people of Merthyr are recognised as belonging to that place whilst walking the streets of Cardiff, Newport, and Swansea; and I can well believe it, for, apart from the above considerations, there are, through the greatest part of the town, reasons not of a nameable kind why the wall should be avoided—such are the consequences which follow, where no powers exist providing for the paving and lighting of a large manufacturing town. For the most part the throng is composed of workmen, their wives, and girls who provide for themselves by labour in the works around the town. They are generally comfortably clothed, the men wearing jackets or coats of coarse cloth, the women warm woollen garments. It is their custom to walk in this manner, after their work, having prepared themselves (as they had need) by ablutions and change of clothes. The shops, which in proportion to the population are few, are literally stuffed with goods. They are inconveniently small and low; but the most is made of space—the windows, and even the doorways in many of them, displaying a profusion of wares adapted to the wants and the tastes of the people. The drapers' shops offer few patterns of cotton goods, but, in lieu of these, every possible kind of woollen texture that can be obtained. The prevailing colours and fabrics are those which old prejudices have endeared to the Welsh; they will have none of your tawdry prints. The same plaids as were manufactured in the country a hundred years ago are still in favour; chocolate brown, with black, indian-red, and deep blue, form the staple colours, and are well adapted, it must be confessed, to the black soil and mud of this neighbourhood. Ironmongers, grocers, druggists, drapers, and last, but not least, booksellers, all thrive here. It is, indeed, a tradesman's own fault if he fails to succeed. I must again mention the booksellers, because I consider them in proportion more numerous than the other trades— that is, taking the usual ratio to population as shown in other places. Even the market-house has two, if not more, bookstalls—a circumstance significant of the tendency to home and fire-side amusements, which deserves notice and encouragement in a place where by far the bulk of the population is made up of the working classes. But a tradesman here need well understand the method of doing business which prevails in the country, and the character of his customers—for a great part of the trade is necessarily on credit, and therefore requires capital, vigilance, and activity. By ten o'clock the streets are cleared, the shops have been long closed, all is darkness (for there are no public lamps) and silence, save the occasional roar of a drunken workman as he staggers home. But I shall have to touch on the social and moral habits of the people hereafter, so for the present I make no further allusion to them.

About a quarter before six in the morning the streets are again alive. Large groups of workmen, habited for the most part in jackets, with corduroy or fustian trowsers, many also wearing small aprons of leather, are on their way to relieve those who have filled "the night turn" in the several callings at the iron-works. Numbers, too, of girls, clad in a rather tightly-fitting canvas dress, with sleeves, reaching from the bosom to below the knees, gathered in round the waist, and worn over a woollen petticoat, are also on their way to the works, where twelve hours of heavy labour, lifting and piling iron, loading and unloading trams, stacking coal at the coking pits, or making fire-bricks, are before them. A small bonnet of coarse black straw (flattened at the crown from the habit of carrying home coal for firing, and other burdens on the head), beneath which, and with a corner pendant over the back, is worn a handkerchief of some bright colour, black woollen stockings, and thick quarter boots, complete the costume of these hard-working females. Can I say they are cheerful? No doubt many are light-hearted, and many resigned to their hard lot. But the instinct of the woman's heart for home duties, for that which is gentle, benign, and good, must revolt at the life of masculine toil and long-tasked physical endurance which they are compelled to undergo. Straggling lines of boys, noisy, frolicsome, and disputatious, also shape their irregular course to the works. After a short interval, similar bands and groups, relieved by those we have just seen, fill the streets on their return from the night's labour, pallid, weary, and exhausted.

At the foot of the ascent to Dowlais, you cross the Morlais, a considerable stream, whose waters—turbid, thick, and black from use in the works above—rush noisily over their stony and precipitous bed, throwing off an abundance of lead-coloured foam. This passed, on the left is a tram-way of singular interest; for on this the first locomotive engine that ever ran was started. It was, I believe, patented in 1802, and placed on this line in 1804. Many persons of the town remember having seen its first essay; it was a rude machine, which barely dragged a weight of ten tons at the rate of five miles an hour. Ten years later, locomotives, having in the interval been greatly improved, came into general use. Judging from what I remember of this district twelve years ago, I think they are not so numerous at present as they were then. However, they are still employed at Dowlais and Cyfarthfa, and it is pleasing to see them running round the mountain-tops, at a prodigious height overhead, and dragging heavy trains of iron ore and limestone to the furnaces below.

Passing the works at Pen-y-darran on the right, and leaving the house and grounds of the chief partner, Mr. Alderman Thompson, on the left, you still ascend, having long rows of workmen's cottages—small, low, and inconvenient—continuously upon one or both hands. Where the view is open to the right, you have an opportunity of estimating the height and extent of the vast mounds of cinder accumulated during many years, and daily increasing, which form one of the most striking features in the environs of Merthyr. The most stupendous railway embankments are insignificant as compared with them. The loftiest of these lines of cinder was computed by an experienced engineer at not less than 300 feet high. The men, trams, and horses, on their flat summits look the merest pigmies imaginable. Placed continuously, they would extend for miles, and they are gradually filling up the hollows which intervene between the acclivities of the mountains and the river. Upon one of these heaps, on the north side of the town, a long row of workmen's cottages has been erected, and the locality has been not inaptly named "Newfoundland." It may be added, that these vast heaps of cinder are years in cooling, and that at night, for a long distance from the extremity where the slag is thrown from the trams, the surface is covered with an attenuated flame of the most beautiful blue.

You observe little more of interest till you reach Dowlais. The distance from the part properly called Merthyr is two miles, but the whole forms a continuous town. As the works of Dowlais are the largest in the world, I directed my attention in the first place to them, because it was there I expected to see the entire economy of the ironworks most fully and palpably developed. On applying to the manager, Mr. John Evans, who received me courteously, I had permission to go through the works; but without authority from the chief partner, Sir John Guest, to whom he referred me, he declined giving me any information. Thus circumstanced I went through the works, accompanied by a friend who fills the office of surgeon in that huge establishment; but until I had permission from Sir John Guest, I did not feel at liberty to put any questions to his men—especially in the absence of an agent or person having authority in the works. Accordingly, by the next post, I wrote to Sir John, who, in his reply, gave me "perfect liberty to see every part of the establishment at Dowlais;" and he added that his agent should "give any information I might wish to have respecting the working classes, more particularly as to their hours of work, wages, and earnings"—concluding with the expression of a wish that the inquiry might benefit those for whose welfare it was mainly instituted. On a second time presenting myself at the works, I had every possible facility afforded me for prosecuting my duties with effect. The books were thrown open to me—the splendid maps and plans of the works, both below and above ground, were unfolded; and whilst thanking Sir John Guest and his agents for their courtesy and attention, I feel it due to them to state that not the slightest reservation was made—on the contrary, they endeavoured to satisfy me on all points; and if I fail to give a clear, accurate, and just statement of the condition of the works, and of those by whose labour they are carried on, it will be from my own deficiency, and not from any want of opportunity to acquaint myself thoroughly with the subject. I have since seen the fine works at Cyfarthfa, and those called Plymouth works (having been refused information and admission at the only remaining works here—those of Mr. Alderman Thompson, at Pen-y-darran); so that, in describing the Dowlais works, I shall have the advantage of alluding to any points of superiority as regards the security and comfort of the workmen which I have observed elsewhere.

At Dowlais, including the Ivor works, there are 18 blast furnaces, 77 puddling, and 66 balling furnaces, besides a large number of refineries. At present there are only sixteen of the large furnaces at work, the remaining two being out of blast. There are employed, under and above ground, no fewer than 6,000 hands, of whom 180 are females. This statement is based on an account taken about eighteen months ago. Up to that time two sets of women were employed, succeeding each other night and day. This circumstance having awakened the sympathy of Lady Charlotte Guest, the nightwork was discontinued, and women now are only employed by day. The entire town of Dowlais, having a population of 8,000, is dependent upon these works. The average amount of wages paid weekly is £4,500. Three years ago the furnaces produced 50 tons each of iron weekly, making a total in the year of 74,880 tons. According to Scrivener (p. 133), the furnaces at Dowlais in 1830, then twelve in number, yielded 32,611 tons, so that the increase in the "make" since is more than doubled; it is true the furnaces have increased one-third in number; but the "yield" from each, to make up the quantity above given, must also have enlarged full 33 per cent., as will appear by calculation from these data. The daily consumption of coal at these works is estimated at 1,000 tons, more or less. Steam at high pressure is entirely used. Several engines of various horse-power up to 300 are employed—some for working the "blowing machines," by which "the blast" is generated, and others for supplying motive power for the ponderous machinery used in the manufacture of the iron. These particulars will afford some idea of the magnitude and importance of the Dowlais works.

I now propose to give a succinct account of the entire process of smelting and manufacturing iron, as observed here—noticing as I proceed every circumstance that strikes me as affecting the labourer. The general view of these works is very imposing. Fourteen blast-furnaces, fifty feet high, stand at the head of the area disposed in a curve something like the form of a horseshoe. Below these stand the refineries, and further down, again, the mills and forges, with their hundred chimneys spouting forth fire. Large engine-houses and regulators (huge globes of iron for equalising the current of blast) stand on the north side of the works. Crossing at several points are pipes of cast iron, varying in diameter from six to thirty-six inches, which convey blast to the furnaces, water for cooling the machinery, the workmen's tools, and for other uses, and steam to supply the requisite power for the wheel-work, squeezers, shears, and saws, used in the several processes through which the metal passes. Besides the workmen engaged in the mills, hundreds are employed in loading and unloading trams, breaking and piling iron, excavating and building, pulling down and repairing, and in divers other occupations, carried on in the open air.

After thus taking a general survey of the works, I proceeded, accompanied by Mr. William Evans, one of the managers, whose intelligence is only equalled by his obliging disposition, to ascend the platform at the head of the furnaces. Here it is necessary to give the reader some idea of a blast furnace. I find it thus described:—"The external form of a blast furnace is that of a truncated pyramid, whilst its interior form has been aptly compared to that of a decanter supported upon a funnel." Popularly it may be represented with enough of accuracy as a huge soda-water bottle, encased up to the shoulders in a cube of compact masonry, being fifty feet in height, and of proportionate diameter, and having at its base, which is called "the hearth," apertures for the flow of slag (vitrified cinder), and for running off the true metal. The back of these furnaces rests against the acclivity of the mountain, and at about twelve feet below their mouths a fine platform of masonry extends and connects the whole. Making our way over the boilers of the steam-engines, amidst the "blowing-off" of the safety valves, we soon reached this platform. Here was a scene of great activity. Trams passing and repassing, laden with coal, limestone, and the various ores used in smelting—kilns for drying fire-bricks, and roasting ore—groups of men and women breaking the limestone and other materials, and wheeling them to the furnace mouths—all attract their share of attention.

The materials being collected near the "tunnel-head" of the furnace (for so the upper mouth is called), the first process is to calcine the ore, in order to dissipate the water and all volatile impurities which it contains. This is effected in kilns, exactly similar to those in which lime is burned. On the flat at the head of these kilns, an old Irish woman was wheeling small coal for stratifying with the ore. Living in an atmosphere of smoke she was necessarily dirty, but her clothes were thick and warm. She told me she had followed that occupation in the same place for two years. I asked her to show me her dinner, and went with her to a hole in the wall where she had placed it. She pulled out a bag from which she drew a large piece of fair wheaten bread. "What, no cheese?" said I. "Devil a bit do I have," replied she, with a smile. "It's five and sixpence a week I gits, and out of it my rent is a shilling. My boots costs me most, because the fire burns them. Since I have been at this work I have suffered much from the sulphur; it makes me cough, and I cannot sleep at night. I had no cough before." The man who managed the kilns, in reply to my questions, said, "I have worked here ten years, and earn 15s. a week. The sulphur fills my lungs, and makes me cough. I get tea, or sometimes broth for dinner. My wife and children have enough of bread, and we get meat once a week. I live as well as others of my class." Returning to the furnace heads, I saw the workmen charging the furnaces. Here the process of smelting begins. Through four large doors, at equal distances in the round and short neck of the furnace, men and women wheel up, in light iron trams, and throw into the flames, the materials with which the iron is made: these are, Welsh iron ore calcined, red hematite (Cornish, Lancashire, or Cumberland ore), raw coal, and limestone, or cinder from the refineries and puddling furnaces, whichsoever may be deemed advisable. The purposes which these materials severally answer should be explained here. The ores of course yield the iron, the coal supports the mass, and keeps up the necessary combustion; and the limestone or cinder acts as a menstruum or flux by which the metal is separated from the earthy parts of the ore—or rather, this combines the materials in a vitrified mass, through which the true metal, by its greater specific gravity, descends to its proper receptacle at the bottom of the furnace. From the apertures where the materials are thrown in, to the dam-plate, whence the iron runs off, the depth is full forty-five feet; and as the melting mass slowly subsides, fresh materials are added, so as to keep the furnace full to the level of the platform, where they are prepared and stored for use. About four feet above the bottom of the furnace, the "blast" is admitted at three points—the two sides and the back. The effect this has on the glowing mass within may be estimated when I say that the pressure of the blast on the square inch varies from two to four pounds, and the nozzles of the pipes entering the furnaces are about two inches and a half in diameter. At Cyfarthfa works I had an opportunity of witnessing this. The founder led me through an arched passage between two furnaces, so narrow as to admit only of one at a time, into a chamber where the blast-pipes divided and entered each furnace. It was utterly dark, save at the two points where the nozzles entered the furnaces. By stooping, I was enabled to see the fluid iron or the slag, or both, trickling down like white threads, but the moment these came within the line of the blast they were dissipated and vanished. The noise was deafening; with the man's mouth to my ear, it was impossible to make out what he said. I should add, that we were followed by a man with a characteristic lantern—a long-handled shovel covered with white-hot slag from the furnace; this, however, served to show the extent of the vaulted chamber in which we stood, and the form and diameter of the iron-bound hose of leather which conducted the blast to its destination. The heat which the "fillers" have to endure is prodigious; yet I have seen women brave it, tilting their iron-trams over in the very flames. The iron-ore, the coal, and the limestone are supplied, in courses, through the four doors; and the furnace, as each successive charge of the material is thrown in, seems agitated like a living thing, sucking them down its fiery throat, and thrusting its fiery tongues through the doors, as if seeking for more.

Great judgment and experience are required for the management of the furnaces, so as to produce a tough and good iron. All the materials are carefully weighed or measured, and unrelaxing vigilance is observed day and night in the progress of the work. It is partly by the flow of iron, but more by the appearance of the lava or slag, which, floating on the true metal, runs off through orifices in the dam-plate over "the hearth," that the whole is regulated. The Welsh ore (called "mine") is by no means so rich as the other ores here employed. The relative values of the several ores mostly used in smelting iron in Wales, as furnished me by a most intelligent practical man, Mr. Joseph, of

Plymouth works, stands thus—Cumberland ore (red hematite) yields from 60 to 65 per cent., Cornish ore, 40 to 50, Welsh ores from 20 to 33 per cent. of iron. Yet, notwithstanding that it produces less in proportion than the other ore, the Welsh makes by far the best grey iron for castings, being much freer from pores and bubbles than the other ores.

The men and women who work on the platform of the furnaces look for the most part healthy and robust. They were well clothed, the girls wearing the peculiar canvas dress above described, over warm woollen petticoats; the men had checked shirts of flannel, some had also jackets and trowsers of Russia duck or fustian. They earn respectively—lime-stone breakers, 24s. a week, out of which they pay a girl for assistance 7s.; the unloaders of coal earn 10s.—the "fillers" 14s. a week. I saw the fillers, men and women, at dinner, and looked into their tins—they had bread and butter (spread) and tea, but in no instance cheese or meat. At night they said they indulged in cheese. House rent and coal cost them 10s. 6d. a month. Nevertheless, heavy as is their labour, and trying the vicissitudes of heat and cold to which they are exposed, they looked healthy. Some of the women were even rosy, as far as the colour could be seen through a coating of black. The men smoke—it is their only indulgence. One of them told me that his flannel shirt cost 5s.—that necessary clothing was so expensive, that, having a wife and four children, what between house-rent and all, they could barely subsist.

Here I must call attention to one particular at least, as regards these men and women—and that is, not the matter of wages, but one affecting the comfort of those who, at the furnace-heads and hearths, are compelled to work exposed to the weather, where, with convenience to all parties and at comparatively light expense, they might have the protection of a roof. At the period of my visit the snow lay two inches thick on the ground; and it may be imagined what must be the discomfort endured by those who for a few minutes are by their duty exposed to a melting heat, and then, removing to a distance from the furnaces, in obedience to the other calls of their occupation, are chilled by the piercing wind which sweeps along these mountains. There is no other excuse for this neglect of the well-being and protection of the labourer than that of expense. But as this touches the question whether or not the duty of the employer is limited to the payment of wages, which it would here be inconvenient to open, I will pass it by with the remark that, in Cyfarthfa works, this consideration has been attended to, and both above and below, at the furnaces, comfortable roofs and walls protect the labourer most effectually.

Descending a long flight of stone stairs we reach the base or hearth of the furnaces. Here the most striking objects are two large jets of flame rushing outwards, through the apertures made for the passage of the slag, with a noisy violence that shows the tenuity of the imprisoned gases within, and in the line which flame takes when acted upon with a blow-pipe. A constant current of lava or slag runs from the orifices in the dam-plate over the hearth, into iron trams placed to receive and remove it. At first it is of a white colour—then it deepens into yellow, and assumes, as it further cools, the most beautiful transparent blood colour. It is from time to time carried off and thrown over the cinder-mounds already described, where, at the top or on the sides, it adheres, preserving a perfect cast of the square tram till covered by succeeding deposits. When cold this lava has a "vitrified, semitransparent," appearance, particularly at the upper side; it is used for road-making, and in the manufacture of glass bottles, so that, though produced in such quantities that a sixtieth part is not used, the very refuse of the furnaces is capable of being turned to serviceable account.

Iron-works, Merthyr Tydfil

Turning to the nearest furnace, I addressed the master-founder. He was a tall gaunt old man, wearing a handkerchief bound tightly round his head, in lieu of a cap, and a woollen shirt of blue check, open at the throat and chest, and tucked up at the sleeves. A pair of canvass trowsers, and huge wooden-soled shoes, completed his dress. At this work, so great is the heat, and so frequent are the splashings of fluid iron amongst the sand, that the men are obliged to go shod with wood. Sometimes, as the surgeon told me, they get the fluid iron over the ankles into the shoe: the effects are terrible. Leaning upon his long iron lever, having first brushed away the big drops of perspiration from his smutted face, he said, "I have been seventeen years a founder, and my health has been pretty good except when I have had the misfortune to be burnt. The work is very hard—it courses day and night; this week I have day-work, the next it will be my turn at night. I earn from 23s. to 25s. a week; on which I support a wife and five children." I asked him to show me his dinner-can, which he did. He had bread and cheese for dinner; but remarked, "I have had meat every day this week till to-day; my wife and children have meat. All the founders get meat, the work is so severe they could not get on without it; most of them earn more than I do." This man informed me that at these works they very properly stop the furnaces on Sundays from eight in the morning till two in the afternoon, in order that the men may all attend Divine service. This is a creditable piece of kindness that, I was told, has not extended to the men at the other works; but it is to be hoped the example of Sir John Guest will for the future be followed there, and that the fireman, instead of having his day of rest and thanksgiving every other week, will be allowed a Sabbath like other men.

Seizing his huge sledge-hammer, and picking up a long iron bar, having a cutting edge in front like a chisel, the old furnace-man called his "underhand," and, addressing me, said, "I'll tap her, and show you the prettiest part of our work." They first opened a trench in the black sand to the refining furnace below—then, having removed a quantity of the "banking-up" at the dam-plate, they inserted the iron bar, and with lusty blows of the "sledge," drove it by degrees through the tough stratum of vitrified sand which closed the orifice of the furnace. Straightway a most brilliant sight presented itself. A stream of liquid iron, almost as fluid as water, and of the most beautiful yellow, bearing a shot of violet colour, gushed forth and followed the course of the channel in the sand, down to the refinery. It was accompanied by a loud snapping noise and small white sparks. But this is not all; large fiery spiders, as it were, leap out wherever the sand is wet, and splash you, to the damage of your clothes and the cost of your skin, if they happen to strike the hands or face. This stream of liquid iron is called "a runner:" at night its light is so intense that the eye cannot endure it. In the present instance the stream was, as I have said, directed to the refinery, which is comparatively a new process; in the generality of cases it is run into moulds on the casting-floor, where it takes the form of the "pig iron" of commerce. A large floor of such castings is called "a sow."

The poor furnace-man seems to regard his furnace as a living creature, and he talks of it as such. He grows in time to have an affection for it, and well he may, for it has fed, and warmed, and clothed him for many a year. The very terms he uses when speaking of it are those applied to animals. When the stream of molten metal runs too thin, he says, "She scours, we must give her more mine." If, on the other hand, the metal flows curdy and thick, he says, "She gobs, and must have more lime." When, again, the stream regains a proper consistency, well pleased, he observes, "She recovers, and runs well." For thirty years together these artificial volcanoes burn on and on, without rest or remission, for the casual interruption of a few hours does not affect them—the fire within is still intense and active. There seems to be no proper limit to the duration of a well-built furnace. Some are now burning, which have been at work thirty-five years without material deterioration. Furnaces built at the same time and of like form, charged with materials in similar proportions, from some circumstances difficult to determine, work very differently, and vary in the quality and even quantity of the iron. So great is this inequality in some cases, that I have been informed Sir John Guest has frequently felt inclined to pull down one of the furnaces at these works, which excels in performance all the others, in the hope of discovering the cause, so as to provide for it in any future furnaces he may build. To set a furnace going, which is called "putting it in blast," is a long and expensive operation: to do this properly takes at least six weeks, at a cost of not less than £100. So many are the hands employed to keep each furnace in full work, from the raising of the ore to the perfecting of the iron for use, that the driving one "out of blast" is regarded, and justly, as a serious evil by the labouring classes. So, on the other hand, the opening of a new furnace is always a day of rejoicing and congratulation.

We have seen the melted iron run into the refinery; it now becomes needful to explain the process there. A refinery is an open square furnace, like a deep pan, having on four buttresses a chimney of some thirty feet high; coal is here added to the fluid mass, and the whole is subjected to powerful jets of blast for two hours, when the metal is run off into what are called "pig-moulds"—large square flakes of iron, of the size and shape of a large tea-tray, but of three inches thickness. It is interesting to observe the liquid metal, which gives un-equivocal evidence of its weight by the ease with which it removes any little obstacle it may encounter, running into these moulds—flowing over when the first is full, and so proceeding to fill the remainder, each of which is successively lower than its predecessor. When the true metal has run off, it is succeeded by such a flood of scum as to give you an apprehension for your feet; however, it settles on the iron, and forms there a crust without advancing further. A man then breaks this coating of cinder with an iron rod, whilst the refiner throws over each mould some buckets of water, the effect of which is astonishing. By this process of refining, the superfluous carbon and oxygen of the metal are, in a great measure, disengaged, and the iron is prepared for the puddling furnace, where it is rendered malleable. In many refiner-ies the old custom of melting the pig-iron with coal is still followed. Refiners earn about the same as founders. Here, as we are leaving this part of the yard, I should say that the "cinder-fillers," who attend to the loading trains with slag—a laborious duty, exposed to great heat—earn on an average, as they told me, 10s. 6d. a week. These men are mostly Irish.

Having cooled, or nearly so, the pig moulds are broken into frag-ments of a convenient size for the puddling-furnaces. This is done with huge and heavy sledge-hammers, each having two handles and wielded by two men. The appearance of the iron when fractured is that of a grey closely-crystallized mass, having numerous pores of a blackish-red colour near and at the surface.

We now come to that part of the process where the cast is con-verted into wrought iron. To witness the operations for this purpose you must enter vast ranges of buildings, called indifferently mills or forges, and consisting simply of roofs perforated by a great number of chimneys from the puddling and balling furnaces, and supported on all sides by pillars of masonry. The floor is paved with cast-iron, and not an inch of space is lost in these works. The effect on the spectator is one of interest and wonder. He sees huge and ponderous wheels in rapid motion; large "squeezers" in action, having a pressure of many tons; enormous shears, always moving, which I have seen cut through a bar of cold iron, as thick as my arm, without sensible exertion; ugly circular saws, whirling round with fearful rapidity, and massive rollers continually revolving; in short, wherever he moves, he has, concealed under his foot, levers, cranks, and shafts in motion; whilst around and above him, he sees machinery at work with unintermitting regularity, of a magnitude to be beheld only at such a place as this.

A puddling furnace is an oven or coffer of brick work, about eight feet long and four feet wide, having a tall chimney. Into one of these, several pieces of the broken refined iron are thrown, and the heat is supplied by coal or coke, and powerful streams of blast. To work each furnace there are two persons, "the puddler" and his "underhand." They work in three courses, so that each set has eight hours' continuous labour. After subjection to the fire for three-quarters of an hour, the iron melts, and gives off copious quantities of gas, boiling up with a frothy appearance. The puddler now introduces, through a small door at the side of the furnace, a long iron bar, with a bend at its extremity; with this he stirs about the mass until it has arrived at a proper consistency, when he again leaves it to the action of the fire. As the tools he uses become red-hot, which is soon the case, he plunges them into a trough of water to cool and harden them. A puddler opened the aperture, that I might see the process, saying, "Look awhile into the furnace, then shut your eyes, and on opening them you will see the iron." I did so. At first I could see nothing but a vapoury flame; however, on closing and suddenly opening my eyes, I saw the iron, white as snow, bubbling up with a hissing noise, like a simmering fluid. On taking his lever into my hand, I found the mass, to my surprise, of a crumbling fineness like snow-powder which will not adhere. I should add, that there were at points on the iron small jets of flame, very much like those produced by the combustion of oil. After a while the iron loses the sandy crumbling nature, and begins to clot and cohere, which the workman calls "coming round"—the fermentation subsides—and the entire mass is divided into five parts, rolled up, and again left for a few minutes to the full force of the fire. During this long process the puddler is either stirring with his lever the iron in the furnace, or regulating the fire, which he is enabled to do at convenience; consequently he is in a bath of perspiration from the heat alone, not to speak of that which follows such heavy labour as he has to perform. These men look sallow and thin. I should inform the reader that at this point I met the gentleman who has charge of this part of the works, who volunteered information respecting the men, in consequence of which I did not like to ask them questions. His accuracy on the whole is unimpeachable; but as I wished to have all particulars direct from the men, I examined some of each class at their own houses. The result will be given in due order. I was here told that puddlers earn about a pound a week, and their "underhands" eleven shillings; they get meat, and, though they perspire so freely, seldom take cold. The contents of the puddling furnace being divided into five parts, as we have seen, and rolled up into balls called "puddler's balls," are now taken, one at a time, to the "squeezers." They are delivered by the "second-hand" to the "shingler," who grasps the white hot mass with a pair of huge pincers, and drags it, at a run, to "the squeezers," where, with a dexterous twist of the arm, he swings it, though nearly a hundred weight, without apparent effort, on the anvil, where it is to be compressed. Formerly, and within my memory, the puddled balls were beaten with a hammer weighing from three to six tons, but the noise and vibration were so inconvenient, that since the invention of squeezers it has been abandoned. Mr. Crawshay, however, informed me that "the hammer makes the best iron—it beats the iron together so thoroughly." The instrument called a "squeezer" consists of a large anvil upon the ground, having a lever joined thereto by a hinge, and alternately raised and depressed by an eccentric, moved by steam or water, as the motive-power may be. The lever forms an acute angle with the anvil, and the glowing iron is, at first, placed just within the sphere of its action, and as the mass, by the pressure, becomes more compact and smaller, it is shifted up towards the hinge, so that a greater force is continually exerted upon it. Most interesting it is to see how the true metal alone can endure this enormous pressure. At each successive compression the dross gushes out from its pores in small streams of a bright yellow, like, to use a homely comparison, buttermilk perspiring through butter under the hands of the dairymaid. A second "shingler," with a pair of tongs, turns the mass after each squeeze, and shifts it gradually to the point where the pressure is greatest. This operation completed, the rough bar thus formed, which is now about twenty inches long and four wide, is next snatched by huge pincers, and swung with a vigorous arm upon iron rollers, of great strength and thickness, and in rapid motion, through which it passes—being grasped on the other side by a man handling huge tongs, suspended by a chain to the roof, who returns it over the rollers to the workman on the other side, who next puts it through a second and smaller groove in the rollers—and so on till the bar is lengthened to the proper extent, and reduced to the required width. In the course of this operation any dross which the "squeezers" failed to eliminate is squeezed out by the rollers. The bar is generally twelve feet long and three inches wide, and whilst still red-hot and flexible as a thong of leather, it is dragged out by boys, or sometimes by girls. The whole of this process takes less time than it has occupied the reader to peruse this account of it. The bars are next presented to the jaws of heavy shears, moved by power underfoot, which cut them into lengths of about two feet, or thereabouts. These are carried on small iron barrows, by boys, to the "piler," who puts together as many of them as the future bar (whether it be a railway iron or otherwise) will require, and each pile is next placed separately in the "balling furnaces," which are similar in size and structure to the puddling furnaces. The men who have charge of this part of the operation are called "ballers." On looking into one of these furnaces, I saw the piles of iron, now called "blooms," exposed to gauzy and waving breadths of flame. When the pile has been long enough in the furnace—which is known by its colour, and by a white paste-like exudation on the iron—it is taken out, placed on a small iron truck, and wheeled with speed to the rollers. These are fluted to the form which the finished bar is to take, whether round or square, or of the shape of a railway iron. Though the bloom often weighs four hundredweight, it is passed through the grooved rollers with astonishing facility and speed. On the other side it is seized with huge tongs, having here a double grasp on the side and beneath the bar, and lifted by the assistance of boys back over the rolls for passage through the next groove; and so on, the bar lengthening and coming nearer the required form, till its completion. In the case of a "rail," the iron passes, after leaving the balling-furnace, nine times through the rollers before it is reduced to its final shape; it is then dragged to the circular-saw, which, with a noise not to be described, cuts off the ends, which are necessarily imperfect. After this it is taken to the "rougher down," who, standing in a shallow pit, files off the jagged edges left by the saw, and the "rail" is dragged away to "the straightener," by whom it is finished. The entire operation, from the presentation of "the bloom" to the roller down to the perfection of the rail, takes a minute and a quarter.

The important invention of the rollers, which at once gave this country an advantage over all others in the manufacture of iron, and enabled us to command the markets of the world, was made by a gentleman named Cort, who is said, however, to have benefited very little by this most valuable discovery. Until then, the smallest sized bar drawn under the hammer was three-quarters square, and, if kept constantly at work, the men could only draw a ton of average sizes in twelve hours; whilst, with a single pair of rollers, they can manufacture in the same time about fifteen tons.

The bulk of the wrought iron made as above shown is what is termed "merchants' bars" and "rails." The former are drawn of the required form, whether round or square; and in the splitting mills, which act much on the same principle as rollers, rods are manufactured for nails, and for any other purposes for which they are available. The "ballers," I was informed, earn about 23s. a week—the "rollers" from £2 to 50s.—the "straighteners" get some £1, some 30s.—and the girls (of whom many are employed amongst the men and machinery, and in the awful heat of these mills, filing the iron) earn 6s. or 7s. a week.

Such is an account of the entire process of smelting and manufacturing iron in Merthyr; it may be taken as applicable to the system everywhere pursued throughout South Wales. I have entered very fully into details for three reasons; first, because I believe that the public is, for the most part, but little informed upon this, one of the most important branches of home industry, and from which, in a great degree, our national opulence has sprung; secondly, because I have not been able anywhere to find a succinct and exact account of the process, and I thought it, therefore, well to place it thus on record; and, lastly, because by means of such a full and particular statement alone can the value of the labourer's services, the inconveniences he undergoes, the dangers to which he is momentarily exposed, and the remuneration he receives, be fully estimated and understood. In my next I shall conclude my notice of these works, and give a statement of the condition of the labourers.

LABOUR AND THE POOR.

————◆————

THE MINING AND MANUFACTURING DISTRICTS OF SOUTH WALES.

[FROM OUR SPECIAL CORRESPONDENT.]

MERTHYR TYDFIL.

LETTER III.

Having described in my last letter the entire process of smelting iron and manufacturing it for mercantile and general purposes, there yet remains for notice a humble but indispensable branch of industry carried on at these works—namely, the making of fire-bricks for lining the furnaces, and, indeed, for all other purposes where a material is required capable of withstanding intense and long-continued heat. There are two substances, found in abundance in the coal and iron districts, which have the property of resisting in a high degree the action of fire; the one is termed "fire clay," a stratum of which is often overlaid by coal—the other is the "farewell rock," a species of stone composed of quartz, blended together by a sileceous cement. Upon this rock repose the whole of the coal and iron-stone "measures." The bricks are used for lining the interior of the blast-furnaces down to "the hearth," or receptacle of the fluid iron, which is always constructed of the stone. Experiments on bricks made of this fire-clay have satisfactorily shown that its capacity of resisting heat is fully equal to that of the better known, and more generally used, fire-bricks of Stourbridge.

The manufacture of fire-bricks at these works is exclusively carried on by women, and a more humiliating and ungenial occupation for the sex is hardly to be found through the entire range of our industrial economy. At Dowlais I found the girls at work making bricks in a low shed having no windows or opening for the admission of light, except the doorway through which I entered. Underneath the floor are flues for the passage of heated air, to dry and prepare the bricks for the kilns, which are built adjacent. The clay is ground in mills by steam power; and the women then saturate it with cold water, in

40

a smaller shed opening by a door from the main building. They next temper it with their bare feet, moving rapidly about, with the clay and water reaching to the calf of the leg. This operation completed, they grasp with both arms a lump of clay weighing about 35 pounds, and, supporting it upon their bosoms, they carry this load to the moulding table, where other girls, with a plentiful use of cold water, mould it into bricks. They have to feed and attend to the furnaces used for heating the floors, in the open air, exposed to the vicissitudes of the weather and the changes of temperature, alternating between the heat of the drying room and the cold winds outside. They told me that on an average they earned six shillings a week when at work, but there are many weeks in the course of the year when, unable to get clay, they are compelled to be idle. To the question, "How do you exist at those bad times?"—"We live as well as we can," said a moulder, still continuing her work; "we are obliged to go in debt at the shop and pay out of our earnings when we are in work." Though they work so much in water, and are subject to such sudden changes of temperature and weather, their health, they told me, is upon the whole good. "It's very seldom I get meat," said the poor moulder; "not once in a month." As they are all young they go to school on Sunday, and work twelve hours a day during the other days of the week. Their dress was similar to that I have already described as worn by the women employed in the works, with the exception that they were bare-legged, and, instead of the flat-crowned bonnet, wore handkerchiefs bound tightly round the head.

This appears the proper place to give full particulars of the employ-ment of women in the iron-works, and to glance at its effects. I stated in my first letter that the returns of the number of females employed in the manufacture of iron in Wales, as shown in the "Occupation Abstract" of the census of 1841, which states them at 182, must, even at that time, have been greatly below the number actually so engaged; and that from personal observation I believed there were considerably more than that quantity employed in the works at Merthyr alone. I have since verified that belief. The number of girls employed in the works at Dowlais, as stated to me at the office, is 180; the number so furnished at Cyfarthfa, 150; the returns supplied from Plymouth works (accurate), 175—making, of females so employed at three works only, an ascertained total of 505. I have no means of learning from of-ficial statements the number working at Pen-y-darran; but as this is the smallest of the four works at Merthyr, it may be put down at 120, which gives us a total of females employed in the manufacture of iron in Merthyr and Dowlais of 625; and that is indisputably within the number actually so engaged. Taking the number of furnaces now in blast throughout South Wales (151), as a criterion for estimating the number of females employed, and calculating the proportion to each furnace as it exists in the above-named works, we shall have a total of females employed in the manufacture of iron in South Wales alone, at the present time, of 2,320—an increase over the official return in 1841, for North as well as South Wales, of 2,188. Of course, since the passing of the statute 5 and 6 Vict., cap. 99, on the 10th of August, 1842, which prohibited the employment of females in mines and collieries, this kind of occupation has been denied them. It is but justice to add that the provisions of this humane statute are for the most part rigorously carried out by the iron-masters and owners of collieries in this neighbourhood; but, with regard to boys under ten years of age, the parents, anxious to avail themselves of their assistance in support of the family, deceive the agents by misstatements of the age of their sons. Not long ago, Mr. Hill, the proprietor of Plymouth works, issued a peremptory order for the discharge of all boys working in the pits under ten years of age, and they were so dismissed, but the fathers in a few weeks brought them back, protesting that during the interval they had attained the statutable age, and begged for their employment. As beyond a doubt their representations are often fraudulent, and the employment of boys of such tender age not only affects their health but deprives them of all opportunity of education, it is much to be wished that the enactment (section 8 of the statute) directing, in like cases of fraud, the summoning and fining of the "parent or natural guardian," were in a few instances enforced, it would probably put an end to a practice by which the benevolent intentions of the Legislature have so long been, and still often are, defeated. If we may credit the last census return, there were thrown out of employment in mines and collieries in Wales, by the above statute, 315 females—a number in all probability as much within the mark as the statement then made of those engaged in the manufacture of iron.

The following particulars of the various occupations of females, and the wages they earn, being the result of personal observations and inquiries, will, perhaps, be read with interest. They are classified under the following names: Pollers, Limestone girls, Coke-girls, Brick-yard girls, Tippers, and Pilers.

The statements made by themselves will be fairer than any abridged version I can give; therefore the reader shall have them as they fell from the lips of the speakers. Here I should state, that, wherever circumstances admitted, I questioned the workpeople of either sex in the presence of the proprietor or agent who accompanied me over the works, in order that there should be a check on both sides for securing accuracy. When, however, I could not do this, and it was necessary for the completeness of my undertaking that I should examine parties at their own homes or elsewhere, I always took the precaution of securing the presence of a professional gentleman well known in the town, to bear witness, if need were, to the accuracy of any statements, and to restrain by his presence any disposition to exaggeration which the speaker might otherwise indulge in.

M—— ——: "I am a 'Poll-girl,' aged 21; my duty is to take 'the *mine*' (iron ore) from the trams, to separate the *rubbish* from it (stone shale), and then to pile it ready for the furnaces. I work eleven hours a day in the open air, and am paid by the ton. My earnings come to 3s. 9d. a week—not more. I clean and stack about four tons of mine a day. The mine is often so flinty that it cuts my hands. [Her hands were horny with calluses.] I live on bread and cheese; often I do not get cheese; sometimes, but seldom, I have some meat for supper. I live at my father's; he is a miner. I cannot read or write. I was working very young to help my father and mother." I saw this girl at her return home from her work on a bitterly cold day. She wore over her canvass frock the tattered remains of a man's coat, which she had thrown on to protect herself from the inclemency of the weather. She added, "There is but one bedroom in our house. My father and mother, my brother, sister, and myself, all sleep in that room. We have three beds. My brother's age is nineteen." A woman from an adjoining house, who was present, here observed, "My husband, four children, and myself, are bound to sleep in one bed, because we haven't got another." Five persons had died of cholera in the row of ten houses where I examined the "poll-girl."

I went next to a house where there lodged a "Coke-girl." The pitiful condition of these girls once very forcibly struck me, when, on a day of heavy rain and high wind, I saw them at work on the mountain side, with the rain literally running off their coal-bedaubed petticoats over their boots, in black streams, to the ground. I wondered why they faced such tempestuous weather, but I have since learnt that they are not paid by the ton, as most workpeople hereabouts are, but by the day; and that, as the furnaces require a given quantity of coke per hour, it must be produced at all hazards and inconveniences. In Dowlais they do not use coke, consequently the following statement does not apply to those works. In all the others I saw girls at their labour in the coke-pits. E—— ——: "I am a coke-girl, aged 24, and have worked in Pen-y-darran three years and a half. My business is to stack the coal for coking in the pits." (This I am told requires considerable skill, or the mass will not burn evenly and make good coke). "I earn five shillings a week, but pay out of that a trifle for the doctor and 'fund' (provision for sickness). I have often to lift from the trams pieces of coal which weigh over a hundred weight, and carry them to the pit. I work eleven hours a day, taking the year through. I go often to my father's, though I live away from him. Without the assistance of my father and mother I could not live. My clothes cost me most, because I must have best and working clothes. My lodgings cost me ninepence a week. I cannot read or write, more shame for me, though I had the chance to learn. I work in all weathers—rain, snow, or frost. I stand the rain and wind often all day long, because we must work." This seemed a very thoughtful girl; she was lodging in a well-furnished house, kept by a most respectable (so I am informed) old couple, who seemed to look upon her with an interest as if she was their daughter.

The "Limestone girls," who work near the "tunnel heads" of the furnaces, breaking the limestone for use in the smelting, said their work was very hard and trying, owing to the heavy weights they carry, and the alternations of heat and cold they have to endure. At Dowlais, where I examined them, they were well clothed and cleanly; they told me their earnings were seven shillings a week, out of which a shilling went for lodging. Their boots, which the work rapidly destroys, were most expensive to them, costing 8s. a pair. They live chiefly on tea, and bread and cheese, but sometimes get animal food.

The next class for notice is the "Tippers." These are girls who work with men and boys in the vast mounds of cinders here called "tip." Their duty is to assist in clearing the trams of their loads of burning cinder. This work is followed in all weathers, and in very exposed situations. Their pay is about four shillings a week.

There is a class, happily not numerous, which I have not mentioned above, and, indeed, whose "class name" I have been unable to learn. They follow their occupation at the mouth of the coal-pits, where they alternately raise the trams loaded with iron-stone and coal, and let down the empty ones to be filled below. These girls work at what are called "balance-pits"—the principle being to raise the full tram by the descent of the empty one, assisted by such a weight of water as will produce an equipoise. As soon as the loaded tram reaches the mouth of the pit these girls drag it away; two of them then step on the platform which supported the tram, and haul at a line passing a pulley over-head, which by a valve lets off the water from the tram at the bottom of the pit. In doing this, one foot of the girl on the open side of the pit's mouth is often suspended over the abyss. One of these girls sets the drum in action, regulating the velocity of the ascending and descending trams by a "break" acted upon by a pulley. I am not able to say whether this system is of frequent occurrence or not; I saw it at one of the pits, and therefore have described it. On referring to the Act, I find that this practice, wheresoever miners or other persons descend or ascend such pits, is clearly illegal. By the 8th section of the statute 5 and 6 Vict., cap. 99 (above referred to), it is enacted, "That when there shall be any entrance to a mine or colliery by means of a vertical shaft or pit, &c., then it shall not be lawful for the owner of any such mine or colliery to allow any person or persons, *other than a male of fifteen years or upwards*, to have charge of any steam-engine, or other engine, *windlass or gin*, whether worked by manual labour *or any other power whatsoever*, or to have charge of any part of the machinery, ropes, chains, or other tackle, of any such engine, by or by means of which, &c., persons are brought up or passed down such vertical shaft or pit, &c., on pain of forfeiting a sum not exceeding £50, nor less than £20." The 17th section distributes the penalties, one-half to the informer, and the other to the overseers of the poor of the parish within which such offence shall have been committed. I invite the attention of the iron-masters to this circumstance, and to the law applicable thereto, of which I suspect they are unaware.

Lastly, of the "Pilers," whose business it is to pile and weigh the iron which has been cut by the shears. These girls work in the mills and forges, scattered about amongst the men, and surrounded by ponderous machinery in rapid motion. They have often to endure intense heat, and their work is very hard. S—— ——: "I am a piler, aged nineteen years. I work by day one week, and by night another. When the mills are working 'rails,' two other girls and myself pile, on an average, 35 tons a day between us. We have to lift up the pieces from the ground as high as my middle. Sometimes the iron is very hot, and we can't take hold of it without thick leathers. I have burnt my hands shockingly, and so have the other girls who do the same work. I live here with my father; sometimes I earn 4s., and at others, 5s. a week."

Such, then, is a faithful account of the condition of the females employed in the iron-works and collieries throughout South Wales, and of the duties they perform. As a class, they are below the middle stature, small, and delicately formed; and the stranger, when he sees them clustered at their dinner in the works, or returning home at the close of the day, congregated as is their fashion together, can scarcely fail to be struck by their prettiness, and by the clear tone of their voices when they chatter or sing, as the impulse may be. I have been assured by a gentleman of observant mind, conscientious and wholly disinterested, that, as a class, the females employed in this mining district are superior in manners, deportment, and conduct, to those who work in the cotton and other factories of the north. Their morals are even better than, surrounded continually as they are by temptations, could be expected. Their ignorance is absolutely awful; yet the returns show in them a singular immunity from crime. Great numbers find an early grave. Exposed to sudden vicissitudes of heat and cold, of rain and wind, on the bleak mountain side or in the fiery atmosphere of the forges, what wonder that consumption should thin their numbers? It is said of them, that they make bad wives and mothers, and I can believe that the fact is so. Accustomed to labour from early youth amongst men, away from the domestic hearth, it is impossible that they can learn the duties and acquire the virtues which beautify the female character, when it is developed and formed at home. Circumstances have unsexed them. Their sympathies and ideas are like those of men more than those properly belonging to women. To bake, and wash, and cook, to make and repair clothes, to keep the house orderly, clean, and comfortable, are accomplishments which must be learnt—they are not intuitive—and where and what have been the opportunities afforded these hard-worked females for acquiring them? No wonder, then, if they make bad wives. And a bad wife is ever a bad mother; the consequence is, that a race of children spring up, who, neglected or misused by the parents, are exposed to the many physical and moral evils which beset infant life in this densely populated neighbourhood. Bad nursing, it is said, annually destroys hundreds; neglect affords early ingress for the seeds of vice, which in due time fructify in crime. Attempts, highly praiseworthy, have been made to improve the condition of these females by education. Adult schools have been established in Merthyr and Dowlais, in which they are taught reading and writing, arithmetic and the rudiments of history, and some other branches of useful knowledge. The zealous and beneficent rector of this parish told me with a smile of satisfaction, if not of pride, that their intelligence and quickness were beyond praise, that they learnt to read in an astonishingly brief time, and that he had sold them many of "the Society's" Testaments. So far this is cheering and encouraging; but though much good must result from this first and most important step, the domestic duties cannot be learnt in schools—the practice of housekeeping can only be acquired in service or at home. It is a fact well known by the local gentry and tradesmen of Merthyr that domestic servants are eagerly sought as wives by the workmen and miners in this neighbourhood. The reason is obvious. The poor man knows that such women are well trained in the economy of the house; and that, having domestic habits, they will make his home comfortable and happy; whereas, if he marries "a working girl," he takes a wife entirely uninformed in the home duties. Without reasoning upon it, and, perhaps, unable to assign a motive for his choice, he intuitively prefers a domestic servant. But the greater number must, per force, marry females engaged in the works; and the results are too often traceable in the drunkenness and profligacy of the husband, the apathy or wretchedness of the wife, and the premature deaths of neglected offspring. Elevate the character of these poor overworked and unsexed females, and you will speedily have a more temperate, regular, and thrifty class of workmen than you have under the system which now prevails.

I have now particularized every class of the workpeople actually engaged in the manufacture of iron, and have shown them at their several employments. But, in addition to these, there are large numbers of artificers pursuing their various callings in different departments of the works. All the machinery here used, extensive, varied, and vast as it is, is maintained on the premises. For this purpose there is always kept a staff of engineers, founders, iron turners, whitesmiths, blacksmiths, mould-makers, forge carpenters, masons, and other necessary hands. These severally earn about the same wages as they would if following their craft in large towns in England. A great many men and boys are also employed throughout the works in what may be called unskilled labour; that is, in loading trams with cinders, and the like simple duties. These are for the most part Irish, and they earn from 9s. to 10s. a week. Having mostly large families, their condition is necessarily abject and pitiable. One of them, an Irishman, said, "I am a labourer in the works. I earn 10s. a week, on which I have to support a wife and five children, and to pay out of it 2s. a week for rent. During the two years that I have been here I have not used a pound of butter or cheese altogether. I contrive to give my family a little meat on the Sunday—some cow's cheek, or that like. I don't know how we shall live after the reduction that is going to take place in the wages." This man talked of going back to Ireland, for, said he, "I've heard that the English gentlemen is buying the land there, and there'll be much money spent in works and improvement; so I shall get work in plenty, and be better off there, because things be cheaper than here." "But how, if you are so poor, will you move there?" inquired I. "That's just what bothers me; but I suppose I'll get back in the same way as I come here." It is a remarkable fact that the Irish, no matter what length of time they remain at the works, never rise to the dignity of skilled workmen. Such a wonder as an Irish puddler was never heard of. They have the same opportunity as others; and, even supposing the jealousy and antipathy of the Welsh in some degree to prejudice them, by patience and good conduct they would surmount those obstacles, and take their place in the front ranks of the workmen; yet, whatever be the cause, they never do so, but remain contentedly in the heavy drudgery to which they are at first admitted.

The impression upon a person who, after having seen Cyfarthfa and the forges at Dyffnyn, visited and inspected the Dowlais works, is certainly unfavourable to them, as regards spaciousness and convenience. The mills and forges appear low, the furnaces crowded together, and, owing perhaps to these circumstances, there is a bustle and seeming confusion which are not visible in other iron-works. I have heard that owing to this overcrowding, and the lowness of the roof, the firemen, during the hot days of summer, are not unfrequently carried out fainting for recovery in the open air. At the Ivor works recently erected, and belonging to the same company, I observed that more consideration had been given to provisions of space and ventilation than in the old works. The furnaces at Ivor having no platform of masonry, and not resting against the mountain at the back, are worked by the hydraulic balance in the same manner as those at the iron-works in Staffordshire. The distance between the two works is about a quarter of a mile; both, however, are included under the general name "Dowlais works." There is a fine new forge erecting at Ivor; and the entire range of workshops for the artificers who make and repair the machinery for both works is there situated.

The various rates of wages paid to the men, as furnished to me by Mr. Howard, the intelligent and experienced cashier and superintendent of the books at Dowlais, to whose kind attention I am much indebted, are as follows:—

Colliers' wages, 14s. a week.
Miners' wages, 13s. a week.
Founders' wages, 25s. a week.
Furnace-fillers' wages, 24s. a week.
Puddlers' wages, 17s. a week (this appears an average of the puddler and his "second hand," who earns less).
Rollers' wages, 25s. a week.
Roughers' wages, 21s. a week.
Ballers' wages, 18s. a week.
Labourers' wages, 10s. a week.
Piling-girls' and mine-charing-girls' wages, 5s. a week.

The reader will, perhaps, remember that in describing the works at Dowlais in my last letter, I was particular in giving the statements regarding wages, as I received them from the men in the presence of an agent belonging to the works. This I did until I came to the puddling furnaces, and I gave the reason why I there discontinued personal inquiries of the men themselves. But in order that my account of the state of things in the works might be as complete as possible, and to give the public an opportunity of drawing conclusions from the particulars furnished by both parties, I examined men of each class at their homes, and before a gentleman whose presence I considered would influence them favourably for my obtaining the truth. The following are their statements:— —— ——: "I am a puddler, married, and with four children. I have worked at Pen-y-darran 30 years. I work twelve hours a day, and at night every other week. I do the first-rate puddling, and have four turns one week and five the next; in all, eighteen turns in the month. I earn 20s. a week, and my 'second-hand' 14s. The second-rate puddlers earn 15s. or 16s. a week, and their 'second-hands' 12s. I could do much more work, but trade is so bad we can't get it to do. In the good times I have earned as much as 50s. a week, and within these two years and a half I earned 32s. 6d. a week. Wages have been reduced twice since then. The first reduction was 4s. in the pound, and the second 2s. 6d., and notice has been given to reduce it again. I hear it is to be 1s. 8d. in the pound. I pay 9s. for rent and 6s.

8d. for coal every month. They stop 6d. in the pound for doctor and 'sick-fund,' and 6d. for clay to repair the furnace. I have had three bad accidents in the works. I fractured my skull, and I often suffer from it now; there is a hole in my head [he showed it]. Next I lost a joint of my thumb; and afterwards I got burnt so badly that I am lame now, and always shall be. I stand the heat pretty well; there are few who live through it so long as I have. My mother died of cholera in this house last September. There were seven persons carried off by it in this row." This man was gaunt and thin, and bore the marks of pre-mature old age; his cottage was comfortably furnished, and his wife seemed more disposed to complain than he did.

A man who worked at the balling furnaces answered me in the following words:— —— ——: "I am a baller in Pen-y-darran, and have worked at it fourteen years. For the last six months I have not earned 20s. a week. The most I ever got in a week was 55s., but that is long, long ago. I have had two severe accidents; once I got my hand mutilated in the rollers, and lost a finger. I pay 9s. a month for rent, 6s. 8d. for coals, 6d. for the doctor, and the same for 'fund.' Though I am better off than hundreds, I can hardly live. But the men are obliged to bear it, they can't help themselves. We all believe the masters can afford to pay us more. This reduction (he meant the reduction of which a month's notice had then been given) hurts us more than others did, because we are already beat down so low; we could better bear the reduction of 4s. in the pound than we can this. We men heard that iron rose 15s. a ton last week, and that makes us think worse of it. We used to get a newspaper between us when we were better off, and we could then see the price of iron; but now we be too poor, and we don't know how the price goes."

Quitting that house, I was next directed to the residence of a "roller," where I found four or five men assembled in a friendly party. They were drinking beer, and, many as have been the houses I have entered in this neighbourhood for the purpose of my investigations, this is the only instance in which I found beer or liquor in use. It is but just to the men whom I thus found together to say, that they were grave and well-conducted, and seemed drinking more for refreshment, after their heavy day's work, than for conviviality.

—— ——: "I am a roller of rails and merchants' bars, married, and with two children. I get from 25s. to 30s. a week. I have been ten years a roller, and have earned as much as 75s. a week. That was in 1846, when there was a great demand for rails. [He gave the same particulars of the two reductions in wages as 'the puddler,' *supra*]. The reason why I earn so much less now is, that I cannot get rail work, otherwise I should earn as much now, less the reductions made since the good times. [He showed me his account-papers of work and wages, in verification of what he had told me. There was in them a deduction of 6d. for doctor and 6d. for 'fund']. I pay 11s. a month for rent and 5s. for coal. My health has stood very well till within the past year. I was laid up with cholera. When we work 'merchants' bars' we make only from 15 to 20 tons a month, but when working rails we make from 30 to 35, therefore we then get much more. I have had some severe accidents—crippled fingers, and injuries to my eyes. The men were never so much distressed as they are now." The other men present, who were "ballers," one being a "gaffer" or superintendent, declared they had earned only from 15s. to 18s. a week during the previous six months. They said they could not bear the reduction; as it was, their wives and children "could not have enough to eat, and what would it be when the wages were lowered?" Two of them had met with severe accidents; one had been laid up, by injury to the legs, for five months. They all worked in Pen-y-darran. "At Cyfarthfa and Dowlais," said one of them, "the men have more constant full work, and therefore earn more than we. If the reduction takes place, we had better go to the parish for help to maintain our wives and families."

These men, and in fact all who come under the denomination of "fire-men," whether founders, refiners, puddlers, ballers, or rollers, have a peculiarly sallow appearance, which enables even a stranger, if he has once been through the works, easily to distinguish them from all other workmen. Even on Sundays, when all distinction of dress is cast aside, I could pick them out without a mistake. Observing this fact to Mr. Edward Davies, one of the surgeons to the Dowlais works, he said he could do more; he could discriminate all the classes with certainty, however they might be dressed. The face of the fireman is often ghastly white, with a peculiar shining waxy texture; his eyes are sunken, and so tremendous and so unremitting is the heat he has to endure that he never shows the slightest particle of fat—his limbs are gaunt and thin, and his muscles dessicated and hard like wire. To supply the place of the fluids exhaled by perspiration, he drinks copiously when at work and afterwards. The beverage he uses for this purpose is mostly tea, of which he consumes an inordinate quantity. Not only are his duties laborious and exhausting to an extent which affects the duration of life, but he is continually subject to accidents of a highly dangerous kind. What between the casualties above and under ground, the very streets are thronged with the maimed and mutilated. In a distance of a hundred yards I once saw three men moving in different directions, two of whom had lost a leg and the other both legs. It is a frequent practice of men disabled in this manner to learn to play the harp, by which means they earn a precarious and scanty subsistence, by playing at public-houses and merry-makings wherever they can find employment. I have seen men recently mutilated practising the harp for this purpose. During the years 1841 to 1847, inclusive, the deaths by accidents and violence *in Merthyr alone* averaged fifty a year. This is shown by the superintendent-registrar's books, from whom I had the information. During the past year, owing to some heavy explosions of fire-damp, the mortality from accidents has been much higher. I reserve the particulars for a letter on colliers and miners, to which it more properly belongs. It will readily be believed that a life such as that of the fireman is necessarily brief. Taking an average of their ages at death during the year 1847, it appears that the life of a fireman extends to no more than thirty-eight years. They generally die from a breaking-up of the constitution; frequently of pulmonary diseases, superinduced by the trying vicissitudes of heat and cold to which they are exposed. Often, when the constitution gives way, and they become unequal to their ordinary duties, they take a humbler employment, and linger for a while as wheelers, ash-fillers, gate-keepers, or in some such occupation. They get, it is true, the best wages of all classes employed in the works, but they barter their life for this increased pay. So subject to accidents, and to the failure of health, are all descriptions of workmen engaged in mining and the manufacture of iron, that an experienced and efficient staff of surgeons and apothecaries is indispensable. And everywhere in this district has this been provided. The companies appoint competent gentlemen, who are members of the "College" and the "Hall," and give them as many assistants and dispensers as are required; all these are paid by a fixed salary, and in some cases the principals are bound not to take private practice. The companies reimburse themselves by stopping a certain sum in the pound out of the wages of their workpeople; but whether there is an overplus or a deficiency at the end of the year, they do not inform them—a circumstance to be regretted, because it gives the men an opportunity for remarking upon it, while there is no doubt that at the least the whole amount, if not more, is expended in this manner for their benefit. A further sum is also stopped from the wages for the "sick fund." At Dowlais, the amount so taken has been for some months past 6d. in the pound. Of this three-halfpence goes to "the doctor," a half-penny to "the schools," and the remainder to "the fund." Each sick workman gets 4s. a week, or thereabouts, for a given time, which is regulated by a committee of workmen. My informant (Mr. Howard) added, "I consider we are now in a condition to return to 4d. in the pound, which was the amount paid before the visitation of cholera compelled us to raise it." The sick and maimed are visited by these gentlemen at their homes, where, unfortunately, the conditions most favourable for their recovery are frequently not to be commanded, and, particularly in the case of accidents, the want of what I may term "professional nursing" is much felt. These circumstances would seem to indicate the necessity for a commodious hospital, which might well be formed and supported partly by subscriptions, but mainly by the workmen's fund.

To complete this account of the business relations between the master and the workman, it should be stated that there is a monthly settlement between them, which is called a "pay." Advances nearly to the amount of the earnings—and in some cases, which I have seen, beyond them, as circumstances may be—are made weekly, and at the month's end (it is always a lunar month) the workman is presented with a ticket on which is a debtor and creditor account, which shows the balance due on either side. Nothing can be more simple or satisfactory than this arrangement, with which the men are, in fact, thoroughly contented. Formerly, when the truck system prevailed, the men were, I believe, paid in bulk at the end of the month, having during the interval to subsist upon credit at the shop belonging to the company. But that evil has long been removed, and the men by the weekly advances are enabled now to go with their money in their hands to the best markets. I understand the tally-system, or something near akin to it, is still carried on at several of the large works in South Wales. I propose visiting these, or at least some of them, and shall faithfully report what I there see.

With respect to the conduct and deportment of the workman in his occupation and towards the master, what I have heard and witnessed is in his favour. He does not indeed always work the first two days after the monthly pay, and sometimes he is slow to begin on the Monday; but when in the works he is industrious, diligent, and pains-taking, respectful to his superiors, and attentive to their directions. You hear him repeat with manifest pleasure and pride the sayings and doings of his masters. In the works he is always temperate, and seldom lags in his duty. Indeed, one of the most remarkable circumstances that strikes the visitor to the works is the astonishing rapidity and regularity with which all the various processes are carried on. All appears hurry and confusion, but, looked into closely, it is found the perfection of method.

The next iron works I visited were those of Cyfarthfa—the model works of South Wales. I did not select these for my description of the process of smelting, and of the labour and condition of the men, because I should have given the public an incorrect idea of the general state of the iron works; but I chose Dowlais as being the largest, and those which presented the average condition of the works in the mineral districts of the Principality.

There are at Cyfarthfa and Ynysfach (works adjacent to each other) 11 furnaces in blast, and four at Hirwain—all being the sole property of Mr. William Crawshay. At these works there are employed, under and above ground, 5,000 hands, of whom 190 are women. By the return furnished me, I find the amount of wages paid at Cyfarthfa and Hirwain alone is £16,000 a month (of four weeks). The make of pig-iron is 72,000 tons per annum. The quantity of bars, rails, and tin plates is 53,000 tons a year. There is used of Welsh iron, and red hematite ores for the production of the above, 166,800 tons a year. The daily consumption of coal is 850 tons. As many as 400 horses are here employed. These extensive works are chiefly carried on by water-power, the supply being procured from the River Taff at a considerable distance up the valley, but steam is used when in summer the water fails. The machinery is very large and ponderous. Those of the water wheels are 36 feet in diameter, and the fly-wheels, which are 60 feet in circumference and of prodigious weight, make ordinarily 70 revolutions in a minute. About three months ago the periphery of one of these wheels flew into pieces, the fragments demolishing the roof of the mill in which the accident occurred, and descending at a distance through the roof of another mill, crushing into pieces large portions of beautiful and costly machinery then in motion, but without further casualty to the numerous workmen than a fracture of the thighs of one of them. One of the steam-engines is of 260-horse power; it has six boilers, and is of nine feet stroke. The above particulars will convey some idea of the magnitude of these works. I was accompanied over them by Mr. Robert Crawshay, whose familiarity with the philosophy of the various processes of smelting the iron is only equalled by his practical familiarity with its manufacture, and to whom I am much indebted for the attention he paid me, and for the lucid and intelligible manner in which he explained everything which I did not at first clearly understand. These works are incomparably the best constructed, the most spacious, well-ventilated, comfortable, convenient, and methodical of all the works, not only in and around Merthyr, but throughout South Wales. Everything has been done on the most liberal scale, and with an evident aim at perfection and completeness. The extensive mills, with their massive walls pierced with large circular openings for light and ventilation, and their arches supporting light and lofty roofs, have an air of architectural grandeur that is quite imposing. The space within the roof of one mill is 82 feet. There is here so much room that the work is carried on without any appearance of that hurry and bustle which I have remarked upon as belonging to other works. I was informed by Mr. David James, a disinterested party, that men who had once enjoyed the comfort, shelter, and convenience of these works would never leave them for others if they could possibly avoid it. I have said *shelter*, because here the men and women employed at the furnace tops and at the hearths have roofs overhead, whereas at Dowlais I have complained that they are wholly unprotected, and such is the case elsewhere. The comfort of such a provision in the windy and rainy climate of these mountains can only be adequately valued by the workpeople who have tried both situations, the exposed and the sheltered. I think it the duty of those iron-masters who have neglected providing such a shelter, to lose no time in following the example of Cyfarthfa and the other works where such conveniences have been adopted. It will be an act of great kindness to the miserables who have now to endure all weathers, and the most violent alternations of heat and cold.

At Cyfarthfa I saw the men belonging to the furnaces, squeezers, rollers, and saws at their dinner. They had good beef or mutton, and potatoes; the boys had broth with a small piece of meat: they seemed pleased to show the contents of their *tins*, observing that the work was so hard and the heat so great that they could not stand it without animal food. This, it must be borne in mind, was in the mills; at Dowlais and in the other works, as I have stated, the workmen also get meat. They were rail-making in two of the mills I inspected. I saw three rails made by direction of Mr. Crawshay. Timed by a watch, they were made in three minutes—that is, from the presentation of the white-hot "bloom" to the rollers to its completion in them. The ends were cut off, filed, and the bars straightened in an additional minute and a quarter—so that altogether the making and finishing of three rails ready for laying down on the permanent way occupied just four minutes and a quarter. It was here I first saw that ingenious but simple invention, "the splitting mill," at work. It was making what is termed "nail rods," which it did by lengthening and dividing a short iron bar into about a dozen rods, eight feet long by a quarter of an inch wide. This most important and useful invention was made in Sweden, and the consequences were most disastrous to the manufacturers of iron in this country, who, having to divide the rods by a long, tedious, and laborious process, could not compete with the new invention. The means by which this difficulty was overcome are highly interesting. I give the story in the words of Coleridge, who particularly delighted to tell it:—

"The most extraordinary and well-attested instance of enthusiasm existing in conjunction with perseverance is related of the founder of the Foley family. This man, who was a fiddler living near Stourbridge, was often witness of the immense labour and loss of time in dividing the rods of iron necessary for the process of making nails. The discovery of the process called splitting, in mills called splitting mills, was first made in Sweden; and the consequences were very disastrous in the neighbourhood of Stourbridge. Foley, the fiddler, was shortly missed from his accustomed rounds, and was not again seen for many years. He had mentally resolved to ascertain by what means the process of splitting bars of iron was accomplished; and, without communicating his intention to a single human being, he proceeded to Hull, and thence, without funds, fiddled his way to the iron foundries of Sweden, where, after a long time, he became a universal favourite with the workmen, and from the apparent entire absence of intelligence, or anything like ultimate object, he was received into the works, to every part of which he had access. He took the advantage thus offered, and having stored his memory with observations and all the combinations, he disappeared from amongst his kind friends as he had appeared—no one knew whence or whither. On his return to England he communicated his voyage and its results to Mr. Knight and another person in the neighbourhood with whom he was associated, and by whom the necessary buildings were erected and machinery provided. When at length everything was prepared, the machinery would not act—at all events it did not answer the sole end of its erection—it would not split the bar of iron. Foley disappeared again, and it was concluded that shame and mortification at his failure had driven him away. Not so: again, though somewhat more speedily, he found his way to the Swedish iron-works, where he was received most joyfully; and, to make sure of their fiddler, he was lodged in the splitting mill itself. Here was the very end and aim of his life attained beyond his utmost hopes. He examined the works, and very soon discovered the cause of his failure. He now made rude drawings or tracings, and having abided an ample time to verify his observations, and to impress them clearly and vividly on his mind, he made his way to the port, and once more returned to England. This time he was completely successful, and, by the results of his experience, enriched himself, and greatly benefited his countrymen. This I hold to be one of the most extraordinary instances of credible devotion in modern times." So far Coleridge. Here, however, they have a different version of one part of the story. They say that the cause of the failure of Foley's first essay was, not that he had copied the machine imperfectly, and therefore that it would not act, but that the heat of the white-hot bar so rapidly softened the teeth and grooves of the rollers, that they bent, and would not divide the bar. To remedy this it was, that Foley made his second visit to the forges of Sweden, where he found that it was by the plentiful use of tallow and cold water, to harden the machinery, that it was kept in working order, which circumstance he had either forgotten or overlooked on the occasion of his first journey to Sweden. The probability is, I think, in favour of this last version, for the machinery is so simple that it could scarcely have been miscopied.

The return made to me of the rate of wages paid at these works, is as follows:—

Colliers, 15s. a week.
Miners, 12s. 6d. a week.
Founders, 22s. a week.
Fillers, 21s. a week.
Labourers, 10s. 6d. a week.
Puddlers, 18s. a week.
Rollers, 30s. a week; rail-rollers, 3*l.* to 4*l.* a week.
Roughers, 18s. a week; ditto, 2*l.* 5s. to 2*l.* 10s. a week.
Ballers, 24s. a week; ditto, 1*l.* 10s. to 1*l.* 12s.; girls, 5s. a week.

The proportion of boys employed under sixteen years of age is about one-sixth of the whole: at Dowlais these were returned as about one-fourth. At one of the mills in these works boys only are employed; it is a training school for them, preparing them for the heavier mill and forge work. I saw them making iron rods for rails, and light work; they seemed to work with great spirit and alacrity. I am told that boys like the work, and I cannot wonder at it, for it gives them early what the spirit of man always loves—independence and the self-respect which accompanies labour.

The next works I visited were "the Plymouth Works," the property of Mr. Anthony Hill. In point of magnitude these rank next after the Cyfarthfa works. They are situated in the valley of the Taff—at two points, the lowest being about two miles below the town of Merthyr. From the mountain at whose foot they stand, these works, like those already noticed, derive their store of fuel and minerals there consumed and manufactured. They comprise eight blast-furnaces (four at Plymouth and four at Dyffryn), 48 puddling and 26 balling furnaces at full work, with three puddling and ten balling furnaces at present idle. The number of hands employed under and above ground is 2,750. Of there 350 are boys engaged in various occupations, as we have seen them at Dowlais, and 175 are women employed in stacking and piling iron, loading and unloading trains, and in separating the iron ore from its matrix of stone or shale. There are here two founders to each blast furnace. The rates of pay, as furnished by Mr. Joseph, the intelligent and obliging manager of the mills and forges, are as follows:—

Founders, about 20s. a week.
Fillers, about 18s. 6d. a week.
Refiners, about 20s. a week.
Puddlers and ballers, 20s. to 25s., according to the quality of their work.
Rollers at puddlers' rolls get 20s.
Ballers at the rolling mill, 18s. to 20s.
Rollers when working rails, 25s. to 35s.
Boys, from 3s. to 15s., according to their work.
Girls, from 3s. to 6s. 6d. a week.

The workmen have their coal at reduced prices here, as at the other works, and the colliers are supplied without charge.

The make of iron here is 500 tons a week of bars and rails; in all, 26,000 tons of iron are here manufactured in the course of the year. The "new forge," erected I believe by Mr. Stephenson, the distinguished engineer, is very spacious and commodious; and Mr. Joseph informed me that one of the furnaces at Dyffryn, which he showed me, was the largest in the Principality. Water is largely used here as a motive power. I saw blowing-machines at work by this agency, but they also employ some large steam-engines. In short, the "lower works" are very complete, with this exception, that the furnace heads here, as at Dowlais, are unprovided with shelter, so that the men and women are exposed to all the vicissitudes of the weather in this rainy and tempestuous climate.

I have now given, in this and my last letter, the statements of the employers and the workmen as to the rate of wages at these, the most extensive, works in South Wales. Compared with each other, these several particulars, as will be seen, differ but very slightly. The variation in the price of labour at the different works is more striking. Wherever there is much "rail" work, the rates are higher, because that description of produce is paid for on a more liberal scale than what is called "merchants' iron;" consequently, any circumstances which depreciate railway property, and limit the extension of lines, have a direct and most baneful effect on the workmen at these works. I cannot close this part of my subject without remarking that the fairness which both masters and men have shown in their statements is the best evidence that each class is conscious of the soundness of its own position, and is willing to afford every reasonable satisfaction to the other. In my next I shall speak of the miners and colliers as I find them in their occupation; after which I shall treat of the morals, habits, and domestic life of all the classes engaged in this mining and manufacturing district.

LABOUR AND THE POOR.

---◆---

THE MINING AND MANUFACTURING DISTRICTS OF SOUTH WALES.

[FROM OUR SPECIAL CORRESPONDENT.]

MINES AND COLLIERIES.

A WELSH COAL-PIT.

LETTER IV.

Although in my first Letter on the mineral basin of South Wales I gave a succinct account of the "coal and iron measures" in this important district, it may be desirable for the better understanding of what I have hereafter to communicate, to recapitulate some particulars, and to amplify others, before proceeding to show the manner in which the mines are worked, and to speak in detail of the life and condition of the intrepid men by whose labour they are rendered productive.

The area of the coal-field of South Wales has been computed at 700,000 acres—having, throughout, of coal, an aggregate thickness of 95 feet, and of iron-stone, workable by level operations, about eight feet. According to Mr. Moses, an experienced mining engineer, the average thickness of iron-stone between the second and third veins of coal, in the ascending order, in the coal measures from Aberdare to Nantyglo (about fifteen miles), on the north crop, is 67 inches—while the average thickness of the same in the south, from the Ebbw River to Carmarthen Bay, is 84 inches. Both minerals are found in separate layers or veins, superposed at various distances above each other. In some instances these veins are so thin and insufficient as to be worthless for the purposes of working; in others they are of such thickness and quality as to be abundantly remunerative. The coals distributed everywhere over this vast field are divisible into three kinds—"bituminous, or caking, coal," "free burning coal," and "anthracite, or stone, coal." Each of these varieties is applicable for a separate purpose. The bituminous coal, which is found in most abundance on the eastern and south-eastern sides of the basin, is saturated with so much naphtha or inflammable oil as to cause "the small," when heated, to adhere and cake; this is the coal mostly raised for exportation, being equally suited for the distillation of gas and for domestic consumption. The quantity of sulphur it contains unfits it for the making of iron. The second variety, "free burning coal," does not cake. Having no sulphur, it is applicable and is largely used for smelting iron, and especially for steam purposes; indeed the experiments recently instituted under Government authority have, as already shown, established the superiority of this coal, above all others tested, for the uses of the steam-engine. It burns freely, as the name implies, with a white or a brown ash, according to the "measures"—whether the "lower" or the "middle"—from which it is extracted. The third and last variety—anthracite—burns without smoke or flame: it is very durable, and emits an intense heat. Its specific gravity is greater than that of the other kinds, and it is used for purposes where a smokeless, flameless, and lasting coal is desirable. It has been tried in the steam navy; but requiring, when used alone, a furnace of peculiar and inconvenient form, it has never come into general favour. It is, however, not unfrequently mixed with other coals, and so used for steam purposes; and it has been adopted in many instances by maltsters for consumption in their kilns. Aided by the "hot-blast" (which is air heated to a high degree before admission to the furnaces), it has been used in the manufacture of iron; but I cannot find that its application in this way is extending.

To Mr. Crane of Ynis-cedwin (whose works are situated on the stone-coal formation, and who was therefore stimulated by that prolific parent of inventions, necessity), belongs the merit of the discovery that this coal, which had been thought unavailable for the smelting of iron, could be rendered serviceable to this end by means of hot-blast. The value of this discovery can only be estimated when the fact is considered that one-third of the coal-field is occupied by anthracite. Whenever the vast districts of South Wales from which the free-burning coal is obtainable shall become exhausted, or, owing to the depth at which it is to be dug, only workable at a loss, there will remain in reserve, for the manufacture of iron, an extensive magazine of anthracite, which our present affluence of other coals causes us in great measure to neglect. The discovery of Mr. Crane has been turned to more profitable account in America than here. In the year 1840 there were, in the United States alone, not fewer than fifty furnaces at work consuming anthracite for fuel. According to

Mr. Crane's statement, this coal would appear far more economical than the other varieties for smelting iron. He says that on an average of three months he made the ton of iron with less than 27 cwt. of anthracite, and that the iron produced was decidedly stronger than any before smelted at his works. Of the ordinary coal, I should say that the quantity required to smelt a ton of iron is about three tons. But it appears (on the authority of Scrivener), that, notwithstanding these advantages, Mr. Crane only used a single small cupola, making not more than thirty-five tons a week, in which anthracite was the sole fuel employed; in his other furnaces he used three-fourths of bituminous and one-fourth of anthracite coal. This is an inconsistency which he may be able to explain; possibly he may now be using this coal more freely, or may have rejected it altogether—a point on which I am not informed, having been unable to pay a visit to his works to look into this interesting question. If I may speak from my own observation of the consumption of anthracite jointly with other coals for steam purposes *in a common furnace*, it does not succeed. I recommended it to a friend in London, who gave it a trial; but his fireman informed me that the mixture made a tough viscous cinder, which adhered with great tenacity to the bars, and so softened them that they were quickly destroyed. The probable remedy which suggested itself to me was, to use brass instead of iron for bars, which I think might be successful. Where anthracite can be used, it is conceded that it is much the most economical fuel. But the other varieties exist in such abundance, are so easily accessible, and are so well fitted for all domestic and manufacturing necessities, that the collier has but a very small field for his labour in this coal.

It is around the edges of the basin, where the minerals are obtainable at comparatively small depths, that the coal is most freely worked. There are, however, collieries at a considerable distance from the "outcrop." Those known as "Sea Coal Collieries" are, for the most part, situated on the south-eastern side of the basin, and their point of export is Newport. But this trade has within the past ten years been pushed with great success, and is yearly extending in and about the Valley of Aberdare, on the north side of the basin—whence, as I showed by figures, in my first Letter, vast quantities are sent to Cardiff, which has become a rival with Newport in the exportation of coals. The mineral is conveyed from the pits to the water's edge by canals, tramroads, and railways. The coals sent to the port of Newport are carried by the Monmouthshire Canal and tramroad; those to Cardiff are conveyed by the

Taff Vale Railway and the Glamorganshire Canal. A striking proof of the increase in the coal and iron trade in and around the Valley of the Taff is afforded by the fact, that since the construction of the Taff Vale Railway, some fifteen years ago—which doubled the facilities for carrying those commodities to the sea, and therefore might have been expected to reduce the profits of the Glamorganshire Canal, which, till then, had been the sole channel for this traffic—the canal, though the railway is exclusively used by the largest works in the world (those of Dowlais, and several others) transports at least the same quantity as it used to carry formerly, if not more. It still pays the shareholders a dividend of eight per cent.—the amount to which it is limited by Parliament—after which there remains so large a surplus as to return the freighters 90 per cent. of the amount charged under authority of their act. To the other towns of export—Porth Cawl, Neath, and Swansea—the coal is chiefly conveyed by railways.

The iron ore is, for the most part, worked in the same pits as the coal, but usually at lower depths. What are called "the ironstone measures," within which is found the white ash coal, lie the lowest of all. The veins of ore vary in thickness from two to ten inches, and are imbedded in a kind of slaty stone. The ore is frequently found in the form of nodules, and what the miners call "pins." I have also seen it in some places quarried in the open air, where it is found in round lumps or boulders, which bear the appearance of having undergone attrition, by rolling, before their envelopment in the matrix of rock which now encloses them. In the "Pennant Series," which is the middle one, the iron is found in a substance called blackband. This discovery was made by Mr. Mushet, the contributor of a series of admirable papers on iron and steel, which appeared some years ago in the "Philosophical Magazine." Until his time, it was not suspected that this abundant material contained iron in such a proportion as would pay for the working. This vein yields, from the raw stone 36 per cent., and from the roasted stone 57 per cent. of iron.

Compared with the depth at which coal is worked in the north of England, the coal-pits of South Wales are shallow. The necessity for working at great depths, owing to the abundance of the veins and the extent of the mineral field, does not exist here. But were the supply, which is now obtained within easy distance from the surface, exhausted, many hundred square miles would remain that might be worked at a less depth than coal is now cut at Monkwearmouth, in the north of England—where there is a pit at which it is raised, with a profit, from a depth of 299 fathoms. I doubt whether there is one in South Wales of more than 125 fathoms. It is estimated by Mr. Moses, that the depth at which coal in this district is workable to advantage is 300 fathoms. The average of Welsh coal-pits, speaking from my own observation, I should say is about 75 fathoms.

Various methods are employed for bringing the minerals to the surface. In most instances steam-engines or "whimsies" are employed; in others recourse is had to the "balance" principle, in which a loaded tram is brought up by the descent of an empty one, assisted by such a weight of water as will set in motion the iron pulley at the top of the pit. There are a few small collieries in which the hand-windlass is still used. Large quantities of coal and iron are also obtained by what are called "levels." These are galleries driven into the sides of the mountains, on an incline into the ground, until the minerals are reached. A preference, from motives of economy and safety, is always given to levels where circumstances permit of their being adopted. The water—of which, as may well be supposed—immense quantities accumulate in the pits—is drained off sometimes through levels, but most frequently it is pumped by steam-engines. In a few instances, where water power is available, it is used for this purpose. Locomotives, often of the most primitive construction (I have seen some with vertical action), and horses, are employed to convey the minerals to the iron works, the canals, or the railways, as their destination may be. Underground, horses are used in all large collieries to convey the coal or iron from the stalls where the miners work to the bottom of the shaft which it has to ascend, or through the levels to the surface. Boys and men perform this office in a few small collieries. Nowhere, since the passing of the 5th and 6th Vict., c. 99, are women permitted to work in the mines. I made particular inquiries on this point, but always found the statute rigorously observed, though the temptation to break it—so great is the competition of females for labour—must be considerable. Some of the steam-pumps which raise the water are inferior only in capacity to the far-famed hydraulic machines of Cornwall.

The colliers earn different rates of wages, according as they happen to find employment at sea-coal or other collieries. They are invariably paid by the ton. The custom is for the overlooker or his assistants to send in as many trams as are required; these are distributed to the men in the mines, who fill them with the produce of their labour, and mark them; and on the arrival of the trams at the surface, the earnings of each man are credited to him in the books of the concern, and he is debited with the cost of gunpowder, mandrils, "helves," and such other tools and conveniences as are from time to time supplied to him. Weekly advances are made, but what is called "the pay" takes place at the end of the month. A balance of the account is then struck—a printed ticket showing the particulars is furnished—and every man is paid the amount which may then be due to him. At the sea-coal collieries a larger sum is paid for cutting coal than at those where it is raised for the use of the iron-works and for consumption in the neighbourhood. For instance, the colliers employed by Mr. Hill in providing coal for his forges and furnaces, get 10½d. per ton—whilst those who work the very same vein, in the valley of Aberdare, at a distance of four miles, get 1s. 4d. per ton, because the coal is there raised for exportation. The reason of this will be stated when I speak of "strikes," which, amongst the sea-coal colliers, are not uncommon. In the particulars supplied to me at the great iron-works, it is stated that colliers engaged in cutting coals for the use of the works earn, upon an average, at Dowlais 14s., and at Cyfarthfa 15s., which agrees very nearly with the statements I received from the men in their workings underground. In addition to this, colliers have their firing supplied free of charge—an indulgence which does not seem extended to miners.

In periods when the trade is depressed, as it has been of late, the men only work half or three-quarters of their proper time. It is the policy of the masters, in the continual hope and expectation of an improved demand, to keep on the same number of hands as when trade is good, so that when the better time comes there may be sufficient workmen available—an arrangement by which the rate of wages is kept at once lower and steadier than it would be if, at the emergency, the number of hands should be unequal to it, and it should be necessary to bid for extra exertions on the part of the men already employed. The number of trams sent into the mines being thus regulated by the quantity of coal and iron-stone required, the workmen get more or less to do according as the demand is brisk or otherwise.

The miners and colliers are almost exclusively Welsh. Although there are great numbers of Irish engaged in rough work above ground, they never undertake the skilled labour of the mines. As a class, the miners are the most provident, temperate, and best affected to their masters; they are also the most regular in their work. During the first and second week after the monthly "pay," the colliers work only about two-thirds of their time, the remainder is spent in idleness, and by many in drunkenness. Various endeavours have been made by the masters to cure this evil, but Mr. Robert Crawshay informed me that they have all failed. At the Dowlais works a regulation was made not long ago, by the sagacious and considerate manager, Mr. Evans, under which those men who should not cut a certain quantity of coal on the Monday, Tuesday, and Wednesday after "the pay," were to be paid at a reduced rate for what they might afterwards raise. This plan, like the others, was found not to answer, for some reason which I could not learn, and it is now, I believe, abandoned. Towards the middle and at the end of the month the men labour most vigorously and industriously, and the masters, in order to provide a stock to carry on the works during the approaching idle time, then send into the pits an increase of trams, proportioned to their wants and to the additional quantity produced.

Whilst it is yet dark the men go to their labour—some at three, some at four, others at five in the morning, as convenience serves, and as the work to be performed requires. Daylight is no consideration to those whose occupation lies perhaps two miles from the aperture through which alone it enters. They carry with them their dinner of bread and cheese, a closed tin jug filled with tea—sometimes, no doubt, with beer—a few candles, and the tools with which they cut the minerals. Their dress is a woollen jacket and waistcoat, trowsers of fustian or canvass, a shirt of checked flannel, and a round-crowned low hat, under the band of which they stick the candle which lights them to and from the stalls in which they work. They enter the mines sometimes by "inclines" leading down to the seams of coal and veins of iron, through which the horses also are led to the galleries where they work. At other collieries they are let down a shaft by steam power; at some, again, they descend by the "balance-pits," which I have already described. Before the men enter the workings, it is the duty of a special officer to examine, with the Davy lamp, every part of the mine which will be occupied in the course of the day. After this, the men and boys enter; each man goes to his "stall," which is the division of the mine where he works; the boys take their places at the doors used for regulating and directing the current of air for ventilation, of which they have charge—or in the "windways" (narrow channels for the draught, which they cut)—or in the "stalls," where they assist their fathers. The work then goes forward actively; the minerals are quarried, as we shall hereafter see, placed in the trams to which the halliers "hook on" the horses, and thus conveyed to the shaft for raising, or through the "level" to the surface, as the case may be. All these operations are carried on by candle-light; very rarely indeed is the safety-lamp used. Accidents, of course, are numerous—sometimes from explosions of fire-damp, but more frequently from falls of earth and stone. This subject, however, will come in more appropriately hereafter, when I treat of the ventilation of the mines, and of the dreadful consequences which result when it is neglected. At three or four o'clock in the afternoon—earlier if his allotted number of trams be filled—the workman returns by the way he entered in the morning, or otherwise, at his pleasure. Arrived at his cottage, where his wife has hot water in readiness for him, he strips and washes from head to foot—after which he takes his evening repast (which is, in fact, the principal meal of the day) of broth, meat, or cheese, as his means afford. This done, the colliers and miners pass the remainder of the evening as they choose—at home, at a neighbour's, or at the public-house. For the most part they go to bed early, having to return to their work betimes on the morrow. The miners and colliers in and around Merthyr are gregarious in their dwellings. Their small four-roomed cottages will be described when I treat of the domestic life of the working classes in this district. Large numbers of miners live in a suburb called Twyn-y-rodin, and there is a large village about two miles north of the town, named Coed-y-Cwmmer, which is principally inhabited by colliers.

There exists in the mines and collieries a system of "middle-men," which requires mention in this place. A man called a "gaffer" undertakes a certain quantity of work at a given price, in the performance of which he employs a number of hands, whom he pays, having generally a profit upon their labour. Sometimes there is a friendly understanding between the gaffer and the men that the former shall contract for the work, dividing the money equally—or at most keeping only a small sum from each, in repayment for the time and trouble experienced in negotiating the undertaking and paying the men. This is an arrangement for mutual convenience, and is therefore unobjectionable. Neither can exception be taken where the work is of such a nature that the masters find it more advantageous to let it by contract—such as sinking pits, driving "horse-ways," and the like, where a fixed sum per yard is paid, instead of so much a ton for the material removed. There is something speculative in this kind of work, which ought, therefore, to have a broad margin of profit to compensate for its uncertainty—whilst the men are secured the pay agreed upon al-

Pit Hands

most as safely as if they worked for the principals themselves. But it is in cases where "the gaffer" employs a number of hands in cutting the minerals, that the system is to be deprecated: here there is no occasion whatever for a middleman between the master and the men. Until lately, many "gaffers" were the keepers of public-houses or beer-shops, where they paid their men, and, as a matter of course, the latter there spent much of their earnings in drink. The iron-masters have very properly ordered that in future no "gaffer" shall keep a house of entertainment of such a kind. But the system of payment in public-houses still continues, and there exists, it is to be feared, in too many instances, an understanding between the gaffer and the beer-shop keeper which virtually defeats the good intentions of the iron-masters and owners of collieries, whose desire is to abolish this temptation altogether. The best conducted and most provident of the men complain of this state of things, and wish to see it remedied. They were utterly unaware that by law all such payments are of no effect— that, having once been paid in a public-house, they could compel the repayment of such amount, and that there is a penalty (not exceeding

£10 nor under £5) attached to "the payment of any sum in respect of wages for work or labour" which shall be made contrary to the provisions of the statute (5th and 6th Vic., c. 99, secs. 10, 11, and 12). The gaffers deduct 3d. from each man for what is termed "getting change"—a matter often of some difficulty where a great number of men are to be paid. The offences committed under this act are cognizable by magistrates; and if the law were put into operation, it is quite equal to the suppression of this baneful practice.

I have given the statements of the masters as to the wages earned by colliers and miners. I subjoin those which I received from the men themselves. The first I examined was a man of great intelligence. He said: "I have been a miner of iron-stone these thirty years. At present I am in the mines belonging to 'Plymouth Works.' I have five children. My earnings are, on an average, 12s. a week, for which I work twelve or thirteen hours daily. I am paid by the ton. Instead of 12s., I have earned 24s. a week for the same work; but that was 25 years ago. The price of bar iron was then £8 a ton; now it is from £4 15s. to £5 a ton. Only three years ago I earned as much as £1 1s. a week. I pay 9s. a month rent for a poor house, and 1½d. in the pound for the doctor's fund. Notice has been given of a reduction of 1s. 6d. in the pound, which I think a great hardship, and the more so as the price of iron is improving. I consider the present pay insufficient, and so do the men. The iron I 'mine' is ninety feet below the coal. I work at a depth of forty fathoms; but there are pits belonging to Plymouth where the depth is 150 fathoms. We blast the rock with gunpowder to get the iron-stone, and we have to displace, or altogether remove, about eight tons of stone rubbish for every ton of ore. The veins I work are four or five, near each other, and the thickness of the whole is about a foot. The ventilation is not bad; but the atmosphere is naturally close and exhausting. I have seen explosions many times; once I was much burnt; twice I was in the fire. I have had persons killed by explosions within a hundred yards of me. When the gas is weak, a red flame rushes with a noise along the top of the mine, increasing in strength as it advances, and then rolls back again. If there is plenty of gas, it keeps burning for days, or perhaps for a week. When explosions occur we run and hide our faces and hands as far as possible in the rubbish. We have for food good wheaten bread and cheese, a little butter, and tea and sugar; but we can only afford meat once, or may be twice a week. Many boys work in the same mine as I do, who are only eight or nine years of age. I have heard them say so, and have known they were right, because I remember the year when some of them were born. I know this is unlawful. Mr. Hill has sent and ordered all boys under ten to leave the pits, but the parents are so poor that they are compelled to apply in a month or two for them to be re-admitted, saying that they had now come to the proper age. I am a member of the Baptist chapel, and belong to a Benefit society; the miners generally belong to such societies, but the men are now too poor to continue their payments, and so must lose the advantage of them. The cholera broke many of the Benefit societies. One evil belonging to them is their being held at public-houses."

It may be well to give the examination of another miner, who worked under a different employer:—"I have worked twenty-nine years as a miner, of which twenty were at Dowlais. I left three months ago, and have taken other employment. I was paid by the ton. During the past twelvemonths I earned only 8s. a week—that is, after the deductions for powder, candles, and the per centage of 4d. in the pound for doctor and Sick Fund. I know men who, owing to bad luck in getting a hard piece of 'mine,' have earned no more than 5s. in a week. I have a wife and six children. I have wanted bread, and so has my family, within the year, though in full work—the rock was so hard, and the pay so bad. The lowest sum I have myself received for a week's work is 6s. 6d.: but the average, taking the year through, is what I have said—8s. Before Sir John's lease was out, I have earned as much as £12 a month; I was fortunate then in getting a stall to work in which required no blasting. I used to get my coal from 'the company,' and paid 1s. for 'a draft' (3 cwt.); they charge a penny a draft more in Dowlais, because they take away the ashes. I worked under William ——, a 'gaffer.' I think the system of employing a gaffer between the master and men is bad; but I must say that Mr. Evans (the manager of Dowlais works) often told us we should have our money, if we liked, straight from the office. It is a bad custom amongst the men. The 'gaffer' charged 3d. for getting change to pay us. *More than half the colliers and miners are paid in public-houses.* The men would rather not be paid there, because, if paid elsewhere, they would only be charged 3d. for 'change,' but now they are bound to pay 6d. for a quart of beer. It is an understood thing that the men must throw back 6d., but they get beer for it. Scores of times I have stayed in the public-house where I was paid till I had spent one-half of my money, and so do great numbers of the men. Many of the 'gaffers' used to keep public-houses and pay their hands in them; but there was an order made twelve months ago that no publican should be a 'gaffer;' they still pay us in public-houses. The men are not aware that such payments are forbidden by law and go for nothing."

At the same time, I took the statement of a "hallier" employed with horses underground, in conveying the trains from the "stalls" to the shafts, where they are raised to the surface; but the only material information he gave was, that his earnings were 12s. a week. This may be taken as the rate of wages of this class of labourers. The scale on which, according to their own statement, colliers and boys are paid, will appear below.

Anxious to describe the miners and colliers as they are to be found in their work—to note down from their own lips such information as they might afford me—and particularly to qualify myself for giving a true picture of the underground life of these classes as it exists in South Wales—I determined on descending into the mines. Facilities for so doing were kindly offered me by Mr. Joseph, the intelligent mining agent of Mr. Hill, and by Mr. Crawshay and Mr. Robert Crawshay, who, from first to last, have thrown open to me every department of their most extensive and complete works, and have placed me under infinite obligations by furthering in every possible manner my wishes with regard to the subjects of my inquiry. I am indebted to Mr. Robert Crawshay for the valuable manuscript returns of the exports of iron and coal during the past year, given in my first Letter, which otherwise I should have found inaccessible.

The pit I descended was at Glynderris, and belonged to Mr. Crawshay. Its depth was seventy-seven fathoms, that is 462 feet. I have been assured by disinterested parties, possessed of the means of judging, that it was one of average quality, being neither what is called a "wet" nor a "dry" pit, neither low, on the whole, nor lofty; and its ventilation much the same as that of most workings in this district. I was accompanied by Mr. Kirkhouse, the mineral agent, for whose obliging attention I owe a grateful acknowledgment. His thorough practical knowledge of the geology of the mines, and of the entire system of working them, together with the readiness and facility with which he explained everything on which I needed information, left nothing further to be desired, and made me thankful that I had the good fortune of meeting with such a guide.

Our road to the pit lay, for about two miles, along a breadth of moor on the lowest slope of the Aberdare mountain. The day was one of the most tempestuous I ever encountered; the wind howled along

the waste with irresistible fury, driving the heavy rain with such violence in our faces as to be almost blinding. The tramroad along which
we advanced was one mass of black water and mud, having treach-
erous holes, which reached over the high boots with which I had
provided myself. The signs of mineral traffic were on all sides visible. Inclined planes worked by steam-engines, and leading to the galleries below—locomotives dragging long trains of trams loaded with
iron-stone and coal—horses similarly occupied on the short lines leading from the various pits to the trunk-line—weighing-houses for the
register of each man's work, and for the regulation of the quantities
raised—halliers, engineers, and other workmen,—all engaged our notice as we passed along. At length the pit we had to descend came in
view. It was a "balance pit," having no inconvenient mound of small
coal and rubbish by its side, such as some pits have, but simply a
small house constructed of iron, for the shelter of those who worked
the machinery of the pit, and in front and behind it, sundry groups
of trams—some waiting to descend and be filled, and others ready
loaded for removal to the weighing-house. Having already described
the principle of the "balance-pit," I need not here repeat it. A loaded
tram having reached the surface just as we arrived, we stepped on the
narrow wooden platform from which it was removed; and the "pitsman" prepared for our descent, by letting into the trough under our
feet the requisite weight of water to counterpoise that of the loaded
train which by our descent we were to bring up. The platform on
which we stood might be about four feet square; it had no cagework;
nor indeed anything to take hold of except the four iron uprights
at the angles, or the cross-bars overhead (rusty with coal-water), by
which it hung suspended on a single linked chain over the abyss beneath. Presently, the trough having been duly weighted, the pitsman
cries "stand-fast," and off we go, steadied by a rope tightly stretched
from the top to the bottom of the pit. The first thing I noticed as we
sunk below the level of the ground was the welcome change from a
fierce rushing wind, with driving rain, to the calmness of the pit—we
had left the turmoil of the elements above-ground. At first we moved
gently—the aperture overhead closing gradually, and the light less-
ening as we receded from it. Presently our speed increased, and at
half way—a point which we recognised by the passing upwards of
the tram that we were raising—we had attained considerable velocity, the rugged, black, and slimy sides of the pit glimmering faintly as
we whirled past them. Still further, and all was darkness. Our speed

slackening, we knew we were approaching the bottom of the pit. The loud splashing of falling water, and the voices of men in the vaults below, were now heard. Looking downwards, I saw some lights, apparently at a vast distance, but in reality near, moving about on the right hand. Our pace by this time was, as it were, a movement of caution, gentle in the extreme, till we struck the ground. Loud clanking reverberations came down the shaft, occasioned by the securing of the tram which had reached the surface. Leaving the platform which had carried us thus safely down, we entered a lofty and spacious chamber cut in the rock, where we were welcomed by the smiling but smutty faces of the men whose duty lay where we thus found them. Stepping back, I took a look at the mouth of the pit from the great depth where I now stood; its appearance was that of a small point, with light playing round it in brilliant pencils, as sunbeams do on a mirror. The valve being now opened in the trough on which we had descended, the water rushed out into the channel which drains the pit, leading to an underground reservoir at a distance, whence it is pumped by a steam-engine. One of the many loaded trams which were waiting to ascend was now placed in the cage—the signal given—and away it went in the usual manner. The occupants of the spacious chamber in which I stood were a few halliers, the men and boys who supply the cages with trams, and some horses, which were quietly munching their provender during a short interval of rest. My guide now drew from a wicker tube, which he carried about him, three small candles; one of the men immediately set them up in a ball of clay, lit them, gave one to the guide, one to me, and kept the third himself. Having exchanged my great coat for a coarse jacket, belonging to one of the men, we now advanced towards the workings—the guide first, myself second, and our attendant bringing up the rear. On leaving what may be called the entrance-chamber, the roadway narrowed and lowered so as to admit of little more than the passage of the horses and trams to and from the workings. Overhead we had in some places a roof of rock; at others, where it was necessary to support the earth, an arched-way like a railway tunnel, with the difference that here the stones were thin, undressed, and not cemented with mortar. The great pressure this archway had to sustain was visible at many points in this pit, where the superincumbent earth had depressed it, displacing the stones so as imminently to threaten a falling-in. The tramway under-foot was sometimes dry, often muddy and wet, but always of a sound bottom.

Occasionally the water reached above the ancles. In this manner we advanced about half a mile.

The system of working coal-pits here—and indeed throughout South Wales—may be thus described. A vertical pit or shaft having been sunk to a point generally below the vein of minerals intended to be worked, a gallery, called "a horseway," along which runs a tram-road, is driven to the spot, where the workings, whether of coal or iron, are commenced. Here other galleries, called "cross-headings," which branch off at right angles, are excavated at a distance of 140 yards from each other. Out of these, and parallel, of course, with the "roadway," run what are called "the stalls," which are the chambers whence the workmen raise the minerals. These are cut to a distance of seventy yards, on both sides of the cross headings, so that they meet midway. About every ten yards, pillars are left, thirty feet square, to support the roof; they are afterwards either removed (and their place supplied with props of pit-wood) or not, as the necessities of the owners require. When abandoned, the old workings are carefully boarded or built up, in order that their secretions of fire-damp may not find entrance to the mine. To these stalls the trams are taken; they are then filled with coal or iron-stone, as the case may be, marked with the miners' initials, and hauled away by horses, in order to be raised above-ground. The ventilation of the pits is carried on for the most part on the principle of rarefaction, by means of a fire at the bottom of what is called the upcast shaft. In the pit I was in, it was dependent upon distant workings—yet it was of such efficiency, that two out of our three candles were more than once extinguished together.

We directed our course, in the first instance, to the iron mines, which are considerably below the coal. Quitting the main "horseway," and proceeding some distance on the left-hand, we entered the quarter where the miners were at work. Here the roof descended so low that we had to advance in a stooping posture, which shortly became painful. The closeness and heat of the pit were sensibly increased, and the difficulty of breathing was aggravated by thick clouds of sulphurous smoke from the blasting of the rock with gunpowder. Rumbling reverberations from successive "blasts" in different directions, mingled with the sharp, short ring of the miners' "picks," echoed through the roof with a strange effect upon the ear. Glimmering red through the smoke, we saw at length, and as it were at a vast distance, a few lights in motion; another hundred yards, and we had reached the stalls where the men were working. Entering and leaving several of these before we found the process by which they obtain the mineral sufficiently formed to witness its perfection, we came at length to one in which the preparation for blasting was all but complete. The miner was boring the solid rock with a long iron chisel, which he plied lustily with a heavy iron hammer, twisting it partly round to disengage the splintered material between each stroke. He was a tall, wiry-made man, of some thirty years of age, clad in a flannel shirt open at the throat, and with the sleeves tucked above the elbows. Fustian trowsers, shoes, and a handkerchief tightly bound about the head, completed his working dress. His face, though besmudged with the muddy water which dripped from the roof, was not black, like that of colliers; in fact, his calling is far more cleanly than that of the latter. It is worse paid, though the work is harder—the greater liability to explosions of fire-damp being, in a degree, compensated to the collier by increased pay. The hole he was boring sloped diagonally upwards and inwards from near the floor; it was a yard in length, and an inch and a half in diameter. He was compelled to work in a stooping posture, having the chisel between his legs, the right foot only resting upon the ground. Seeing us enter he redoubled his exertions, and after awhile, handing the tools to our attendant—who, that no time might be lost, supplied his place—he went for his charge of powder. He returned with a brown paper cartridge about 15 inches long, and containing about half a pound of coarse gunpowder; this he coolly held within two inches of my candle, to satisfy me, I presume, that it was full. The powder they use is of a grey colour, and though cheap is very strong. Having screwed up the mouth of his cartridge, the miner carefully deposited it at the furthest end of the hole. He now made, by wetting the rock-dust which had fallen from his boring, a sort of clay, which he rammed with much care upon the cartridge. The hole being filled in this way, he took a slender "tap," or gimlet, which he inserted through the clay until he reached the powder. This done, he took a piece of paper and folded it so as to make a little trench; along this he laid a short train of gunpowder, and placed it in the mouth of the hole made by the tap; he then smeared another piece of paper with tallow from his candle, and screwed it on to the first, by which his preparations were completed. Giving us notice to retire, he set fire to this fusee, and rejoining us, about fifty yards below, assured us we were at a sufficient distance for safety; we therefore stopped, and leaning against the side of the stall on which the discharge was to take place, waited the result. In a few seconds the explosion happened; there was a half-stifled roar, a gush of smoke and flame, the rattling of a few missiles against the opposite rock—and the miner then stepped briskly forward, pronouncing it a successful blast. About a ton of stone rubbish had been displaced, leaving the vein of iron-stone above clean, smooth, and flat, as though it had been levelled by a carpenter's plane. He had now only, with his crowbars and wedges, to break this down, and place it in the trams for removal. Seeing the nicety required to avoid smashing the left hand with the weighty iron hammer used in boring, I asked him if he did not sometimes injure himself by a false blow. He replied, "I have had accidents, but not of that kind; I can do it even in the dark. Many's the blast-hole I have finished after my candle was burnt out." This man told me that his earnings, after paying for powder, &c., were 12s. a week.

The workings I first visited were in what is called "the blue vein," which is about four inches thick. We next proceeded to "the black and spotted vein," considered the richest in this district. There are more than one vein running parallel at various distances, and looking like ribbons of a dark colour upon the face of the rock. The uppermost vein, being six inches in thickness, is most productive, it is black, spotted with yellow spars radiating from the centre, and yields nearly 50 per cent. of iron. On our way we passed what is here called "a thread." It is a dislocation of the strata—beyond doubt, in this instance, by upward pressure. The veins of iron have been snapped through, and one side lifted a height of 2 feet 6 inches. When the displacement is more extensive, it becomes "a fault," of which there were instances in this pit, extending to 33 feet. In the "black vein" we saw much the same process as above described—with this addition, that in several of the stalls the men were engaged building up the space behind them with the stone which they had blasted or otherwise removed in getting the ore. So much of it as cannot be so employed they have to load in trams, and send above ground.

At one place we saw a miner working a driving-way for horses. Observing the note-book in my hand, he jocosely said, in good English, "I hope, sir, you are not come to put me down for the militia." In reply to my questions, he said, "I like this work well enough if I could get more at it. The rock is so hard that I make only six yards way in a month, and that by the use of 40 lbs. of powder in blasting. I get from 6 to 7 tons of 'mine' (ore) in that distance, for which I am paid 6s. 10d. a ton; for cutting the rock, I earn 6s. 2d. a yard; but the cost of gunpowder must be deducted. I have worked 25 years in the mines, and never had a burn, but have been injured by cutting and by falls of earth and stone."

Leaving the iron mines, we directed our steps to the quarter where the coal is raised. The change, as regards roominess, was agreeable: but, in other respects, for the worse. The temperature of the workings is here considerably higher than in the iron-mines, and the air, though moving with the pressure of a gentle breeze, is charged with gas and minute particles of coal-dust, equally unwholesome for respiration. Passing several doors for regulating the draught, we steadily ascended at a low gradient, kicking up clouds of small-coal at each step we took, until we reached the stalls where the colliers were at work. On our way one object struck me, which, at the risk of irrelevancy, I must mention. Drawn boldly on the smooth shale, in chalk, I saw the outline of a prancing horse. The accuracy of the proportions, the propriety of the action, and the fidelity and spirit of the lines, were such that I stopped to examine this really striking performance. The hand that produced it was evidently practised and sure in the art. Though disposed to wonder at even a creditable performance in so strange a place, I could not but admire this drawing for its intrinsic merits, and I concluded that its author had profited by the French lithographs which I had seen abundantly displayed in the shops of Merthyr. Mentioning this matter to the colliers when we reached them, two or three voices exclaimed at once in Welsh, "It is the work of Noah Jones." But Noah Jones was not then to be found, so I lost the pleasure of witnessing a further performance. I may state that the boys in the coal-pits have in general a taste for drawing. The poor boy who has to attend all day one of the doors above mentioned, takes in his pocket—for the purpose of whiling away the tedium of his situation—a farthing's worth of happiness in the form of a piece of chalk. The doors are invariably covered with their productions, and I could detect the peculiar likings of each by his performances—one, drawing horses and animals; another, men fishing; and a third, architectural objects, such as churches and houses: every one of these subjects I saw displayed on different doors.

On reaching the stalls we found the colliers busily employed. Entering one of them, I observed the method in which they work. They use picks for cutting, and wedges for separating the coal. Sometimes they work seated—at others sideways—and occasionally lying, as necessity requires. They cut the coal to an acute angle, and then wedge off the mass to the square. The grain of the coal dips north and south

(I believe, in the line of the magnetic pole)—a circumstance which favours the miner, who, thus enabled to calculate with certainty the line in which the mineral will split, directs his operations accordingly. The miners call these lines "slips." In one stall, after clambering over some trams, I saw a mass thus detached with a single wrench of a crowbar, which weighed upwards of a ton. There exists an emulation amongst the colliers as to the masses they can raise entire. At this time, there is on the lawn, before Cyfarthfa Castle, in one solid mass, as it was raised from the pit, a block of coal, weighing 4 tons 3 cwt. 1 qr. 8 lb. It was cut a few weeks back in the nine-feet vein. In reply to my inquiries, this collier, whose dress was like that of the miner before described, informed me that "he had worked fifteen years in the pits, and it pretty well agreed with him. He had sometime got *singed* with explosions of fire-damp, and had had a few bruises from falls of earth. He had a wife and three children, and earned from 12s. to 15s. a week, according as he worked. He got bread and cheese for dinner, and sometimes meat. They always had meat on Sunday." The roof was wet and dropping—my face, note-book, and clothes were by this time very freely bespattered—so, as I could scarcely make matters worse, I sat down on a block of coal to recruit myself. Behind me I heard a uniform and monotonous singing noise, like the humming of a gnat, only much louder. I inquired what it was; he told me it was occasioned by the fire-damp, which made this sound in rushing through the fissures into the workings. I asked him to show me the place where it so came in. Holding his candle to the floor of the coal, and sweeping away the rubbish with the other hand, it immediately fired, and continued burning over the crevice till he trampled it out. I had long before remarked the peculiar lengthening of my candle; and the blue halo surrounding it, which is occasioned by the combustion of the diluted gas, had been pointed out to me. I wished to see a slight explosion, if it might be attempted without danger, and I was gratified. Cautioning us to stoop, the collier raised his candle with a rapid movement towards the roof, and as suddenly withdrew it, but without effect. The second time it fired, flashing like gunpowder, and moving with great velocity, and a whizzing noise a few yards forwards and backwards, and then it died out. The vein I was now in is called "the five-foot vein;" it is, however, interrupted by a band of black-stone, about fourteen inches thick.

The serviceableness of boys struck me very forcibly in the coal-pits, as well as in the iron works. The "windways," made for the purpose of ventilation, are entirely cut by them. They are 3 feet wide by 2 feet 6 inches high; within these narrow limits, without the means of working out the coal in masses, these boys work, doubled up of necessity into the most painful and inconvenient postures. They are paid at the rate of 1s. 2d. per yard. The other employments of these boys are, keeping the air-doors, attending upon the horses, loading the trams, or assisting their fathers in the stalls. They earn from 4s. to 6s. a week.

At this point we were distant from the shaft we had descended about a mile and a quarter, having traversed the workings, including those of iron and coal, to an extent of several miles. Having now completed this branch of my inquiry, by taking the statements of the men whilst actually at their labour, I retraced my steps towards the "upper earth."

Here I may remark that in this pit I could not get a sight of any of those beautiful fossils which, twelve years ago, I saw in a coal-pit on the southern rise of this mineral basin. There I was gratified by the sight of *sigillaria calamites*, and especially ferns—the latter impressed upon the shale with a distinctness that showed every leaf with surprising minuteness. I inquired anxiously for similar remains, and was informed by my guide that fossils are very rarely found at such a depth, and that, in descending the shaft, we had passed through the vein in which they are met with in most abundance.

On our way back we passed, at the junction of a cross-heading with the main "horse-way," a circle of colliers at dinner. Their smouched faces relaxed into a smile on seeing us; for my visit, and its object, had created a lively interest amongst them. They sat like North American Indians, squatting upon their hams—a position which they are much accustomed to by the nature of their work, and can maintain even with comfort for a long time. They were eating bread and cheese—their only aliment in the pit; their drink was cold tea, milk, or water. Above them, upon nails driven into the sparkling wall of coal, hung their respective stores of candles. We soon reached the bottom of the shaft, and took our stand on the cage. The signal given, we started off, and gliding smoothly and swiftly upwards, soon reached the surface, where we landed after an interesting sojourn of four hours in the depths below.

The following is a table of the deaths by accident (including the explosion at the Llelty Shenkin Colliery) which occurred in the coroner's district for the division of Merthyr, between the 21st

June and 14th December, 1849. This district comprises the following five parishes, some of which are agricultural:—Merthyr, Aberdare, Ystrad, Llanwonno, Llanvabon, and Gelly Gaer. A great portion of the mining and manufacturing districts of South Wales is under the jurisdiction of other coroners, whose papers I have not had an opportunity of abstracting from:—

Colliers killed by explosion of fire-damp	54
Colliers killed by falls of coal, stone, or earth	11
Miners killed by falls of stone and earth	9
Cutter killed by fall of fire-clay	1
Engineers killed by machinery (two accidents)	2
Colliers and others killed by fall into coal pits (three accidents)	3
Ditto ditto killed by fall of bucket	1
Ditto ditto killed by fall of chain	1
Workmen suffocated	2
Miners, colliers, and others, killed by various accidents	6
Firemen	2
Killed by trams	5
	97

The number of accidents in which the above 97 persons met their death is 46. This of course does not show anything like the number of accidents that occurred in this one district within the above-stated period of 25 weeks. The cases of fractured limbs, of burns, and other injuries—some disabling the parties for life—have been, to my knowledge, numerous, but the particulars are not obtainable. Here I must thank Mr. Overton, the coroner, for the obliging offers he made to give me any information in his power; and I must especially acknowledge my obligations to Mr. Morgan, his very efficient deputy, who assisted me in extracting the above statement.

The average life of colliers and miners, accidents included (as calculated from the register of deaths for the Merthyr district), is 42 years. I am aware that Mr. Tremenheere, in his Report for 1846 on the mining population of an adjacent district, has said, "The colliers and miners of this district *usually* preserve their vigour till near 55, and a large per centage may be found capable of doing a good day's work at 60." I know, however, of no circumstances which should make a difference between the district of which he speaks (it is only six miles off) and that of Merthyr. My comment on this statement is a reference to the register which gave the age I have stated as the duration of life in these classes. The year for which the particulars were extracted was 1847; the account for last year being at that period unavailable, and that for 1848 in an inconvenient state for examination.

There exists no material difference, in the statistical value of life, between colliers and miners. Both die, for the most part, of pulmonary diseases, of which the most frequent is phthisis. Their occupation sufficiently accounts for this. From a third to one half of their time is passed in the depths of the earth, amidst an atmosphere contaminated with gases inimical to human life, and loaded with highly comminuted particles of coal-dust, which irritate the delicate textures of the lungs. Mr. Edward Davies, whose opportunities for observation have been as large as his sagacity is vigilant, informed me that, in making *post mortem* examinations of the bodies of colliers and miners, he often found small black patches in the tissue of the lungs, which he believed were portions of carbon from the coal. But even if the above were insufficient to account for this proneness to pulmonary complaints, another cause is to be found in the vicissitudes of temperature to which these classes, like the firemen, are subject. The districts in which the minerals are deposited being mountain or moor-land, the climate, taken altogether, is extremely cold. In the winter it is very severe. On the other hand, the temperature of the pits and mines in which the men work is always high, increasing in proportion to the depth, according to a fixed and ascertained law. But here the miner is, in part, himself to blame; for the only care he takes for the preservation of health, on emerging from the warm and sulphurous chambers below, to perhaps a freezing sky, is the slight one of putting on his flannel jacket, and buttoning his checked shirt, so that his throat and chest remain almost wholly unprotected. Considering the vicissitudes of temperature which they have to encounter, and their careless habits, we cease to wonder at the deaths by consumption which decimate the ranks of those who work under-ground.

A few words on ventilation—a subject which I have hitherto only incidentally alluded to—may be of service in this place. I confine myself to the plans adopted in the Principality; the contrivances of Mr. Goldsworthy Gurney have not, that I can find, been tried here. The general system in use is extremely simple. The air in a colliery is heated both by the increased temperature below the surface, of which I have just spoken, and by the caloric given off by the numerous men, boys, and horses who are therein employed. Air becomes

lighter as it is heated, and therefore ascends—the space which it occupied being, in turn, filled with the cold air which descends. In the
mere sinking of a pit, this operation is sufficient of itself, without mechanical aid, and may even be relied on to a small extent when the
horizontal workings are commenced below; but as they proceed, two
pits become necessary—one called *the up-cast*, for the ascending of
the upward and impure current of air—the other *the down-cast* shaft,
for the downward supply of pure air. As the workings become larger
and more intricate, artificial means have to be resorted to, in order
to augment the draught; these have generally been the construction
of a fiery furnace at the bottom of the up-cast pit, to heat, and consequently to increase the velocity of the air in the ascending column.
I have already described the oozing of *fire-damp* into a coal-pit. This
is carburetted hydrogen gas (nearly same as the distilled gas used
for illumination), which, when mixed with a certain quantity of common air, becomes highly explosive. We have seen that the Davy-lamp,
invented for the purpose of saving life and of enabling the workman
to pursue his occupation in the dark recesses of the mine, is rarely
used in this district for any other purpose than examining the state
of the pit before the men commence working in the morning. Accidents from explosions of fire-damp are, unhappily, too numerous in
South Wales, as well as in the coal-fields of England. It is obvious
that the greatest danger must exist when a stream of this ignitable
and fatal gas comes into contact with the fire of a ventilating furnace
at the bottom of the up-cast pit. The dread of this recently occasioned,
in all human probability, the loss of many lives in a pit at Aberdare,
distant about two miles from the one I inspected. It is believed that
out of 52 persons who were there killed, two-thirds might have been
saved if the bystanders at the mouth of the pit had not been afraid
to descend and explore the workings, until the fire in the ventilating furnace beneath had died out for want of fuel. Mechanical means
have, therefore, been applied to accelerate the upward current in the
up-cast pit. In these districts this has been effected in two modes—
the one invented by Mr. Struve and the other by Mr. W. Brunton.
Mr. Struve's plan for increasing the current is by the application of
two cylinders or pumps working into water, like a gasometer, and so
drawing up the air from beneath through pipes, which afterwards discharge it by the opening of valves for that purpose. The machine of
Mr. Brunton is on a different, a simpler, and, I think, a better principle. It consists of a fan, or drum, moving rapidly on a vertical axis, and

having, at its periphery, compartments radiating inwards to a central tube, which collect the air from below, and disperse it above. In both inventions the top of the up-cast pit is closed to bring the machine into operation. However, inasmuch as the first mover, whether it be a steam-engine or other power, is liable to be stopped for repairs, that plan is clearly preferable which (other things being equal) shall not interfere with the current of upward air due to the natural heat evolved from the earth or other spontaneous causes. In a late accident at the Eskyn colliery the apparatus for ventilating was that which I have first described (Mr. Struve's), and a most ingenious invention it is; but, being stopped for the necessary repair of the engine, the suction of the pumps ceased, and the current of air being in this manner obstructed, an explosion ensued. As soon, however, as the air below became respirable, the men descended, instead of waiting as at Aberdare, and extricated their burnt companions—happily in this instance without loss of life, but with most extensive injuries to about a dozen of them. The plan to be preferred is certainly that which, even in its temporary suspension, does not prevent the natural ascent of the heated air; and the apparatus of Mr. Brunton, recently applied at the colliery of Mr. Powell, of Gellygaer, seems to effect this object most completely. The machine had been taken down at Gellygaer to make room for a larger one—itself being removed to another pit, where it had not been completely set up, so that I failed to see it working on a large scale. But I was favoured with an inspection of a model which I saw at work, and it fully sustained, in my opinion, the merits which its inventor has claimed for it. The machine is extremely simple—it has no parts liable to derangement—and all the friction resolves itself into a foot pivot moving in oil. It is capable of being made to exhaust the atmosphere of the mine, during the night, of its noxious gases, and thus to prepare it for the reception of the workmen by day. To do this, all that is needed is simply to stop the mouth of the downcast pit; and, the power of the machine being sufficient to exhaust the heaviest of the gases which are fatal to human life, the place will be found filled with pure air to be respired by the workmen, when they descend to their labour in the morning. The operation of this ventilator has, I understand, been witnessed by Mr. Blackwell, the Government inspector of mines, who for that purpose visited the pits at Gellygaer; it was submitted to the committee of the House of Lords last session, and as the inventor freely and disinterestedly offers it for public use, it is to be hoped that it will be generally adopted. I may add that I heard it spoken of by one of the most experienced mineral engineers in South Wales in terms of unqualified praise, coupled with a wish, such as I have here expressed, to see it in universal use. But wherever mechanical means are employed for the purpose of ventilation, no colliery should be unprovided with some *secondary* means for sustaining it—such as a horse-gin, or a capstan for manual power—which may be resorted to in the event of a temporary stoppage of the original ventilator from accident or repair, such as occasioned the first of the two explosions which recently occurred at the Eskyn colliery.

LABOUR AND THE POOR.

—◆—

THE MINING AND MANUFACTURING DISTRICTS OF SOUTH WALES.

[FROM OUR SPECIAL CORRESPONDENT.]

ABERDARE.

A "STRIKE" OF COLLIERS.

Letter V.

Having heard that "a strike" had just taken place amongst the "sea-coal" colliers in the Aberdare valley, I proceeded thither to inquire into the cause which had originated, and the circumstances which attended, so serious an evil. Out of the materials which I gathered I hope to frame a clear, impartial, and complete account of a dispute which has occasioned grievous privation and suffering to the men and their families, much harassment and loss to the masters, and no little detriment and inconvenience to the public.

The valley of Aberdare is separated from that of the Taff, where Merthyr lies, by a bleak and rocky mountain, 1,500 feet high, beneath which are found vast stores of the minerals which are worked with so much success in the neighbourhood. Over the crest of this mountain, along a precipitous and stony bridle-track, inaccessible to carriages, lies the shortest road to Aberdare—the distance from Merthyr being four miles. This course, mounted on a sure-footed horse, I took early in the morning of a cheerful, bright, and frosty day—such a one as is rarely seen in the winter season in this tempestuous and cloudy region of the mountains. On the Merthyr side there were, in every direction, abundant evidences of life and bustle. As I crossed the successive lines of rail and tram roads which lead from the "pits" to the "works," locomotives and horses, dragging long lines of trams heavily laden with coal and iron, were passing and repassing continually. Arrived almost at the summit of the steep, before I faced the icy breeze that always prevails at this season where the air currents divide, I took a glance at the landscape I had left behind me. The town of Merthyr, with its white and yellow-washed houses and grey-tiled roofs, its massive square-towered church, and its flaming and smoking "works," stretched up the hill-side opposite, nearly to a level with the point at which I stood. On the right, the valley of the Taff—its narrow sides roughed and darkened with underwood—curved away towards the sea. On the left, under the lofty precipices of the Keven, the collier village of Coed-y-Cwmmer, with its picturesque old bridge and its background of drooping leafless birches, stood out brightly in the frosty air. My attention being distracted from this scene by the sound of voices above me, I turned, advanced, and presently met a party of five men, who proved to be some of the colliers who had "struck" in Aberdare. They saluted me with that respectful demeanour which is universal among the labouring population of these hills, and (when I accosted them) informed me they were going to visit their friends in Merthyr. They were dressed in their Sunday clothes, and I fancied I detected in their countenances traces of anxious thought, such as their position was well calculated to give birth to. Afterwards, in the course of the day, I saw unmistakeable evidences of mental suffering amongst these unhappy, and, I fear, misguided men, and their wives and families. At various points further on my road, I met like groups of colliers, also on their way to Merthyr. They had, in fact, two motives for this journey; one was, to while away the tedium of idleness, and dissipate the anxieties of reflection—the other, to see whether they had any chance of employment in the iron-trade collieries around Merthyr. Whilst going over the works at Cyfarthfa a few days previously, Mr. R. Crawshay pointed out to me many men whom he knew to be "strangers," dispersed through his mills and forges: he at the same time informed me that an uneasy feeling existed amongst the colliers around Merthyr, on the ground that they did not raise as much coal as they might, and that his furnaces had been stopped eight hours the day before, owing to that circumstance. This no doubt was attributable to the men's sympathy with the colliers who had "struck," though theirs was a wholly different branch of commerce from that of the iron-trade collieries which supply the works.

Arrived within view of Aberdare, I was astonished to find a large town, stretching a couple of miles down the valley, where, only ten years before (which was the last time I had visited the place), there stood a mere village. I believe the growth of Aberdare—owing to the extension of old workings of coal and iron, and the development of new ones, consequent upon the general advance of these important branches of manufacturing industry—has been more rapid than that of any other town in the kingdom, Liverpool and Birkenhead not excepted. In all county histories and topographical works the place is spoken of as an insignificant "village;" and such it was till within a few years past. The valley is broader and more favourably inclined towards the sun than the adjoining vale of the Taff; it has, consequently more cultivation; the mountain-slopes are less precipitous, and they are better clothed with wood. The parish is ten miles in length, with an average breadth of four miles. The population in 1831, according to the census returns for that year, was 3,961. In 1841 it had advanced to 6,471, being an increase of 2,510 in ten years—nearly as much as 75 per cent. The population of what is called in the census return "the village" of Aberdare, in 1841, contributed 1,322 towards the above total. At present the number of souls in this extensive parish is calculated at 13,000, which doubles the population during the past nine years; and looking at the extent of the new town which has sprung up during this interval, I have no doubt that the next census will verify the accuracy of this statement. This population is almost wholly made up of persons engaged in, and dependent upon, mining and the manufacture of iron. It may be distributed into two classes—those employed in and about the iron-works, including the raising of coal and "mine" for consumption there—and those engaged in the "sale," or sea-coal, collieries, where the coal is raised for exportation. Of these by far the least provident and well conducted are the Sea Coal Colliers. These were the men who had "struck," the others still following their regular occupation.

Of the iron-works, which at present include 14 furnaces, with their proper complement of mills and forges, I need say nothing in this place—the method of smelting and manufacturing the metal, the wages of the workmen, and all other particulars, being similar to those I have already described, when treating of the works in and around Merthyr. Second in importance to the iron-works are the sea-coal collieries, where the mineral is raised for shipment at Cardiff. Of these there are at present eight pits, usually in full work, and others are now sinking. The average of men and boys employed in each is from 110 to 120. The coal is carried from the pits by the Taff Vale Railway, and the Glamorganshire Canal, down to the port of Cardiff, where it is sold and shipped, chiefly for steam purposes. The particulars of the enormous increase of this trade in the valley of Aberdare I shall give when the subject of the "strike" is disposed of. The veins of coal chiefly worked here are two. The first, or "four-feet seam" (so called), is found at various depths from 34 to 120 yards, and has a uniform thickness of five feet, with an inclination of three inches in the yard towards the south. The second, or "nine-feet seam," is mined at a depth of 90 yards from the surface (increasing as you advance south); it is regular, and has the thickness which its name indicates, with the same inclination and direction as the "four-feet seam." This is the coal employed at the works for the smelting and manufacture of iron; it is also in demand for exportation, being admirably adapted for steam purposes.

I mentioned in my last Letter the fact that there exists a disproportion between the wages of an "iron-trade" and a "sea-coal" collier, amounting to a full third or more of the total sum, in favour of the latter; and I instanced the circumstance of the "four-feet seam," which, in October last, was cut in the Merthyr valley for the iron-works, at 10d. a ton—whilst the same vein was worked by the sea-coal colliers, in the valley of Aberdare, at 1s. 6d. a ton. It is necessary to account for this. The main cause is to be found in the uncertainty of employment to which the sea-coal colliers are subject. The trade varying with the demand, when many ships are in Cardiff docks for the purpose of loading coal, the men work hard and earn high wages, out of which they must make provision for the dull season, when the demand is slack and they earn little or nothing. If it were convenient to work "to stock," the masters might regulate the quantity to be raised, so that it should be equal, or nearly so, all the year round, in which case the wages would be steady; but the "sea coal" being liable to deterioration by exposure to the air, when it softens, crumbles, and spoils, the masters are compelled to vary the amount raised according to the existing demand at the place of shipment; hence the fluctuation in the quantity of work to be performed within a given time. Another consideration, taken no doubt into account in the estimate of the value of labour in sea-coal collieries, is the increased danger which the men there incur, owing to explosions of fire-damp in those pits, the ventilation being more difficult and less perfect than in the collieries belonging to the iron-works. A third element in this disproportion of wages is, perhaps, the circumstance that the "sea coal" is an article of commercial export, on which a more liberal profit is obtained by the master than upon the coal raised and used in gross for the manufacture of iron in the immediate neighbourhood.

I have said that the least provident and well-conducted of these two classes are the sea-coal colliers—and, I might have added, the most mutinous also. Let us consider why this is so. Their want of providence explains the whole. Out of their earnings in good times they have to save and provide for the bad. Here lies the mischief. The temptation to spend freely when money is in hand affects colliers like other men, and their money melts away speedily under such circumstances, leaving them to an unwelcome dependency on credit, and too often to the humiliating shifts and devices of penury. Add to this the fact that the idle time must in some way be disposed of; the necessity for excitement of some kind or other, whether of labour or recreation, lawful or vicious, must be supplied. If he has not work to go to, the collier resorts to the public-house; and should he not do this, he has leisure to think, and to make himself miserable; he feels the pressure of the times without taking into account his own improvidence, and is ever ready to listen to and second the complaints of his fellows, who likewise suffer, and to entertain the suggestions of interested incendiaries, who are base enough to support themselves by the wages of agitation, scattering disaffection on all sides in the districts through which they travel.

Aware that it is stated in Mr. Tremenheere's Report for 1847—on the authority of Mr. Hall, the secretary to the Miners' Association in the north of England—that the miners in Wales had formed a "union," and had applied to them for a delegate, I made inquiries, but could obtain no intelligence that such an association exists here. It is true that the men act in concert, and perhaps subscribe a trifle to retain a professional person to support their interests before the magistrates; but I believe it ends with this, and that they provide no funds for enabling them to stand out against the masters. The distress they suffer during a "strike," and the fact of their then mostly living on credit, support this belief. Neither have they here any such combination as that known in the north, under the name of "the limitation of the vend." On these subjects I may here quote the following passage from Mr. Tremenheere's Report above named:—

> "The public is probably quite unaware, and it would be impossible, perhaps, to calculate with any accuracy, to what an enormous extent it is frequently mulcted by the combinations amongst the colliers, to which their want of intelligence is so often betraying them. At this moment, over large portions of the coal-fields of the kingdom, the men are only working on an average of the month, four or five hours a day, in order to keep up the price of coal. The effect of these combinations in embarrassing trade and manufactures, and ultimately in bringing

unmitigated loss and suffering upon the colliers themselves, must be obvious to whomsoever considers the subject. General reasonings and the lessons of experience appear to be equally ineffectual in preventing their constant recurrence."

The manner in which the public are inconvenienced by such a strike as that at Aberdare is this. Relying upon a supply, vessels come from various ports, coastwise and from foreign countries, to Cardiff, to load coal. Arrived there, they find, owing to the strike, no coal available—consequently they take their departure for Newport, Neath, Swansea, or Llanelly, as the case may be. But they lose, at least, one tide; consequently there are a day's demurrage and a day's wages of the crew in Cardiff—dock dues in two places—and the loss of time, perhaps another day, taken up in going to a fresh port for loading—all to be added to the cost of the cargo, which increase falls not upon the shipowner, but on the consumer. Besides this, the additional demand in other ports, where there cannot yet be an increased supply, raises the price—by which also the consumer suffers, to the detriment of trade and the augmented cost of our manufactures.

The circumstances of hiring, and the mutual obligations of the masters and men, from a conflict of which the strike had arisen, next claim attention. The usual method of hiring in the Aberdare valley is the simplest, but perhaps the least satisfactory, imaginable. The collier addresses himself to the agent and asks employment. He is told to "go below," and nothing more is said on either side. The rate of payment is perfectly well known: a copy of the month's notice expected to be given on either side is hung up in the company's office, and posted about the "tool-house," and the new comer is presumed to know, or at once to acquaint himself with, all the other *customs* of the colliery. No pit-bonds, such as are used in the north of England, are ever signed here; and I have been informed on good authority, that the men would not consent so to bind themselves. The men are expected to work whenever there is a demand for coal—which, as I have shown, is variable, and their wages fluctuate accordingly. The masters do not hold themselves obliged to find employment for the men at all times, nor to pay them when unemployed; neither do the men expect to be paid when no work is done. The higher rate than that paid in the iron-trade collieries is, as above stated, the compensation for this uncertainty and inequality in the wages of a slack or a busy season.

The relation of master and servant being thus loosely established, the work goes on. The following is a copy of the terms of notice posted on the premises of one of the largest of the sea-coal collieries—that of the Aberdare Coal Company:—

"TO THE COLLIERS AND ALL OTHER WORKMEN EMPLOYED BY THE ABERDARE COAL COMPANY.

"Notice is hereby given, that the Aberdare Coal Company engages every workman employed by them, in every branch of the works, subject to his being dismissed on a month's notice, and without notice for any misconduct; and that every workman must, before he can quit the service of the Aberdare Coal Company, give them a month's notice of his intention to quit their service.

"EVAN DAVIES,
"May 31, 1845."   for the Aberdare Coal Company.

It was understood, but never expressed, in these agreements, that the masters were only to employ a certain number of men in each colliery—so that, regard being had to the demand, the wages might average throughout the year about 60s. a month or more; but there was nothing really to restrain the masters from employing as many hands as they might please. Even though the effect of this might be to reduce the wages to 20s. a month, the workman would have no remedy; he must work out his month's notice, or be carried before a magistrate to answer for his default. When I was made acquainted with the precise terms of this one-sided contract, I expressed my belief, to the Rev. John Griffith, vicar of Aberdare, that it was bad for want of mutuality, and could not be enforced—an opinion which has since been verified by a legal decision.

On the 18th of October last the colliers in the Aberdare valley, without giving the month's notice, "struck," and carried in their tools. The alleged cause of the strike was the employment of extra hands at a time when, as the colliers asserted, and as the fact proved, work was getting slack. An attempt was thereupon made by the Aberdare Coal Company to enforce the contract against one of the men, whose case, as a matter of course, would govern the others. A summons was granted by Mr. H. A. Bruce, the stipendiary magistrate for the district of Merthyr and Aberdare (a barrister), against Rees Rees, one of the colliers in the employ of the company. The alleged offender was defended by Mr. Owen, an attorney in Newport. As the particulars of this case illustrate most thoroughly the nature of the relation between the master and the collier in this district, I shall abstract so much of it as is material. My abridgment is made from a very full report in the *Cardiff and Merthyr Guardian.*

> "The summons recited the information upon the oath of John Jones, cashier of the company, that the defendant did, on the 16th of July last, contract with David Davies to serve the said company as a collier, subject to being dismissed from the said service at the end of the month, after receiving from them a month's notice, and without notice for any misconduct,—being himself bound to give the like notice to the said company before leaving their service: that he did then and there enter into the said service, under and according to the said contract; and that, on the 18th October, he left the said service without giving such notice, and without any cause or lawful excuse."

In support of this it was proved, by an underground agent of the company, that the defendant applied for work five years ago, and was employed; that nothing was said about wages or a month's notice, or the other terms of the contract—these being presumed to be well known, and a printed notice being posted in the office (as above) respecting the notices which were to determine the service, a knowledge of which was fixed upon the defendant. It was further proved that the defendant was paid by the month, at the rate of 1s. 6d. per ton for the coal he raised, and at various prices for such other work as he might do; and it was admitted, on cross-examination, that the amount of his earnings depended upon the demand for coal, which sometimes supplied him with full work—sometimes with little—and, not unfrequently, for days together, with none at all.

Upon this evidence the company called upon the magistrate to adjudicate against the defendant. On the other hand it was urged in defence, first, that no contract had been proved, such as was contemplated by the statute 4 Geo. IV., c. 36, s. 3; secondly, that if proved, it was void for want of mutuality; and lastly, a technical objection was raised (in reality of not the slightest value), that there was a variance between the *information* and the *evidence*—the former laying the contract of service with one agent of the company, and the latter showing it to have been made with another. I need hardly say the decision was adverse to this objection.

With regard to the first point of the defence, the magistrate said:—

"The statute gives validity to contracts, whether in writing or not. I am, therefore, clearly of opinion that (supposing the contract not to be otherwise defective) the demand for employment, followed by the granting of such employment, constitutes a valid contract, and that evidence of clear and well-ascertained custom may be let in to explain its nature. It is, however, urged on behalf of the defence, that the only contract proved by the evidence is a contract to raise a ton of coal, and that there is no proof of that exclusive right to the collier's service which constitutes the relationship of master and servant, the existence of which relationship alone gives jurisdiction to the magistrate. From this view of the case I entirely dissent. The evidence clearly proves that the company's agents insisted upon the regular daily attendance of the men during the usual hours, and that the men acknowledged their right to do so, and the question whether the payment be by the day or the ton does not at all affect the right of the master over the servant's time."

This plea disposed of, the second and substantial point came under review. The following is the judgment on this important question:—

"The objection to the want of mutuality in the contract is far more serious. Not that I attach much importance to the argument, that because the men were bound to find labour at all times, while the masters were not bound to find employment at all times, the contract is necessarily void. This inequality could be, and in the case before me, actually was compensated for by a higher rate of payment per ton than would have been allowed had the employment been steady and certain, and unaffected by the fluctuations of trade. The case of Williamson v. Taylor, 5 Q. B., 175, is precisely in point; and Lord Denman, on confirming the contract, is reported to have said, 'I do not find anything in the terms of that agreement to make it imperative on the defendants to keep the pit at work any given time, or to find employment to the defendant all the year round. It may be that such a stipulation was omitted, as it would be generally thought that the interest the defendants had in keeping the pit at work would be a sufficient protection to the plaintiff in that respect.' In the cases of Pilkington v. Scott, 15 M. and W., 657, and Hartley v. Cummings, 5 C. B., 247, contracts of nearly the same description were enforced. But these were written contracts, and the right of the workmen to employment, when employment could be furnished, was clear and distinct. Has such a right been established in this case? or, supposing that it has been established, what is there to prevent the masters, after a temporary discontinuance of employment, from bringing in any number of fresh hands, utterly disproportioned to the demand for coal, so as to reduce the earnings

of their former workmen to little or nothing? It is not enough to establish the right of the masters to the service of the men, unless the
masters also be amenable to justice for any breach of contract on their
part—for instance, for dismissal without notice, refusal to employ, or
for the introduction of fresh hands to such an extent as to leave little
or nothing for the colliers first employed to do or to earn—it is clear
to me that a magistrate has no jurisdiction. In order to enforce such
a remedy against their masters, it would be necessary for the colliers
to show a contract, determining, with sufficient precision to be acted
upon in a court of justice, in what particular state of the trade, or at
what period in particular, the employers were bound to find work for
them, and when not. I do not think that these points have been, or
can be, made out with sufficient clearness by a mere reference to customs which could only have been in existence for a very few years, and
which may, and probably do, vary in some particular in every colliery
in the district. I am, therefore, of opinion that the contract is void, for
want of mutuality, and I am fully impressed with the importance of the
subject, and with the consequences which may arise from my decision
throughout this populous manufacturing district. It will affect, more or
less, far the greater part of the contracts so loosely entered into between
the masters and workmen in the iron-works as well as the collieries. I
have, therefore, not only given the subject my most anxious attention,
but I have availed myself of the opinions of learned and able men, accustomed to the consideration of this complicated branch of the law.
It is consolatory also to me to reflect that there are two remedies open
to the masters, if dissatisfied with my decision. They can either prepare
a written form of contract, to be signed by their men, and so framed
as to meet the difficulties of the case—or, on my refusal to entertain a
complaint founded upon alleged contracts of the nature I am now considering, they have an easy way of testing the correctness of my opinion
by application to the Court of Queen's Bench."

Such was the judgment delivered by Mr. Bruce in the above case.
The masters, satisfied that they had nothing to hope from an appeal to
the Court of Queen's Bench, adopted the other alternative suggested
by the magistrate, and prepared a form of contract for future hirings,
which I shall give in the proper place.

In the interval between the hearing of the information and the
delivery of the judgment, the men in some, if not all of the collieries,
resumed their work; but shortly afterwards, on another ground, they
again struck. In addition to the oral statements I received from the
men, I am enabled to give the particulars of their complaints from a
printed account of the occasion of the strike published by themselves.

It was posted about the town of Merthyr, and exhibited in many of the shop windows:—

> "WORKMEN, STOP AND READ!—As there are so many different reports gone over the country, about the stoppage at Aberdare, we, the colliers of Aberdare, feel it our duty to make known unto our fellow-workmen, and all others, why we have ceased to work, and what is the reason of the present strike. On the commencement of last November, all the masters belonging to the sea coal at Aberdare, gave us notice to leave our employment at the end of one month; at the expiration of the said notice, the terms that were offered us were, twopence per ton reduction, *and to bind ourselves to work on the said reduction for one year,* and the masters to have liberty to discharge six men in each month, on giving them a month's notice; and six of the workmen, and no more, to have the power of giving notice within the same month, and therefore they would have the power to manage the notices, so that the year would always be up on the slowest time on the sea coal.
>
> "From the COLLIERS OF ABERDARE SEA COAL."
> "Dec. 14, 1849."

From the above it will be seen that this strike was occasioned by acts of the masters, and did not arise from any discontent with the existing state of things on the part of the men. I found that opinions differed in the neighbourhood as to the reasonableness of the terms insisted on by the masters. Some of the ironmasters in the Valley thought that the masters, in requiring the men to bind themselves to work for a twelvemonth at the reduced rate of wages, asked more than they justly had a right to expect or demand. I am of the same opinion, because the masters do not engage to find the men during this period as much work as will secure wages sufficient for the support of themselves and their families, and because the reduced rate of wages, though fair for the dull time of year, would, on the average throughout the year, be altogether insufficient.

About 840 men and boys were thrown out of employment by this strike. In company with the worthy vicar of the parish, I visited some of their houses. When the subject was mentioned, I found the women in tears, and the men universally thoughtful and downcast, but resolved. They seemed convinced of the justice of their cause, and confident of receiving approval and sympathy. When I saw this eagerness for consolation, this desire to be strengthened by the good opinion of others, I was forcibly reminded of the circumstances attending the

Pensher strike, in the north of England, "where the men had regularly, once a week, prayer meetings at the chapels in the colliery villages, to pray to God to give them success. The men said they went there to get their faith strengthened. Prayers were offered up for God's blessing and support during the strike, and that he would give them the victory." The men whom I saw at Aberdare very probably made like appeals for comfort and support, for there is a strong religious bias in the colliers, and indeed among all the working classes in these mountains.

I subjoin the evidence of one of the men I examined; his statement elucidates every point in the unhappy dispute:—

"I am a sea-collier, and have worked so for twenty years. I have earned as much as 30s. a week; but the last few weeks I worked I got no more than 7s. 6d. a week. The works were so full of men that I could earn no more. There was little or no demand for coal. The occasion of the strike is this: the masters gave us notice to drop 2d. a ton for cutting, and the men objected to it. There is another reason, which is that the masters wanted us to sign an agreement to work twelve months at the reduced rate of 1s. 4d. a ton; but they won't engage to employ us what we call an average working time, even at that rate. The men are quite willing to go back to work at the reduced wages, but they won't consent to sign the paper, and the masters refuse to give us work unless we do. We can't anywhere get employed hereabouts. Though I have only been three months at work in ——'s pit, I have seen in that time three boys burnt and a horse killed by fire-damp. I have twice been in the fire and burnt, and have sometimes had injuries from falls of earth and stone. I lost my wife three months ago of cholera. I have five children to support, and being now out of work a fortnight, we are badly off. When I am employed we get meat once or twice a week. I pay 7s. a month for rent, and have my coal as all colliers do, for nothing. Only one of my children is in school."

The appearance of this man was one of extreme dejection; he leaned, with his hands in his empty pockets, against the 'dresser' of the neighbour's house where I examined him, and spoke only when he was questioned, looking at other times stolidly at the fire, as a man does in a reverie. The poor widow in whose house I saw him, assured me he was prudent and careful. Her own story was touching:—"I am a poor widow. Two years ago I had a dear boy, who helped to support me, carried home to me a corpse. He was only twenty-three years old, and was killed by fire-damp in his pit. His two younger brothers are working now, and support me; they are out of employ through this strike, and I don't know what will become of us."

At the time I visited Aberdare the distress of the men and their families had not yet affected their little property in furniture and clothing—they were living in part upon credit; but their subsequent privations must have been dreadful. The usual consequences of a strike soon manifested themselves in the importation to the district of other workmen, and in vagrancy, but I did not hear of any serious depredations on property. Some petty thefts more than usual had, however, occurred. The most earnest endeavours had been made to call back the men to their work, by one of the most able, zealous, and benevolent magistrates in the Principality—Mr. Henry A. Bruce, a gentleman who has conciliated the esteem of all parties and sects in the neighbourhood, as I had abundant opportunity of witnessing. It was Mr. Bruce's opinion, that the strike was kept up by the active exertions of a few men who controlled the remainder. I give below the particulars of a melancholy case of vagrancy (arising out of the dispute), on which Mr. Bruce had to adjudicate, together with an exhortation to the men made by him from the bench, after delivering the judgment which I have quoted above. I was informed that this address was to be translated into Welsh, and to be printed and distributed amongst the men. Mr. Bruce laid before them the history and results of the great strikes in the north, as reported by Mr. Tremenheere; these, however, are too lengthy for insertion here.

> "Mr. Bruce said he was exceedingly sorry yesterday to have had to adjudicate on a case which made him almost ashamed for his neighbours. It was the case of a Cwmbach collier, who was brought up before him on a charge of vagrancy—begging in the streets—and that was a man who was able to earn from 16s. to 18s. weekly, if he could get employment; but he was deprived of the means of obtaining a livelihood by what he (Mr. Bruce) believed was nothing more than a combination of a mischievous minority of workmen. He believed that man would have been too glad to work—he believed that nine-tenths of the workmen would be too glad to have gone back to their work if it were not for the mischievous tyranny of a minority. It was most painful, in the case he referred to, to see a young man who was only about twenty-three or twenty-four years of age, begging for his bread under the circumstances he had referred to. And as there were a great many men in the room, he (Mr. Bruce) would like to say a few words to them on the course they were pursuing. They had been standing out for some time. The Abernant colliers had been standing out for nine weeks; and the

rest of the men for three or four weeks? Did they think that any good would be the result of those strikes? In the history of strikes was there a single instance upon record where any good accrued for the men by it? He could tell them something respecting strikes, as he had taken, and continued to take, great interest in the condition of workmen, and had considered the manner in which they were affected by these attempts to improve their condition,—attempts which had always ended in utter failure. Look at the effects of the great strike of the Durham and Northumberland colliers in 1844, which was a combination between all the workmen of those extensive districts, who commenced it with a great deal of money in hand, with a determination, on their part, to raise the price of coal, when, at that time they might earn 3s. 8d. a day, besides having a cottage and garden rent-free and their coal. It was not easy to conceive why those men should engage in a strike; but they did: it began on the 5th of April, and continued to the end of July, during which time not one stroke of work was done. The consequence was, that collieries were opened in Derbyshire, in Wales, and in various other parts, which would not have been opened had it not been for the conduct of the men. The price of coal never rose for one moment in London, for the demand was supplied by fresh collieries. At the end of the period he had just named, the 22,000 men and boys who had turned out went back to their work at the wages offered to them in the commencement; but by that time there had been a great number of new men introduced into the works, which lowered the price of labour; and it had continued lower ever since. The strikes of 1826, 1831, 1832, and 1844, had reduced wages at least 30 per cent.; that is, workmen now received 70s. instead of 100s. In the northern districts, finding the men obstinate, the masters sent for men from Wales, Derbyshire, and Staffordshire, by which means the rate of wages was permanently lowered, the number of collieries was permanently increased, the consequence was a fall of price in coal; and, of course, if the price of coal fell, workmen could not expect masters to give such high wages. And that would be the effect of a strike in Cwm Cynnon. He understood that from forty to fifty new men had been taken on at Cwmbach; and every fresh workman that was employed in a district added to the competition for employment, and tended to reduce wages.

"At Abernant, the strike of the colliers had compelled Mr. Fothergill to use coke, which he had never done before, which would save him the necessity of raising such a great quantity of coal as was formerly required; and so every one of the men would be losers by that, as there would be less demand for their labour, and consequently their wages would fall."

This admonition to the men having been closed, Mr. Bruce then addressed himself to the masters as follows:—

"He would like to say a few words which might reach the masters. His opinion was, that the cause of those strikes was the ignorance of the men, who were not able to judge of the real state of the question, and were misled by a few idle, profligate fellows, who tried to live on the proceeds of agitation. Nine-tenths of the workmen would much rather go back to work, and take the present wages; but a few active fellows, who worked on their spirit of pride by telling them to stand fast together, prevented their doing so. If men were properly educated—and the means of education were in the masters' hands—if sober and temperate habits of thought were cultivated—those strikes would not occur as they now did; honest workmen would take those mischievous fellows by the neck and turn them out, telling them, 'We are honest workmen, desirous of earning a fair livelihood, and can now obtain from 15s. to 18s. a week; let us alone.' He (Mr. Bruce) believed that workmen would have intelligence enough to do that. In the north of England masters had taken great interest in their men; and schools had been provided for the general diffusion of education, from which the best consequences had proceeded. Savings banks had also been established, which had been found highly useful. Men in those works had refused to join strikes which had taken place in neighbouring concerns. He did not mean to blame any particular master. The works in the Aberdare valley had not long been in existence; but if masters would show their men that they were anxious to treat them with strict fairness, would sympathise with them and interest themselves in their welfare, in every sort of way, the men would be far less likely to engage in any objectionable courses. Instead of jealousy, suspicion, and distrust, the men should be taught to feel confidence and good trust; and they would not then so easily believe any wild theory which mischievous persons were so anxious to promulgate. Men should be taught that the price of labour, wages, did not depend on their combinations, but on the state of the market."

This advice to the masters was judicious and well-timed. In the case of strikes, the men no doubt are often wrong: it is impossible to read Mr. Tremenheere's Report for the year 1846, without coming to this conclusion. Much, however, might be done in the way of promoting a good understanding, by explicit and kindly statements of the condition of trade by the masters; for no workman would be so insane and suicidal as to revolt in the face of truth and facts. I believe that many strikes would have been averted, and much loss, distress, embarrassment, and inconvenience avoided, by frank explanations on the part of the masters as to the actual state of the trade, if proffered when the men first showed symptoms of uneasiness and discontent. I find a passage in Mr. Tremenheere's Report for the past year, which bears out these views. It is a comment upon the manner in which the "Consett Iron Works," near Newcastle, are conducted:—

> "A course of open and straightforward dealing on the part of the resident manager and the agents, with the workmen, on the subject of wages, has had the effect of gradually establishing a very satisfactory degree of confidence between them. The latter have seen that though wages have fallen elsewhere, *their own have not been reduced while the company were engaged on contracts made before a fall of prices.* They have therefore submitted to reductions without a murmur when the company found it necessary to make them; and they have found that wages have been raised without their asking for it, the moment the time came when it was equitable that the advance should be made. On this subject the resident manager, Mr. William Cargill, said, '*We make it a point always to tell them the truth; we never deceive them, nor allow any one to do so.* Sometimes agents will imagine they are serving their employers by such a course. We never permit it, and should turn off any one who did so.'"
> (Report, 1849, page 7.)

The following is the form of contract prepared by the masters and submitted for Mr. Bruce's approval. It neither satisfies him nor the men. I discussed the matter with him more than once, and shall append his objections to the several clauses of the contract, *seriatim.* They are those of a magistrate experienced in all the relations of master and servant in this district, and therefore deserving of considerate attention:—

> "MEMORANDUM OF AGREEMENT, made and entered into this .... day of .... one thousand eight hundred and .... between .... on the one part, and the several other persons whose names or marks are hereunto subscribed on the other part.
> "1. The said .... do hereby retain and hire, and the said several other parties whose names or marks are hereunto affixed do hereby agree to serve, subject to the several conditions and stipulations herein contained, from the .... day of .... one thousand eight hundred and forty-nine, or from any subsequent period, to the .... day of .... one thousand eight hundred and fifty, to cut, work, and fill, at one shilling

and fourpence for every 2,640 pounds of clean large coal (120 pounds of which is to be allowed for breakage), to be cut as large as the coal vein will admit, and to be entirely free from small, rubbish, brass, or clod.

"2. To drive levels	feet wide at	per yard.
Cross or rise headings	wide at	per yard.
Deep headings	wide at	per yard.
Windway	wide at	per yard.
Four yard stall at		per yard.
Turning stall		
Setting double timber		per pair.
Posts and bars		

and to do all other such work as comes within a collier's customary business, at such prices as may hereafter be agreed upon. And to do and perform when required, except when prevented by sickness, or some other unavoidable cause, a full day's work in each and every working day, or such quantity of work as shall be fairly deemed equal to a day's work, and not to leave their work until such day's work is fully performed, and finished to the extent of each man's ability.

"3. It is hereby provided that, when from the slackness of trade, or other cause, the said colliers whose names are hereunto affixed are unable to earn, with all due diligence on their part, fifty-five shillings per month on an average, per man, it shall be lawful for them after seven days' notice to the said . . . . to determine by ballot of the whole of the said colliers the reduction of their number (such number to be fixed by the agent or proprietors), so as to make their wages amount to not less than the said sum, and the colliers so balloted out shall be held free from this contract, and have full liberty to remove elsewhere. In case, however, the whole of the colliers at any time agree, instead of balloting, that those of their number who last entered the colliery should be the first, to leave, it shall, under such circumstances, be allowable for them to do so.

"4. And it is further provided and mutually agreed, that should, at any time during this contract, any collier be desirous of being freed from it, and of leaving his work, he shall be at liberty after . . . . written notice to the . . . . to do so. Provided always, that not more than notices from six of the said colliers shall be given during any period of . . . . and that should more than six of the said colliers tender notices to leave within the said time, the first six only shall be accepted, but the next, not exceeding six in number, shall be placed the first on the list of notices for the ensuing period of . . . ., so that not more than six colliers shall have power or be permitted to leave under such notices during any period of . . . .

"5. And the said .... reserve to .... the power of discharging any six of the said colliers at the expiration of a like notice of .... and of engaging an additional number of colliers equal to supply the demand for coal, whenever the number of colliers in the said colliery shall fail to cut the quantity of coal required of them.

"6. All differences which may hereafter become matter or subject of dispute to be settled by a reference to the stipendiary magistrate for the time being for the Merthyr district, and his decision to be final and binding on both parties.

"It is however mutually agreed, that the whole of the parties whose signatures are hereunto affixed shall be entirely free from this agreement, on and after the expiration of the thirtieth day of November, one thousand eight hundred and fifty."

With regard to the first clause of this agreement, which the masters propose to fill up so as to make it binding for a full year, Mr. Bruce remarks that it ought not to be insisted on. The men object to being hired for a year, at a rate per ton which they, for the most part, admit to be fair for the dull season, but which would be too low during the summer months. In a letter I lately received from Mr. Bruce, he says, with regard to this subject:—"The masters naturally wish to protect themselves against the frequent strikes of the men, who always seize the time most inconvenient to them to demand an increase of wages. On the other hand, it seems unfair that the price proposed for cutting coal throughout the year should be the lowest price at which the colliers have been accustomed to work. A medium price should be fixed—say 1s. 5d. per ton; and to this I do not think the men would object."

As to the second clause, fixing the price for cutting cross-headings, windways, driving levels, &c., Mr. Bruce considers that the price had much better be left for arrangement in each particular case, it being impossible to fix beforehand the proper value of the work, which will vary with the nature of the soil, shale, or rock to be penetrated. The reader has seen in my previous letters the statement, of miners and colliers who, taking work by the yard, and having miscalculated the hardness of the substances they had to penetrate during the period they were occupied upon it, have been kept, with their wives and families, at "starvation point;" and the clearest judgment and the most mature experience are often at fault in "takings" of this nature.

To the 3d clause Mr. Bruce objects, specifying his reasons thus:—

"I object to this plan of reducing the number of the men by ballot, although voluntary on their part. In the first place the number *so to be balloted out is to be fixed by the masters,* who, of course, might violate the spirit of the agreement by fixing two or three when ten or twelve men ought to be removed, so as to allow sufficient earnings for the remainder. In the next place it is to be expected that the younger men will be always clamouring for a reduction of their number on every fall of wages, whilst the elder and steadier men will be content to work on at low prices, in the hope of better times, which are not long in coming round."

With respect to the 4th and 5th clauses, Mr. Bruce observes:—

"I do not think that the 4th or 5th clauses ought to be insisted on. The men ought to be allowed to leave when they please, after giving the proper notice, and the masters to dismiss as many as they please upon like notice. I have suggested the introduction of a clause enabling the colliers to leave after one week's notice only, when the wages shall fall to 55s. per month."

As to the 6th clause, making Mr. Bruce mutual referee, and his decision final and binding on both parties, that gentleman declines the honour, on the ground that the offices of arbitrator and judge are not quite compatible.

Some idea of the vast extension of the coal trade, in and near the valley of Aberdare, may be formed from the following statements, which, as I procured them in manuscript from the proper officer, may be relied upon as strictly accurate:—

A STATEMENT OF THE QUANTITY OF COAL BROUGHT DOWN THE GLAMORGANSHIRE CANAL TO THE PORT OF CARDIFF, DURING NINETEEN YEARS LAST PAST.

			Tons.
In 1829 the coal conveyed to Cardiff was			83,729
In 1838,	„	„	189,081
In 1848,	„	„	281,966

This shows an extension of the trade amounting in the above period to very nearly 200,000 tons, which is upwards of 10,000 tons a year. Nor is this by any means the extent of the increase, for a large quantity of coal is sent down by the Taff Vale railway, the returns of which I have not yet been able to obtain.

The following particulars of the export of each colliery sending coal by the canal to the sea, at Cardiff, may be useful for the statistics of the coal-trade in South Wales.

There were sent by the under-mentioned proprietors, down the canal, in 1838, the following quantities of coal:—

In 1838.	Tons.
Thomas Powell and Co.	62,186
W. Coffin and Co.	45,285
Lucy Thomas	16,777
George Insole	21,628
Morgan Thomas	12,926
John Edmunds	12,840
D. Davis and Co.	9,020
Duncan and Co.	6,299
E. Evans	2,120
Total	189,718

There were sent down the canal to Cardiff, by the undermentioned proprietors, in 1848, the following quantities:—

In 1848.	Tons.	cwt.	Tons.	cwt.
Waun Wyllt Coal Company ...	8,889	5		
Graig Coal Company	13,814	10		
William Thomas	23,547	10		
			46,251	5
Aberdare Coal Company			29,512	10
D. Davis (Hirwain)			16,245	19
John Nixon and Co.			18,855	10
Thomas Powell (Duffryn)	34,493	0		
Thomas Powell and Co.	11,331	14		
			45,824	14
Duncan and Co.			12,838	0
John Edmunds			26,558	2
D. and T. Thomas			2,349	0
George Insole and Sons			13,176	10
Morgan Thomas			9,074	0
Evan Evans			10,315	10
Thomas and Joseph			718	15
John Calvert			45,373	15
Price, Bassett, and Co.			2,682	0
Sundry collieries			2,191	4
Total			281,966	14

This gives the particulars of increase during the ten years ending the 31st December, 1848, and will serve to show the vast amount of labour employed in the sea-coal collieries. Three of these, during the year 1848, raised and exported upwards of 45,000 tons each. A reduction in the rate of wages, such as the masters have required (2d. a ton), would therefore make a difference in the profit at each colliery of nearly £400 a year.

That the trade—now that the superiority of the Welsh coals over those from the other coal-fields of this country has been established by parliamentary inquiry and scientific investigations—will be indefinitely enlarged, there can be no doubt. I think it due to the collieries in South Wales, to give the following statements of the calorific and economic values of a few of them. All the varieties here specified are worked in or close upon the Aberdare valley. I should add that I take from the tables, in each of the cases, only the practical results most interesting to the consumer:—

Names of the Coals employed in the Experiments.	Economic evaporating power; or number of pounds of water evaporated from 212° by 1 lb. of coal.	Weight of one cubic foot of the coal as used for fuel.	Space occupied by one ton in cubic feet.	Evaporating power of the coal, after deducting for the combustible matter in the residue.
Thomas's Merthyr (Aberdare)	10.16	53.0	42.26	10.72
Dyffryn (Aberdare) ..	10.14	53.22	42.09	11.80
Nixon's Merthyr	9.96	51.7	43.32	10.70
Hill's Plymouth Works	9.75	51.2	43.74	10.18
Aberdare Coal Comp.'s	9.73	49.3	45.43	10.27
Gadly's nine-feet seam	9.56	54.8	40.87	10.46
„ four-feet seam	9.29	51.6	43.41	10.73

This table would, however, be of little value, if I did not give the results of the experiments on the sample which proved to be the best of all the English and Scotch coals tried. The best by far of all these varieties is the "Andrew's House, Tanfield," Newcastle coal, the result of which is shown as follows, distributing the figures under the above table—viz., 9.39—52.1—42.99—9.80.

The various coals from the mineral basin of South Wales, principally shipped and in request at the several ports of outlet along the northern shores of the Bristol Channel in Monmouthshire, Glamorganshire, and Carmarthenshire, are (according to the statement of Professor Wilson, who was appointed to inquire) the following:— At Newport, the Cwm Risca, Porthmawr, Cwm Brane, the Tredegar Company's, the Dyffryn, the Varteg, and others. At Cardiff, the Ynis-cynon, the Aberdare Valleys, and Blaengwawr. At Porthcawl, the Bryn-ddu and Bethvos coals. At Taibach and Port Talbot, the Roch Vawr vein and two other sorts, belonging to the Governor and Company of Copper Miners. At Neath, the Bryndowy Pwllfaron, Tyr-Edemed, Abbey Graigola, and others. At Swansea, the Forest Graigola, Petrepoth, Pentrefelin, the Graigola Company, with a few others of good repute as steam-coals. Lastly, at Llanelly, the Llangennech, the Binea, Oldcastle's vein, Ward's vein, and Webb's, with the anthracite coals of the Gelly Ceidrim and Garnant mines.

The foreign countries to which coal is chiefly exported from the South Wales coal-field are, France (which carries on a large trade with Swansea), Spain, Portugal, the different countries on the Mediterranean, Brazils, and ports in South America, the East and West Indies, Africa, &c.

Though I have in a former letter treated of the subject of accidents in the coal-mines of the Principality, I cannot close this account of the collieries in and around Aberdare without alluding to the circumstance, that in this valley, within five years past, there have been killed not fewer than 100 persons from explosions of fire-damp. Unless one of these catastrophes includes a score or two of human beings, it passes away unnoticed by the public. Many fatal explosions are never reported in the public papers. Ventilation is still very imperfect in what are called the "fiery pits." Nowhere could I find in use Mr. Foudrinier's admirable apparatus for preventing the cage being drawn over the pulley, and for stopping the cage in its descent, should the rope break. I have pointed out the insufficiency and the danger of ventilation by furnaces at the bottom of an upcast shaft, and the necessity that exists for a capstan or horse-gin, to be resorted to as a motive-power for increasing the flow of pure air, whenever an accident may disable such a machine as Mr. Struve's from working.

In the year 1845 an explosion occurred in Aberdare valley, in which twenty-five lives were lost; and again, at the close of last summer, a second tremendous explosion (this time in a colliery not far distant, called the Llelty Shenkin Colliery), by which fifty-two human beings were killed. It is right the public should know that, within five weeks

after the last-mentioned frightful accident two more explosions occurred in the same pit, by which two men were burned; this was kept
as private as possible. I made some inquiries into the distress which
the Llelty Shenkin accident occasioned, and I found that there were
remaining in the parish nineteen widows, of whom four were left each
with five children, the respective ages of the *oldest* being 19, 12, 11, and
9; others were left with four—three widows with two—young children. There were four families left without either parent, the mothers
having died before the accident. All these were left wholly unprovided
for, and I was informed that nothing whatever had been done by the
proprietor, either towards assisting the widows or the children. It is
only just that I should state what he actually did—he paid for a coffin,
with handles, for each corpse. In the former accident alluded to, the
proprietor of the colliery made the widows and children a weekly allowance; and he showed some sagacity in promising and giving each
widow a small fortune of £15 on marriage—a stroke of policy which,
I have been assured, was eminently successful, for in due time he married off every one of them.

Aberdare contrasts in many respects favourably with the neighbouring town of Merthyr. It is, of course, a newer town. The streets
are wider, and they are drained, and lit with gas. Here it was I first saw
workmen's cottages three stories high; there is a row of such on the
mountain-side, above the furnaces of Mr. Fothergill. But the builder,
notwithstanding the increased height and breadth of frontage, has
confined himself, as regards the windows and doorways, to the proportions of the low and small cottages—the effect is, therefore, well
nigh ludicrous. I have since seen other three storied rows at Sirhowy,
to which the same remark applies.

With a population of 13,000 souls, there is in Aberdare, strange to
say, church accommodation provided for no more than 200 persons,
and there is not a single free sitting in the parish church. I was struck
with the circumstance that the church, which should form the centre
of the town, was at one end of it, and had few houses near it. On
inquiring the cause, I was informed that the owners of the glebe land
would not grant building leases; by which means the town, which is
rapidly enlarging, has extended down the valley instead of surrounding the church, as it otherwise would. The impropriators of the great
tithes, and owners of the glebe land, are the Dean and Chapter of
Gloucester. The living is a vicarage, the clergyman receiving £10 a
year of the vicarial tithes. The clergyman's income is made up of small

tithes, Parliamentary grant, and Queen Anne's Bounty, amounting to £180 gross; and the surplice-fees make about £20 more. It has been calculated that the glebe land, if properly turned to account, would bring in £2,500 a year. Three years ago, when the present clergyman, the Rev. John Griffith, was inducted to the living, there was school accommodation for 120 children. Since then, by untiring and highly praiseworthy exertions, he has raised the means for educating 1,000 children. More than once he applied to the Dean and Chapter of Gloucester, as owners of the glebe land and impropriators of the great tithes in this very large and populous parish, for assistance in this behalf; but he never received from them one farthing. His success in other quarters has been remarkable. The parishioners, according to the clergyman's statement, have seconded his exertions in the most cordial spirit.

I visited and inspected the schools. The girls' school is held in a spacious, well-lighted, and airy room. There are 165 girls on the books, varying in age from five to fourteen years. They are taught—in addition to the usual feminine accomplishments of sewing and knitting—reading, writing, arithmetic, and singing. For some time there was no school for the daughters of the middle classes in the town, and the tradesmen's children then attended this school. But that want has since been supplied, and the scholars I saw were the children of the working classes. They were strikingly clean, and neatly dressed and well-behaved. The governess, a very intelligent and superior woman, is from the training-school at Westminster. She is unassisted, though the attendance sometimes amounts to ninety-six scholars. The average, however, is eighty. Two of the girls have passed the "Government Examination" for apprenticeship—and that very creditably; they will be indentured in February. Some of the children are taught singing on Wilhelm's system. The entire school sang for me a little song—the multiplication and addition of money tables in verse—and acquitted themselves extremely well.

From the girls' school I went to that of the boys. The house accommodation of both is temporary; proper school-rooms will soon be ready. There are 124 boys on the books; the average daily attendance being 90. The boys all belong to the working classes. I found them healthy and strong, comfortably clothed, and looking like true schoolboys, with their slates slung around their necks, and their books in their hands before them. They pay at different rates, from one penny to threepence a week—very few pay the largest sum. They learn reading, writing, and arithmetic. The regular course here followed is that recommended by the Committee of the Privy Council for Education, called "Baker's Circle of Knowledge," comprising natural history, and some other of the useful sciences. The boys are drilled daily; they went through their exercise for me with great spirit and exactness. They learn singing—a few of them on Wilhelm's method. One master, who has his classes in excellent order, and three monitors, have the management of the school. At present it is inconveniently crowded; but there will be accommodation afforded for 400 boys, in the course of a few months. There will be an equal, if not a greater, extension of the girls' school. It is proper here to add, that in neither of these educational establishments is it compulsory on the children to learn the Church of England Catechism, if the parents object.

When I saw the vast amount of good which this clergyman had effected in the brief space of three years, and witnessed the satisfaction with which he regarded the result of his labours, I could not help envying him his feelings. He passes so much of his time amongst them, that, numerous as they were, he called any boy or girl whom he addressed by the proper name. The children in their turn were frank and communicative; they were such as one would expect to do what those children did who, when overlooked by the village pastor—

"Plucked the good man's coat, to share the good man's smile."

LABOUR AND THE POOR.

———◆———

THE MINING AND MANUFACTURING DISTRICTS OF SOUTH WALES.

[FROM OUR SPECIAL CORRESPONDENT.]

MERTHYR AND DOWLAIS.

LETTER VI.

Having in my former Letters minutely described the workman as I found him in his labours below and above ground, in the mines and iron-works of this productive and important district, I purpose, in this and my next communication, treating of his domestic and social life—showing him in his character of father, husband, and neighbour.

And first, it will be necessary to premise a few remarks on the subject of wages. I have already compared the particulars on this head furnished me by the masters, with the statements of the men. The difference between them is small and unimportant. Both concur in showing that the price of labour has recently been lower than, with one exception, has ever been known within memory of man. It is less by full 40 per cent. than it was two or three years ago, and about 20 per cent. below what is considered the average and usual rate in this neighbourhood. Various causes have combined in producing this result. Three years ago, owing to the vast extension of railways, and to considerable activity at that time in the foreign trade, the price of iron was very high, and labour being in great demand, wages rose in a proportionate degree. That was, indeed, a prosperous season, and the evidences of it still remain visible in the well-furnished cottages of the prudent and thrifty among the workmen. "In the good time," said a roller (at Pen-y-Darran) whom I examined, "I earned sometimes as much as £3 15s. a week. That was in 1846, working rails. I now earn from 25s. to 30s. a week; never more, because we have no rail-work, only merchants' bars. Since then there have been three reductions in wages. The first was a fall of 4s.—the second, 2s. 6d.—and the third 2s. in the pound."

The great commercial depression from which we are now recovering, the cramped and unsatisfactory condition of the railway interest, and the check given to the foreign trade by the revolutionary disturbances on the Continent, have been the main causes of the depressed condition of the iron-trade during the past year and a half, which necessitated these reductions. A consciousness of these circumstances has made the men patient under their reverse, still hoping for better times. But they complained to me of the last "fall," as having been made in the face of an improvement in the price of iron. Thinking that their dissatisfaction might possibly not reach the master's ear, I informed Mr. Hill, the proprietor of Plymouth Works, of its existence. He admitted the advance in the price of iron, but said:—"What are the masters to do? They are as considerate as they can be. But, for the past year, the trade has been carried on actually at a loss; this must be recovered, and the present seems the best time for the purpose. As the trade improves the men well know, from former experience, we shall not be backward in giving them their share of the benefit."

The method of payment followed in this neighbourhood— and, in fact, not only here, but throughout the iron-works of the Principality—next challenges attention. It is on what is called the "long system" that the workmen are paid. In the books of the "company," as the proprietors are generally called, a debtor and creditor account is kept with each workman (except in cases where a middleman or "gaffer" intervenes between the employer and the labourer), which is balanced and settled once a month—the occasion being called "the pay." An advance is made once a week, and this is termed "a draw." But though professedly this is named a monthly payment, different works have different customs, and the "pay" is in very many instances a five weeks' balance instead of a monthly one. However—be it of four, five, or six weeks—when the "pay" comes round, each workman is handed a printed note, on which is a statement of his account. On the left side he is debited with gunpowder, iron, helves, doctor, and "fund" (as the calling of the workman may require), and with the amount of weekly advances which have been made to him. On the opposite side he is credited with the amount of his earnings, a particular statement of the items being at the same time therein given. A balance is struck, and the amount due upon the account, if any, is then paid. In more than one instance I saw notes where the advances overtopped the earnings, and the workman was the debtor; but they were cases where men, having taken underground work at a contract price, had met with unexpected difficulties in the cutting, and had earned much less than they hoped for when they entered upon the undertaking.

It is to be wished that this "long payment system" were abolished. It originated in the odious and censurable "truck-system"—the object then being to compel the workmen, by means of few payments, at long intervals, to depend upon the company's "store" or "shop" for the supply of their daily wants, by which practice the masters made a double profit on labour. Happily, in none of the great works in and adjoining Merthyr does this oppressive practice now exist; the workman can now carry his wages to the best market, and has the benefit of the competition in trade which his custom engenders. But over the hills, at no great distance from here, the "truck system," under arrangements presumed to be sufficient to defeat the intention of Parliament in legislating for its suppression, still prevails. As I purpose, however, devoting some space hereafter to remarks upon this subject, I shall not further allude to it on the present occasion.

Perhaps the greatest mischief resulting from the "long-payment system," where "truck" does not exist, is the temptation to intemperance which it holds out to the men. A "pay" is a kind of jubilee for them, occurring every month or five weeks; they pass the two or three days following in idleness and intemperance. For this their families suffer, by the loss of the money spent in the public-house, and the men themselves suffer likewise, by the increased labour they have to perform within a given time in order to make up for their dissipation. But if the pay was, like that of other artisans, weekly, and if it was made (as at Mr. Vivian's Copper-works in Swansea) the evening before market day, the families would have the benefit which ready money in various ways ensures; the more frequent recurrence of the pay-day would also deprive the event of its importance, and the *Saturnalia* of the month would no longer be celebrated as at present. Besides this, I believe that habits of thrift and saving would thereby be promoted. Instead of relying upon the balance of his monthly pay for the payment of his rent, his small bill at the shop, his subscription to the "benefit club," and the like, as he now does—the funds for which frequently melt away in the public-house before he reaches home from the pay-office—the workman would have to provide for these weekly out of the six days' earnings, and thus would naturally become more careful. There is not, that I can see, or on inquiry could learn, any practical difficulty attaching to a system of weekly payments. The

The Market

same staff of officers would suffice for a weekly as for a monthly pay; for I was expressly informed that no extra hands were employed in preparing for the occasion when the monthly day of reckoning comes round. I am convinced that it is only the prejudice of long-settled habit that continues this system; and I hope that, as the cause in which it originated has, in the best-class works, for many years past ceased to exist, the masters will ere long come to a determination to pay wages in future on the evening preceding market-day. This would make the system pursued at the works where "truck" prevails so conspicuous that it would probably die out for shame, even were no more powerful influence in the meantime applied for its extinction.

In a former Letter I gave the evidence of some men as to the evils of payment in public-houses, and made some remarks on this practice, and on the effect of employing middle-men or "gaffers." Since then I have met with the following passage in one of the Reports of Mr. Tremenheere on this district, which, as it fully corroborates my views and statements, I quote here:—

"On my arrival in the district, I found that the practice of paying wages in public-houses was very general. Most of the large works make use of contractors to raise the iron ore; some few are also engaged to raise the coal. Each of these contractors may employ from 10 to 100 men. At one of the extensive works there are thirty contractors, and the sum paid to them weekly may not be far short of 2,000*l.* The sums due to the men as wages are paid in gross to each contractor, at the office of the company, and the men are then assembled by him at some convenient place to receive their respective shares. The proprietors and managers of some of the works have, with due consideration for the interest of the men, made arrangements to prevent their being taken to public-houses for that purpose; by furnishing their contractors with a sufficient quantity of gold and silver, and by providing a proper place where the payments can be made. But in the great majority of cases, these aids are not given, and consequently the injurious practice is continued of adjourning to a public-house, where change is provided, and the accommodation paid for by a certain per centage spent in drink. This, of course, usually leads to much more, and must powerfully encourage the already excessive tendency of the population of these hills to habits of sensuality; drawing also many of the better-disposed into a snare which they might otherwise be inclined to avoid. Little could be added to what has been already submitted to Parliament in previous Reports, in reprobation of this practice, of which the Legislature has also marked its sense by laying it under penalties; and it is remarkable that the proprietors of these great works, whose interests are apt to be most injuriously affected by the drunken habits of their men, should not have shown an active desire to avail themselves of this among other means of leading to their improvement. The change, however, in the mode of payment will no longer be a matter of choice. I took care to inform the managers of all the works, and I requested them to apprise their contractors, that steps would forthwith be taken to enforce the penalties of the Act against those who should continue to disregard it."

The intimation contained in the last sentence of the above extract was made about four years ago; yet, though the statute, as I have elsewhere shown, is quite equal to the suppression of this baneful custom, it still exists wherever my inquiries have yet extended, and, I believe, throughout the entire mineral district of South Wales.

Out of the month's wages there are stopped, at most of the works, certain amounts—in part authorized by Parliament—for the purposes of providing medical attendance, a fund for support during sickness, and for the education of children. These items vary at different works.

Some have only a "doctor's" fund, leaving the men to provide for sickness by benefit societies; others have no educational fund, but one for the doctor and another for sickness. Some have only a doctor's fund. At Dowlais the deduction from wages for the above purposes amounts to 6d. in the pound, of which 1½d. is appropriated for the doctor, ½d. for the school, and 2d. goes to the sick-fund, which is very properly under the control of a committee of workmen—the general allowance being 4s. a week during a certain period to any workman who is disabled by accident or sickness. It is but justice to the masters to say that the arrangements they have made for medical attendance are on the most liberal scale, and are abundantly efficacious for the purpose. They have secured the services of extremely able men (some of them, I believe, not merely members, but fellows of the College of Surgeons), a competent staff of assistants, dressers, and dispensers, with all the necessary appliances for surgical and medical skill, ever ready for any emergency which may arise. It is no undeserved compliment to Mr. White, and Mr. Edward Davies, of Dowlais works; Mr. Russell, of Cyfarthfa; the gentleman who has charge of Plymouth Works (his name I forget); and Mr. John James to say, that a more efficient and skilful group of professional men is rarely to be found within an equal area—the metropolis, perhaps, alone excepted. Let me also give the workmen and their families the praise which I have heard the medical officers accord them. Mr. Edward Davies, speaking of their conduct under sickness, once remarked to me "They are patient under suffering, and attentive to the instructions of their medical man. Their confidence in him is great, and their power of endurance extraordinary. If it is necessary I should operate, and I say, 'My good man, I am sorry to tell you, but you must lose your leg,' or 'have your arm off,' as the case may be; he does not cry out, as I have usually known patients under the circumstances in the English and French hospitals—'oh, dear, don't do it now; can't it be put off till to-morrow;' but submits without an objection—sometimes saying 'Well, doctor, you know best'—and they bear the knife with heroic fortitude." The number of accidents in the works below and above ground, resulting in amputation, is very great. I believe there are in Merthyr more men with wooden legs than are to be found in any town in the kingdom having four times its population. I once passed in the street three, within a hundred yards, and five in going through the entire street, which was not a long one.

The rate of wages, as will be seen on reference to my former letters, has recently ranged from 10s. up to 35s. a week, according to the
value of the services rendered. There are very few who earn the largest
amount, and those are engaged upon the highest class of skilled work
which is here performed. By far the largest proportion of the workmen earn a less sum than 20s. a week. But, low as is this rate, the
men are unquestionably better able to sustain this depreciation than
they were to bear the reduction of wages which preceded the last fall.
An intelligent puddler whom I examined said—"When we was reduced 2s. 6d. in the pound, the price of food and such like was very
high, but now it is as low as ever was known hereabouts." This circumstance greatly alleviates the condition of the lowest class of workmen.
Though, I believe, even with this in their favour, they have difficulty
in living, yet such is the patient endurance of these classes, that they
will undergo great bodily privations rather than dispose of their little
furniture, as long as it can possibly be retained. I could not find that
the pawnbrokers, of whom there are just twelve in Merthyr, had per-
ceptibly increased their business owing to the depressed state of wages
in this district. The houses were still crowded with furniture, and the
men with their families lived on, denying themselves in some degree
the quantity of animal food they used to consume, and reducing their
expenditure in other ways. There have been a few instances, no doubt,
where the vices of drunkenness and improvidence already existed, in
which the low rate of wages has brought affairs to that crisis when the
disposal of the household goods and apparel is unavoidable; but it is
not of such exceptional cases I speak, but of the mass of the labouring community, to whom those reproaches, I am happy to say, do not
apply.

The markets of Merthyr and Dowlais are abundantly supplied
with provisions and such miscellaneous articles as are in demand
amongst the working classes. They were established by private
speculators, and are no doubt abundantly remunerative. The local
act for Merthyr vests the property in the market in two private
gentlemen, whose shrewdness suggested the value of such a project;
that of Dowlais belongs to the Dowlais Company. Thus, owing to
the want of a corporation in this town of 40,000 inhabitants, whose
duty and care it would have been to provide a market-house, the tolls,
producing (in Merthyr, at all events, and I presume in Dowlais) a
very handsome yearly income, which might have been appropriated
to the draining, cleansing, and lighting this dark, unsewered, and

filthy town, have been for ever alienated, or are redeemable only at a cost which would not make them worth the purchasing. The butcher's meat is supplied from Breconshire, Monmouthshire, and the grazing parts of this county bordering the sea; the poultry comes from Carmarthenshire; and the vegetables, strange to say, are nearly all imported from Bristol, by the way of Cardiff. I wonder no speculators have hit upon the idea of establishing extensive market gardens on the southern slope or at the bases of the mountains facing the sea, for the supply of the great iron-works. The soil about Llandaff and Cardiff is abundantly rich, and there are annually thousands of tons of the finest manure thrown into the Taff at Merthyr, because there is in the neighbourhood no use for it, which might be had at the mere cost of removal, and turned to profitable account in growing vegetables. The shops of Merthyr are numerous, well furnished, and show all the bustle and activity of a thriving trade. The market-house, which is very capacious, may be termed a "bazaar of shops." The scene from six to ten o'clock on Saturday evening is one of the most extraordinary I ever witnessed. In this interval what one might suppose the entire labouring population of Merthyr passes through its crowded halls. All are dressed in their Sunday clothing, clean, warm, and comfortable. It is not only the field of supply, but evidently the promenade of the working classes. Every face is smiling; pleasant greetings and friendly jokes are freely exchanged. All is happiness; the week's money is in the pocket, and the pleasurable excitement of bargain-driving, in which the Welsh are proficients, goes bravely forward. One division of the market is appropriated to butcher's meat; another to vegetables; a third to poultry and butter; a fourth to dried stores of bacon, cheese, and herrings; a fifth to apples, eggs, and fruit. Of the first-named in this division, judging by the quantities for sale, there must be a large consumption. There are also stalls of every description of hardware and other shop-goods. Hatters, drapers, shoemakers, tinmen, ironmongers, and even booksellers, here drive an active and thriving trade. Wandering about amongst these, accompanied with their wives bearing baskets, you see the sallow-faced, hollow-eyed firemen, the noisy colliers, the prudent and saving "miners," the jovial Irish labourers, all intent upon business, which they make a pleasure. Vociferous groups of boys set loose from the works rudely rush through this motley assembly, to the disturbance of the "stocking-men," who, with their woollen wares depending from a horizontal stick, half obstruct the way, and to the annoyance of the red-cloaked, hat-covered women, who pay them back with blows if active enough to reach them. Outside the market-house are booths and shows, with their yellow flaming lamps, flaunting pictures, and obstreperous music. Groups of Welsh ballad-singers, shouting with stentorian voices, and a row of stalls where the fathers put their boys to shoot for nuts or gingerbread at a wide-mouthed puppet or a well-worn target, complete this lively and striking scene.

The prices of provisions in the markets, and the necessaries in the shops, which I took pains accurately to obtain, I found to be as follows:—

Beef and mutton (good) 4½d. to 6½d. per lb.
Pork, 4½d. to 6d. per lb.
Fowls (per couple) 2s. to 3s. 6d.
Bacon (Welsh, home cured) 9d. to 10d. per lb.
　　　" 　(American) 6d. per lb.
Cheese (Gloucestershire and Caerphilly) 3d. to 7d. per lb.
[Immense quantities of cheese are consumed. The miners and colliers exclusively use the best; they give preference to an article of tough quality, because it is not so liable to crumble and break in carrying. The "navigators," and such as work above ground, use the common qualities.]
Butter (salt) 7d., 8d., and 8½d. per lb.
　　　" 　(fresh) 10d. to 1s. per lb.
Flour (best quality) 3s. 4d. per 28 lbs.
　　　" 　(seconds) 3s. to 3s. 2d. per 28 lbs.
Oatmeal (chiefly used by the Irish) 3s. 6d. per 28 lbs.
Indian meal (not much used) 2s. 6d. per 28 lbs.
Potatoes, ¾d. per lb., or 8 lbs. for 6d.
Candles (prodigious quantities consumed in the mines and houses) 5d. to 5½d. per lb.
Sugar (also largely used) 4d., 5d., and 6d. per lb.
Coffee, 10d. to 1s. 6d. per lb.
Tea, 3s. 8d. to 4s. 6d. per lb.
Soap, (yellow) 5d. per lb.

On my inquiring why oatmeal was dearer than the best flour, it was accounted for by the fact that flour was very cheap. When flour is dear more oatmeal is made, and it is then lower in price than wheaten

flour. The Irish prefer it. "The habits of the people in the neighbourhood," said Mr. Morgan, the proprietor of the largest provision shop
in Merthyr, "are, to use the best of everything, particularly flour. Of
sugar, for instance, there is much more of the 6d. than of the 4d. quality disposed of. Bacon is not so much used just now, because butcher's
meat is so cheap. The people don't yet understand Indian meal, or I
am sure there would be more sale for it. The consumption of tea is very
large; coffee is sparingly used, probably because in this town milk is
dear, scarce, and of indifferent quality. The custom is to sell everything by weight."

I consider the dearest item, and the greatest hardship the labouring classes have to contend with in the way of living, is that of house-
rent, which is here disproportionately high, considering the scanty accommodation afforded. The houses of the workmen are built in rows
of uniform height and size. They are of three classes. The best are of
two stories, have four small sash-windows (which, by the way, are
never opened), two above, and one on each side of the door. On the
ground floor there is a roomy kitchen with a stone floor; adjoining is
a small room, just large enough to contain a four-post bed, a chest
of drawers, a small corner-cupboard, two chairs, and a window table,
which usually form its contents. The ceiling is not plastered, and the
rafters are used for hanging up the crockery and household utensils.
Above stairs are two bed-rooms, one large and the other small; the
ceiling here is of lath and plaster. This is all, except, perhaps, a narrow cupboard, cut off from the lower bed-room, and dignified with
the name of "pantry." There is no strip of garden, no back-door or outlet, no place of accommodation, no drain to carry away house refuse,
nor any pump or pipe for the supply of water. The street in front is
consequently made the receptacle of every kind of abomination con-
ceivable. Such are the residences of the best-class workmen in and
around Merthyr. These houses are, for the most part, the very type
of cleanliness and order. They are stuffed with furniture, even to superfluity; a fine mahogany eight-day clock, a showy mahogany chest
of drawers, a set of mahogany chairs with solid seats, a glass-fronted
cupboard for the display of china, glass, and silver spoons, forming
indispensable requisites for the principal room. The other apartments
are equally well furnished. The habits of the women, in respect of their
houses, are those of cleanliness, decency, and order. They are always
scrubbing the rooms, polishing and regulating the furniture, or with
long brushes laying white or yellow washes upon the front of their

house. In short, the people themselves do their duty; but there being no town authorities to look to cleansing, draining, and scavenging, the streets are in a state of disgusting filth, abounding in fermenting and putrefying substances, equally offensive to decency and injurious to the public health. For such a house the workman pays from 10s. to 13s. a month.

The second-class houses have but two rooms, one above stairs and one below; for these the rents vary from 6s. to 8s. a month. There are third-class houses having only one room, for which the rent is about 4s. a month. It will be seen from the above particulars, and from the following statement of the cost of building, that in the best and second-class houses, the rent, considering the accommodation afforded, is unreasonably high. The houses are built of a peculiar grey sandstone, raised in abundance by the "patchers" who quarry for the nodules of iron ore which are found near the surface of the ground. This stone costs little more than the price of carting; consequently labour, wood, and iron-work form the most expensive items in the construction of these houses. In Dowlais, I am informed, one-third of these habitations were built by and are the property of Sir John Guest and his partners. A house which cost in the building £45, lets for, at least, 10s. a month (of four weeks) or £6 10s. a year, thus returning upon the outlay about fourteen per cent.

Let us now take the case of a "second-hand" puddler, with a wife, and four children under the statutable age for work; and consider the circumstances of his wages and expenditure. He earns 15s. a week, which may be regarded as the medium price of labour in and around Merthyr at the present time. Out of this he pays:—

Rent (8s. a month), weekly	2s.	0d.
Coal (6s. 6d. a month), weekly ..	1s.	7½d.
Doctor and sick-fund	0s.	4d.
Clay for repairing furnace	0s.	4d.
Total	4s.	3½d.

This sum, deducted from his weekly wages, leaves just 10s. 8½d. to feed and clothe six persons; his fiery and exhausting labour requiring that he should himself use animal food. One wonders how it can be done; yet, with the arts of thrift and good management, it is done by hundreds. The condition of labourers who earn only 10s. a week is, of course, proportionably straitened and worse. This analysis of the cost and means of living amply corroborates the statements made to me, of the scanty and hard diet of these classes.

The domestic habits of the workman, his character and conduct, are largely influenced by the wife it has been his fortune to meet with. If he has married a maid-servant (there is large competition for females of this class, from a belief that they make the best wives), and if he has not some inherent vice, such as idleness or drunkenness, to contend against, he is, taking times in the long run, a prosperous and happy man. His home is comfortable, his children and wife are well-clothed, and of good repute. On the other hand, if he has married a "working girl," ignorant as she is of household duties and the obligations of a wife, the chances are against him; though often, in course of time, these poor girls become domesticated and learn the arts of housekeeping, which, bred entirely in the society of men, at the pit's mouth, on the mountain side, or in forges and mills, they had previously no opportunity for acquiring. Children, when they arrive at the age of ten, instead of being a burden, are a strong help to him, for boys and girls alike earn from 4s. to 7s. a week, out of which their allowance for pocket-money may be 4d., or perhaps 6d. a week. He is often provident and saving; the wealth of furniture he loves to have around him, and the fact that in numerous instances he buys or builds his own house (not by the aid of Building Societies, but with his own proper and ready means), sufficiently attest this. I was curious to learn what amount of savings had been invested by different classes of workmen in savings banks. I was told that there *had been* a savings bank in Merthyr, but that it was misconducted, and the trustees having to pay for the defalcations of an officer, it was broken up, and no new bank established. I was also told that the men, from an apprehension that the masters might learn the amount of their savings and lessen their wages, never favoured establishments of this nature.

Whilst treating of the subject of his provident habits, I should mention the fact that the workman is always a member of one, sometimes of two, Benefit Societies. The Loyal and Independent Lodge of Odd Fellows numbers within its ranks many hundreds of this class. By such means, in addition to his allowance from "the fund" at the works, he provides additional resources for the hour of sickness, or when he may be disabled by an accident. This has been found to work badly in cases where a man subscribes to two Benefit Societies, and is idle and dissolute. It is then an adjutant to those vices. I knew one case—and Mr. David James, the chairman of the board of guardians, told me of another which came before him privately on that day—where a man who, whilst in full work, earned only 14s. a week, when certified by the medical officer as sick, came at once into the receipt of 18s. a week; that is to say he had 7s. a week from each Benefit Club to which he belonged, and 4s. from the Sick Fund at the works. This, with dishonest men, acts as a premium on idleness and imposture. A system which works in this manner, by encouraging fraud and indolence, ought to be, and it easily might be, put down. All that is necessary is to make one rule of the club, requiring a declaration from every new member that he does not belong to any other Benefit Society, and another for the forfeiture of his interest in the concern, in case of his having made a false statement in this particular.

The domestic habits of the workmen in the iron-works are peaceful and simple. During a stay of several weeks in the town I neither saw nor heard of altercations or fighting. The man, on his return from labour, usually washes (the colliers and miners invariably wash every day from head to foot), puts on another coat, and sits down to his meal of potatoes, meat, and tea, or broth, and bread and cheese, as the case may be. His wife and children, comfortably clothed and cheerful, sit down with him. Afterwards he goes to a neighbour's house, or receives some friends in his own, when they discuss the news and light gossip affecting their class, or talk over the success or difficulties attending their work and their prospects as regards the future. Visiting many of their houses at night, I saw numbers of such groups; in one instance only I saw them drinking beer, and that was at a kind of housewarming, one of the body having that night taken possession of the neatly furnished house where I found them assembled.

But there is no doubt that many betake themselves to the public-houses, which are very numerous and hold out every kind of temptation to induce custom. If the man's home be, owing to a bad wife, cheerless and neglected, what wonder that he flies when he can to the beer-shop and the public-house! There he is always welcome—its portals admit him to gaiety and pleasure. At nightfall, as you pass the doors, you hear the tuning of the harp in preparation for the coming dissipation. Two hours later, if you again pass, the twinkling strings are ringing merrily, and you hear the rapid shuffle of feet on the sandy floor. I obtained an account of the number of public-houses and beer-shops in Merthyr and Dowlais. There are, of

Public-houses and Inns   98
Beer-shops 207
                                        ───
              Total 305

The number of rateable houses is 7,500; therefore, according to the above statement, there is one public-house or beer-shop to every 24½ houses. Out of seven adjoining-houses in one of the streets I counted five public-houses and beer-shops. On analysing the list of persons entitled to vote for the borough, I found that, out of a total of 643 voters, one in every 3½ was a publican or beer-house keeper! In Dowlais alone there are not less than 75 of these houses. The proportion of voters and rateable householders is 1 to 11½. The clergyman at Dowlais remarked to me, "The 'kidliwinks' (beer-shops) are the greatest curse of this place. But the nuisance is abating; there was at one time upwards of 200 in the town." On all hands I heard it admitted that this abundance of beer-houses (for the public-houses are better conducted and are by no means so pernicious) was a fruitful cause of the intemperance and vice which exist in this neighbourhood. The purpose of the Legislature in passing the statute for the regulation of beer-houses, was to ensure by a high-rating the respectability of the house. At that time it was admitted that the number and low character of the beer-houses throughout England and Wales had worked a serious mischief upon the labouring population. To remedy this it was enacted that no householder should have a license for a beer-house unless he was rated to the relief of the poor as high as £15, if the population was above 5,000; the object being to have responsible and respectable householders, as far as possible, for the keepers of these houses. In addition to this there was continued the old certificate and bond, but the first of these is easily obtained by any man from his neighbours, and the latter, so far as I know and believe, is never enforced. (In speaking of the provisions of the Act I am relying upon memory, a copy of the statute not being at hand, but I believe I have correctly stated them.) The manner in which the spirit and intention of the Act is violated in this neighbourhood is this. A man living in a row of workmen's houses, whose rent is £7 a year, determines on keeping a beer-house. He goes to his neighbours who certify he is a respectable man. He then builds a small shed at the back of his house to give colour to his application to be rated at £15. He now goes to the overseer and calls on him to rate him at that sum, saying he has made additions to the premises. Only too happy to have a contributor to the rate in this increased amount, the overseer rates him as requested; he next applies to the Excise who have nothing to do but grant him a license, and there is at once another source of temptation created in the neighbourhood. I may add, another voter is also made, who may be easily controlled. I noted in Dowlais the names of two beer-shops of the same height and size, and of the same roofage, as the houses adjoining in the same row, the rents of the neighbouring houses being, as I learnt from the tenants, from £7 to £8 a year. If the beer-house had been doubled in size, its rental would not have amounted to the statutable requirement, for the population of Dowlais is thrice 5,000. I may add that I have reason to believe, from my own recollection of "a pay" in this place about a dozen years ago, and my observation of one now, that drunkenness is much less rife than it was at that period, and this opinion has been corroborated by that of gentlemen who have passed much of their time in Merthyr. The growing intelligence of the masses, even here, where so few means of intellectual recreation are offered them, is operating favourably, and will, no doubt, continue to lessen this evil.

Not a few of the working men here are men of strong natural genius, which they have proved by self-elevation from the lowest ranks of labour. The underground mineral surveyors are frequently self-educated, and so are the agents to whom are confided various responsible situations in the works. A Mr. Henry Murton, who till lately was himself an operative, gave a lecture in Dowlais a few evenings ago upon chemistry. There are, however, and it is a fact to be regretted, scarcely any opportunities afforded them for self-improvement. Adult schools there are, indeed, which I shall notice hereafter, but there are no places well lit, decently furnished, warm and comfortable, to which the workman might resort after his day's labour to read and converse, and so entertain himself. There is what is called "a Tradesman's and Workman's Library" in Dowlais, and another in Merthyr. The latter I visited; it was a comfortless and dreary place.

Anxious to acquaint myself with the literary tastes of the inhabitants of Merthyr, I applied to Mr. White, an intelligent bookseller with an extensive business, for his assistance. He supplies all classes. The following are the particulars I extracted from his books; they curiously show the interest taken in the physical sciences affecting the operations of trade in this neighbourhood. Mr. White's present sale of serials and periodicals is as follows:—

The Artizan, 5 copies.
The Mechanic's Magazine, 6 copies.
Tredgold on the Steam Engine, 3 copies.
The Practical Mechanic's Journal, 10 copies.
The Builder, 6 copies.
Rudimentary Treatise on the Steam Engine (Lardner), many copies.
Rudimentary Treatise on Well-digging and Boring (Swindells), many copies.
Rudimentary Treatise on Blasting and Quarrying for Stone (Burgoyne), many copies.
Rudimentary Treatise on Mineralogy (Varley), many copies.
Art of Building (Dobson), many copies.
Art of Constructing Cranes (Glynn), many copies.
Family Herald, 19 copies.
Chambers's Journal, 5 copies.
Eliza Cook's Journal, 2 copies.
Art Journal, 10 copies.
People's Journal, 2 copies.
Pendennis, 6 copies.
David Copperfield, 9 copies.
Bulwer's Works (in parts), 6 copies.
Banker's Magazine, 2 copies.
New Monthly and Bentley's, a copy of each.
Blackwood's Magazine, 7 copies.
Eglwysydd (Penny Church publication in Welsh), 150 copies.
Churchman's Penny Magazine, 50 copies.
Church of England Magazine, 7 copies.
Christian's Penny Magazine, 20 copies.
Baptist Magazine, 11 copies.
Baptist Reporter, 8 copies.
Juvenile Missionary Magazine, 30 copies.
 Ditto   ditto   Herald (Baptist), 63 copies.
Christian Witness (Independent), 15 copies.
Child's Companion, 55 copies.

I next called upon Mr. Wilkins, the bookseller, who supplies the market-houses here, at Dowlais, and in the neighbouring works. He told me that if the cheap publications were in Welsh the sale would be enormous. While conversing with Mr. Wilkins, I was forcibly struck with the circumstance that the sellers of cheap publications can lead as well as follow the taste of the labouring classes. A heavy responsibility is in their hands. Mr. Wilkins disposes of—

	Weekly.		Weekly.
The Family Herald	360	The Domestic Journal	12
The London Journal	360	The Northern Star	12
Eliza Cook's Journal	18	The News of the World	189
The People's and Howitt's		Dipple's Miscellany	12
Journal	18	The Physician	24
The Home Circle	18	Lloyd's Miscellany	24
Reynolds's Miscellany	60	The Brigand	6
Reynolds's Political Instr-		The Hebrew Maiden	12
uctor	36		

These particulars give a tolerably clear insight into the literary predilections of the inhabitants of this populous neighbourhood—which, it will be seen, run equally in the direction of their worldly and spiritual necessities, the learning of the sciences on which they depend for bread, and the comforts of religion which form the *pabulum* of the soul.

Wisely endeavouring to improve the intellectual character of his workmen by means of a refined amusement, Mr. Robert Crawshay has established amongst them a brass band, which practises once a week throughout the year. It is entirely composed of workmen. They have the good fortune to be led by a man (one of the roll-turners) who must have had somewhere a superior musical education. I had the pleasure of hearing them play, and was astonished at their proficiency. They number sixteen instruments. I heard them perform the Overtures to *Zampa, the Caliph of Bagdad,* and *Fra Diavolo, Vivi tu,* some concerted music from *Roberto, Don Giovanni,* and *Lucia,* with a quantity of Waltzes, Polkas, and dance music. The bandmaster had them under excellent control; he everywhere took the time well, and the instruments preserved it, each taking up his lead with spirit and accuracy; in short, I have seldom heard a regimental band more perfect than this handful of workmen, located (far from any place where they might command the benefit of hearing other bands) in the mountains of Wales. When I was informed of the existence of this band, I knew how to account for a circumstance that had puzzled me—hearing the boys in Cyfarthfa works whistle the best airs from the most popular operas. The great body of men at these works are extremely proud of their musical performances, and like to boast of them. I have been told it cost Mr. Crawshay great pains and expense to bring this band to its present excellent condition. If so, he now has his reward. Besides this, he has shown what the intellectual capacity of the workman is equal to, and, above all, he has provided a rational and refined amusement for classes whose leisure time would otherwise probably have been less creditably spent than in learning or listening to music. I greatly wish his example were followed at other works. Give a man an instrument to learn or play, and his spare time is employed in a manner equally entertaining and improving, whilst his family benefits by an occupation which, in a great degree, keeps him out of temptation.

Whilst they are respectful to their superiors, and even regard with something like veneration their masters, when the latter come amongst them, the workmen, as a body, have a high spirit, and resent anything which they consider in the light of a meanness. In proof of this I will relate an illustrative story. It appears to have been a long-established practice in Merthyr for the tradesmen to present each regular customer at Christmas with a sufficient quantity of rice, sago, or groats, with currants and lemon-peel, to make the Christmas pudding. Last year they determined on abandoning the rule, and issued a notice headed "Christmas Boxes," wherein they stated that, whereas the said practice usually occasioned dissatisfaction equally to the party who gave and the party who received the present, and whereas such a custom was "totally opposed to a sound system of doing business," they, the undersigned (there were two long columns of names), had determined on discontinuing it. Almost immediately on the appearance of this placard, the workmen issued the following remarkable handbill, one of which I obtained.

"OH DEAR! OH DEAR!! WHAT CAN THE MATTER BE?

"We, the workmen of Merthyr, having our attention drawn to a placard posted in our town, headed 'Christmas Boxes,' informing the public the intention of our shopkeepers not to give Christmas boxes this year, as usual; we, the workmen, knowing there must be a reason for the same, and, judging from appearance, our shopkeepers must be desperately impoverished, and in many cases poverty leads to crime; therefore, as a preventative is better than a cure, we, the workmen, judge it unsafe to deal with such suspicious characters, and deem it expedient to form a fund, in order to procure our provisions from the cheapest markets, or deal with those whom we can rely on.

"THE WORKMEN."

This was succeeded by a doggerel poem, in seven stanzas, of which also I obtained a copy. This gives me an opportunity for remarking that there is a great disposition for versification amongst the working classes in Wales. Here, in the iron-works, they have an abundance of what I may call "native songs," many of which, in Welsh and English, are in praise of the works and their employers. The poem above referred to commenced and concluded as follows:—

"THE POOR'S LAMENT, FOR THEIR CHRISTMAS PUDDING.

"Alas! alas! bad news, indeed,
To all who want their rice and seed,
The news is shocking bad to read
    About the Christmas Pudding:
For by going down the street one day,
Large bills we saw of great display,
Which appeared unto us for to say,
    You'll get no Christmas Pudding.

CHORUS.
Oh dear! Oh dear! what times are these,
The shopkeepers do as they please,
The poor they're trying for to tease,
About a Christmas Pudding.
* * * * * *

"Now all good folks advised be,
And mind where you do buy your tea,
And get a Christmas box do you see,
    Where at the shop you're dealing;
They'll soon come round to beg and pray
Saying, 'twas all a joke, do of us buy,
Them don't believe when so they say,
    But mind what you are after."

I have said that the workmen regard their masters, when the latter come amongst them, with something like veneration; I may add, that where the habit of the master is to pass much of his time in the works, this feeling ripens into affection. And it has always been so in the Welsh iron-works. The rejoicings upon every marriage or other festive occasion in the families of such masters are as sincere as they are universal. I cannot forbear relating, as I had it from a gentleman on the spot, the following incident, which perhaps changed the destiny of one of the most influential and important houses in the manufacturing interest of this kingdom. Many years ago, when the Cyfarthfa Works were not the sole property of the Crawshay family, there was a difference amongst the partners, which disgusted Mr. Crawshay, and he proposed retiring from the firm. As this vast concern had been established by the enterprise of a Crawshay, and had ripened to perfection under the superintendence of that family, the men heard this piece of news with great regret. In the meantime, negotiations for the dissolution of the partnership went forward, and Mr. Crawshay, accompanied by his son, the present proprietor of the works, who was then a boy, went down to Cyfarthfa, from which place he had for some time been absent, for the purpose of completing the act by which he was to take his share and retire. The deed was at the counting-house of the works, but not quite ready, the testature clause or something having to be added. Whilst this was being done, Mr. Crawshay entered the works for "a last look at them." He was received everywhere with the accustomed respect, and with a cordiality which seemed increased by the prospect of a severance of the relations that had existed between himself, his family, and the workmen. At length, after eager running to and fro and hasty consultations by the men, a grim old puddler, who had grown grey in the service, left his glowing furnace, approached, and, wiping his sweaty face, addressed Mr. Crawshay:—

"We have heard, sir," said he, "you are going to leave us."

"I am so, Daniel," said Mr. Crawshay, for well he knew the old man, "but what of that? You'll have others who will be as kind to you, and whom you'll like as well."

"That may be so, sir," rejoined the furnace-man; "but the men can't endure it. A Crawshay came here, and made the works; he did great good here abouts. The people have always been used to a Crawshay, and they can't bear the change. There have been more talk about this amongst the men than you know of."

Many voices assented to this; those who were out of hearing, aware of the prevailing sentiment, divined what was going forward and came flocking round. They begged Mr. Crawshay not to leave them. For a few minutes he was absorbed in thought, then turning to his son he exclaimed:—

"By Jove, Will, we'll not sign; there is no harm done to any one. All parties are in the same position as before the negotiations. I cannot leave the men."

The news spread instantly through the works, causing great satisfaction; and Mr. Crawshay, with his son, posted straight to London,
where, expecting a suit in equity for a specific performance of the
agreement, they at once retained Sir Samuel Romilly. Whether such
a suit was instituted I cannot say, but shortly afterwards Mr. Crawshay bought out the other two partners, and became sole proprietor
of the works. Such is the story as it was related to me.

The influence of Chartism, which once was great over the population of these hills, as witnessed by the sanguinary conflict at Newport, has not only lessened, but nearly died away in these districts.
This statement is supported by the paucity of Chartist works taken
by the people. From the account above given of periodicals sold by
Mr. Wilkins, emphatically "the workmen's bookseller," the reader
will find that, though Mr. Wilkins attends the markets all through the
iron-works, and supplies the wants of a population of some 80,000,
his sale of the *Northern Star* is but one dozen copies a week. Itiner-
ant orators and delegates sometimes come amongst them. Even at
the period of my visit, when wages were at a low ebb, and they subsisted with difficulty, yet in the iron works all was peaceable, and quiet,
and orderly, and there were no indications whatever of disturbance,
though some dissatisfaction existed, as I have heretofore shown, with
the cause of the reduction.

In support of what I have above said of the furnishing of the
cottages and the condition of their inmates, I will give the particulars
I observed in two or three houses belonging to different classes of the
workmen. —— ——, Cyfarthfa-row. This was one of the roomiest
and best cottages I had seen in the iron works. It was new. It had
a fine large kitchen, a good parlour, a convenient pantry with a
window, and two lofty ceiled bed-rooms upstairs. There was a small
strip of garden behind, and *(mirabile dictu!)* a privy at command;
there was one to every six houses in the row. Nevertheless the rent
was only 8s. a month. In this case there was evidently a diminution
of rent in consideration of services. The house was literally crammed
with furniture. In the kitchen were two mahogany chests of drawers,
each of which supported a looking-glass, a tea-tray, bread-basket,
tea-caddies, and some books, amongst which I observed Burhitt
on the New Testament, folio, and Bagster's Comprehensive Bible.
There was also a well-polished eight-day clock, and a set of good
mahogany chairs. On the walls were a quantity of prints in gold

frames. Between two pieces of needlework was a portrait of our Saviour upon one of the walls. Another had a good looking-glass, a coloured portrait of the Duke of Wellington, and a large print of the Battle of Waterloo. From the rafters of the floor above hung a canary bird in his cage, a lanthorn, and a quantity of jugs enough to have supplied a harvest-home supper. Over the fireplace there were displayed a bottle-jack, and small bellows, an Italian iron and flat irons, extra tongs, poker, and shovel, and a variety of useful little articles, all kept bright as silver. The window was filled with a large myrtle. [Here I may remark upon this habit of cultivating flowers in doors, which is universal amongst the labouring classes. I have seen everywhere an abundance of *arums*, geraniums, cinerarias, myrtles, and the like, which thrive most luxuriantly, owing, I presume, to the warmth of their apartments, which have always a large blazing fire.] In the parlour there was a good four-post bedstead, a French-polished chest of drawers, covered with a profusion of glass and other articles, including a cruet-stand and decanters, with small figures of the Queen and Prince Albert in chinaware, a neat work-box, and some ornamental shells. In a corner was a glass-fronted cupboard, filled with china and glass, and displaying ostentatiously silver sugar tongs and a set of spoons. There was also a mahogany table, with a bright copper teakettle reposing on it. On the walls were framed prints of St. John and St. Luke, with a portrait of King George the Fourth between them. Behind the door hung a quantity of male and female wearing apparel, and beside it were some shelves loaded with books, amongst which were "Bunyan's Pilgrim's Progress," the "Complete Works of Flavius Josephus" (in Welsh), *"Haver Bedyd-dwyr"* (History of the Baptists), M{c}Donald's "Family Cook," "The Evangelical Rambler," a Welsh Bible, "Cydymarth-y-bibl" (Bible class-book), and an English "Book of Common Prayer." A slate, a hat, a bonnet, and a pair of child's boots, completed the inventory of this room. The apartments upstairs were equally well furnished. They had a four-post, and a stump bedstead, mahogany chairs and tables, looking glasses, coffers for keeping clothes, a pair of scales for weighing flour, a spinning wheel, and other conveniences. The floors were as white as snow, and all the furniture was polished and kept with great care.

I should state that in selecting that house I took the first that I met with, where the furniture appeared remarkably good. I next took an average second-class house. It was inhabited by a collier working at Pen-y-darran; and though it had but too small rooms, the rent was the same as that of the last house, namely 8s. a month. The wife kept a small huckster's shop—a common practice hereabouts. She sold apples, gingerbread, herrings, bacon, and a few other articles which did not require a license. In reply to my questions, she said, "My husband is a collier, working at Pen-y-Darran; he earns about 10s. a week; sometimes he gets 11s., but never more. My mother died in this house of cholera." I was amused with some odd-looking characters in chalk on a cupboard-door. She told me she could not write, but nevertheless could keep accounts. She had symbols of her own for that purpose. I asked her to read her accounts, and she did so readily. I cannot pretend to describe the marks she had for names, but the notation of a shilling was expressed by a ring, that of sixpence by a circle with a spike issuing from the centre; straight strokes expressed a penny, and horizontal lines a halfpenny. Among the furniture of this house I noticed one chest of drawers, on which stood a tea-tray, two waiters, and a few books, including a "Bible," "the Young Woman's Companion," "the Popular Story Teller," &c. On the books were a clothes and hair brush; and, hanging on the wall above, was a small looking-glass. One round and one square deal table, three chairs, a wicker cradle, a Dutch clock without a case, and a few useful articles over the fireplace, consisting of brass candlesticks, a coffee-pot, and the like, constituted the whole of the furniture of this room. In a small back window there hung a canary in his cage, and a flower, which the good woman informed me was a "nettle geranium." There was an infant in the cradle, only three months old. A few small pictures decorated the walls; among them was a tribute of affection to the memory of the woman's little brother—it was a coloured French lithograph, cleverly executed, of a child reclining his head upon his hands. It had been bought from a fancied resemblance to the deceased brother.

I shall resume this subject in a future Letter.

LABOUR AND THE POOR.

——◆——

THE MINING AND MANUFACTURING DISTRICTS OF SOUTH WALES.

[FROM OUR SPECIAL CORRESPONDENT.]

MERTHYR AND DOWLAIS.

PUBLIC HEALTH—THE IRISH—RELIGION IN THE IRON-WORKS.

LETTER VII.

A memorable event in the annals of Merthyr was the visit of the cholera to the town last summer. It was a four months' reign of terror and desolation. Go where you will—but especially amongst the labouring classes and the poor—the people still speak of it as of a heavy trial, and a frightful calamity. Remembering the virulence with which the disease raged at its former visit in 1834, and aware that no substantial improvement had since been effected in the sanitary condition of the place—that the houses and streets were still undrained—that the supply of water was precarious and insufficient—that the roads were one mass of decomposing rubbish—and, in short, that the town, in various other ways, presented a favourable field for pestilence—the parish authorities exerted themselves most strenuously in anticipation of its coming. They built temporary refuges on the surrounding hills; they removed vast heaps of house refuse, which had been accumulating and decaying for years around the dwellings; and they limed, and washed, and purified every stagnant hole and corner, as diligently as activity, backed by competent means, could perform those duties. Nor were the great iron-masters backward or parsimonious in their arrangements to meet the exigencies of the time. They strengthened their medical staffs by the addition of competent assistants, and furthered the endeavours of the parish authorities in removing the augean nuisances which abounded everywhere throughout the town. Scarcely had these preparations been completed ere the cholera came. It broke out on the 25th of May, attained its height in

133

August, and ceased on the last day of September. During those four months it swept away nearly 1,500 out of a population of 40,000 souls. The number of houses in Merthyr and Dowlais is 7,500, while the total of persons attacked was 3,260; so that, assuming that only one person in a house had been smitten by the disease (and the instances were not numerous where there were more, because immediately on a death the medical officers removed the inmates to the temporary refuges on the neighbouring hills)—and excluding the residences of the tradesmen and professional men, whose inmates passed comparatively unscathed—the disease must have visited nearly every other house. The streets were black with funerals, and resounded all day with the hymns sung, according to immemorial usage amongst the Welsh, at the burial of friends and relatives. The following is the official return of the ravages of cholera in Merthyr:—

"CHOLERA AT MERTHYR TYDFIL.
"RETURN OF CASES—MONDAY, OCTOBER 1, 1849.

	Attacked.	Dead.
Merthyr:		
Total from commencement (May 25), as per last report, corrected by registration returns up to ten a.m., yesterday	1,788 ...	749
Pen-y-darran:		
Total from commencement (June 5), up to ten a.m., yesterday	272 ...	170
Dowlais:		
Total from commencement (June 10), up to ten a.m., yesterday	1,200 ...	501
Total	3,260 ...	1,420

"FRANK JAMES, Clerk to the Guardians."

According to this statement, there was 1 person attacked in every 12¼—equal to 8 and a fraction per cent. of the population; and 1 person in every 28 1-5 died—equal to 3½ per cent. of the entire population. Some idea of the destitution and suffering occasioned by the pestilence may be formed from the fact (mentioned in my first letter, but which I think it proper to repeat here), that at the period of my visit there were dependent upon the parish 182 widows having 411 children, and 51 orphans, who had lost both father and mother—making a total of 644 persons, whose means of subsistence were utterly cut off, and who became chargeable to the parish entirely through the ravages of cholera. Nor does this by any means show the extent of the losses sustained by widows and children, many of whom now support themselves, or are assisted by relatives.

It is, I know, the opinion of many—and some medical writers of eminence (including one of the victims to the disease, the late Mr. Aston Key) have concurred in it—that greatly too much importance was attached to sanitary precautions during the prevalence of cholera throughout the country last summer. The instance of the town of Merthyr affords some significant facts bearing upon this question. In the divisions of Dowlais and Pen-y-darran, which lie higher, more open, and better disposed to the sun than Merthyr-Proper, but are infinitely more neglected and more filthy, the disease raged with far more deadly virulence than in the lower part of the town. This is best illustrated by actual returns. The town is divided, for the purposes of registration, into two divisions—the upper, including within it Dowlais, Pen-y-darran, and Fynnon Tydfil—the lower consisting of what is properly the town of Merthyr. The population of each district is about the same. In the quarter extending from the 1st of July to the 30th of September last, the births were, in the upper district 226, in the lower 215, which is nearly equal; whilst the deaths, from all causes (but mostly from cholera), which ought to have been as evenly balanced, were, during that interval, in the upper district 1,022, in the lower 495. Such are the results as furnished by the registrars' books. But there is a further testimony in favour of the value of sanitary measures, which, though I cannot claim for it official authority like the above, I give, on the faith of a gentleman of unimpeachable veracity— Mr. Joseph, of Plymouth Works. At a distance of a mile and a half below Merthyr, and near the New Forge at Dyffryn, Mr. Hill has built 300 cottages, which, with the exception of Mr. Crawshay's new houses at Cyfarthfa-row, are the loftiest, roomiest, and best arranged of the workmen's dwellings that I examined in this neighbourhood. They have pumps which supply water, ovens for baking, and covered privies. At the approach of the cholera, ventilators were put in the ceilings, and proper arrangements made for the daily removal of house refuse. Not less than 1,100 of the workmen were living in these houses, of whom only 25 died of cholera; whilst of 1,700 workmen, who resided in the ill-ventilated and waterless town of Merthyr, 150 died of that disease. Can anything be more conclusive in favour of pure air, abundance of water, and wholesome streets, than the contrasted statement I have here given?

Desirous of learning what attention the great iron-masters paid to the comforts and interests of the working classes, when the cholera actually prevailed (I have already stated their preparations for it), I inquired of a gentleman, wholly independent and of some standing in the town, with respect to their conduct. His answer in writing is now before me. I give the following in his words:—

> "Mr. Crawshay organised and kept a staff of house visitors, gave away soup to workmen and the poor, carted away filth, and gave much lime away.
>
> "Mr. Hill was active, and through his principal agent, Mr. Wolridge, did much service. His men were visited daily, and provided with little necessary comforts. He *limed* the bottom of the town, where his men chiefly live, free of expense to the parish.
>
> "The Dowlais Company did all that could be done, but the previous condition of Merthyr was too bad to admit of great benefit. They charged the parish for lime and cleansing to the extent of nearly 200*l*., although one-third of the houses in Dowlais are their own.
>
> "Thompson and Co., Pen-y-darran, evinced much apathy. Though the disease was awfully fatal at Mount Pleasant, Pen-y-darran, there was here no organization of visitors or scavengers. They did sprinkle a small quantity of lime, but, in fact, beyond this they did nothing. The men died like rotten sheep. It is true they made advances to the men who were debilitated *after cholera*, by way of loan, which of course is paid back. They charged the parish for all lime had by the authorities."

In the meantime the medical officers were worked past reasonable endurance; for many days and nights they were never in bed. Two of the principals, at least, suffered sharp attacks of the disease, one of whom it was thought would not recover. Too much praise cannot be accorded to these gentlemen for their invaluable services at that trying season. Their humane conduct was not lost upon the poor. In several places I heard it spoken of with admiration and thankfulness. Some curious exceptions, however, here occur to me; these, however, did not show themselves *during*, but *after*, the disease. Mr. Edward Davies told me, that in some cases where he found patients labouring under cholera, in rooms insufficiently ventilated, he knocked a hole in the roof for the admission of air and the benefit of the sufferers. In no one instance, during the prevalence of the disease, was complaint of this made by the landlord; but since then he has been called upon (in some cases saucily) to repair the roofs he had thus broken, and has actually been threatened with actions of trespass on his refusal to accede to such demand!

The conduct of the rector of the parish, Mr. Campbell, throughout this fearful visitation, calls for notice in this place. In him were seen the beauty of faith, the constancy, courage, and humanity which distinguish the Christian character. His services were as arduous, and his duties even more responsible than those of the medical officers, nor was the risk he incurred less than theirs. Though he had, in Mr. Rowland and Mr. Evans, efficient curates, to whom he might have confided his flock—himself, like some clergymen under similar circumstances, seeking safety in a distant place—he never deserted his charge, but remained stedfastly in it to the last. He encountered his duties cheerfully and performed them zealously. There was no house too wretched, no den of crime and misery (there are many such here) too repulsive for his care. Wherever there was a cry for spiritual comfort which reached his ear, there, braving the disease, he was to be found by the bedside of the dying, ministering consolation and encouraging hope. Often, whilst engaged in prayer, the hollow voice of the sufferer suddenly ceased to follow him; and the spirit, with his benediction, took its flight. On all sides, and from all classes and sects, I heard this clergyman's conduct spoken of with unqualified commendation.

The antipathy which the Welsh entertain against the Irish was notably increased at this time, from a belief that the latter, whose habits are as filthy as those of the Welsh are cleanly, imported the disease to Merthyr. A Welsh maid-servant, in the house of Mr. David James, the chairman of the board of guardians, who was most indefatigable and fearless in attending the sick Welsh, carrying them every comfort which Mrs. James thought needful, could not be prevailed upon to enter the house of an Irishman. The conduct of the people of these two nations, as remarked to me by the clergyman, was equally at variance and remarkable. The Welsh showed strong sympathy for their fellows, and the difficulty was to keep them out of the sick-room; whereas the Irish fled, leaving their relatives to the care of the men-nurses and others engaged by the authorities to give assistance. There were instances where the inmates of an Irish house, on a death occurring, fled, carrying with them the key of the front door; and it was necessary, in order to save breaking in the door, to get out the corpse for interment through the front window.

Ireland is now prostrate, and it seems hard to strike her. But Truth has neither predilections nor antipathies, and recognises no distinction of nations. My duty is to describe the labouring classes and the poor; and the Irish must not be overlooked. What, then, can I say of them? They are laborious, patient, and light-hearted. On the other hand, I have found them here filthy, sensual, crafty, quarrelsome, and brutish in their habits. Their houses are unfurnished, foul, and stinking; their children uncared for—barefoot, ragged, unwashed, and uneducated. And this not from necessity, but from natural habits. They are compelled to segregate in their dwellings, for the Welsh will not reside amongst them. They inhabit the lowest and worst quarters of the town. There is in Pen-y-darran, on the high road, an "Irish colony," in which the passer-by may see, through the open doors and in the street, the striking difference that exists between the same class of labourers in the Irish and the Welsh; the houses and children of the former being such as I have just described, whereas the dwellings of the adjoining Welsh are neatly and comfortably furnished, and the children clean and warmly clothed. In this quarter of the town I have seen Irish children of six or seven years of age rush to the doors of the houses when the omnibus was passing, stark naked; though the frost was severe, they seemed happy in their nudity, and equally to disregard decency and the sharpness of the cold. But a few extracts from my note-book, of particulars jotted down upon the spot, will convey the justest impression of the Irish labourers as they exist in Merthyr.

The day after my arrival here I went round with Mr. Edward Davies on his visits to the patients under his care as surgeon to the Dowlais Iron Works. In the houses inhabited by the Welsh, whatever were the wages of the owner, we found a sufficiency—often a superfluity—of furniture; and cleanliness and comfort were everywhere visible. In the first house we entered, inhabited by an Irishman, there sat hovering over the fire a man swollen with dropsy; the house had no other furniture than a three-legged table, a small bench, two stools, and a few utensils for cooking, such as saucepans, basins, plates, and crockery. Up-stairs were three beds of hay, without a single article of furniture. The second house we visited was one in Pont-y-Store-house—the worst quarter of the town. A measured plan of this dwelling now lies before me. Originally it was a one-roomed house; but the boards overhead had been cut away to convert the slope of the roof into a second room. On entering, we found three bare-legged women, a man, and some children, squatted round the fire. On a string stretched before the fire-place there hung, drying, a quantity of black woollen stockings, almost footless, for want of repair. The dimensions of this room were 12 feet by 8, and the only furniture it contained was one rickety three-legged table, a low bench, and a log of wood. A cracked tea-pot, a blacking jar, and a broken lamp were on the chimney-piece, and two tin pots on the fire. One of the women ran out, and soon returned with a candle, which she lit, and carried before us up a ladder, into the loft above. It was not without difficulty we squeezed ourselves through the narrow opening cut through the boards, but having done so we were fairly in the bedroom, the unoccupied space of which we pretty well filled. The room was formed simply of the slope of the roof; there was no window, but a tile had been displaced to admit a little light and air. The cobwebs hung in black films from the roof. On the right and left hand of the entrance were two beds: each might be touched when standing on the ladder. Stooping down with the candle over the bed on the right, the woman pointed to the man ——, who was in a raging fever. When the doctor had examined him, the woman threw up the clothes at the foot of the bed, and showed us a poor child, emaciated with dysentery from fever, and shivering on its sudden exposure to the air. Mr. Davies gave attention to the child, and in the meantime I put some questions to the man and woman. The man told me he worked at the Dowlais Iron Works, and earned 11s. a week, and that he had been ill four days. The woman informed me that two families slept in that room, ——, his wife, and two children in one bed; her mother, her sister (grown up), her brother (aged 12), and herself in the other. In the room below there lodged two single women and one illegitimate child, aged seven years. On what these slept I did not hear; certainly they had no proper bed. I was importuned to give them money. Statements were made that they were all destitute, and that the sick man had not "had bit nor sup for two days." Mr. Davies told them that the poor man wanted nothing but toast and water, and directed them to call for medicine at his surgery. The stench of this house was unendurable, and we were glad to get away from it. On our road home we were overtaken by a man who asked if he must bring a bottle? Notwithstanding he was answered in the negative he still followed us; he had something more to ask, but hesitated at putting the question. At length he inquired, "*Is it taking the disease is, your honour;* the woman wants to know?" He was told the man and child were ill of fever, and he then left us. The next day another of the children was smitten with fever. Going round with the clergyman, Mr. Campbell, about a fortnight afterwards, I called to inquire how —— was. He was still in bed, but recovering; the child whom I had seen was also recovering, but the other had died, and its funeral took place the day before my second call.

The next case which I noted was that of a house in Pen-y-Darran, the owner of which, —— ——, was also employed under the Dowlais Company. He was from home when Mr. John James and myself called; but his wife informed us that he earned 10s. a week as "a patcher" or quarrier of iron-stone. The house consisted of two rooms, and was inhabited by two families and a lodger. The rent was 11s. a month. In the upper room were three straw beds on the floor. The men and their wives severally occupied two of them, and the children the third. There was not a table in this house; the only furniture of the principal room was a cradle made of a bottle-hamper, and three small benches. A tea-pot, a tin kettle, a can, two jugs, one candlestick, a basin, three pickle-jars of green glass, and an ornament over the fire-place, in the shape of an illuminated card, announcing that "Mark-wich's patent Epithems" were to be had there, formed—with the exception of a brown pan, in which a kneeling woman was kneading dough upon the floor—the *entire* contents in the shape of furniture and utensils which this house contained. There were four ragged children, who, with the women, were barefoot and dirty. Both mothers had infants, still suckling. A boy aged six, of a fine ingenuous countenance, was playing with the fire, which had no fender to protect the children. He told me he had never been in school. The women were light-hearted; they spoke of the difficulty they had to live, but laughingly, as if life were nothing more than a joke. One admitted she had buried three children, the other had lost two. In a closet in this room there was an old woman, bedridden, and supported by the parish. She lay on a mass of woollen rags, spread on the floor, and she completely filled the closet. If it were not for the open door, she must have died of suffocation. Her allowance was 2s. a week, out of which she paid 6d. for lodging; upon the remaining 1s. 6d. she subsisted and paid for attendance. The women said they "looked to her" more for charity than what they had from her; and I believe the case was so, for the old woman spoke favourably of this attention to her. I have notes of other cases, which would, however, only repeat, in other forms, much the same kind of evidence as that above given. Enough has been given to support the general statement I have advanced respecting the Irish, as seen in the iron works.

But before quitting the subject I must caution the reader against supposing that because the Irish are naked or in rags, with their houses unfurnished, their children uneducated, and themselves professing poverty, they are necessarily poor, improvident, or intemperate. Many instances of drunkenness and improvidence no doubt are to be found amongst them; but these vices are not so general as to produce the universally low state of domestic life in which I found them. They are content to live in this abject and loathsome condition from two causes, of which the first and most powerful is habit—they have been unaccustomed to a better state, and are content to live as they have always lived before; the second is, that they do not look upon themselves as permanent denizens of the country, but hope to save enough to return in comfort to "Ould Ireland," and settle where their inclination leads them. Often they save and sew up money in their clothes. They resort to various and numerous devices to obtain assistance from the parish for their wives and families, whilst they are themselves in full work—in which sometimes they succeed, but more frequently are foiled. Mr. Edward Davies gave me two instances of this kind; and Mr. Roger Williams, the relieving-officer, can probably furnish abundance of others. Only a few days before I visited Merthyr an Irishman was killed by falling into a coal-pit; he was always thought a poor man, but on stripping the body about sixty sovereigns were found sewn up in his waistcoat.

To show that the Irish are equally unpleasant neighbours in other manufacturing districts, I extract the following from Mr. Tremenheere's Report on the Ironworks of Lanarkshire (1848). Speaking of strikes, and their effect in importing to the works large numbers of Irish labourers, he says:—

"The large proportion of Irish introduced of late years among the mining population, chiefly in consequence of the strikes of the Scotch colliers and miners, obstructs greatly the progress of the work of raising the habits and condition of the people."...

On the page following are these further remarks:—

"But the most serious result is, the great number of Irish that these strikes have been the means of introducing into the whole district. Of the miners, it is now estimated that upwards of two-thirds are Irish, and of the colliers about one-fourth. Every successive strike adds to their number. They remain in the country as competitors with the Scotch population for the lower kinds of employment, and their presence is greatly felt in this respect the moment that trade becomes dull. Mixed up as they are with the Scotch in the mining villages, their habits have an injurious effect upon their neighbours, and make it more difficult for well-disposed and decent families to preserve order and cleanliness about them. Their presence in so great numbers has been a cause of serious anxiety to the authorities, who, in March last, were obliged to quarter three troops of yeomanry and a detachment of military among them to prevent the public peace being disturbed."

But numerous as are the Irish in the mining and manufacturing districts of South Wales, the *morale* of the Welsh, their cleanly habits, and their love of comforts, render them proof against the contagion of bad example, even were the antipathy which the Welsh bear towards the Irish, of no account in this particular.

Before I close the subject of the labouring classes and address myself to the questions of religion, education, crime, and pauperism, which yet remain to be noticed, I will advert to a conversation I had with Mr. White, the able and experienced surgeon at Dowlais, upon the subject of the health of the women and children in the iron works. I have already shown by statistics that the rate of infant mortality in Dowlais is alarmingly high. The following is Mr. White's opinion of the cause:—"The mortality," said he, "under the age of six is absolutely frightful. Much of this is, in my opinion, attributable to bad nursing. The women bred in the iron works make, as a general rule, bad mothers; they have a poor idea of the duties of a mother. The health of the married women throughout this district is decidedly bad. They suffer from dyspeptic complaints more than from any other. About two years after marriage they fall away and look quite old. They suffer much, beyond question, from the diseases which result from constipation, owing to a want of proper domestic conveniences. (This has also been stated in one of the Government Reports.) This in its turn affects the children. If the mothers have not healthy milk the children must be unhealthy. The total want of drainage and scavenging greatly affects all classes. The ventilation is less perfect than it might be without additional expense, owing to a sad habit which the people here have of keeping their windows shut. The cholera was aggravated by this circumstance, and I believe many more deaths occurred than would have happened if that custom had not prevailed." At the same conversation Mr. Edward Davies remarked that the children of firemen were, taken altogether, less robust than those of other workmen—in fact, they are often emaciated and unhealthy.

I now come to the important subject of religion in this densely-populated and interesting district; and, first, of the Established Church. There were, until within the past three years, only two churches, one in Merthyr and another at Dowlais, for the accommodation of 40,000 inhabitants. Here I feel bound, for the sake of the English church, and in order to show the reason, in part, why the Established religion has not kept pace with Dissent in Merthyr, to make some allusion to the dead. The rule *de mortuis nil nisi bonum* should apply only to private life. A man's public character, be he living or dead, is open to remark. Society may profit as well by bad as by good example; therefore I shall not scruple to state the facts which have retarded the progress of the Church in Merthyr. The late incumbent, Mr. Maber, for the last thirty-two years of his life was non-resident in his parish. During that time he derived an income from it of about £1,000 a year; but he never paid a visit to the parish—once only excepted, when he came in a post-chaise (almost as great a curiosity at that time to the townspeople as the sight of their rector), *to vote for a church-rate*. The consequence was, that the charge of the parish being confined to curates who were continually changing and had no permanent interest in the place, the congregation fell away almost to the clerk and sexton, and dissent gained what the Church lost. In the meantime the parsonage was allowed to become dilapidated; one half of it had fallen to the ground; the other half, though unsafe, was, on Mr. Campbell's appointment to the living, inhabited by a policeman. Having been so grossly neglected, and the population having largely increased, especially in the up-lying district of Dowlais, the parish, on the death of the late incumbent, was divided into two—Merthyr Proper and Dowlais—the latter being endowed with one-fifth of the tithe and glebe. When the present incumbent of Merthyr, Mr. Campbell, took possession of the living in 1844, the whole accommodation in the Church was for 860 persons. A subscription had been opened some years before for the erection of an additional church, and considerable sums promised, but difficulties had arisen respecting the plan and other details, and it was not until the 24th March, 1846, that the foundation stone was laid. This church, which is an exceedingly handsome Norman structure, built of blue-stone faced with free-stone, was consecrated in September, 1847; it contains

1,200 sittings, of which one-half are free and unappropriated for ever. Before the opening of the new church there were four services every Sunday in the parish church; two in the English and two in the Welsh language; the English services being at 11 a.m. and 2 p.m.; those in Welsh at 9 a.m. and at 3 p.m. This distribution of hours was obviously unfair to the Welsh portion of the population, which consists almost entirely of the labouring classes; "The consequence was," says Mr. Campbell, in a communication he addressed to me, "that at my first coming here the Welsh congregation varied from 70 to 100 in the afternoon, and was even less in the morning. My wish then was to devote the parish church entirely to the Welsh, and the new church to the English congregation; but this was disagreeable to some of the latter, who occupied in the old church large pews, secured to them by faculty—so I consented to meet their wishes so far as to have an English service in the parish church at three o'clock in the afternoon. This service, indeed, was badly attended, but not worse than I had anticipated. On the other hand, the new distribution of services has been attended with the happiest results. Instead of an average congregation of about eighty, there are now nearly 400 *communicants*, while the evening congregation is only limited by the size of the building. I must, however, add that the zealous labours of two successive curates, Mr. Griffiths and Mr. Rowland, have contributed largely to this result."

About three years ago a district was formed out of this parish, and endowed by the Ecclesiastical Commissioners, under Sir Robert Peel's Act. It is called "the Cyfarthfa District." The number of souls it contained in 1841 was about 6,000, but it has since shared in the general increase of the population of this town. To meet the spiritual wants of this district, a large "school-room," capable of containing some 250 persons, was licensed by the late Bishop of Llandaff, and service is there performed twice on Sunday and once in the course of the week, in Welsh. The populous district of Pen-y-Darran, lying between Merthyr and Dowlais, whose inhabitants cannot amount to less than 4,000, is without either church or school, except some in-significant private schools. There is also a rapidly-increasing popula-tion springing up near Dyffryn, about two miles down the valley (as I have already remarked), which, numbering at present about 1,200, is unprovided with efficient means for the ministration of the Church. There was, indeed, service performed, by the permission of the pro-prietor of the works, Mr. Hill, in a small cottage-room, but this is obviously insufficient for the spiritual wants of so thickly-peopled a locality. Such is the provision made for the accommodation of a vast and rapidly-increasing population, by the Church of England, in this important district. It well deserves the consideration of all who believe that the moral improvement of the people depends upon the extent of spiritual accommodation provided by the Established Church. I need hardly point out how utterly inadequate are the means at the disposal of the Church to meet the wants of this district. Even now the new church remains unprotected by railing—the committee being incumbered with debts for gas-fittings, and therefore wholly unable to fence in the churchyard. The present net value of the living of Merthyr is about £500 a year, out of which £54 is paid to the treasurer of Queen Anne's Bounty, in repayment of money borrowed for rebuilding the parsonage-house.

The up-lying district of Dowlais next claims attention. With a population of 16,000 souls there is only one church, which affords accommodation for only 480 persons. There are here four services every Sunday; three in English, and one in Welsh. One service is devoted exclusively for the benefit of the soldiers, whose barracks are in Dowlais; this was necessary because there was no room for them at the other services. The Rev. J. Jenkins is the present incumbent, and he has one curate to assist him. There is one Welsh service by the bishop's license on Sunday evening, at the girls' school-room, which is, however, not large enough to contain the congregation. The clergyman contemplates arrangements by which there will be service at 11 a.m., at 2 (for the soldiers), at 3 (in Welsh), at 5 (in English), and at 7 (in Welsh). This distribution of service has been rendered necessary by the insufficiency of the school-room to accommodate the Welsh congregation. The Dowlais Iron Company have promised another church. In the course of the week there is an English service on Tuesday evening; and one in Welsh every Wednesday throughout the year. There is, further, on Wednesday, a Welsh service at one of the schools. It will be seen by the above that there are eight services every week, and these performed by two clergymen. Besides this, there is not a single evening of the week in which there are not cottage lectures, meetings for prayer, and readings of the Scriptures. I give the following in the words of the Rev. J. Jenkins, the incumbent:— "There is not a single locality in South Wales, where church accommodation is more wanted than in this neighbourhood. The feeling of the great mass of the population towards the Church has been, of late, rapidly improving. In proof of this there is the fact of a great increase of communicants. In my church, which accommodates 480 persons, the communicants, English and Welsh, average 350. There was an increase of 200 at the visitation of the cholera, and I am happy to say they all remain steadfast to their faith."

After digressing to educational matters, we returned to the Church, and discussed the subject of dissent; when he said—"The Church in these mountains, so long as the people have two separate languages, will never prosper unless there are distinct places of worship for each nation. The Welsh are fond of their own language. There is but one spot, Merthyr Old Church, where the Welsh can be said to have a church of their own; but see the result—it is crowded to an overflow."

The promise of the Dowlais Iron Company to build a church where one is so urgently needed, will, I hope, not be forgotten. The obligations of the company to their workmen are so heavy, that they can hardly be too liberal in making provision for the spiritual necessities of the town of Dowlais, a full third of which belongs to them.

The labouring classes and the poor amongst the Welsh are decidedly religious; if not actually communicants, they nearly all attend with great regularity some place of worship. They are mostly Dissenters; the cause of this has partly been explained above; at present I forbear going further into the question, which will more properly arise and be treated when I come to describe the people, their habits and customs, in the counties of the Principality; it is enough here to state the fact that Dissent greatly preponderates. But Merthyr, even whilst a mere village, and before the establishment of the iron-works, was always the abode of Dissent. Here it was that the first dissenting congregation in Wales was formed and established. It was founded by Vavasor Powell, a man of unquenchable zeal, sincere convictions, and great natural eloquence, in the year 1620. This man, famous in the annals of Nonconformity, was not, as his name might lead one to suppose, of purely Welsh extraction—his mother being of the Vavasors of Yorkshire, who settled in Wales. About 64 years ago there was, however, only one chapel in this place, which belonged to the Welsh Independents; but the Welsh Baptists preached occasionally about that time at Gwenllwyn, a farm-house in Dowlais. In 1815 there were 11 chapels in Merthyr and Dowlais. At present there are 35. Some of these structures are of very large dimensions, and are capable of accommodating 1,500 persons. Though they have no pretensions to architectural beauty, their immense roofs form a prominent feature in the view of Merthyr, as seen from the surrounding hills.

I wished to obtain an accurate account of the religious accommodation afforded by the churches and chapels, as well as the educational provision made by them, for the 40,000 inhabitants of this town. I obtained these particulars from the Church, and I called on the leading ministers of the three principal sects here, and asked their co-operation, which was promised me, but from one minister only—Mr. Fletcher, of the English Wesleyans—did I obtain what I required. I have seen a statement which showed that in 1845 there were 6,000 Dissenters in Merthyr and Dowlais, and that the places of worship would contain 18,000 persons. Obviously, from the number of chapels and the church accommodation here, both particulars are understated. I give the names of some of the chapels as I find them in a list before me; they are characteristic:—Bethel, Zion, Tabernacle, Ebenezer (two), Zoar, Adulham, Bethesda, Siloh (two), Elim, Pennsylvania, Carsalem, Hebron, Bethania, Hermon, Carmel, Tabor; the others bear the name of their locality. The English Wesleyans have two chapels, and the Welsh Wesleyans two; the congregations of the English Wesleyan Society in Merthyr and Dowlais are returned to me at 510—the number of communicants, 270. Beyond this I can give no exact particulars of the numbers of the congregations in these chapels. The English Baptists have one chapel, whilst the Welsh Baptists have not less than eight. The English Independents have one chapel only; the Welsh Independents have ten. The Welsh Calvinistic Methodists have five chapels. The Primitive Methodists have two chapels. The Unitarians have two chapels. Besides these there is a Catholic chapel, supported mainly by the Irish; and the Jews have also a place of meeting. Strange as it may appear, after the exposure of the frauds of Joe Smith, there are in and around Merthyr many Mormonites; they call themselves "Latter-day Saints." There has been some emigration of this sect to Nauvoo, their Holy City in America. Regarding the number of chapels as a criterion for judging of the relative extent of each sect in Merthyr and Dowlais, they will take numerical precedence as follows:—

1. English and Welsh Independents.
2. English and Welsh Baptists.
3. Welsh Calvinistic Methodists.

4. English and Welsh Wesleyans.

5. Primitive Methodists.

6. Unitarians. (The number of Primitive Methodist chapels and of Unitarian chapels is the same, but the congregations of Primitive Methodists being the largest, I have given them precedence).

7. Roman Catholics.

8. Mormonites, or Latter-day Saints.

9. Jews.

I could not learn that the "Plymouth Brethren" have any followers here, a circumstance that, considering the proselytizing zeal of that body, somewhat surprised me. There are no Quakers here.

It is impossible to advert to these particulars of the number and variety of dissenting chapels in Merthyr and Dowlais without being struck with the preponderance of Welsh over English services. Taking the instance of the four most popular sects, as stated above, it will be found that in twenty-five out of twenty-nine of their meeting-houses the Welsh language alone is used. This is the best and most conclusive argument that can be urged in favour of the adoption of Welsh services in the Church of England. The general intelligence of the people and their knowledge of the English language are not ripe enough to enable them to appreciate the English service. The practical sagacity of the elders and authorities in the dissenting congregations perceived this; they recognized the predilection of the people for their own vernacular tongue; and saw that, to be efficacious, their system must be accommodated to that circumstance. Many of the preachers are wholly uneducated men—that is to say, their learning extends no further than to simple reading and writing. Some of them—indeed I may say many of them—were, at the outset of life, daily labourers, like the classes whom they now lead. I was told that there are more miners in the dissenting ministry than any other class of workmen. But zeal, earnestness, and energy of character supply the place of educational acquirements with the rude, untutored masses who are here to be worked upon. The preacher who has himself been a labourer knows best the labourer's nature, and adopts the most likely means of affecting and ruling it. There is a world of native eloquence in their sermons; they are, in consonance with the genius of the Welsh language, abundantly figurative; and the preacher himself, unaccustomed to close reasoning, which would indeed be ill adapted for his audience, appeals more to the feelings than the understanding. He affects the heart, which he can touch—and not the head, which is above him, and beyond his reach. The sight of one of these huge meeting-houses during service is memorable. Next to the violent and rude gesticulation of the preacher, as in a sonorous and guttural language he denounces, expostulates, persuades, and comforts, one is struck first with the vast throng of cleanly and well-dressed people that literally fills the chapel, and in the next place with the circumstance that they express sympathy with the sentiments of the discourse or prayer by ejaculations, and sometimes groans. The effect upon a stranger, accustomed to the well-trained congregations of England, where there are no such audible expressions of emotion, is peculiar.

The singing in these chapels is generally very good; in some of them great pains are taken to keep up an educated staff of singers. As I was walking one evening, I saw two girls of about twelve years of age, their arms twined round each other's necks, and singing as they advanced, a Welsh duet to the old-fashioned tune of "In my cottage near a wood." Their voices were clear and equal; the second preserved an interval of a sixth below the first voice, and whenever the laws of harmony (of which, no doubt, they were blissfully ignorant) required a change, it was made with unerring accuracy. I stepped up and asked them where they learnt singing? Unfolding their arms, and ceasing their song, they answered, preserving the Welsh allocation of words, "It was in Chapel Bethesda."

At the time when the cholera raged here, one effect it had was to increase three-fold the number of communicants in the churches and chapels. This had the effect of settling, to one or other of the denominations of Dissenters, many who previously had wandered from sect to sect without any definite or fixed notions on religion. The increase of church communicants in Merthyr during the cholera was 230—that in Dowlais 200—as stated to me by the clergymen.

LABOUR AND THE POOR.

———◆———

THE MINING AND MANUFACTURING DISTRICTS OF SOUTH WALES.

[FROM OUR SPECIAL CORRESPONDENT.]

MERTHYR AND DOWLAIS.

PUBLIC CHARITIES—EDUCATION—PAUPERISM.

Letter VIII.

With the exception of a small bequest made in 1735 to the Welsh Independents of Ynysgau Chapel "for religious and benevolent purposes," there are no endowed charities in Merthyr. There are no almshouses for the support and shelter of the poor, nor is there an hospital. This is the more remarkable considering the wants of such a population, and the fact that many and large fortunes have been here accumulated.

The vitally important subject of Education next claims our attention.

According to the returns of school attendance, given by Mr. Lingen, one of the Commissioners of Inquiry into the state of Education in Wales, there were, in 1847, in the parish of Merthyr (including, of course, Dowlais and Vaynor)—

Attending day-schools (both sexes)	2,301	
Attending Church Sunday-schools ...	961	
Attending Dissenting Sunday-schools	5,941	
		6,902
Total		9,203
The number of schools he returns as being—		
Day-schools	41	
Sunday-schools	36	
Total	77	

I have no doubt that the attendance is here over-stated. According to some particulars of the school accommodation afforded by the several chapels (as supplied in a small laudatory pamphlet called "A Guide to Merthyr Tydfil"), the numbers educated in their Sunday and day schools amount to no more than 5,126. And it must be borne in mind that nearly the whole of this is *Sunday-school education*, no provision being made for education on week-days. The number of private schools is insignificant, and the scholars there accommodated are few. As regards education, everything here depends upon the exertions of the Church and the Dissenters, and the co-operation of the iron-masters—there being, as I have elsewhere said, no middle-class for the support of good day-schools. Mr. Lingen states the proportion of those educated in day-schools as 6.7 per cent. on the entire population. I subjoin the following remarks from his report:—

"The stoppages upon the people's wages (for the schools) vary considerably in amount, as ½d., 1d., or 2d. per week; 2d., 4d., or 6d. per month; ½d., 1d., or 4d. in 1*l*. (in the latter instance the sick fund is maintained from the same source). For these payments, books, but not stationery, are generally found. The stoppage is compulsory, and is made irrespectively of the number of children sent to school, or of a man's having any to send. In one instance only did I find a difference made between married and unmarried men. The contributors are not furnished with any means of auditing the school account, neither have they any control over the expenditure of the funds. There is a kind of tacit understanding that, in consideration of the stoppage, the proprietors will keep open the school as long as they keep on the works.

"The gigantic character of these works is a feature not to be passed over. It has rendered the ancient divisions of the country a dead letter. The basis of the old parochial terrier was the manor; the basis of the new one is the works. I regard, therefore, a workmen's school in no other light than as a parochial school, and I regard works to which no school is attached in the same light as a parish containing no school. Nor can it be justly deemed an exaggeration to speak of these works as parishes: *e.g.*, four proprietors employ all the labouring population of Merthyr and Dowlais, representing some 40,000 souls. So that, just as when parishes were first instituted, it was every man's interest to think what parish he belonged to, because his rights of relief, employment, and redress were all parochial or manorial, so now does the same interest make him think of these or those works, and not at all, or very remotely, of the parish. In the works is his sick fund, sometimes his benefit society; in the works is his hope of employment; in the works (by a tolerated system of fining) is his ordinary court of justice.

"I dwell upon these circumstances, because, as long as there is such contradiction between the parochial and the veritable distribution of the population, it is impossible to deal with its educational necessities through any adaptation of the existing parochial machinery. But not only the physical distribution—still more the moral and social relations of this mining and manufacturing community—require new and special provision. It contains no middle class, such as those who commonly constitute a vestry. For although the absence of the truck system from my district is allowing the growth of shopkeepers, yet these are only an offshoot. The works themselves contain no middle class. There are the proprietors and their agents of administration on the one hand, the mass of operatives on the other. The elimination of a middle class is rendered still more complete when, to the economical causes tending to produce it, is superadded the separation of language."

With this I close my reference to Mr. Lingen's report. I now give the results of my own inquiries.

As I wished to know what increased accommodation had of late years been provided, through the instrumentality of the Church, for this rapidly growing population, I inquired of the rector of Merthyr what was the state of things in this particular when he came here, and what had since been done. I give his reply:—"When I came here there were only two 'National Schools'—one for boys, and the other (that now licensed in the Cyfarthfa district) for girls. Between them, these were capable of containing about 350 children; but they were neither of them well filled, and one (the boys' school) was in a bad state of repair. I am happy to say that, in more efficient hands, there has been a considerable improvement both in the attendance and in the progress of the children. As soon as the new church was completed, I began to solicit subscriptions for new schools, and for this purpose I obtained the necessary permission to convey to the National Society a piece of ground adjoining the new church, which also was built on glebe land. These schools contain accommodation for 300 children—150 boys and 150 girls—and they have been well attended. Their cost was about £800, of which £300 was supplied by the Committee of the Privy Council for Education, and £100 by the National Society; the remainder being made up by private subscriptions. Before they were used as day-schools, they were opened as *night-schools for adults*. The plan we adopted was one struck out by Lady Charlotte Guest, and already tried with success at Dowlais. The services of competent persons to superintend were retained at moderate salaries; but *the greatest amount of work was done by voluntary teachers*, who gave their services for one or more nights in the week. The female school was held in

the new school-room, and that for men at the old school-room. The
number of volunteer teachers amounted to about 120, and for a time
the rooms were crowded to excess; for instance, there were counted
at one time 396 women in a school built for 300 children, and the
men's school was not less crowded. This, however, did not last. In the
long days of summer the attendance gradually decreased. The adult
schools were, therefore, discontinued on the 1st of May, and it was
intended to recommence them in September, but the cholera intervening, everything was disarranged, and the meeting of these schools
was postponed to the second week of October. The attendance has
since not been so full as formerly, yet much good is done by them."

There was no infant-school here attached to the church, if indeed
there was any other—at least I heard of none. But a club-room had
been taken for the purpose of an infant-school in connexion with the
Church, which, I was told, would shortly be opened, and would accommodate about 170 infants. There is no school whatever connected
with the church in the populous district of Pen-y-darran. About a year
ago Mr. Alderman Thompson announced to Mr. Campbell his intention of establishing an infant school for the benefit of the children of
persons employed in Pen-y-darran works, but this purpose has not
yet been carried into effect.

It is to be hoped that sympathy for the infant population of
Merthyr will induce the public to assist in making provision for a
school-house where they will be better accommodated than in the
private room now hired for the purpose. The rate of infant mortality
is higher here, I believe, than anywhere else in the kingdom. I have
already given the local statistics on this point. It is above all things
necessary that infants should have every provision for ventilation,
warmth, and comfort made for them in the school-room. This cannot
well be done in a private apartment not built for such a purpose.

I visited the new schools and examined the children. The following is the substance of the notes I made. The exterior of the building
is neat, and of the "ancient almshouse" style, with slate roof and high
gables. It struck me, however, as being low—an objection, the importance of which Mr. Wyatt, who is the architect, will, I hope, consider
when he next designs an edifice of this kind. I first went to the boys'
school. On examining the books I found that the average attendance
was about 120 daily. The boys were mostly well-clothed and clean;
only one of them was barefoot. The master, who is from the training-
school at Westminster, observed that they were children who, "but

for the school, would have been running the streets." The course of instruction at present comprises reading, writing, and arithmetic, geography, and the outlines of history. When the highest-class boys are sufficiently advanced, they will be taught grammar. I tried the second class, consisting of boys from seven to nine years old, in the Gospel of St. Luke, and they acquitted themselves very creditably, reading without hesitation, and correctly. One boy in the head class was working a sum in practice, another in reduction, a third in subtraction, and so on. As a body, the master informed me, the children show great acuteness and capacity. "The only difficulty I have," said he, "is to get them to attend regularly; when they stay away for a few days of course they fall back. Mondays and Fridays are the worst days for attendance." He could give me no reason why on these days the attendance was small. On turning suddenly from the master, I asked the boy nearest me (who might be about nine years old), "What kindness did Mary Magdalen do for Christ?" He replied, without a moment's thought, "She washed his feet, and wiped them with the hair of her head."

From the boys', I went to the girls' school. The room has a timber roof, and is in all respects similar to the other. The schoolmistress is also from the training institution at Westminster. The books showed the average attendance to be about 150. The course of instruction is nearly the same as in the boys' school, with the addition of the feminine arts of sewing and knitting. The children were extremely well clad, neat in their appearance, and clean. Most of them were sewing when I entered. They may bring work of their own, but they are mostly occupied on work for a town charity for supplying the poor with clothes. They read for me the 21st chapter of Genesis, which was in the course for the day. I examined them by questions on that chapter, and they answered with remarkable quickness and general accuracy. Two of them were strikingly superior in intelligence, and these answered questions that were put to them on other than scriptural points. There were 491 children admitted in the course of the year. "The worst of it," said the rector, who accompanied me, "is that they come and go in so irregular a manner." This I think an evil that will in time abate. It must be more the fault of the parents than the children, for it is in their power to compel attendance. But in reality the people have not yet begun to feel the advantage of these schools, as they have been only opened a year. When they see the striking improvement in manners, language, and turn of thought which these schools eventually must bring about, they will then properly estimate the value of such institutions and will be anxious to profit by them as largely as they can. The children sung a hymn, the clergyman read prayers, and we separated. The holidays at both schools are a fortnight and three days, at Midsummer and Christmas.

I took an opportunity of visiting the *Adult Schools*. I could scarcely credit my senses when the governess told me that the girls I saw were those whom I have formerly described as stacking coal for coking, loading trams, and cleaning ore on the slopes of the mountain, black, coarsely clad, and repulsive. Here they were clean, orderly, and well dressed. The average attendance at present is 60. They meet five nights in the week. The full season lasts from October to June. The governess, a very intelligent woman, of many years' experience, speaking of the aptness of these grown-up women for learning, said:—"You would be surprised to see how rapidly they get on. Even married women have learnt to read the Testament and to write well, in one season." They were mostly writing when I entered, using steel pens and copybooks— a far preferable system to the slate and pencil, which I think are too much used in some of these schools. A lady of the town—one of the voluntary teachers—was here engaged in her beneficent duties. The school for men being at a distance, in George Town, Cyfarthfa, I had not an opportunity of visiting it. The average attendance, I was told, is about 90.

The efforts made by the Church, assisted by Sir John and Lady Guest, for the extension of sound and useful education in Dowlais, have been very great, and are as praiseworthy as they have been successful. I need not give the particulars with the same minuteness as I have with respect to education in what is properly called Merthyr. An outline of the arrangements will here suffice. There is here a boys' school, under three masters from the training institution at Battersea. This school, unlike the boys' school in Merthyr, is not connected with the National Society. In the upper school there are 40, in the second school 130 scholars. Those in the head class learn algebra, mechanics, and others of the useful sciences; the others learn reading, writing, arithmetic, geography, and history. The girls' school is nominally in connection with the National Society, but I believe receives no aid from it. It is under the superintendence of three schoolmistresses, selected with great care, and who perform their duty very satisfactorily. Before the visit of the cholera, the average attendance was 150; since then it has fallen off, and has been reduced to about 110. There are three infant-schools here. The first, under charge of a master and mistress, has at present an average attendance of 170; the second, under a mistress and an assistant, has an attendance of 120; the third, which is governed by a mistress, averages just now 40.

It was here that the plan of adult schools was first tried in South Wales. There are in Dowlais as in Merthyr two adult schools—one for each religious denomination. The average attendance of men was for some time 170; it has been now reduced to 110; this was accounted for to me by a statement that there had been a want of efficient teachers, but I was told that this would be obviated in future. It was cheering to learn that this falling off was not the fault of the workmen, but owing to a defect which attention can, and it is to be hoped will, remedy. The adult school for women has an average attendance of 100. There are two teachers—one paid and the other a volunteer—to each class. It was remarked to me of these adult schools by the incumbent, Mr. Jenkins, that he thought that they had done much good. "The shopkeepers," said he "have more than once in the course of conversation intimated that the effect of them has been greatly to improve the language and conduct of young men and women in the streets and everywhere."

So much for the day-schools of Dowlais, which are mainly supported by the fund accumulated by deductions from the wages of the workmen. There are three Sunday-schools in Dowlais for adults, having an attendance of 311; in these the Welsh language is used. Further, there are two English Sunday-schools, in which the average number of scholars is 120.

Everywhere I found a great falling off in the attendance since the visitation of the neighbourhood with cholera, as compared with the numbers previously to the coming of that destroyer. This reduction was generally one-fourth, and sometimes nearly a half, of the former average attendance. The Rev. Mr. Jenkins observed of it, "The cholera has unhinged and broken up everything."

The Dissenters' schools in Merthyr and Dowlais are mostly Sunday schools. The English and Welsh Wesleyans educate 550 scholars. The Welsh Baptists have 1,554 Sunday scholars; the English Baptists 180. The Welsh Independents have 2,067 (one school at "Bethania Chapel" has 600 Sunday scholars); the English Independents 100. The Welsh Calvinistic Methodists educate 810 scholars; one chapel alone, "Hermon Chapel," accommodates not less than 500, and has 105 teachers. The Primitive Methodists have 40 scholars, and the Roman Catholics 60.

The particulars I have here given on this most serious and interesting question show with tolerable accuracy the provision made for the education of the rising generation in Merthyr and Dowlais. For many years the workmen were almost entirely helpless with regard to the instruction of their children. The private schools were utterly incompetent and insufficient, and the wonder really is, how and where the labouring classes who were bred in this district obtained so much knowledge, not to say learning, as they possess. Great praise is due, of late years, to Sir John and Lady Guest, who, fortified by the assistance of the Legislature in giving a power to the employer to create an education fund out of the wages of the workmen, have rendered infinite service to the cause of social advancement in Dowlais. Neither must the exertions of the Rev. Mr. Campbell and Mr. Jenkins, and of the various ministers of the Dissenting chapels, be overlooked. I have been particular to give all their due. The benefit of this great movement, though it has been going forward only a very few years, is already visible, and it will from time to time enlarge.

I have next to speak of pauperism in and around Merthyr. Considering that the population is almost entirely dependent upon manual labour—that employment, fluctuating with the prosperity or depression of the iron-trade, is unsteady, and often insufficient—and that wages have been for a long time unusually low—it is rather a matter of surprise than otherwise that pauperism is not more prevalent than I found it in the mining districts of South Wales. This speaks well for the provident habits of the workman, and attests his aversion to receive parochial assistance, except in the last extremity—a fact I have heard mentioned with praise by more than one observant person in Merthyr. The "Sick fund" and "Doctor's fund" at the iron-works, with the "Benefit societies," which are here very numerous, have been of essential service in this particular—at once limiting the burden of the rates, and preserving the self-respect of the workman, who, but for these provisions, would, in cases of severe sickness or accident, be reduced to the humiliating necessity of obtaining relief from the parish.

The Poor-law Union of Merthyr comprises nine parishes—some purely agricultural, and others manufacturing. It was created in 1836. At that time Chartism had a stronghold here amongst the mountains, and it will be remembered that the New Poor-law was violently denounced by the leaders of that party as inhuman, monstrous, wicked, and detestable. This was not without its effect upon the classes who

were most likely to be personally affected by the change. In addition to the influence of Chartist orators, the prejudices of the Welsh
in favour of old-established institutions, and their distrust of novel-
ties, made them regard the new system with jealousy and disfavour;
it was therefore thought unadvisable to erect a union-house for the
district of Merthyr. There was, moreover, a desire on the part of the
guardians to see how the new law would work where union-houses
had been erected, previously to committing themselves by building.
Fourteen years have elapsed, and no union-house has been raised at
Merthyr. The hostility of the working classes has dwindled to insignificance long ago, so that we must look for other causes to account for this backwardness to give the New Poor-law full efficiency
in the Merthyr Union. As I have been informed, the fault lay with
the country guardians, who pertinaciously opposed the erection of a
workhouse on the ground of expense. The folly of this obstinacy I shall
show by a comparison of the expenditure of the adjoining Union of
Abergavenny with that of the Merthyr Union:—

COMPARISON OF EXPENDITURE BETWEEN THE MERTHYR AND ABERGAVENNY UNIONS.

POPULATION IN 1841.

Merthyr Union 52,864
Abergavenny Union 50,674

EXPENDITURE DURING FOUR YEARS ENDING WITH LADY-DAY, 1849, FOR THE MAINTENANCE AND RELIEF OF THE POOR, &c.

	1846.	1847.	1848.	1849.
Merthyr	£8,552	£8,882	£14,016	£19,365
Abergavenny (workhouse expenses included) . . .	6,393	6,818	8,592	9,201
In favour of Abergavenny	£2,159	£2,064	£5,424	£10,164

I should here remark that it is quite fair to contrast these unions,
their component elements being precisely similar; that is to say,
they equally comprise manufacturing and agricultural districts—the
Abergavenny Union containing, at the time the above statement was
drawn up, Rhymney, Tredegar, Beaufort, Ebbw Vale, Nantyglo, and
other iron works.

By this table it will be seen that (the population of both unions
being of the same classes, and nearly equal) the expenditure of the
Merthyr Union, without a workhouse, exceeds that of Abergavenny
Union with a workhouse, by the enormous sum of £10,164; being

actually more than double what it ought to have been, as compared with the latter union, if affairs had been as judiciously conducted at Merthyr as at Abergavenny.

Struck with the sudden and large increase of expenditure in both unions in the year 1848, and curious to learn the occasion of it, I inquired, and was informed that this was mainly attributable to the "Irremovable Act." Here again the advantage is on the side of the Abergavenny Union, where the increase was only £1,774, whilst in Merthyr it was not less than £5,134.

Thus much for the *folly*, as regards the ratepayers, of not erecting a union house, and giving the New Poor-law full operation at Merthyr—I have now to show the social mischiefs of this purblind and mistaken policy. The privilege of personal freedom is nearly the only set-off that the poor can urge in favour of out-of-door relief as against provision in the workhouse. We shall afterwards see, when visiting the dwellings of the poor, how the old system works in Merthyr; in the meantime I may remark, in general, that, left to themselves, the poor are half-starved, in rags, ill-housed, squalid, diseased, and filthy; whilst in a union house their condition, if not entirely the reverse, is greatly ameliorated. But there is another and a more crying evil resulting from the present state of the poor-law regulations in Merthyr—and that is, the neglect and ruin of the many children whom circumstances have thrown upon the parish. In the Merthyr union there are 150 orphan, deserted, and illegitimate children, "relieved without their parents." For many of these there are no means of education provided; they are boarded and lodged in the worst quarters of the town, often in the filthy houses of the Irish, where the only society is that of thieves, prostitutes, and vagrants, so that their training is derived from the example of vice, recklessness, and infamy. The consequences are enough to make one shudder. Yet, with these perpetually before the public, a humane endeavour made by Mr. H. Bruce—supported by Mr. D. James, the chairman of the board of guardians, and a few others—to remedy this alarming evil by the establishment of an industrial school where these children would, in a great measure, support and educate themselves, was defeated at a meeting of the board of guardians in November last. No doubt an education in a workhouse would be vastly preferable to an education in crime, such as these neglected children at present receive—and that, *primâ facie*, is a reason for a union-house comprising a school. But it has been found that the association of adult and infant paupers in a

workhouse has not been without ill effects; and we have the authority of the Poor-law Commissioners for the fact that all endeavours
at separation within the house have failed. This being the case, and
education apart from the union-house being desirable, perhaps no
system has ever been proposed better calculated for bringing up children at a moderate expense, and at the same time in such a manner
as to make them useful and exemplary members of society, than that
of industrial schools. As the advantages of these institutions are but
imperfectly understood by the general public, I take this opportunity
of extracting from the speech delivered by Mr. Bruce, on proposing
an industrial school in Merthyr, a passage which will serve to make
them more widely known:—

"I have taken," said he, "some pains to watch the workings of industrial schools; and from all that I have read, am led to believe that
children placed on a farm, the boys being taught useful trades, and
the girls trained in the practice of housekeeping, would themselves defray the cost of their maintenance. And when of an age to shift for
themselves, boys accustomed to brave the inclemencies of the weather
would become strong, robust, and healthy, and when skilfully trained
to useful arts would make a superior class of workmen, and find no
difficulty in getting employment; while girls so trained would form a
class now greatly required. The welfare of society depends upon good
wives—good wives provide comfortable homes and made good husbands; and no class of women would be more likely to make good
wives than those whose minds had received the advantages of early
cultivation, and who from their infancy had been instructed in the art
of domestic management. Establish an industrial school for 300 children, and the result would be both immediate and permanent benefit.
There can be little doubt that under such a system the rates would be
greatly relieved, as the children would, by the produce of their labour,
defray at least part of the cost of their own keeping; but industrial
schools were recommended by other and still higher considerations.
The criminality of this country has now risen to such a height as to
be quite alarming. In Liverpool alone, it is calculated that 700,000*l.* a
year are lost either by actual pilfering or in protecting the inhabitants
against crime and dishonesty, much of which would inevitably be saved
were proper care taken to give the children of their destitute population good moral training and early industrial instruction. A case had
lately occurred at Dowlais where destitute children had been proved to
be the principal instruments in robbing the company of scraps of iron
to a very large amount. Had care been taken of them when young, this

would probably not have occurred. I do not mean to say that, on the establishment of industrial schools, all crime would disappear, but where so many children are left to grow up unheeded and uncared for, and exposed to the vicious contamination of crowded cities, crime must be the fatal and necessary consequence. We are answerable for the orphans of this parish. The germs of good exist in all of them, and if these are developed, it will be well for us, and well for them; but if we neglect them, I feel quite satisfied that we shall hereafter have to pay dearly for their punishment in various forms—for their prosecution, their maintenance in gaol, their trial—probably for a repetition of all these expenses before they are finally transported—then for their maintenance in the hulks, and for otherwise carrying out the sentence of transportation. It is no exaggeration to say that 200*l.* may and will be expended upon many of the children whose fate we are now discussing, unless something be done to reform their characters, and to fit them for honest employment. It is impossible for us to be any longer indifferent to this matter. The manner in which the children of these parishes are brought up is a scandal to us, and let us therefore remedy the evil without delay."

To the general objection that industrial schools were visionary and impracticable—and, more pointedly, that they had never been tried in a manufacturing district—Mr. D. W. James at the same meeting thus replied:—

"It had been said that no industrial school has been established in a manufacturing district; but the assertion was not correct. Such a school had been established at Kirkdale, in Lancashire, in a cotton manufacturing district. [He then read the report.] Some boys had been trained to agricultural pursuits, some as gardeners, tailors, and shoemakers. A few had been taught the management of the steam-engine; and it was proposed to train a few sailors. Were fifteen boys, trained to the management of steam-engines, turned out annually, would they have any difficulty in finding employment? None whatever. While to us and to them the difference would be great, between fifteen robust and skilful workmen, able and willing to work out their own independence, and fifteen ignorant and dissolute men, who, unable to rise to good positions, would ever and anon fall back into their cradle—the workhouse. The one class would regenerate society, the other would sink it still lower than it is. The cost of establishing an industrial school and purchasing the necessary ground would not be more than 3,000*l.*; and as that amount would be spread over twenty-one years, the annual charge upon the union would only be 200*l.*; and who is there that thinks that too large a sum to pay for so great a benefit? We have to pay relief to these children; and would it not be wise and prudent to make them self-supporting?"

So nicely balanced were the supporters and opponents of an industrial school at Merthyr, that the motion in its favour was only lost by a minority of one. It is, however, to be hoped that the defeated party will not relax in their endeavours to overcome the prejudices of those who opposed them; and, whatever may be the ultimate result, they have the consciousness of knowing that the wishes of a majority of the intelligent classes of this neighbourhood are in their favour, as was unmistakeably shown by the memorial to the guardians praying for the establishment of such a school.

The following is a return of the pauperism in Merthyr Union on the 1st of last July. An analysis of this table, which I shall afterwards make, will throw some light on the social condition of the labouring classes in and around Merthyr:—

A STATEMENT OF PAUPERISM IN MERTHYR ON JULY 1, 1849.

		Merthyr.	Vaynor.	Total Merthyr and Vaynor
Able-bodied, or the families of Able-bodied.	1. Adult Males (married or single) relieved in cases of their own sickness, accident, or infirmity	178	6	184
	2. Adult Males relieved on account of sickness, accident, or infirmity of any of the family, or of a funeral	29	1	30
	3. Adult Males (married or single) relieved on account of want of work, or other causes	—	—	none
	4. Wife .... ⎧Families of adult males,	171	7	178
	5. Children ⎨ in columns 1, 2, 3, resident with the father under 16 ⎩ ident with the father	469	27	496
	6. Widows	207	9	216
	7. Children under 16, dependent on widows	434	21	455
	8. Single women without children	18	1	19
	9. Mothers . ⎰Illegitimate children and	37	4	41
	10. Children ..⎱ their mothers	43	4	47
	11. Wives ... ⎧Families relieved on account of parent being in gaol, &c.	5	—	5
	12. Children ..⎨ count of parent being in gaol, &c.	19	—	19
	13. Wives ... ⎧Resident Families of other non-resident males relieved	44*	1	45
	14. Children ..⎨ non-resident males relieved	112*	2	114
Not Able bodied.	15. Males	154	11	165
	16. Females	442	38	480
	17. Children under 16, relieved with Parents	69	4	73
	18. Orphans or other Children under 16, relieved without their Parents	73†	3	76
Lunatics, Insane Persons, and Idiots.	19. Males	5	—	5
	20. Females	2	—	2
	21. Children under 16 ...	—	—	none
22. Vagrants relieved out of the workhouse		29	—	29
				2,579

* Where husbands run away. There are here many of these cases.
† This is the total of orphans deserted and illegitimate children.

Taking the population at the last census return as 52,864, the amount of pauperism in this union is not quite 5 per cent.; whereas I find that the average of paupers relieved throughout England and Wales, in proportion to the population, was, in 1847, as high as 10.8 per cent.

The first remarkable circumstance which strikes the reader of this table is that there are here no adult males chargeable on account of "want of work." Applications of this kind are infrequent, and when made, the party is ordered to break stones, by which he earns his own and his family's subsistence. The reader must bear in mind that the population of this union was 52,864 at the last census in 1841, and that it has since very largely increased. Of the 184 males relieved in cases of their own sickness, accident, or infirmity, the greater portion are chargeable through accidents. Some, having exhausted their "sick fund" or "benefit society" allowance, become burdensome to the parish; others, again, have not the advantage of any such provision for casualty or illness, and are therefore chargeable from the first. The 4th and 5th items show the number of women and children whose proper means of support have been cut off by sickness or accident to the father and husband, or by some heavy affliction in the family. As regards illegitimacy, the morals of Merthyr, if they are not above, are certainly not below, the average of towns of equal size. For instance, I find by the Ninth Annual Report of the Registrar-General that the number of illegitimate births in the district of Merthyr (a manufacturing one) in 1846 was 127—whilst in the city of York (which has no manufactures of any consequence), with a population less by several thousands than Merthyr, the number was 128, a contrast obviously in favour of morals in the latter town. Neither is the number of children chargeable through the imprisonment of the parent by any means large. Looking at items 13 and 14, where is shown the number of women and children destitute through "non-residence of males," it appears large. These, I am told, are all cases where the husband has run away, leaving his wife and family to the care of the parish. There are many of such instances; but when the fact is called to mind, that numbers of men of bad character flock to the iron works from the surrounding counties (when by misconduct they have need to fly), where they are followed by their families, our surprise is lessened; and it is nearly always men of bad reputation, who have to fear the law, that thus abscond. The number of infirm old men (165) and women (480) is not great, considering that this is a manufacturing population; the women are mostly widows past work. Lastly, with reference to the number of orphans and other children under sixteen years of age, relieved *without* their parents, I should observe that this statement is considerably below the actual number at present chargeable—the cholera, having intervened since the date of the above return, has largely extended the ranks of these fatherless and unfortunate sufferers. The number of lunatics is small. They are provided for at a private establishment near Briton Fury, this county having no public asylum. I may mention that I one day saw in the streets of Merthyr, under charge of the police, on his way to the magistrates for an order for confinement as a pauper lunatic, a fine old man who, lifting up his hands and turning round like an Eastern dervish, kept crying out in Welsh, "I am the son of the great God!" I learnt on inquiry that his was a religious madness, and that he belonged to the sect of Mormonites, which, as I have already stated, number a not inconsiderable congregation in this town.

The following is an account of the amount of money expended in the relief of the poor in the Merthyr Union during seven years ending with the 29th September last, as obligingly furnished me by the assistant overseer, Mr. Edward Lewis:—

Year ending 29th September,	1843 ...	£8,599	18	4
„ „	1844 ...	8,371	1	2
„ „	1845 ...	8,432	7	1
„ „	1846 ...	7,081	3	5
„ „	1847 ...	8,727	5	4
„ „	1848 ...	12,487	11	0
„ „	1849 ...	10,034	2	5
Total of 7 years		63,733	8	9

This, it should be observed, is only the expenditure in the actual relief of the poor, and does not include the disbursements for law charges, magisterial and medical expenses, payments to the county or borough rates, &c., all of which are included in the table contrasting the Merthyr and Abergavenny Unions above given. How large a portion of the rates is borne by the proprietors of the iron works will be seen by the following statement:—

POOR-RATES PAID BY THE MERTHYR IRON-MASTERS FOR
THE QUARTER ENDING 25TH DECEMBER LAST.

Dowlais Iron Company	£697	11	0
Pen-y-Darran British Iron Company	345	10	0
Cyfarthfa	559	16	0
Plymouth Works	381	11	6
Total of the quarter	£1,984	8	6

To conclude this subject, and substantiate my remark that pauperism is not more prevalent in the Merthyr district than elsewhere,

I will extract from the fourteenth report of the Poor-law Commissioners a statement of the receipts and expenditure of West Bromwich union—the population of which is engaged in manufactures, like that of Merthyr, and is nearly equal in point of numbers, the first being 52,596, and the last 52,864:—

Total amount of money received for the relief of the poor in the year ending 5th March, 1847.			Total amount of parochial rates, &c., expended in the relief of the poor, &c., in the year ending 5th March, 1847.		
West Bromwich ... £15,497	1	0	£15,085	11	0
Merthyr Tydfil 14,660	3	6	12,843	3	0
£836	17	6	£2,242	8	0

By this it appears that pauperism is more expensive—and, it is fair to presume, more abundant—in West Bromwich than in Merthyr; though the population of the former is actually less than that of the latter town. The difference in the total sum expended, amounting to upwards of £2,200, is very remarkable; and as I have shown, if Merthyr had a union-house, and the parochial affairs were conducted there as economically as they are in Abergavenny, the charges in Merthyr being proportionably reduced, the contrast between the cost of pauperism in that town, as compared with that of West Bromwich, would yet be more striking. With this I close my remarks on the statistics of pauperism in and around Merthyr.

LABOUR AND THE POOR.

—◆—

THE MINING AND MANUFACTURING DISTRICTS OF SOUTH WALES.

[FROM OUR SPECIAL CORRESPONDENT.]

MERTHYR—TREDEGAR.

EDUCATION OF PAUPER CHILDREN—PAUPERISM—CRIME.

LETTER IX.

Wishing to satisfy myself of the authenticity of certain statements I had heard, that the pauper children in Merthyr were confided to the care of the low Irish and others living in the worst quarters of the town, and being desirous to examine into the condition of the poor in their own houses, I set apart a day to this duty. I was accompanied by the rector of the parish, the Rev. Mr. Campbell, who kindly undertook to be my guide. We called in the first instance at the offices of the "union," where we obtained the addresses of a number of illegitimate and orphan children farmed out by the parish, after which we commenced our round of inspection.

There is a quarter of the town extending along a flat on the right bank of the Taff, from the lowest point of High-street, towards Cyfarthfa—the proper name of which is Pont-Storehouse; but, like the unhappy and lawless people who inhabit it, the place has an *alias*, and is generally known by the name of "China." The houses are mere huts of stone—low, confined, ill-lighted, and unventilated; they are built without pretensions to regularity, and form a maze of courts and tortuous lanes, hardly passable in many places, for house refuse, rubbish, and filth. In some parts they are considerably below the level of the road, and the descent is by ladders. Such houses are called "the cellars." Here it is that, in a congenial atmosphere, the crime, disease, and penury of Merthyr are for the most part located. Thieves, prostitutes, vagrants, the idle, the reckless, and the dissolute, here live in a miserable companionship. This neighbourhood formed the main scene of our inquiries; and what I that day saw of misery, degradation, and suffering, I shall remember to the end of my life. After an ineffectual endeavour to see a pauper child at the house of an Irishman, which we found closed, we called at the dwelling of an Irishwoman named W——, where were placed by the parish two orphan children, whose parents had lately died of cholera. An old table, two chairs, and a stool formed the only furniture of the main room of this house. The woman was out, and we found four children squatted round a handful of fire which was burning in the grate. The oldest of them might be about nine years of age. There was no fender to protect them from the fire, nor was there any one in charge of them. The house was filthy and stinking; the floor, which was strewed with the sweepings of coal, had not been washed, I should say, for weeks; the window was in several places broken, and the holes were unstopped. The eldest girl had a look of intelligence. I judged her to be about nine years old. Like the others she was barefooted, and in rags; her hair was matted, and her hands, face, and neck were black with dirt. She answered me as follows:—"My name is Biddy N——. I and my sister are put here by the parish. My mother and father are dead. I can't tell what my age is. I cannot read, for I was never in school. I sleep with three or four other children in that room." She pointed to an adjoining room, which I entered. The only furniture it contained was a stump bedstead, with a net-work of cord in lieu of sacking; on this there was a bed of straw. Here, without sheets or blankets, and with only a filthy counterpane to cover them, these children passed the bitterly cold nights of winter. I thought of the high mortality of infant life in Merthyr, and it seemed to me a mercy, rather than otherwise, that children should be taken away young from such hardships, neglect, and sufferings.

We next called at the house of an Irishwoman named W——, which, though dirty, was perhaps less loathsome than the one we last inspected. The house consisted of two rooms. The first thing we saw on entering was the corpse of a child in a winding-sheet, laid out upon a table; a white handkerchief, folded small, covered its eyes, but did not conceal the features, which, waxy and pallid, death had composed to a smile. Though the child had been dead two days, it was unprovided with a coffin. The odour of the house was almost insupportable. Before the fire were three or four children; amongst them was a boy named Martin B——, 11 years of age, who had been placed there by the parish, the allowance being 2s. per week. This boy had no shirt;

he was barefooted, in rags, his hair bristled up, and he was literally black with filth. He sat with the others on a low bench near the fire, and seemed more to vegetate like a plant than to live like an animal. I made him stand up, and questioned him, but could get no answer. He stared with an air of stupefaction at the fire, and, unlike the other children, appeared to take not the slightest interest at the entrance of strangers, or in the questions I put to him. Yet the woman told me he was not idiotic, as at first I supposed. His father, she informed me, had run away, and his mother was an "unfortunate woman." "He has been to school," said she, "for this fortnight past. I pay for him 1d. a week, and he knows his A B C." On looking into the adjoining room I saw three beds; two of these were occupied by two married couples, and the third by the children I had seen round the fire.

Leaving that house, we next called at Mrs. Davies' of "the Cellars," where we found two pauper children under far more favourable circumstances than the others whom we had visited. The house was neat, clean, and remarkably well-furnished. The good old woman brought forward a boy and girl, for the first of whom she was allowed 2s. 6d., and for the other 3s. a week by the parish. "The girl," said she, "is now six years old: they brought her to me an infant with only a shift on her back. The boy is four years old; and they are both good children, they give me little trouble." When I looked upon these healthy, comfortably clothed, and well-behaved children, for such they were, I could not help remarking how much there is in human affairs dependent upon destiny. The contrast between the personal appearance, the intelligence, and the behaviour of the children whose good fortune it had been to be sent to the care of this woman, and the squalor, rags, filth, and stupidity of those whom we have seen entrusted to the Irish, could not well be greater; and the widely different circumstances in which they are thus placed must operate materially in the formation of character in after-life. The old woman told me she had sent these children regularly to school, and they could both read. She accounted for the superior comfort of her house by saying that she owned a number of the adjoining houses, on the rents of which she subsisted. Whilst we were in the house, some women of the neighbourhood gathered round the door, and beset the clergyman with requests that their children might be admitted to the new schools; he sent away some smiling faces and gladdened hearts, with a promise that if they would send them at once, and pay attention to their children's habits, they should have the benefit which these excellent institutions afford.

Passing down a lane, we saw an instance of the truth that the poor
pay more dearly for accommodation than the rich. In a small hovel,
about nine feet by six, with a low tile-roof, unplastered and unceiled,
we found a young man in bed, and just recovering from a long sickness. His wife was attending him, and what with the bedstead, a table,
and chair, which formed the only furniture, there was scarcely room
to turn; yet for this small accommodation the poor man told me he
had to pay 2s. 6d. a week. I have since heard that, in proportion to the
likelihood there is that the tenant will be unable to pay regularly, the
price is raised to provide against such contingency. But as I have already shown the disproportion existing between accommodation and
rental in Merthyr, I will here say no more on this subject.

The lodging-houses next had our attention. In an up-stairs room
of the first we entered, we found, lying in a bed on the floor, a fine
young man, whose thighs had been fractured a few days previous by a
fall of earth. He lay under the fire-place, which was covered by a piece
of old carpeting. There were not less than five beds in this one room;
and it required care to make one's way through them to the side of
the disabled man. The owner of the house admitted to me that often
there lay two or three of different sexes in each bed. Upon the whole,
this house was tolerably clean, but the lower rooms were thronged
with the lodgers. The statement of the sick man was as follows:—
"My name is Robert Lavender. I was at work a few days ago with
some others lowering the side of a hill to make some new coke-ovens
for Mr. Joseph, when the earth above us gave way and came down. It
buried four of us; one was killed, and I got both my thighs broken;
the others were much hurt. I have here no friends or relations. The
doctor (Mr. J. James) is very kind to me, and so is this poor woman,
or I should not be able to live. The bed-sores hurt me cruel; and I can't
get any ease because my limbs are strapped, and must not be moved."
The woman complained that the weekly parish allowance (which was
6s.) was insufficient. "The poor man," said she, "wants a bit of fresh
meat, but as I have only what I get from these beds to live upon, I can't
afford it for him; but he should not want for good attendance, out of
pity, if I got nothing for him from the parish. I have been obliged to
keep somebody to watch him; and candles at night and other things
comes expensive."

The next lodging-house we visited was that of Mrs. S——, in
Caedraw. The floor was broken and unwashed, and the rooms stinking and filthy in the last degree. A small barrel, which served the

purposes of a chair, a round table, two stools, a bench, a few pots and kettles and pieces of crockery, a couple of japanned waiters, and a double line of blackened knives, forks, and spoons, sticking in leather straps behind the door, formed the entire contents of this room. The price for beds was from 2d. to 4d. a night. We here saw a stout Irish-woman, barefooted, in a blue cloak, with one child on her back, and five around her. She came in not to stay, but to ask assistance. This woman told me that she had come from Cork to this country by way of Newport; she had no husband, she said, to work for her, and no other object than to wander through the country, subsisting on beg-ging and parish relief, as she best might. This gives me an oppor-tunity for stating that since I treated the subject of the Irish in the iron-works, and mentioned the frauds they perpetrate on the parish officers in seeking relief when they are really not destitute, I learnt from one of the authorities of the Newport union that cases of decep-tion in this form were frequent there; and that only a short time ago, on an Irishman's applying for relief as one of the casual poor, they put into force the clause in the statute which confers power of search— when they found on his person 16s. 6d.; he was then taken before the mayor and committed to prison.

From the last we went to another lodging-house kept by a man of the name of ——. Here we found one of the children placed out by the parish. She was an orphan aged four years; the weekly allowance for her clothing and maintenance was 2s. 6d. She had a fine, open, and intelligent countenance; but was barefooted and dirty. The man promising to get her some shoes, the clergyman directed him to send her to the Infant-school, where for a part of the day she will be re-moved from the vicious society amidst which ill-fortune has placed her. There were four rooms in this house, but the man was unwilling that I should examine those upstairs, so I did not inspect them. He told me there were only three beds in each of the upper rooms—a story which, considering the manner in which the lower rooms were thronged, I did not believe. I counted sixteen persons in the two small rooms below stairs. This man admitted that four persons slept in one bed; he was the owner of the house, and, though that circumstance made it probable that he had saved money, he declaimed violently against the burden of the church and parish rates.

Through the open door of a house a few paces further, we saw a hollow-visaged, attenuated, and feeble old man seated on a block of wood. I entered, and conversed with him. He was making wooden skewers. There was scarcely any furniture in the house: two saucepans and a table were all I saw. The following is his statement:—"My name is Richard J———. I live in this house by myself, and work hard making skewers, and anything else I can do to earn a penny. My wife died of cholera in this house. Five years ago I had a paralytic stroke; but I got over it in part. The parish allows me 2s. 6d. a week: out of that I pay 1s. 6d. for rent, so I have 1s. a week to live on, besides a penny or two that I can earn. I am now 62 years of age. Many days I am without victuals. I paid rates and taxes for 30 years, but I don't get much return now. In the first 20 years I saved £300; but my wife started a shop, and was too good-natured in bailing (giving credit), and with one thing and another we lost all. I am starved of cold; if I had a bed-tick for my straw, and a rug to cover me, I should do." I went upstairs; the only furniture of his bedroom was a brush, a small tub, and a candlestick. A heap of straw in a corner formed his bed, and his only covering was some dirty bagging. I should add that I was informed that this man was addicted to drinking. If this be so, no wonder at his distress.

From thence we went to a house where a woman lay ill, of whose condition Mr. Campbell had already been apprised. The neighbours expressed to us on our way the strongest sympathy for her condition. Her name was M— H———, and she had an only son, whom every tongue reprobated for the neglect and cruelty with which he treated his unhappy mother. On entering the house, which consisted of a single room, we found gathered up, on a bed of cloth rags spread upon the floor, a woman whom at first sight I thought was dying; for she breathed short, quick, and with evident difficulty. Her face, neck, and arms, were emaciated to the bone; her thin white lips were compressed tightly, apparently from pain; and her large eyes gleamed out from their hollow sockets with that peculiar luminous glare that often accompanies the last stages of pulmonary disease. By her side, resting on a broken jug, which in its turn was supported by a lump of coal, was a plate with a piece of toast. A mere handful of fire was expiring in the grate unheeded. Two saucepans, a teapot, a cup, and a few onions on the mantel-piece, formed literally the entire contents of this desolate room. Though we cautioned her not to exhaust herself by talking, she made strong efforts to explain her unhappiness. Uttering a word with each breath, she said, "That wicked boy, he uses the victuals and lets me starve. I have from the parish 3s. a week, but my rent is 1s. 3d. My son does not work, or I should not be so perished; he does not mind to do anything for himself or me." A sight more piteous or painful

I never witnessed; for, as if the sufferings of this poor creature were not enough from disease and want, they were aggravated by, perhaps, the most horrible and unendurable of all afflictions—filial ingratitude. Whilst we were yet in the house, the neighbours who surrounded the door raised a cry, "Here the son is, the bad fellow!" Finding attention thus directed to him, he took to his heels, and, supposing we would not follow, ran up an adjoining street, which, happening to be a *cul de sac*, the clergyman and myself quietly followed and came up with him. He was a well-made, sharp-looking lad of about 18, by trade a tailor; and he excused himself for being out of work by saying his master had gone for a few days to Brecon. On being remonstrated with for his unnatural conduct to his dying mother he cried freely, but protested that he had not neglected her. He promised better conduct for the future. How this has proved I am unable to say; but death no doubt has ere this released that heart-broken woman from her sufferings in this world.

With this sorrowful picture I close my account of pauperism in Merthyr. The additional notes I have gathered furnish details of various other forms of suffering, but I do not care further to dwell on so painful a subject. Enough has been given to show what pauperism is in Merthyr, and to support my statement that the poor, left to themselves, "are half starved, in rags, squalid, diseased, and filthy;" whilst in a union-house—if such had existed in this place—they would at least have been well housed, well fed, warmly clothed, and clean. In quitting this subject, I feel bound to make my warm acknowledgments to the humane and independent chairman of the board of guardians, Mr. D. W. James, and to Mr. Frank James, the active and very efficient clerk of that board, for the facilities they afforded, and the valuable assistance they rendered me in every branch of my inquiries in this town. I have also to thank Mr. Roger Williams, the relieving-officer, for some useful information which he communicated on the state of the poor in this union.

With regard to the important subject of crime in the iron districts of South Wales, it is much to be regretted that accurate statistics are nowhere obtainable. The Parliamentary tables of criminal offenders, published annually, give with much minuteness the particulars of every county, but not of each parish or hundred, as they ought to do. The returns for Glamorganshire, Brecknockshire, and Monmouthshire, obviously afford no proper criterion by which to judge of crime in the iron districts; because they comprehend offences committed by the agricultural, as well as by the mining and manufacturing population, and there exist no means of distinguishing one class of criminals from another. However, I have done all in my power to lay the foundation for statistics of crime in the iron districts of South Wales, by procuring an elaborate and accurate return, for the past year, of the offences cognizable by law in the most important division of the iron works—the district of Merthyr. In the absence of the like information for preceding years, I am unable to say whether crime has increased or decreased of late years.

In a useful book, published by Mr. Jelinger Symons (one of the Commissioners of Inquiry into Education in Wales) "On the Condition and Treatment of the Dangerous Classes," the various districts of England and Wales are thus classified:—

> "BELOW THE AVERAGE IN CRIME.
> Mining Districts.
> Silk ditto.
> Agricultural ditto.
> "ABOVE THE AVERAGE IN CRIME.
> Cotton Districts.
> Iron ditto.
> Metropolitan ditto.

"The iron districts," he proceeds, "are not only more criminal than the others (except the metropolis), but they possess features of moral debasement and abandonment peculiar to themselves. There is no class of industry in which the welfare of the labourers is more grossly neglected by the employers. ... The masters are generally looked upon as the natural enemies of the men; the intimate relation between capital and labour, and the identical interest which links their fate, are neither understood nor believed; both classes imagine that they are necessarily antagonistic. ... Until last year (1847) there was this marked feature in favour of the iron district; namely, that though its crimes of *theft* exceeded those of other districts, its crimes of violence fell short at least of the cotton district. Not so in 1847; its crimes of violence were in that year greater than in the cotton district. Not only are these iron districts noted for crimes, but for all that fertile disorder and reckless improvidence which beget degradation of every kind. The people are essentially animal in their habits."

I have given these remarks a place, because it is well that the public should have the opinion of more than one inquirer into the moral and physical condition of the iron-works. That crime is far more rife in the mining and manufacturing than in the agricultural districts of Wales, is undeniable. The opposite conditions of society—the one crowded, forced, and artificial—the other scattered, untempted, and peaceful— sufficiently accounts for this; but on the assertion that "the masters are generally looked upon as the natural enemies of the men, and that the iron districts are noted for crimes and for that fertile disorder and reckless improvidence which beget degradation of every kind," I join issue; and I point to the facts and details I have given in my former letters to vindicate my position against that of the writer who has made an assertion so sweeping, so severe, and withal so unsupported as this.

Not a small amount of the crime in the mining and iron districts is that imported from the surrounding country. The facility with which work can generally be obtained, and the opportunity of baffling pursuers in the multitude of workmen and the maze of the works, induce those who, for poaching, larceny, orders of affiliation, and the heavier offences, are compelled to quit the localities of their crime, to seek shelter amongst the collieries and iron works. The leaven of vice these men import is not without its effect in promoting crime.

In any table which may hereafter be constructed of crime in the iron districts, care should be taken to discriminate the sexes of the offenders. I have already shown the degradation of women owing to their being bred from childhood amongst men in the works, away from the softening and elevating influences of the domestic hearth. Since then I have found that the offences by females in the iron districts are higher in proportion to numbers than in any other district, the metropolis not excepted. Here is another and a strong argument for the emancipation of the sex from the laborious, unnatural, and degrading duties they now perform at the collieries and the iron-works.

By the Merthyr Police Act, a stipendiary magistrate and an adequate body of police were constituted for the protection of person and property in the surrounding district. At present, the police force is, I believe, as well organised, and as well trained and efficient, as care, steady discipline, temper, and good judgment can make them. I inquired of more than one well-informed person, and the character given them was uniformly good. In a town of some 40,000 inhabitants, of whom nearly all the males are workmen, the police must, as a body, be exposed to great temptations, and often to personal danger, which always aggravates the passions—and perhaps this circumstance makes them the more circumspect, cool, and cautious. Be this as it may, their reputation stands good for forbearance, moderation, firm-ness, and courage, and they have undoubtedly a strong moral effect upon the masses whom they have to keep in order.

I am indebted for the following useful and interesting table of crimes, misdemeanours, and fiscal offences in the Merthyr district, during the year 1849, to Mr. Wrenn, the superintendent of police. The ingenuity and completeness which characterise this return will be acknowledged by all who examine it. A succession of similar tables for future years will be a most valuable addition to the criminal statistics of the country—which are now, as I have above shown, incomplete, as not affording proper means for distinguishing the crime of one district from that of another, without which the influences of wages and education can never be properly ascertained.

RETURN OF THE NUMBER OF PERSONS APPREHENDED AND SUMMONED BY THE GLAMORGAN CONSTABULARY IN THE MERTHYR POLICE DISTRICT FROM THE 1ST JANUARY TO THE 31ST OF DECEMBER, 1849:—

No.	Sex	C/D	Offence	No.	Sex	C/D	Offence
1	M	C	Robbing Post-office.	43	M	C	Larceny.
1	F	C	Attempt at child murder.	34	F		
2	M	C	Assault on Sheriff's baliff.	29	M	D	
8	M	C	Offences against Highways Act.	10	F		
2	F			16	M	C	Larceny from the person.
13	M	C	Offences against Railway and Canal Acts.	4	F		
4	M	D		13	M	D	
6	M	C	Cruelty to animals.	6	F		
1	F			6	M	C	Burglary and housebreaking.
1	M	D		1	F		
9	M	C	Fraudulent removal of goods.	4	M	D	Sheep-stealing.
2	M	D		3	M	C	
2	M	C	Deserting army.	1	F		
1	M	D		1	M	D	
28	M	C	Leaving families chargeable to parish.	1	F		
1	F			2	M	C	Cutting or wounding.
3	M	D		2	M	D	
1	F			3	M	C	Forgery.
30	M	C	Misdemeanor in service.	8	M	C	Uttering base coin.
12	M	D		2	F		
30	M	C	Offences against Sanitary Act.	3	M	D	
3	F			1	F		
1	M	D		1	M	C	Obtaining money and goods by false pretences.
3	M	D	Poaching.	1	F		
				5	M	D	
				4	F		
				6	M	C	Larceny by juveniles under 14 years old.
				3	F		

Explanation: "C" means convicted, or committed; "D" means discharged; "M" means males; and "F" means females.

Informations against

No.	Sex	C/D	Offence
14	M	C	Refusing money out of benefit clubs.
1	M	C	Offences by pawnbrokers.
1	F	C	Illegal pawning.
1	M	D	Illegal pawning.
15	M	C	Publicans.
1	F	C	Publicans.
2	M	D	Publicans.
56	M	C	Beer-house keepers.
4	F		Beer-house keepers.
4	M	D	Beer-house keepers.
4	M	C	Selling beer by unlicensed persons.
1	M	D	Selling beer by unlicensed persons.

Number committed for trial.

No.	Sex	
21	M	Assizes.
7	F	Assizes.
61	M	Quarter Sessions.
44	F	Quarter Sessions.
133		Total.

Total apprehended and summoned.

No.	Sex	
1,190	M	
217	F	
1,407	Total.	

No.	Sex	C/D	Offence
2	F	C	Robbing Fields and gardens.
9	M	C	Vagrants.
11	M	D	Vagrants.
7	F	C	Disorderly prostitutes.
228	M	C	Common assaults.
62	F	C	Common assaults.
56	M	D	Common assaults.
18	F	D	Common assaults.
39	M	C	Assaults on police-officers.
2	M	D	Assaults on police-officers.
5	M	C	To find sureties of the peace.
4	M	D	To find sureties of the peace.
2	F		To find sureties of the peace.
57	M	C	Malicious injuries to property.
10	F		Malicious injuries to property.
8	M	D	Malicious injuries to property.
58	M	C	Drunken charges.
1	F		Drunken charges.
69	M	D	Drunken charges.
10	F		Drunken charges.
49	M	C	Bastardy.
10	M	D	Bastardy.
28	M	C	Disobeying orders in bastardy.
1	M	D	Disobeying orders in bastardy.
82	M	C	Non-payment of wages.
23	M	D	Non-payment of wages.
47	M	C	Refusing to pay rates.
4	M	C	Offences against Market Act.

HENRY WRENN, SUPERINTENDENT.

From Merthyr I made an excursion of one day to Tredegar, a town of rising importance on the borders of Monmouthshire—passing through Sirhowy, a kind of suburb to that town. The Tredegar Iron

Works are extensive; they comprise seven furnaces, all of which are in blast. They belong to Messrs. Homfray and Thompson, who carry them on under the name of the Tredegar Iron Company. At Sirhowy there are five furnaces, one of which is out of blast. Messrs. Derby and Brown are the proprietors of these works. The rate of wages and the hours of work are the same as in Merthyr, neither is there any noticeable difference in the morals and habits of the people, or in the condition of their dwellings. Some improvements have, since the advent of the cholera, been made in the sanitary condition of the town by draining and cleansing; but much remains to be done before the town can be said to be well-drained and scavenged, well-paved and lighted. Much the same inconvenience from the want of privies is felt here as in Dowlais and Merthyr; and the people suffer much from an insufficient supply of water. I saw water sold from a barrel drawn by a horse in the streets—a bell being used to inform the inhabitants that this necessary of life was near, and to be obtained for money. It seems that formerly there were several wells in the town, but the ground being freely undermined in every direction for minerals, the wells, which used to yield abundantly, became dry. There are many persons who earn a good living by the sale of water in Tredegar. "This," said a gentleman with whom I talked on the condition of the town, "is our most crying deficiency." It is to be hoped that the Health of Towns Act will be applied to this place; the benefit to the inhabitants would be incalculable. Many of the houses—and the lodging-houses more particularly—are sadly overcrowded; indeed, house accommodation should be extended—a subject well deserving the consideration of the Tredegar Iron Company. There is no "truck"—or at all events no violation of the right of the workmen to go to what market they please with their money; but there is a large shop called "the Company's Shop," the proprietor of which is a tenant of the company, and the men understand their obligations to this establishment. There are no beer-houses in Tredegar. In this respect the town has a palpable advantage over Dowlais and Merthyr, whose greatest curse is the abundance of these nurseries of crime. I heard a remark made of the Tredegar Iron Company, which, as it redounds infinitely to their honour, I have pleasure in repeating: it is, that when their steady workmen grow old and past labour, they provide for them by a competent weekly pension. The population of Tredegar, Sirhowy, Ebbw Vale, and Victoria, at the last census was 13,000. Now it is probably 20,000. For these important towns and iron-works there is but one church, together with two school-rooms licensed for religious worship, affording accommodation for 1,420. The nearest point of Ebbw Vale and Victoria Works to the church is two miles, and the furthest three miles and a half, the road lying over a lofty and bleak mountain. With such church accommodation as this, no wonder that the people frequent the dissenting chapels, which are built conveniently for them. There has lately been opened a licensed school-room at Ebbw Vale, but there is no place of worship belonging to the Church of England at Victoria. The population of these two places is about 6,000. There would not have been even so much as this licensed school-room had it not been for the assistance rendered by the Pastoral Aid Society. There are in all nine full services every week, besides prayer meetings and communicants' assemblies. Of the services, there are at Tredegar three in Welsh and six in English. The attendance at the church, including children, is about 1,000, and the communicants number fully 300. A gentleman who 25 years ago passed through these densely populated districts assured me that at that time there was not a church to be seen between Abergavenny and Merthyr. The improvement is manifest; but even now the exertions of the Church of England do not keep pace with those of the Dissenters; consequently, her congregations are smaller and her influence is less than they might have been.

I was glad to find that the cause of education is warmly advocated and advancing in and around Tredegar. There are at this place three schools—for boys, girls, and infants. They are on the system of the National Society; the average attendances are—boys, 135; girls, 110; infants, 75. At Sirhowy there is a school, and the company are building five school-rooms, at a cost of some £2,000. At Ebbw Vale there are two schools, accommodating about 160 scholars. I was informed that they are well conducted and that already, though not long established, they have effected much good. There are not in this district any adult schools. Remembering the service these institutions have rendered in Merthyr and Dowlais, I was sorry to find no provision of this kind made for the working classes in and around Tredegar; and I hope that another season will not be permitted to pass without the establishment of one or more of these most humanizing, and in every sense desirable, institutions.

LABOUR AND THE POOR.

---◆---

THE MINING AND MANUFACTURING DISTRICTS OF SOUTH WALES.

[FROM OUR SPECIAL CORRESPONDENT.]

"TRUCK" IN THE IRON-WORKS AND COLLIERIES.

LETTER X.

I proceed now to speak of "truck" in the iron-works and collieries of South Wales. Fifteen years ago I made a visit of curiosity to this district; at that time the "truck system" was in almost universal operation through the iron-works; and I remember being led to the "Company's Shop" at Dowlais, and also to that at Tredegar, as places affording an insight into a peculiar feature of the economy of the iron trade which should not be overlooked. It was a curious sight. A spacious room was fenced off on three sides by counters, having lofty iron railings, with sliding wickets, through which the articles furnished were handed to the parties who applied for them. The centre of this area was occupied by a throng of men, women, and children, each with a book and order for the register and supply of goods; and they were served with meat, flour, grocery, shoes, drapery, or ironmongery, as they required, at different compartments of the counters, and in their respective turns. Happily, in Dowlais, and at the large works in and around Merthyr, this hateful practice has long since been abolished. Wages are always there paid in cash, and the workman has, in his shop dealings, the benefit which results from ready-money payments, as compared with credit, and also of the reduced prices which a competition of trade in the same town naturally produces.

But in several of the iron-works eastward of Merthyr, and in many of the sea-coal collieries which export their minerals at Newport, the truck system, under arrangements which are presumed sufficient to evade the legislative penalties attached to it, is in full work. The plan usually adopted to defeat the Act is this:—An agreement is made and entered into between the company and an individual who acts as shopkeeper (sometimes bringing in capital, and sometimes trading on the resources of the company), under which the company engage to send the men in their employ to the shopkeeper for goods, and the latter agrees to divide the profits of the business in such a proportion as may be mutually arranged between them. It is difficult, of course, to ascertain the terms of these agreements; but the prevalent belief in the country is, that from two-thirds to three-fourths of the profits are taken by the company. The shopkeeper is usually the tenant of the company. When a workman applies to his employers for money, he has an "order" given him for the payment of a certain sum at the shop. The man or some member of his family proceeds to the shop and asks for such goods as may be needed, up to the amount of his "order;" before these are delivered to him, he goes to a part of the shop occupied by the cashier—there he presents his "order" and is paid— he then re-crosses to the counter where his parcel of goods is made up, hands in the money, and the goods are delivered to him. In this manner the money paid for wages makes a perpetual circle in the same hands, never passing out of the shop—the sum of ten pounds in cash paying in its course for perhaps several thousand pounds' worth of labour. It is a well understood thing, wherever there is what is called a "company's shop," that if a workman on cashing his order does not lay out the full amount, or very nearly so, in goods, he must no longer look for employment as before, but may expect his dismissal.

In the case of the Rhymney Ironworks, the Ebbw Vale Works, and those at Sirhowy, where the system is followed, I have been informed—and, I believe, truly—that the resulting evil is less grievous and injurious to the workmen than it is found to be in the sea coal collieries; and that, upon the whole, a fair article, at not unreasonable prices, is supplied in payment for labour. But assuming this to be true, it is not denied that goods of the same quality are something higher in price at those shops than in the neighbouring towns of Abergavenny, Pontypool, and Merthyr— whilst the objections remain, that the workman, compelled to deal at the company's shop, is denied the opportunity of cheapening and bargaining which he would enjoy if he carried money in his hand to an open market; that he is excluded from the advantage of low prices resulting from the competition of trade already mentioned; and lastly, that the company have, by this means, a double profit on his labour—a circumstance which, though it ought to increase, in reality diminishes the rate of wages.

The condition of the labouring classes in localities where this system is pursued is at all times worse than that of their fellows in districts where the men are paid in money. This difference is very perceptible at present, and is sensibly felt by both classes. The workmen who are paid in cash have the benefit of low prices in the markets, by which they are better able to sustain the depression which exists just now in the value of labour; but their less fortunate brethren who are paid at the "tommy shop" experience no favourable change in the markets—they derive no advantage from a fall in the price of provisions and clothing. Another, and not the least in magnitude, of the evils attendant upon this state of things, is that all habits of thrift and economy—all endeavours to provide for sickness and old age—are not only discouraged, but utterly extinguished by it. Take an equal number of workmen, at the same nominal rate of wages, in Merthyr and in Rhymney—in the former of which towns the men are paid in money, and in the latter in goods—and inquire which of the two has built or bought the largest number of houses; the reply will be greatly in favour of the workmen in Merthyr.

It is the policy of the confederated parties where this system is pursued, to supply every want of the men, and to give them as little cash from one monthly "pay" to another as they can. Goods the men may freely have, up to the value of the "orders"—but the workman who takes away money must be prepared for his discharge. Every variety of articles is kept on hand at the shops—grocery, drapery, and hosiery, flour, and salted provisions, ready-made clothes (including boots and shoes), butchers' meat, ironmongery, oils and paints, vegetables, (including potatoes, cabbages, beans, and peas); in short, all requisites for household consumption (except spirits, beer, and cider), are supplied on demand. The extent of one of these establishments may be imagined, when, as at Rhymney, a population of some eight thousand persons mainly depends upon it for the supply of their daily necessities.

But it is in the collieries on the South-Eastern border of the Welsh coal field that "truck" exists in its worst forms; there it occasions hardships and injustice of the most vexatious nature, as will be seen from the statements which I shall presently give. Here it is necessary to make some explanations, in order that the right parties may be saddled with this offence. Although the reproach of "truck" apparently lies upon those who *work* the collieries, and upon them alone, the fact is not so—for the blame in a large degree ultimately rests upon the lessees and owners, who reside at a distance, and are not seen to take part in the conduct of the business. It is right the public should be informed of the arrangements made between these parties and the men who work the collieries, which form such fruitful sources of hardship and inconvenience to the workmen and their families. I will take the instance of the sea-coal collieries in the valley of the Ebbw river, which send their produce for shipment at Newport.

Many of the merchants in whose hands lies the vast export trade in coal carried on at Newport reside in or near that town. They are generally the lessees of collieries at some point or other in the adjacent coal-field. Others, too, there are, the proprietors of collieries, who derive a handsome income from ownership, without intermeddling with the coal-trade. The system adopted by these parties is as follows:—A man of wealth and substance, or, at all events, having a reputation as such, obtains the lease of a tract of minerals for a term of years, or possibly buys a colliery. In either case he does not work it himself, but takes the biddings of *contractors* for raising and supplying a given quantity of coal in a certain time at so much a ton. These contractors are in most cases men of no capital; generally they have themselves been miners, who, possessing more enterprise than their fellows, and having nothing to lose, take the chance of bettering their condition by entering upon a speculation of this nature. The lessee of the colliery plays off one of these men against another in bidding for the contract, taking such offer as appears most eligible, which, in the usual run of cases, is the lowest. The party whose tender is accepted now looks about him for the means of carrying on his undertaking. A large number of hands must be employed, and in some way paid. True, he has little or no money to commence with, but the difficulty must be overcome. He can obtain four months' credit for grocery and provision stores in Bristol; before this period has expired, he will be in receipt of heavy payments from the lessee with whom he has contracted, and in this manner he will be enabled to get along. A "tommy shop" must be started—but not in his own name, for that might entail inconveniences; so he opens one in the name of a friend or relation, and there his men are paid in goods. He probably soon finds that, in his eagerness to obtain the contract, he has set his price too low. He is not unprepared for this. Some one must suffer, or he cannot live. Who must it be? Not the owner of the colliery, for his position and the terms of the contract protect *him*. No—it must be the workman; he is defenceless, and must endure the hardship. Larger profits must be exacted through the tommy shop. The beerhouse-keeper whom he has set up, and from whom alone his workmen can obtain credit for drink, must yield a larger tribute. In this manner he makes up for his imprudence, or his recklessness, in having taken the contract at too low a sum. Every possible device is resorted to for the purpose of squeezing profit out of the workmen. Yet these contractors rarely do well. They live by shifts and expedients—by extending credits, and by bills—for a while, till the evil day comes, when they sink, and are succeeded by adventurers of the like character.

In this manner it is that all the evils of "truck" are wrought by a baneful system of middle-men in the sea-coal collieries of South Wales. Go wherever you will through the iron and coal districts—if you find a middle-man between the proprietor and the labourer, the latter is always seen to suffer by it. But as I have, in a former letter, expressed myself strongly on this subject, I will say no more at present. One word, however, to the lessees of collieries in and around Newport who thrive by this hateful and iniquitous system. To make money is, no doubt, a desirable thing; but wealth may be bought, as it is in slave countries, at the sacrifice of that which should be above all value—the esteem and good opinion of the world at large. The poor man's capital is his labour; whoever unnecessarily depreciates that, is guilty of a sin which is not the less black because it is done under the semblance of a voluntary and honest, but in reality, a forced and unfair competition. By means of this system of employing contractors, who in their turn make their profit upon the workmen, those lessees and owners of collieries who are shippers are enabled in some degree to undersell the parties who follow the more honourable and old-fashioned plan of working the mines themselves, without the intervention of a contractor. It is to be hoped, for the sake of humanity, that this *collier sweating system* will be brought to an end, and that speedily. But this may not be hoped for from the voluntary action of the lessees themselves, or the mere indignation of the public—it must be by making the Truck Act more effective. Do this, and you knock on the head at once the whole brood of contractors, who, without capital, subsist by "truck," to the infinite injury of the honest labourer.

A conviction under the Truck Act is very rarely heard of in South Wales. In the absence of any power to examine the parties, the law, as it at present stands, is wholly inoperative. By a colourable and transparent device the intention of the Legislature is effectually defeated, and the evils attendant upon payment of wages in goods are now as rife, as enormous, and pernicious as if the Truck Act had never been passed. It may be well to specify a few instances, which have been communicated to me by the sufferers, of the mischief resulting from the intervention of contractors between the proprietor and the workman. Wherever the truck system prevails there is what is called a "monthly pay;" but this is merely nominal—the men (owing to inability on the part of the contractor to meet his engagements, and the interest he has to make his payments entirely through the shop), frequently going as much as thirteen weeks without the settlement called "a pay." Not unfrequently during this period they receive no more than 5s. in money, and they are compelled—when they want a shilling to pay for the repair of shoes, their "sick club" money, or for anything that cannot be supplied at the shop—to get goods and sell them for half their value amongst their agricultural neighbours, in order to possess themselves of the required amount in cash. The difference in the quality of the provisions furnished at the "tommy shops," and those obtainable at the same price in the neighbouring towns, is from 1d. to 2½d. per pound; and in the same proportion for articles of drapery and the like. Strong in their monopoly, and conscious of the utter helplessness of the men, the keepers of the tommy shops treat them haughtily, and sometimes rudely; they must take the goods delivered to them or go without. Statements to this effect, taken from the lips of the complainants, will be laid before the reader presently.

It may reasonably be asked, why do the men endure this state of dependence and slavery? The answer is, they do so under the pressure of necessity. The competition in the labour-market, amongst the iron-works and collieries, is so great and urgent, that men are constrained, by the dread of being out of employment, to put up with these hardships and inconveniences—they have to choose between two evils, and they prefer the least. Some, no doubt, bred in the neighbourhood, and accustomed to the system from their childhood, are less impatient under it than others who elsewhere have experienced the happiness of a sounder state of things. Again, not a few have associations of relationship which they are averse to sever by leaving the neighbourhood where they are located. One man, in reply to my question why he did not push his fortune in another quarter, informed me that, of himself, he should long ago have done so, but his wife, in whose native place they lived, was unwilling to quit her relations. The general effort, however, is to get employment in respectable collieries, or in iron-works where the wages are paid in cash; and, in several of such places, I heard men who had once lived under the truck system, on its being alluded to, speak loudly in condemnation of it, and congratulate themselves on their emancipation from its hardships.

Determined to make investigations upon the spot, and to take a statement of their grievances from the sufferers themselves, I visited the collieries in the valley of the Ebbw, where "truck" most prevails. I stayed a short time in Rhymney, where I took the examination of a shopkeeper, reserving that of the men for the colliery district I was about to visit.

The town of Rhymney is of modern date, having grown up with the extension of the iron-works. Like Merthyr, it is a town of workmen's houses. The streets are tolerably spacious, but the houses are small, ill-drained, and without the convenience of privies. Water, I was told, is very scarce in Rhymney. On a hill beside the town there has been lately erected a handsome church. The iron works appeared compact, well arranged, and in good order. There were eight smelting furnaces in full blast. They are the property of the Rhymney Iron Company, of which, I believe, the Marquess of Bute is a large shareholder. At one time these works were the property of Sir Benjamin Hall. On the death of his father he offered them to the Marquess of Bute for £55,000, which was then declined. Subsequently he sold them for £80,000, but, owing to some informality or to a forfeiture, they came again into Sir Benjamin's possession, and he ultimately disposed of them for £130,000, being considerably more than double the sum he originally asked for them. They are now understood to be very successful. Near the works stand what is here termed "the Company's Shop." Outwardly it bears the name of Mr. Andrew Buchan. I entered it, and found a very spacious room, with an iron-tied roof like that of a railway terminus. The counters were railed with iron, and the business of serving the workmen, their wives and children, was going actively forward. As may be supposed, with such a leviathan establishment and such a system to contend against, the shops, in this town of 8,000 inhabitants, are few and insignificant. The statement made to me by one of the shopkeepers was as follows:—

"The men here get their goods at 'the company's shop,' managed by Mr. Buchan. The system is this: The forge-men, or 'gaffers,' take to the shop a list of the names of the several workmen under their control, informing the conductor how much goods they are to supply to each workman or his family. The men apply for goods, and a quantity is set out for them; the clerk in the shop, who serves them, adds up the amount, and tells them what it is; they then go to the 'pay-room,' which is an office having the same frontage wall as the shop, but a separate roof, where they receive the money. This done, they return to the shop, pay for and take away the goods. They are not allowed to remove anything from the counter till the money is paid. They keep every article at the company's shop which a poor man's family may want, except coal and drugs. They sell butchers' meat, grocery, drapery, ironmongery, oils and paints, flour, potatoes, cabbage, onions, beans, peas, and other vegetables. On the 'pay-ticket,' the sums advanced in this way for goods are entered as 'cash advanced;' but when money is had at the office, as it sometimes is, for other purposes than for goods, the debit is entered in a separate account; this, I suppose, is to show the men the different manner in which they have been paid—in goods so much, and the remainder in money. The men well know the meaning of this, though 'goods' are not expressed in the account. The people, when they come here to lay out a trifle, often say it is a hard case they cannot go where they like for their goods. I have known them say this in other shops than mine. There are 'Company's Shops' at Sirhowy, Ebbw Vale, Blaina, and Clydach."

At a distance of some miles across the mountain I entered the district in which lie the sea-coal collieries that supply the port of Newport with coal. Here, in the valley of the Ebbw, it is that the truck system most luxuriantly flourishes. Previously to entering on my inquiries, I secured the company of a gentleman of standing and high character in the neighbourhood, as a check upon the men, in case they might be disposed to mislead me by extravagant statements. I took every man's name and address, and at the close of his examination I read over to him his evidence, and received his approval of it. The first collier I examined was one who until very recently had worked in the Cwm Brain Collieries and Iron-works, the property of Mr. Reginald J. Blewitt, the member for Monmouth. He said:—

"I am a collier, and worked in the Cwm Brain Collieries for eight years. I was employed by a contractor named ——, who raises the coal, and supplies it to Mr. Blewitt, the proprietor, at so much a ton. The system followed at that colliery is this: A man goes and asks for work; he is given a job, but nothing is said as to when wages are to be paid, nor as to the rate for cutting coal; all this is understood by the men. In collieries where 'tommy shops' are kept, the workmen are not paid a better rate of wages than in other collieries. Different veins bring various prices for cutting, from 1s. 10d. to 2s. 10d. a ton. When I had been at work a few days, and wanted money, I went to the contractor for an order. He gave me a note for what I required—perhaps 10s.— to go to the shop, where they did not give me silver for it that I might pocket, but I was compelled to take the amount in goods. The cashier in the shop gave me the money, which I had to hand to the man who served me before I had any goods. All this took place in the shop. If a man wants to keep a shilling or two in the shop they sometimes knock him about. I have known this done. They set their dog on J— B—. I myself had law on them for beating a boy who worked in the colliery, because he kept a shilling of the money paid him by the cashier in the shop. The boy is in Cwm Brain now. They make some kind of a 'pay,' which is called 'monthly,' but the month often extends from ten to thirteen weeks. —— told me yesterday that the 'pay' has now run twelve weeks. In the course of that time there is supposed to be 'a draw.' These draws vary from four to seven weeks. We were allowed to have 'shop notes' for goods once a week. At the intermediate 'draws' the collier gets whatever sum the contractor puts in the order. The money at the 'pay' and at a 'draw' is taken by the contractor from the office to a public-house. The men get from 10s. to 15s.; out of this the contractor stops 6d. for beer, giving the man an order on the publican:—'—— Inn. Give the bearer a quart of beer.' They make this stoppage for getting 'change.' When we have the quart of beer we seldom stop at that, but drink more. Sometimes the men spend in this way all their money, and their wives and children suffer for it. Many times I have found great difficulty in getting on, through not being able to obtain payment in cash. I have gone and taken things out of the shop many times, and sold them for half-price in order to get a shilling or two to pay my 'sick club' money. If we have not some earnings in advance they will on no account let us have goods at the shop. A fellow-workman of mine, whose wife was ill, was told by the doctor to send for some vinegar to bathe her temples. He had no money, so he sent to the shop for a pennyworth on trust. They put the vinegar in the cup, but when they found there was no money they took it back from the child's hand, and she returned without it. The man's name is ——; he was then at work with me, and complained of the circumstance. The goods supplied us were very much worse for the money than we could get at Pontypool. There was a difference of 1½d. or 2d. a pound at least. I could get at Newport or Pontypool as much for 15s. as here for £1. I have very often heard men complain of the hardship and injustice of this system; the general remark was, that elsewhere provisions and goods could be procured much cheaper and better. They do not pay the same attention to us at the 'tommy shops' as we have in other shops. At the —— Company's 'tommy-shop' (iron-works ——) my brother obtained his goods. On a cold day in the winter, his wife went to the shop for her week's supply, and she was kept there waiting, on a damp floor, from six to eight hours. Feeling faint and wanting some refreshment, she asked for 6d. out of her order to get something to take, she was so weak and cold. She was refused, and having further to wait, she became so benumbed and exhausted that she fell to the ground, and they had to carry her out of the shop. She was taken home, and never recovered. She died in a few days. When I lived at Cwm Brain, I tenanted a house belonging to the proprietor of the colliery: it had neither a privy nor a drain."

I next examined a second miner from the same colliery. He said:— "I am a miner, and worked in the Cwm Brain collieries twelve months. I heard ——'s statements, which you have just read over to him, and they are correct in every particular that I can depose to. I mean all his remarks upon the 'tommy shop' at Cwm Brain. The contractor does not himself keep the shop, but it is generally believed through the works that he shares the profits. The 'tommy shop' at Cwm Brain belongs to Mr. Blewitt, the proprietor of the colliery, and is let out by him. The contractor told me I must deal in the shop, or leave my employment. I have known instances of men being turned away because they did not take goods at the shop. I can mention one. P—— had an order to receive £1; he went to the shop and had his goods put up. He received the money from the cashier, and, wanting cash very badly, he pocketed it instead of paying for the goods and taking them away. A clerk was immediately sent from the shop to the works, where he informed the contractor of the circumstance. P—— was at once discharged; he never did a stroke in the works afterwards. I have known instances, at 'a draw,' where, owing to a quarrel between the contractor and proprietor, the contractor has failed to obtain money, and we have been sent away without a farthing after waiting several hours. When my wife goes to the shop and wants cheese, they do not let her choose it, but they weigh it, throw it down (as good as to say, 'here it is'), and she must take it or leave it behind. Good cheese or bad, all is there charged alike, 8d. a pound. I'll tell you a case that shows the difficulty there is to get a payment in money when needed; it is that of T——, who lives close by me. His child died, and he had no money to pay for its grave. He went to the contractor, who gave him a shop-note for the price of a bushel of flour. He sold the flour to get money to pay for digging his child's grave. I know this from my own observation. When I have wanted money to pay for mending shoes, and such as that, my wife has been compelled to get candles at the shop and pay in that way. When there have been no potatoes to be had at the 'tommy shop' my wife has taken goods in order to exchange for them at other places. I would work for much less money at a colliery where the men are paid in cash and not in goods, and I should be better off. I have heard many other men say the same thing. I have proved the difference when I have saved a few shillings at 'the pay,' by buying goods at Newport and Pontypool. I lived in one of the houses belonging to the proprietor of the colliery; it had neither a privy nor a drain."

This man furnished me with a contrasted statement of the prices of articles of the same quality in the tommy shop and at Pontypool. It is as follows:—

	Tommy Shop.	Shops in Pontypool.
Sugar	7d. per lb.	5d. per lb.
Butter	11d. per lb.	9d. per lb.
Flour	10s. to 11s. a bushel.	8s. to 8s. 6d. a bushel.
Bacon	11d. per lb.	8d. per lb.
Cheese	8d. per lb.	7d. per lb.
Ham	1s. per lb.	10d. per lb.
Candles	7d. per lb.	5d. per lb.

By the above it will be seen that the extra profit over the ordinary per centage taken by the legitimate trader amounts, in several cases, to 30 per cent. This, added to the fair dealers' profit, which may be taken at 20 per cent., gives 50 per cent. clear profit to the tommy shop; and this is below rather than above the mark.

A collier from Cwm Tillery Colliery next had my attention; the following is his statement:—

"I have worked five years in Cwm Tillery Colliery. The proprietor is Mr. Francis Adams. He does not employ a contractor, but his brother is 'gaffer' under him. There is a 'tommy shop' at Cwm Tillery, kept by one Lewis Richards. The men are compelled to deal there. We have a 'draw' once a fortnight, and a 'pay' every month. The proprietor keeps a public-house, and the men are paid there. The colliers are in the habit of drinking there. The men can have as much drink as they like, but it is always stopped out of the monthly pay. I have spent there sometimes 15s., and, once or twice, £2 of my earnings in the course of the month—that is pretty nearly all I got. I have been as much as six or seven months without receiving one penny in money. I have often been forced to sell goods I obtained at the shop, in order to pay for my clothes and other necessaries. I lived in one of the proprietors' houses, and my rent was stopped out of my earnings. It was a poor house, very much out of repair, and without conveniences for decency or drainage. I have very often heard the men complain bitterly that they could get no money—what between the shop and the public-house, they were always in debt, and there was not a shilling to be had. If a man keeps a few shillings when he has the luck to have money at the 'pay,' and spends it elsewhere, the consequence is that when he next looks for trust at the public-house, they tell him to go where he spent his ready money. The goods at the 'tommy shop' in Cwm Tillery are much dearer than in the regular shops. I have proved this on leaving the works and going to Pontypool. There is full the difference between 15s. and £1, if not more. It would be a great change for the better if we were paid in cash, because the men could then go with their money in their hands to the cheapest market."

The last workman I examined on the subject of "truck" was one who had just left the Barcella Colliery. He said—

"I am a collier, and have recently come from the Barcella Colliery; I left it last week. The proprietors are Latch, Cope and Company; the contractor's name is Thomas Thomas. There is a 'tommy shop' at which the men are bound to get their goods. When we wanted money it was very seldom we could get any—we must take goods. We had a 'draw' at the end of every month to square up our shop account; we had then to wait for the 'pay' till the second Saturday in the month, when our accounts were balanced. The shop would not let us have goods except on a Friday, because they did not know till then what would be coming to us, and were afraid we might overdraw. If we wanted cash badly at any time, and ventured to ask the master, he would give us perhaps a couple of shillings—never more. I am not a married man, but I have frequently seen men and women carry candles to sell in order to get a little ready money. I have myself had to go barefoot in the middle of the month when my shoes were worn out, because I could not obtain money to pay for repairing them. The prices of goods at the Barcella 'tommy shop' are much higher than in other shops. I believe there is as much difference on some articles as from 1½d. to 3d. a pound, particularly upon bacon."

The above is the substance of what I collected on the subject of "truck" in the iron-works and collieries of South Wales. I have laid bare a very oppressive and iniquitous system—I hope effectually— and I trust that the publication of the statements made by the sufferers will awaken public sympathy in their favour, and eventually be the means of correcting this monstrous evil. I have said that the law, as it at present stands, is inoperative, but with a slight alteration it may be made effective. This, however, is not the proper occasion for remedial suggestions; therefore I reserve them. In the meantime, I commend this matter to the attention of the honourable member for Marylebone, Sir B. Hall (himself an extensive proprietor of Welsh collieries), whose zeal and ability were very conspicuous the last time this subject was before Parliament. I have here furnished him with some startling facts, showing that a vast amount of hardship is entailed upon the helpless labourer under the present system—hardship, moreover, which the law is at present altogether unable to alleviate.

LABOUR AND THE POOR.

THE MINING AND MANUFACTURING DISTRICTS OF SOUTH WALES.

[FROM OUR SPECIAL CORRESPONDENT.]

ABERCARN AND GWYTHEN COLLIERIES.

LETTER XI.

Having heard from various quarters much in praise of the Abercarn and Gwythen Collieries, on the south-eastern border of this mineral basin, I determined to visit them. In forming this resolution I was actuated by a two-fold motive:—First, as I had described, in Mr. Crawshay's admirable forges at Cyfarthfa, a model iron-work, I thought my undertaking would be incomplete unless I also described a model colliery—if such a thing, indeed, were anywhere to be found in South Wales. Secondly, aware of the objectionable arrangements in operation at many of the large Welsh collieries (of which I noticed some of the most censurable in my last Letter), and grieved at the culpable apathy with which their proprietors too generally regard the physical and social condition of the mining population dependent upon them, I was anxious to contrast the working of a good system with that of a bad one, in order to show that, considered in every way, the master's true policy is to provide for the comfort, health, and convenience of the classes upon whose labour he has embarked his capital. The result of my inquiries in this matter will, I think, successfully refute the argument of those masters who justify the neglect of their workmen's well-being by the assertion that all social and domestic arrangements are best left to the workmen themselves, and form no part of the obligations of the master.

The Abercarn and Gwythen Collieries are situated in the narrow and picturesque valley of the Ebbw, at a point distant a few miles from the "outcrop" of the "seams," on the south-eastern border of the great Welsh coal-field. They are the property of Sir Benjamin Hall, who owns an extensive tract, comprising farm, wood, and mountain lands, everywhere underlaid with minerals in this district.

Fully alive to the enormities of "truck," and to the various other evils existing amongst the surrounding sea-coal collieries, Sir Benjamin was desirous of forming upon his property a large colliery, which might become the germ of a sounder and more humane system in this neighbourhood—an establishment where the workmen should enjoy their inalienable right of being paid, at short and regular intervals, in cash—where they might have every appliance needed for the preservation of life and health—and where their domestic comfort, their intellectual improvement, and the education of their children, should be anxiously studied and liberally provided for. This wish he has seen abundantly gratified; and it must be a most pleasing reflection to him that there exists on his property, in the centre of a district where the well-being of the workman is shamefully neglected, and where "truck" is rife, a colliery having a contented, industrious, temperate, thriving, and improving population—where, but for his exertions and those of the company to whom he has leased the collieries, there would have existed the same unhappiness, discontent, embarrassment, dependence, and slavery, which I have already described as disgracing the neighbouring coal-works.

The ride from Newport to Abercarn lies through varied and interesting scenery. The distance is eleven miles. At first the ascent is steep for about a mile. Arrived at the summit of the hill, if you look back, a grand panoramic prospect lies outspread before you. In front, at the extreme distance, rise the bold and wavy outlines of the Mendips; stretching down to the distant horizon on the right are the diminishing undulations of the Quantock hills. On the left, in swelling masses, are the heights of the Forest of Dean; and still further eastward the Graig and Blorenge, at the extremity of that magnificent chain, "the Black Mountains." Running across the picture, and separating the Somersetshire from the Monmouthshire coast, lies the Bristol Channel, expanding westward in its course, and seeming to mingle with the sky beyond the rocky islands called "The Flat and Steep Holmes." Numerous vessels, of every size and denomination, bound for various destinations, up, down, and across the Channel, impart life and interest to the sea-view. Two lines of these are distinctly traceable; one stretching from the mouth of the Bristol, the other from that of the Newport river. Still nearer the foreground is a fine breadth of cultivated land and salt-marsh, through which winds lazily the yellow Usk; while at the foot of the hill stands the busy, wealthy, and rapidly-extending town of Newport, with its docks and forest of shipping, its canals, railways, bridges, and churches, and its handsome streets stretching far upwards towards the point at which you stand. In the year 1791 Newport was a mere village, containing only 750 persons, and having an insignificant trade in coal (it amounted to just 6,939 tons), carried on by means of mules. The following year saw the opening of the Monmouthshire Canal, by which the minerals could be conveyed in any quantity, with speed and facility, from the collieries to the wharfs for exportation; and from that time the town dates its prosperity. Passing over the several causes which, in the interval between that and the present year, have contributed to increase the trade of Newport, I will content myself in this place, for brevity's sake, with remarking that the population now numbers some 20,000, and that the quantity of coal sent coast-wise and exported in the year 1848, as shown by a Parliamentary return, is not less than 554,102 tons.

Resuming our journey to Abercarn, after passing through the strictly preserved estate of Sir Charles Morgan, and crossing a bleak but well-cultivated tract of land, we enter upon the valley through which flows the swift-rushing and noisy Ebbw. The hill sides are precipitous, and, for the most part, agreeably clothed with wood. In the flat besides the river are some watery meadows, interspersed here and there with alders. Following the devious road along the bank of the river, you soon enter upon the coal-field. Its boundary is recognizable by a cliff of the red sand-stone (which material always underlies the mineral) appearing through an oak wood on the right hand. The evidences of an extensive traffic are now visible on all sides. Long trains of trams, dragged by powerful locomotives, pass downwards, laden with coal—or upwards, to be refilled at the collieries—in rapid and frequent succession. The trade on the canal, though less noisy and less active, goes steadily forward, and claims its share of attention. Presently you pass some tin-works, and, I believe, some chemical works; after which the road leads *under* a viaduct of many arches, extending across the valley and the river, the beauty of which reminds the spectator of the noble aqueducts of Italy, one of which, as I have been informed, served as its model. The extensive collieries of Mr. Russell are now seen occupying a favourable position on the left bank of the Ebbw. Yet a few miles further, through larch groves and amidst beautiful scenery—and the place of our destination is attained.

Here I met Mr. Ebenezer Rogers, the resident director of the company who work these collieries. He obligingly conducted me over the works and through the residences of the men. To this gentleman belongs the praise due to the complete and admirable arrangements everywhere visible throughout this extensive concern. Possessing a mind enlarged by liberal views, and animated with a fervent desire to improve the condition of the labourer—a task for which the experiences of travel through the various mineral districts of the Continent and America, with the purpose of studying their several characteristics, eminently fitted him—this gentleman has founded in Abercarn a happy, industrious, and prosperous colony. The wisdom of confiding the management of an undertaking of this magnitude to such a man, and of supplying him with ample means for carrying out his ideas, has been proved by the fact that the company, after several years' trial, have been very successful. Indeed, I may say here, that, complete and liberal as are the provisions made for the well-being of the workmen and their families at these collieries, they have never entrenched upon, nor in the slightest degree endangered, the legitimate profits of capital. So far, indeed, from this having been the case, the balance, I was assured, is in favour of capital. And I can well believe that uniformly steady conduct on the part of the men, which at these collieries can with certainty be calculated upon, together with superior intelligence—a result ensured by their training here—would give the proprietors an advantage over others, having a discontented, mutinous, and dissolute set of men in their employ, more especially at seasons when a sudden and extraordinary demand for coal exists at the shipping ports—a circumstance of not unfrequent occurrence.

The collieries stand on the right and left-hand of the road on the south-side of Abercarn. The pit to the right is on the Mynyddysllwyn or "red ash" measures, and is worked at a depth of seventy yards; that to the left works the iron-stone vein in the "white ash" measures. The former yields bituminous coal for household purposes and the distillation of gas—the latter a strong and enduring coal, which gives out an intense heat, and is largely used for steam purposes. Its superiority has been officially acknowledged by its free adoption in her Majesty's steam navy.

The first circumstance which struck me at these collieries was the total absence of the noise and bustle usually characteristic of such establishments. At each colliery I entered the house in which work the powerful engines which raise the coal and pump the water from the pits. The ponderous machinery (entirely designed and erected by Mr. Rogers) was in the finest condition imaginable; it worked with-

out the slightest perceptible jar or vibration, and with all that delicate precision and gracefulness of motion which are indicative of the
most perfect design and faultless workmanship. The arrangements
for the prevention of accidents at the mouth of the pits were new
to me; they seemed quite effective for this purpose. The organization
of duties and the subdivision of labour are here so judicious that from
four to five hundred tons of coal are sometimes raised daily, without
hurry, noise, or confusion. All goes on quietly, orderly, yet vigorously.
From the collieries the trains, as they leave the pits, pass to an inclined plane, which they descend; and, by means of machinery at the
lower end, they deposit their stores of coal unbroken on the wharf,
whence a single motion places them on the rail for Newport. I visited
the counting-houses, the carpentery and smithery, and the "turning
and model house," where every provision had been made for execut-
ing work soundly and with celerity. Lastly, I visited the "head-office,"
where I found engineers engaged upon designs for machinery, and in
mapping the underground excavations. Beautiful sectional diagrams
of the strata, and costly maps, showing with geometrical accuracy the
true lines and bearing of every horse-way, cross-heading, stall, and
waste in the workings below, were unrolled and spread out before
me. Scattered around, in various directions, were curious specimens
of fossil plants, impressed upon the shale of the coal-measures, and
here collected for scientific purposes.

On leaving, I could not forbear expressing my gratification at the
very complete arrangements I had witnessed—acknowledging that,
of the various collieries I had visited in the course of this inquiry, I
had seen none to compare with those of the Abercarn and Gwythen
Company.

We next proceeded to the workmen's houses, which for the most
part, if not indeed entirely, were built by the company, and remain
their property. Mr. Rogers's first care on commencing this new
town—for such it is—was to provide an effective deep sewerage, for
which the elevated situation of the ground afforded acceptable facilities. This done, the houses were erected. They are two stories high,
consist of four rooms, and stand in double rows, having a wide street,
properly drained, between them. They have privies and receptacles
for house-refuse; and each is furnished with a coal-bunker, where the
week's supply is regularly delivered and stowed away. On entering
the houses I found the rooms lofty, with ceilings, and having, below
stairs, floors of flag-stone and convenient fireplaces. The windows

were all furnished with ventilators. I found the houses extremely clean, and in most cases orderly; and on complimenting a woman for these virtues, she replied, "Ay, sir, there is some encouragement for work in such houses as these; they almost keep themselves clean, the floors are so good." Coal ashes and rubbish are removed daily, at the expense of the company. I observed in these houses the same disposition on the part of their inhabitants to accumulate showy and good furniture, which I have described as existing amongst the workmen in the iron-works at Merthyr. The houses were literally crammed with furniture, and the walls were bedecked with a profusion of coloured prints and lithographs. From the houses, I went to the public "bakehouse," where I found a number of women making up their dough for the oven. This bakehouse is provided for the use of the workmen's families, free of charge, the company finding attendants, fuel, and every requisite. I was next led to a range of very convenient public baths and wash-houses, also provided gratuitously by the company for the use of their dependants. Public urinals and privies for the general accommodation of the town are also built and kept in order at the expense of the company.

With sanitary arrangements so complete, the reader will not be surprised to learn that the cholera, though it ravaged collieries on all sides, found no resting place in Abercarn. I believe not a single case occurred in the neighbourhood.

Having thus described the very complete arrangements generously and humanely provided for the health, comfort, and convenience of the working classes at Abercarn, I have next to specify the opportunities for intellectual gratification and improvement which the wisdom of their employers has laid open to them. And first I must notice the "Abercarn Scientific Institution." On referring to a description of the objects of the institution, the statistics of attendance, and the nature of the books mostly used by the workmen—obligingly furnished me by Mr. Jonathan Rogers, a gentleman who has taken a lively interest in everything conducing to the happiness and improvement of the population of Abercarn—I find these so clearly set forth that I transcribe his communication verbatim.

"THE ABERCARN SCIENTIFIC INSTITUTION.

"This institution was established for the purpose of affording opportunity and means for the acquirement of rudimentary learning to the working population of Abercarn, whose early education has in many instances been wholly neglected; and also to supply sources of intellectual enjoyment to those who, having had greater advantages, have made proportionally greater progress in the acquisition of knowledge.

"In connection with the institution there is a Reading-room, open from seven to half-past nine o'clock every evening, and supplied with books of an entertaining and instructive character. Two daily and eight weekly metropolitan and provincial newspapers, seven periodicals, including *Chambers' Journal, Hogg's Instructor, Seren Gomer,* (Welsh), *Bentley's Miscellany,* the *Edinburgh, Westminster, Foreign Quarterly,* and *Eclectic Reviews,* are taken in. The average attendance of members numbers from thirty to forty.

"Classes are held on five evenings in each week for the instruction of the members in reading, writing, arithmetic, grammar, geography, mechanical drawing, and chess. The average attendance of the classes is from five to twenty.

"Lectures are delivered monthly on interesting subjects, to which all members have free admission. As a general rule, the lectures are delivered in as plain and simple a manner as possible, in order to place the subject within the comprehension of every listener. The average attendance is from 150 to 350.

"An Essay and Debating Society meet twice in each month. This branch of the institution is kept up with much spirit, and forms a powerful focus of attraction. It has been carefully inculcated among the members, that the object of such a society is not to cultivate a taste for disputation or wrangling, but to promote a spirit of research, and stimulate inquiry after truth; to enable them to classify their ideas and express them fluently; and, lastly, to lead them to the acquisition of knowledge through industry and emulation. The establishment of such a society would probably be dangerous and imprudent among the working classes in England; but the Welsh are essentially a reasoning people, great essay writers, poets, and cultivators of Bardism in all its forms.

"The business of the institution is conducted by a committee of management, the greater part of whom are elected from among the more intelligent of the workmen or mechanics residing in Abercarn.

"The number of members is at present 112, and it is rapidly augmenting. More than three-fourths of the members are adults. The rate of subscription is 1s. 6d. per quarter. With the funds thus arising, aided by subscriptions of honorary members, and donations already promised, the committee confidently expect that before the end of the present year they will be enabled to make such additions to the library as will justify them in allowing the books to be circulated at home among the members of the institution.

"The reading-room is given, free of rent, by the Abercarn Colliery Company.

"As an institution professedly and *really* devoted to the improvement of the working classes, I believe this is a new feature of educational development in this part of the country. The neighbouring Mechanics' Institutes exist only in towns of considerable population, and in every instance are attended, not by mechanics and labourers, as would be inferred from the name, but by clerks, shopmen, and others who have already made material progress in the rudimentary branches of learning."

At night I visited the reading room of the institution. The curate of the parish, a proprietor of some neighbouring tin works, and Mr. Jonathan Rogers, formed the visiting attendants on duty. I there saw some fifty workmen, well-dressed, clean, and orderly; some amusing themselves after the day's labour with the recreation of reading, and others practising writing. I examined the copybook of one of these adult scholars. The man informed me with a smile of pride, on my praising his performance, that he was 43 years of age, and had learnt to write in the institution. On looking at the titles of the works then in request, I found one man reading a "history of India," another a book of voyages and travels, and the third a magazine.

When I saw this, and remembered a remark before made to me that Mr. Rogers exercised a discrimination in his choice of workmen, giving character its due preference (which, I am sorry to say, is not generally so much considered as it should be by masters in the collieries and iron works), I ceased to wonder at the paucity of public-houses, in proportion to inhabitants, which I had noticed in Abercarn. That craving after excitement which forms an element of the human mind, and which must be satisfied, I here found ministered to in a manner at once harmless and elevating, while the family at home were absolutely benefited by such a disposal of the workman's leisure; for the man who reads good books can hardly fail to become gentler and kinder, a good husband, and a good father. If any one should object that these arrangements are not enduring—that they charm chiefly by their novelty, and are insufficient to fix permanently the liking of the workman (as I have heard some contend), the answer is, that though the system has now been in operation a long time, there is no falling off in the attendance, nor in the interest expressed by the members. The reverse is rather the case. No doubt the variety of the lectures, debates, new books, and concerts (for they have these also) which are from time to time provided, tends in no inconsiderable degree to keep alive interest, and to divert men from sensual and degrading indulgences; and, for judiciously studying their alternation of amusements, great praise is due to Mr. Jonathan Rogers and the other managing visitors, who have never allowed the succession of these intellectual exercises to suffer interruption, or even to flag.

I next visited and inspected the schools. The company's school is held in rather a small, but a thoroughly ventilated room, well furnished with maps, diagrams, and all the needful appliances for scholastic discipline. Both sexes were gathered in the same room, the girls occupying the desks and forms nearest the master. I understand that better school accommodation is in preparation. I found all the children neatly dressed, clean, and well behaved. Like most Welsh children, they had fine open and intelligent countenances. The master (Mr. Jones) appeared proud of his charge, and spoke highly of their capacity for learning. The system followed is that of the Welsh normal school, with some slight alterations which the experience of the master has suggested. The number of children on the books is 65, but the attendance when I called was 45; this decrease was accounted for on the ground of the inclemency of the weather. The boys were called into class, and exercised on mental arithmetic; they astonished me by the quickness and accuracy of their calculations. The entire school then sung the "Multiplication" table, and the "Addition of Money" table, in verse; after this they were marched round the school-room, and practised in exercises of the hands and arms. Two girls then sang for me "The Death of Llewellyn," in Welsh; this was followed by the beautiful song, "Hedyddlon;" and the "National Anthem" closed this pleasing exhibition of the school-room.

But, thanks to the beneficence of Lady Hall, the above is not the only educational establishment in Abercarn. Her ladyship has established a school in which 40 children of poor Welsh parents are received as free scholars, and provided with a sound and useful education. When I inspected this school there were 80 children upon the books. The average attendance was 60. The system adopted is one devised by her ladyship, and comes nearer, perhaps, to "Chambers' Educational Course" than any other. Children come from a considerable distance in the surrounding country to enjoy the benefits of this school; and in my subsequent excursion through some neighbouring farms to inquire into the state of the agricultural labourers, I heard in more than one place grateful allusion made to her ladyship for her beneficence and liberality in establishing and supporting this school. Those children who are not on the free list pay from 2d. to 6d. a week, according to their age and position. No distinction whatever is made between the free scholars and those who pay. The Welsh and English languages are both taught. The children learn reading, writing, arithmetic, grammar, singing, and the rudiments of geography. I was particularly struck with the specimens of writing which the master pointed out to me as the result of the day's lesson.

As late as eight in the evening I visited the singing class, where I found a large number of young people, including several married men and their wives, practising chorus singing. They were all neatly dressed, and seemed to enjoy themselves very heartily. They were led by an elderly miner, who had a fair knowledge of music; he gave the time, whenever a change was marked, with great emphasis and accuracy, and conducted with confidence and spirit. The class sang for me Spofforth's animated old glee, "Hail Smiling Morn," Webbe's "Glorious Apollo," and one or two others. After this I was gratified with an example of Welsh Penillion singing, with the substitution of a violin for a harp—which latter instrument was not at command. It was in Welsh, and took the form of dialogue, the contention being between a young girl and a middle-aged bachelor—the former advocating matrimony and decrying the single life, while the latter defended celibacy and attacked the married state. As may be supposed, the lady came off victorious, and the gentleman was too happy to be convinced by the united force of beauty and wit. Preparations were in progress that evening for a public concert, which was to take place in a fortnight's time.

The following day I descended into the pits, where I saw and questioned the men at their work. This appears to be the proper place to state the arrangements existing between the employers and the workmen in these collieries. In a former letter on the "Strike at Aberdare," I alluded with censure to the loose, unsatisfactory, and informal contracts made between these parties in many of the sea coal collieries of South Wales. That objection does not apply to these works. Here everything is rendered clear and definite. The workman before he enters the pit has delivered to him a printed form of the contract he makes, and the rules he must abide by. The competition that exists on all sides to obtain employment in these collieries forms the best evidence of the high estimation in which all the arrangements made by this company are regarded by the working classes in the neighbourhood. A "draw," or payment in cash, is made to the workmen every Friday evening, so that their wives may go money in hand to market on Saturday; and at the end of every month a statement of his account, with any balance that may be due upon it, is handed to each workman. Each man is required to contribute at the rate of sixpence in the pound of his earnings to the "works fund"—of which one-half is applied to the payment of the doctor of the works, for attendance during the illness of such workman or any member of his family, and the other half is used as a "relief fund" for his support during accident or illness. The works fund is managed by a committee of workmen elected from the general body. A number of visiting inspectors, consisting also of workmen, are appointed, whose duty it is to see that the relief-fund is properly distributed, and that none but such as are incapable shall receive its benefits. A long printed list of the rules and regulations for the management of the workmen's sick fund now lies before me. They have evidently been maturely considered, and they have proved most efficacious in practice. I extract the rule limiting the scale of relief:—

"8. Every workman who from sickness or injury received on the works is incapacitated from following his usual employment, shall, upon his handing in to the visiting inspectors the surgeon's certificate of such incapacity, and making application in accordance with these rules, receive from the fund a weekly allowance as specified in the following scale:—

When the Balance in the hands of the Treasurer shall amount to	1st. Men on full Wages.	2d. Boys under 18 years of age.	3d. Boys under 14 years of age.
£10 and not exceed £30	6s. 0d.	... 3s. 0d.	... 1s. 6d.
30 and not exceed 60	8s. 0d.	... 4s. 0d.	... 2s. 0d.
60 and not exceed 100	10s. 0d.	... 5s. 0d.	... 2s. 6d.
100 and upwards	12s. 0d.	... 6s. 0d.	... 3s. 0d.

If any workman shall be killed or receive injuries which may cause his death during the pursuance of his proper occupation on the works, it shall be in the power of a majority of the workmen, at a meeting regularly convened, to direct such sum as they may deem expedient, not exceeding 5*l.*, to be paid over to the widow or nearest relative of such workman, to assist in defraying the expenses of his funeral."

This system of self-government, in the instance of the doctor's and sick fund, has been found, according to the statement of Mr. Rogers, to work most beneficially. It at once flatters and gratifies the work-man to have the control of a fund, created compulsorily from his own labour, which in other places is administered by strangers. I have shown that in the iron works no account is rendered of the expenditure of this fund; a circumstance which affords an opportunity for ill-natured remarks, though there can be no doubt that, in those places, the whole proceeds are honestly expended. Here the men have the distribution of the entire fund; a fixed amount is set apart for the doctor, and the remainder is watched over with the most jealous care—so that skulkers and idlers have not here the chance of living, as they do in places where no such wholesome supervision exists, at the expense of the honest and industrious labourer.

I thought it well to take down the statement of the circumstances surrounding and affecting the workmen, from the lips of individuals of their number. I transcribe them as follows:—

William Jenkins: "I am, as you see, a collier. I have worked under the Abercarn and Gwythen Company nearly four years. There is no contractor here, neither is there a public-house or shop in any way connected with the company. We are paid weekly on Friday night, so that our wives may go to market on Saturday. There are no stoppages out of our wages, except for doctor, sick-fund, and tools. A committee of workmen manage the sick-fund; they meet monthly, and by care have saved a considerable sum of money. I live in a house of the company's; it has four rooms, is well drained and provided with a privy. The rooms are light, lofty, and well ventilated. I pay 8s. a month rent, and the company pays the taxes. My family use the public bakehouse. My children go to the school, where I pay for each 2d. a week. Where a man has a large family, and cannot afford to pay for education, his children are admitted free. I am a member of the Mechanics' Institution, and frequent the library daily. There are singing and writing classes, also classes for mechanical drawing, at the institution. I learnt to read and write there, though I was thirty-two years old when I began. The men are very proud of their institution. I often hear them bragging of it to strangers. I was in these works when they were carried on by the Victoria Company, who kept here a 'tommy shop.' At that time I had no money for months together. There is a happy change now. The men are contented and comfortable, and their families see the difference between some other works and these."

Thomas Kenver. (This man chiefly corroborated the statements made by Jenkins, but spoke to the state of the underground workings.) "The underground workings are, as you have seen, very roomy, safe, and well ventilated. I have worked here four years without the slightest accident. The roof in the White Ash Pit is not naturally good, but with the precautions taken by the company, it is rendered as safe as the roof of the other pit."

The first pit I descended was the "Rock Vein Pit," which has a depth of 210 feet. The "red ash" coal is there raised. I traversed the workings, which are very extensive, throughout. They were spacious, dry, and thoroughly ventilated. So clear and direct is the drift way for the passage of air through the workings from the downcast to the upcast shaft, that all necessity for artificial ventilation is unnecessary. The pit effectually purifies itself by natural means. The heat of the mine, by rarefying the air, causes a smart current of dense and cold air to enter the pit by the downcast shaft. This action, once set up, continues, and is abundantly sufficient in pits where no interruption to the flow of this ventilating current takes place, nor any *break in the circuit*. In this pit I recognised the leader of a singing-class I had visited overnight, cutting a horse-way. He expressed himself thoroughly happy in his employment, and thankful for the benefits the company had conferred on the entire body of workmen in their employ. I found these sentiments everywhere prevalent where I made inquiry. In this pit I was gratified by an inspection of the rich fossil Flora of the Mynyddyslwyn coal measures. Everywhere impressed upon the shale, with wonderful distinctness and minuteness, were splendid specimens of the vegetation of a former world. These have a brilliant jet-black surface, and, relieved by the dull slate-coloured rock upon which they are flattened, they form extremely interesting objects for examination. Gigantic ferns, and broad-leafed waterflags, lepidodendra, with their curious bamboo joints, stigmaria, calamites, and a host of the tribe juncaceæ, were visible upon the roof of the mine in every direction. I saw also, in three or four places, what the miners term "bells." These are fossil-trees, resting with their roots upon the coal, the stems remaining upright, as they grew, and encased in rock. The bark, in every instance, has been converted into coal, while the heart of the tree, by the mysterious process of fossilization, has changed to stone. These trees run from a foot to eighteen inches at the base. The lower part of the trunk being something wider than the upper, and the connection with the surrounding rock cut off by the thin layer of coal which occupies the place of bark, these trees often slip down into horseways or cross-headings, and serious injury has occurred to men and animals by coming into contact with them in the darkness of the mine. To lessen the probability of these accidents, the miners, when they find such a tree, generally cut away the base as far as they can reach with their "picks," which gives the hollow thus made in the roof the appearance of the inside of a bell—hence, I presume, the name.

I then descended the "White Ash" steam coal-pit, where I found the same perfect arrangements for the protection of life and health, and heard the same expressions of satisfaction, and thankfulness on the part of the workmen, as in the workings I had just left. The depth of the pit is 420 feet. I must not omit to notice a plan here adopted for steadying the descent of the cage, which I believe is peculiar to these works (I have not seen it elsewhere), and which may be adopted in other collieries with the best effect. Instead of the hempen or wire rope usually employed, they use here a line of railway irons laid vertically, and pinned securely to the bratticing and side of the shaft; a proper shaped groove in the cage, which is kept well greased, traverses the rail, and the effect is to impart greater smoothness and steadiness than are obtainable by the old-fashioned system.

Here I close my notice of the Abercarn and Gwythen collieries. I have called these works "a model colliery," and I hope the reader will approve the title. Certainly if he had seen, as I have, the lamentable neglect of the happiness, comfort, and well-being of the workmen and their families which is evinced in too many of the Welsh collieries, he would agree with me that a lesson may profitably be taken by their proprietors from these works.

It will be, perhaps, remembered that, in the absence of returns of the number of tons of coal annually shipped and exported from the ports in the British Channel west of Cardiff, I estimated the whole export trade of the Welsh ports at 2,000,000 tons a year. Since then I have found means for making an accurate table of the quantity of coals sent coastwise and exported abroad, and of the "declared value" of the exports, as made at the Custom-houses. I had very little over-estimated the shipping coal-trade, as will appear by the subjoined tables—the difference between my estimate and the actual trade being only 35,874, in a calculation of 2,000,000 tons:—

WELSH COALS, BRISTOL CHANNEL PORTS, 1847.

Coastwise.	Tons.
Cardiff	432,726
Newport	436,099
Swansea	373,307
Llanelly	204,391
Milford	52,713
	1,499,236

Exported Abroad.

	Tons.	Declared Value.
Cardiff	81,032	£41,137
Newport	116,098	57,683
Swansea	46,715	19,529
Llanelly	14,178	5,585
Milford	439	243
Total	258,462	£124,177

WELSH COALS, 1847.

	Tons.
Sent Coastwise	1,499,236
Exported Abroad	258,462
Total	1,757,698

1848.

Coastwise.	Tons.
Cardiff	546,961
Newport	429,217
Swansea	392,371
Llanelly	239,886
Milford	55,502
	1,663,937

Exported Abroad.

	Tons.	Declared Value.
Cardiff	117,674	£58,444
Newport	124,885	62,323
Swansea	42,114	18,013
Llanelly	15,251	6,372
Milford	265	245
Total Tons exported	300,189	£145,397

WELSH COALS, 1848.

	Tons.
Sent Coastwise	1,663,937
Exported Abroad	300,189
Total	1,964,126

	Tons.	Declared Value.
Total of 1848	1,964,126	£145,397
Ditto 1847	1,757,698	124,177
Increase of the trade ending in the year 1848	206,428	£21,220

LABOUR AND THE POOR.

—◆—

THE MINING AND MANUFACTURING DISTRICTS OF SOUTH WALES.

[FROM OUR SPECIAL CORRESPONDENT.]

SWANSEA AND THE COPPER-WORKS.

LETTER XII.

From Merthyr I came to Swansea, which is a flourishing, populous, and increasing town, situated at the mouth of the river "Tawey," on the north coast of the Bristol Channel. Swansea, it appears, was at a very early period a place of some importance. From allusions made in existing Welsh poems to persons who lived, and events which happened, as verified by history, in the eleventh and twelfth centuries, it is certain there was a stronghold here before the erection of the castle (whose blackened towers and mouldering walls still overlook the town), in or about the year 1113, by Henry de Beaumont, the conqueror of Gower. It was created a borough by charter, in the reign of King John, and, being walled and fortified, was the subject of frequent contention between the Royalists and Roundheads, in the civil wars, when it was taken and retaken several times. Ultimately, it fell into the hands of the Parliamentary army, and its fidelity to the cause of Charles does not appear to have been regarded vindictively; for Cromwell, who marched here in 1648, conferred a second charter upon the inhabitants.

But it was not until the extent and value of the South Wales coalfield came to be known and appreciated that Swansea began to enlarge and to show evidences of enduring prosperity. It is remarkable that the development of those branches of manufacturing industry in South Wales which depend upon coals took place nearly simultaneously in the early part of last century. Until that period there were no iron-works of any consequence existing in South Wales, and copper-works were entirely unknown; since then, both trades have advanced *pari passu*. The insignificance of the trade of Swansea about that time, and the prejudices of its inhabitants, are so well described in a small pamphlet, called "A Description of Swansea," published some thirty years ago, that I give place to the paragraph here:—

> "The state of Swansea about 100 (now 130) years ago may be easily conceived by the following anecdote:—At that period coal in bags of no more than two Winchester bushels was conveyed from the pits to the shipping wharfs *on horseback*—a practice so dilatory and injurious that Robert Morris, Esq., father of the late Sir John Morris, determined upon the use of waggons, which had no sooner made their appearance in the streets of Swansea than the inhabitants, *one and all*, determined to indict these cumbrous machines as a nuisance, declaring that their rumbling noise and agitating motion caused the beer to turn sour in their cellars, and it required no small address to persuade them to the contrary."

When attention first began to be directed in this country to the smelting and manufacture of copper, it became a consideration with the adventurers who embarked in the trade to ascertain where it might be carried on at the lowest cost, and with the greatest advantage to themselves. A sketch of the history of the copper-trade will show the endeavours that were made to discover such a locality, and the reasons why this place was fixed upon as the most favourable for the purpose. That the arts of mining and manufacturing copper were practised in Britain by the Romans, there can be no reasonable doubt. Antiquarians have agreed in assigning to that people some ancient workings discovered in Anglesea, and (with less certainty) in Cumberland. Indeed, miners and mines were held in high esteem by that sagacious and thrifty people; and it was the policy of the civil law to confer upon them many privileges and immunities—it being alleged, as a justification for these preferences, that miners were a very useful body to the commonwealth. The abundance of brass remains which have survived in this island to our own times, in their domestic implements and utensils, and in their coinage, testify to the fact that they had large stores of copper somewhere at command; and since, previously to the tenth century, we have no record of copper being worked nearer than Rammelsberg, in Lower Saxony, it is fair to assume that, as the metal existed in abundance in this country, and as the Romans here largely used it, they obtained their supplies in England, and not from abroad. "It is supposed," says Mr. Watson, in an interesting paper on Ancient Mining, contributed to the Mining Almanac, "that copper was first found in Britain during its occupation by the Romans, brass-foundries having been erected by them in various parts of Britain, where their weapons of war and other articles were made. Ignorant of regular mining, and without the means of exploring far beneath the surface, the Pary's Mine in Anglesea is generally believed to be that from which the Romans derived their ore; and this supposition is strengthened by the fact that, *among the vestiges of ancient mining*, one of the mountains is termed 'the Roman Work.' The labour consisted in quarrying huge masses of ore which rose to the surface of the ground on the summit of a hill, and, for a prodigious extent, exposed to the glare of day." I may here, in passing, throw out a hint to any reader of *The Morning Chronicle* residing near Ross, in Herefordshire, that, according to Fosbrooke (vide *Ariconensia*) and other distinguished antiquaries, Bollatree, near that town, was the *Birmingham* of the Romans. He may very probably be able to settle this question, by searching the heaps of slag that still remain there, for traces of copper, which, if the metal was smelted in that place, will no doubt be found.

It is on record that copper was mined in Cumberland in the thirteenth century. It appears, by the "Close Rolls" of Henry III., that some rich veins of ore were worked about the year 1250, at Newlands, near Keswick, in that county. Speaking of those copper works, Camden says that "they were not only sufficient for all England, *but large quantities of copper were exported every year.*" Indeed Cumberland, for two centuries and a half at least, was the principal if not the only seat of the English copper trade; this we learn from the Rolls above alluded to, and from a charter granted by Edward IV., about 1470, to the town of Keswick, which recites that the town was then famous for copper-works. Long subsequently to this there appear to have been apprehensions entertained that the mines would become exhausted. "In the reigns of Henry VIII. and Edward VI.," says Watson, "we find several acts of Parliament were passed, prohibiting the exportation of brass, copper, bell and gun metal, under penalties; the reason given being, 'lest there should not be metal enough left in the kingdom for making of guns and other engines of war, nor for household utensils.'" Probably our county histories, if diligently searched, would add some valuable facts to the scanty stock of mining history already collected. Dr. Plot, in his History of Staffordshire, published in 1686, states that long before his time copper was worked at Ecton-hill, in that county, where the ore was found near the surface in great abundance. It is stated by Cliffe, in his "Book of South Wales"—on what authority I know not—that the art of making copper was lost in this country for a long period, but he does not say when. Probably he followed the compiler of the "Swansea Guide," who says that it was lost from the time of Queen Elizabeth to the year 1670. But we have already seen that it was worked in Staffordshire in 1686 and long previously, and it was obtained in such abundance in the reign of Elizabeth, that the supplies of ore, on which the art depended, could hardly have been exhausted at her death. This Queen took the rich copper mines of Keswick from their then holder, the Duke of Northumberland; and, as Fuller, in his "Worthies," &c., remarks, "By taking these rich mines from the duke, it came to pass that the Queen left more brass than she found iron ordnance in the kingdom." This statement shows that the copper trade must have flourished to some extent in the reign of Elizabeth.

But although at the present day the quantity of British ores annually sold in Cornwall, as compared with that sold in Swansea, bears the proportion of 860,228 against 68,268 tons, and although from Cornwall the largest supply of ore is obtained, the prodigious stores of the metal which existed in that county were overlooked or neglected down to the 17th century. That much of the ore was thrown aside amongst the rubbish from the tin mines, so late as 1735, is certain; for in that year, according to Dr. Paris, "one Mr. Coster, a mineralogist from Bristol, who then visited the tin-mines, observed a quantity of ore, which the miners called *Poder*, lying amongst the heaps of rubbish around the tin-mines, and he formed the design of converting it to his advantage; he accordingly entered into a contract to purchase as much of it as could be supplied. The scheme succeeded, and Coster long continued to profit by Cornish ignorance." A like discovery, and a productive one, took place as late as 1846. "Copper," says Cliffe, "generally occurs at a much greater depth than tin; and the first Cornish miner, in the latter half of the seventeenth century, who discovered it, abandoned the mine, because he fancied that it '*spoilt the tin*'—an expression long used."

The honour of being the first person who turned the Cornish copper mines to productive account belongs to a Sir Clement Clarke, who, about the year 1670, built some furnaces in Cornwall; but the price of coal, which had to be carried from Wales, and which was augmented by the cost of transport to the water and by the want of accommodation for shipping on the Welsh coast, was so high, that he could not carry on the works profitably in Cornwall; he therefore removed them to Clifton, where he had coal in abundance from the Bristol coal-field. But Sir Clement eventually failed; whereupon his manager, Mr. Wayne, and the before-mentioned Mr. Coster, embarked in the trade on their own account. The former, in partnership with Sir Abraham Elton, erected works at Screws-hole, near Bristol, where they soon realized a profit of £60,000; and Mr. Coster erected his works at Redbrook, on the river Wye, where, notwithstanding the fact that the situation was not favourable, being on a shallow river far above tides-way, yet, owing to his good luck in the above related purchase of neglected *poder*, he also accumulated a fortune. We have seen that copper-smelting could not be successfully carried on in Cornwall, because of the dearness of coal. As it would not pay to carry coal to the copper, the question naturally arose, would it pay to carry the copper to the coal? Even before the general use of steam engines in Cornwall, this last plan was found to succeed. Since the adoption of steam-power for pumping the mines, the change has been found even more profitable than it had been previously, because now the shippers have the advantage of *back-freight*, which they had not before; they carry the ores from Cornwall to Wales for smelting, and convey on their return coals to Cornwall for the use of the engines which pump the mines. Three great advantages, united in Swansea, seemed to point to this place as the locality best fitted for copper works on the Welsh coast. First, it offered a cheap and abundant supply of coal raised literally at the water's edge; secondly, it possessed a sheltered and secure roadstead for vessels; lastly, it had the advantage of proximity to the mines of Cornwall, which lessened the expense of carriage to and fro. Eventually these circumstances secured for this town a preference over all other places for the establishment of copper works.

In the year 1700, a Mr. Turner erected a copper-smelting work near Neath Abbey, distant from here about eight miles. This was the first established in South Wales. Shortly afterwards Sir Humphrey Mackworth, with a company called "The Mine Adventurers," built smelting-houses at Melyngry-ddon, Neath. About the year 1719, a Mr. Pollard (the owner of considerable copper mines in Cornwall), in partnership with a Dr. Lane, erected works near where the Cambrian Pottery now stands above this town. At the bursting of the "South-Sea Bubble," Pollard failed, and the works were purchased by Messrs. Lockwood, Gibbon, and Morris, by whom, and their representatives, the copper trade was here carried on in conjunction with extensive collieries, for nearly a century. I may, in passing, observe that this Mr. Gibbon was the grandfather of the historian of "The Decline and

Redbrook

Fall," &c. The Landore Works (now the property of Messrs. Williams, Foster, and Company) were next erected; and at various intervals, as this branch of productive industry progressed, and called for increased accommodation, the several works which are now in operation here were established.

In this manner, during the course of a century, the copper works sprung up in Swansea. The effect produced here by this location of the copper trade was equally striking and beneficial. From being an insignificant town, lying between verdant hills, near the mouth of the river, with only two prominent objects to vary its outline—a massive church tower, and an old Norman castle—and having only small trade in coal, carried on by smacks and sloops, with the opposite coast— Swansea enlarged tenfold. Extensive piers were built, enclosing a capacious harbour; ships, barques, and other vessels of heavy burden, trading with the most distant parts of the globe, thronged the river; commodious quays and lines of lofty warehouses were constructed, which became the scene of active enterprise and thriving business. Instead of the long trains of mules, laden with sacks of coal, which formerly were seen winding their way, with something of Spanish picturesqueness, along the slopes of the adjacent mountains, down to the crazy shipping stages at the water's edge, canals were cut, and rail and tram-roads were opened, to the sources of all this prosperity— the coal-pits and works up the valley of the Tawey. Internally, the change was no less remarkable. New churches and chapels, a spacious market-house with a lofty and prominent tower, a Philosophical Institution, and spacious law courts—all having greater or less architectural pretensions—were built; and the town, stretching away from the river along the foot of the mountain, parallel to the bay, presented a new face of elegant villas to those who approached it by the sea.

The increase of population during the present century has been six-fold—itself a conclusive proof of the thriving condition of the town. The population and house returns were:—

1801	Males and Females	6,420	... Inhabited Houses	1,182
1811	Ditto	8,515	Ditto	1,591
1821	Ditto	10,669	Ditto	2,049
1831	Ditto	14,253	Ditto	2,582
1841	Ditto	20,152	Ditto	3,166

At present the population, inclusive of the district of the copper-works, is calculated at about 40,000.

The increase in the shipping trade, relative to which the returns are conflicting, has been also very great. The best statement I have been enabled to extract is as follows:—

VESSELS TRADING WITH THE PORT OF SWANSEA.
In 1768	Inwards	694
In 1819	Do.	1,652
In 1830	Do.	2,277
In 1840	Do.	2,728
In 1845	Do.	4,569

I take the following particulars of the foreign trade with Swansea from Cliffe's "Book of South Wales":

"The foreign trade, which has chiefly arisen since 1827, when the first cargo of foreign copper was brought here, has advanced very rapidly. The number of ships trading to foreign ports in the year 1814 was only four; in 1834 it was 46; in 1840, 328; in 1844 it amounted, inwards, to 168, and outwards, 437, with cargoes. In 1847 not less than 158 foreign vessels of an aggregate burden of 38,967 tons, with cargoes, and 148 vessels of 15,296 tons, in ballast, entered Swansea. The following is a statement of the number and registered tonnage of vessels entered 'inwards,' frequenting the port during three years, not engaged in the foreign trade:

In 1844, inwards 4,017 registered tonnage 261,698
   1845   „   4,132   „   268,243
   1847   „   3,651   „   217,882

The duties paid at the Custom-house in 1831 were 4,767*l.*; in 1846 they exceeded 70,000*l.* About 140 vessels belong to the port."

To this I may add the following returns of the shipping trade for the past year, 1849, as just published:—

"FOREIGN TRADE.—Number of vessels entered inwards with cargoes, 205, bringing 48,000 tons; outwards, with cargoes, 438, taking 50,000 tons. Inwards, with ballast, 112; tonnage, 9,000; outwards, with ballast, 16; tonnage, 3,600.

"COASTING TRADE.—Numbers of vessels entered inwards with cargoes 4,000, bringing 263,000 tons; vessels outwards with cargoes 6,000, taking 355,000 tons. In addition to the above about 100 vessels arrived in ballast, and about 200 cleared out in ballast. Out of 205 vessels entering inwards from foreign parts, 18, of 600 tons burden each, brought copper ore and wool from Australia."

The principal trade is of course in copper ores, with South America, Cuba, and Australia, in foreign parts—and with Cornwall and Ireland for home-raised ores. But this port also enjoys no inconsiderable trade in coal.

There were shipped, of coals, culm, and cinders—

In 1847.	Tons.	In 1848.	Tons.
Coastwise	303,307	Coastwise	392,371
Exported in foreign		Exported in foreign	
vessels	46,715	vessels	42,114
Total tons	350,022	Total tons	434,485

Thus the increase of the coal trade here in the year 1848, over the preceding year, notwithstanding the depression of trade and the unsettled state of the Continent, was not less than 83,463 tons. But it will be observed that the increase was entirely in the coasting trade; and that, from some cause—probably that of the disturbances abroad—the export trade from this one port in 1848 was reduced by about a tenth. Taking the instance of France, I observe there was a great falling off in the total quantity of coal exported from England to that country in 1848, as compared with 1847; the numbers for the year 1847 being 640,010 tons, whilst for 1848 they were 565,965 tons, showing a decrease in 1848 of 74,045 tons, or about one-eighth of the total quantity annually exported to that country. The declared value of the exports of coal and culm from Swansea to foreign ports was in 1847 £19,529, and in 1848 £18,013. The above particulars, which I have abstracted from the last parliamentary return, include, I believe, under the name "Swansea," the shipments from the ports of Neath and Port Talbot, in Swansea bay—for in the returns there is no mention made of the export of coal from those places.

The number of vessels engaged at the present time in the foreign and home copper trade with this port I endeavoured to obtain, but failed. We have seen that 18 vessels of 600 tons burden each entered with copper ores from Australia in 1849; but a great many ships and barques of 500 tons burden trade in copper ores with Cuba and South America. The vessels which trade with British ores are very numerous; they average about 100 tons, make from 18 to 20 voyages a year, and are each worked by five men.

It is to be regretted that no accounts are available of the total quantity of copper made from ore raised in the United Kingdom previously to 1820. "No statement," says Porter, "can be given of the total quantity of copper raised in the United Kingdom before 1820. From that year until 1834 the produce was:—

Yrs.	Tons.	Yrs.	Tons.
1820	8,127	1828	12,188
1821	10,228	1829	12,057
1822	11,018	1830	13,232
1823	9,679	1831	14,685
1824	9,705	1832	14,450
1825	10,358	1833	13,260
1826	11,093	1834	14,042
1827	12,326		

"Since 1834, the produce of copper smelted from British ore cannot be accurately distinguished from that of foreign origin. The value of this metal now annually raised in the kingdom *exceeds one million sterling*, being more than double the value of the quantity annually produced at the beginning of the present century."

With regard to the produce of the Cornish copper mines, which forms the heaviest branch of the shipping trade in ores with this place, I find in the "Mining Almanac" the following interesting details:

"Previous to the 17th century, few records exist of the production of copper in Cornwall. The first sale on record of copper ores was in 1729, when 2,216 tons were sold for the year; in 1730, 2,832 tons; in 1731, 2,555 tons; in 1732 only 1,714 tons; and in 1733 the quantity increased to 3,113 tons. Of these years no records exist to show the produce or per-centage of the ore, nor even of the quantity of ore raised from 1733 to 1764. In the latter year the quantity was 16,437 tons, yielding a produce of 11 3/8. The quantity raised kept gradually increasing from 1764 to 1773, in which latter year 27,654 tons were raised, yielding an average produce of 11 per cent. From 1773 to 1800 no records exist. In the latter year we find the quantity was 55,981 tons, yielding 5,187 tons of copper and 550,925*l.* 1s. in money, average produce, 9¼, standard, 133*l.* 3s. For ten years the quantity varied from 60,000 to 78,000 tons per annum; and in 1805 I find the standard was 169*l.* 16s., with a produce of 7 7/8. This is the highest I can find, and was, I suppose, before the smelters could boast a monopoly. In 1822 the annual produce had reached 100,364 tons, yielding 638,715*l.* 9s. 6d.; produce, 8 5/8; standard, 106*l.* 14s. In 1830, 141,263 tons; 802,979*l.* 9s.; produce, 8 1/8; standard, 103*l.* 2s. In 1840, 147,266 tons; 792,758*l.* 3s. 6d.; standard, 108*l.* 10s.; produce, 7½. It will be observed that although in 1840 the quantity of ore raised was much greater, yet the money realized was much less than in 1830; indeed, it appears throughout the tables to which I have referred, that the quality of the ore deteriorated almost annually, for which I can only account by the supposition, that as the mines became deeper the ores became poorer. To bring these statistics to the present time, we find that in the year ending June 30, 1848, the quantity of copper raised in Cornwall was 155,616 tons, yielding in money 825,080*l.* 2s. 6d., average produce, 8¼, and standard 97*l.* 7s.

"The largest amount of money realized for the produce of Cornish mines in any one year from 1729 to 1848, I find was in 1836, when 140,981 tons brought 957,752*l.* 8s. 6d., at a standard of 115*l.* 12s., produce, 8¼."

The quantities of Welsh copper ores bought in Swansea during twelve years past, with the value and average price per ton of 21 cwts. (ores are always sold by 21 cwts. to the ton), are shown by the following table:—

Years.	Tons.	Value.	Average Price.
1837	2,064	£13,384	£6 9 8
1838	2,237	14,638	6 10 10
1839	2,830	18,832	6 13 1
1840	1,795	9,747	5 8 8
1841	1,456	7,020	4 16 5
1842	556	2,728	4 18 1
1843	737	4,260	5 15 7
1844	1,688	8,479	7 15 10
1845	681	3,175	4 13 3
1846	1,389	6,639	4 15 7
1847	434	2,378	5 9 7
1848	68	570	8 8 0

By the above table it will be seen that the produce and value of Welsh mines within the last twelve years have fluctuated in a most extraordinary manner, and that the quantity of ore raised has vastly diminished within that period—being, in 1839, as many as 2,830 tons, whilst in 1848 it had dwindled down to 68 tons. The variations in price during the above interval were from £7 15s. 10d. per ton in 1844 to £4 13s. 3d. in 1845.

The Irish ores form an important branch of the copper trade. The quantities of those ores bought in Swansea, with the value and average price per ton during twelve years past, are shown in the following table:—

Years.	Tons.	Value.	Average Price.
1837	20,436	£130,823	£6 8 0
1838	22,705	139,586	6 2 11
1839	22,290	143,447	6 8 8
1840	23,412	135,293	5 15 6
1841	16,538	137,442	8 6 2
1842	14,030	115,570	8 4 8
1843	16,523	115,791	7 0 0
1844	19,385	127,898	6 12 11
1845	18,597	113,566	6 2 1
1846	17,264	110,159	6 7 7
1847	14,463	88,760	6 2 8
1848	14,554	78,024	5 7 2

It remains to show the extent of the trade in foreign ores, which I believe were never used in this country prior to the year 1827. At present it will be seen, by the subjoined interesting tables, that the imports from abroad are very large:—

SALES OF FOREIGN COPPER ORES AT SWANSEA, IN THE FIVE YEARS ENDING 30TH JUNE, 1848; WITH THE QUANTITIES AND VALUE OF ORE SOLD, THE AVERAGES IN EACH YEAR OF PRODUCE IN METAL, QUANTITIES OF FINE COPPER IN THE ORE, PRICES PER TON, VALUE IN MONEY, &C.

		Tons. of 21 cwt.	Average Produce per cent.	Fine Copper. Tons.	Average Price of Ore. £ s. d.	Value. £	Total Value of Foreign Ore. £	Quantities of Ore. Tons.	Average Produce per cent.	Fine Copper. Tons.	Average Price. £ s. d.	Value of Ore to a Ton of Copper. £ s. d.
1844	Total sales at Swansea	65,520	16 15-16	11,108	13 9 4	882,568	745,724	44,936	20·872	9,387	16 11 11	79 8 11
	Less British ores …	20,584	8·363	1,721	6 18 0	136,844						
1845	Total sales at Swansea	62,950	16 7-16	10,349	12 1 5	759,999	643,995	43,924	19·967	8,770	14 13 3	73 8 8
	Less British ores …	19,026	8·301	1,579	6 1 11	116,004						
1846	Total sales at Swansea	64,987	15 1-16	9,788	11 10 6	748,915	633,371	46,758	17·703	8,278	13 10 11	76 10 3
	Less British ores …	18,229	8·282	1,510	6 6 9	115,544						
1847	Total sales at Swansea	53,284	16 ⅝	8,857	12 13 9	676,069	584,929	38,387	19·834	7,663	15 4 9	76 6 8
	Less British ores …	14,897	8·015	1,194	6 2 4	91,140						
1848	Total sales at Swansea	50,731	17	8,645	12 8 2	629,660	533,721	36,109	19·804	7,151	14 15 7	74 12 9
	Less British ores …	14,622	10·215	1,494	6 11 3	95,939						
	Total quantities …	210,114	…	41,249	…	…	3,141,740	210,114	…	41,249		
	Average amounts, &c.	…	…	…	…	…	628,348	42,023	19·632	8,250	14 19 1	76 3 3

In order to allay the apprehensions of those who may feel alarmed lest this immense importation from abroad should affect the working of British mines, I may here state that, notwithstanding the increased consumption of foreign ores during the past few years, it has not been more than commensurate with the demands of trade; for I find that, before foreign ores were used, the total of copper made from British ores in the three years ending in 1826 (the last, I believe, before the importations from abroad) was 31,156 tons—whilst, in the three years ending with 1848, it had increased to 41,462. The money value of foreign and British ores smelted in the five years ending with 1848 was—British ores, £4,748,672; foreign ores, £3,141,740; which leaves a balance on the money value of £1,606,932 in favour of English ores reduced into metal in this country in the last-mentioned period of five years. Of course I am not prepared to say that, if no foreign ores had been imported, our own mines might not have been more actively worked, and therefore rendered more productive; all I have endeavoured to show is, that they have not been neglected or thrown back in consequence of the competition of copper ores from abroad.

I give in the next place a most valuable and useful table, showing the actual number of tons of foreign and British ores smelted, with the average price per ton, the total produce in metal, and the money value of the whole, during the interval extending from 1833 to 1848. It is, in fact, a summary of the entire trade during that period. I have extracted it, with the omission of some particulars of less general interest, from the "Mining Almanack":—

AN ACCOUNT OF THE SALES, BY PUBLIC TICKETINGS, OF BRITISH AND FOREIGN COPPER ORES IN CORNWALL AND SWANSEA RESPECTIVELY, IN EACH YEAR, FROM THE 30TH JUNE, 1833, TO THE 30TH JUNE, 1848, SHOWING THE PRICES AND VALUE IN MONEY; WITH GENERAL AVERAGES FOR THE WHOLE PERIOD, AND THE TOTAL PRODUCE IN METAL, AND MONEY VALUE OF THE WHOLE. ALSO GIVING THE VALUE OF ORE COMPUTED TO PRODUCE A TON OF COPPER, FROM THE ENTIRE SALES, AND FROM THOSE OF CORNWALL AND SWANSEA RESPECTIVELY.

In the Years ending (30th June)	CORNWALL			SWANSEA			Total produce of the whole in fine copper.	Total value of the whole in money.	CORNWALL AND SWANSEA AVERAGE.		
	Computed quantity of ore, in tons of 21 cwt.	Average price of ore per ton of 21 cwt.	Total value in money.	Computed quantity of ore in tons of 21 cwt.	Average price of ore per ton of 21 cwt.	Total value in money.			Average value of the qty of ore to make a ton of copper.	Average value of Cornish ore to make a ton of copper.	Average value of Swansea ore to make a ton of copper.
	Tons.	£ s. d.	£	Tons.	£ s. d.	£	Tons.	£	£ s. d.	£ s. d.	£ s. d.
1833	138,300	6 1 6	858,709	13,101	7 5 0	95,008	12,343	953,717	77 5 4	76 15 5	82 0 10
1834	143,296	6 4 0	887,902	18,112	7 7 6	133,821	12,805	1,021,723	79 15 9	79 2 0	84 14 0
1835	150,617	5 18 6	893,403	28,771	7 15 6	223,990	15,105	1,117,393	73 19 5	72 15 10	79 1 3
1836	140,981	6 17 0	957,752	34,366	9 17 6	340,025	15,489	1,297,777	83 15 8	82 5 7	88 6 9
1837	140,753	6 9 1	918,614	34,216	9 18 0	338,976	14,783	1,257,590	85 1 4	84 17 6	85 12 0
1838	145,688	5 17 6	857,780	42,931	11 4 6	481,323	17,433	1,339,103	76 16 3	74 8 3	81 9 11
1839	159,551	5 17 0	932,298	49,474	12 1 6	597,996	19,747	1,530,294	77 9 10	74 1 5	81 19 3
1840	147,266	5 7 6	792,758	56,279	11 19 6	674,012	19,511	1,466,770	75 3 6	71 16 5	79 10 11
1841	135,090	6 1 6	819,949	59,378	14 14 6	871,248	20,277	1,691,197	83 8 1	82 2 0	84 13 4
1842	135,581	6 1 6	822,871	56,821	14 5 0	808,182	19,274	1,631,053	84 12 5	83 3 0	86 3 7
1843	144,806	5 11 0	804,446	60,554	13 6 4	805,213	20,788	1,609,659	77 18 8	73 12 7	81 13 0
1844	152,667	5 6 10	815,246	65,520	13 9 4	882,568	22,355	1,697,814	75 18 9	72 12 3	79 9 0
1845	157,000	5 6 3	835,351	62,950	12 1 5	759,999	22,588	1,595,350	70 12 6	68 5 0	73 8 10
1846	158,913	5 11 7	886,785	64,987	11 10 6	748,915	22,236	1,635,700	73 11 2	71 6 4	76 10 3
1847	148,674	5 11 9	830,739	53,284	12 13 9	676,069	20,823	1,506,808	72 7 3	69 8 6	76 6 7
1848	155,616	5 6 0	825,080	50,731	12 8 2	629,660	21,514	1,454,741	67 12 4	64 2 2	72 16 8
Total Amt in 16 years.	2,354,799	—	13,739,683	751,475	—	9,067,005	297,071	22,806,689	—	—	—
Average pr Annum.	147,175	5 16 8	858,730	46,967	12 1 4	566,688	18,567	1,425,418	76 15 5	74 15 6	80 0 2

I observe, by the last published Parliamentary paper, that the total quantity of foreign copper *ores* imported into this country during the year ending June 30, 1849, was 50,053 tons, and of *regulus* (ore partly manufactured) 124. Of this, not less than 35,753 tons came direct to Swansea. The following are the countries from which the bulk of those importations arrived, with the quantities they severally contributed (rejecting fractional parts of a ton):—

		Tons.
Cuba		30,679
Chili		4,503
South Australia	7,783	
New South Wales	3,688	
Van Dieman's Land	543	
New Zealand	70	
		12,084
Peru		1,882
China		388
Italy		126
Spain		120
Western coast of Africa		101

As to prices, those of the British and Irish ores are given in the above tables; the following shows the averages during the four years ending 30th June, 1847:—

TABLE OF THE AVERAGE PRICES OF COPPER ORES IMPORTED FROM CHILI, CUBA, AND AUSTRALIA AND OTHER BRITISH POSSESSIONS, IN THE FOUR YEARS ENDING JUNE 30, 1847.

Price per Ton in	Average Price of Ore from Chili.	Average Price of Ore from Cuba.	Average Price of Ore from Australia, &c.	Average Prices of Ores from the three Places.
1844	£21 5 7	£15 2 5	—	£16 16 7
1845	22 12 9	13 1 0	9 7 0	15 1 10
1846	25 17 6	12 9 7	16 16 2	14 3 4
1847	24 12 4	12 5 4	18 2 0	15 15 0
Annual } Average }	23 6 3	13 5 5	17 7 3	15 9 1

Of the Cornish and Devon mines the most productive are the following. I have thought it desirable to give the sum paid up per share, and the market price. This statement relates to the year 1848—the last for which data are available:—

Name.	1848. Produce in Tons.	1848. Money returned.		Paid up per share.	Market price per share.
Great Devon Consols (Wheal Maria) ...	16,374	£94,418	6	£1	£230
Great United	12,822	48,293	0	1,000	250
Carn Brea	10,432	62,631	0	15	100
Par Consols	8,884	56,549	0	55⅜	1,000

Having now seen pretty clearly the extent of the *Imports* and of the home produce and manufacture of copper, we will next turn to the *Exports*. The only tables accessible to me, of the exports previously to 1849, include brass as well as copper. The declared value of exports of copper and brass was in the year 1846, £1,558,187; in the year 1847 it was £1,541,868; in 1848 it was £1,272,675. By the last parliamentary return, the exports of copper from the United Kingdom in the year ending 5th January, 1849, were (rejecting fractions):—

	Tons.
Unwrought copper in bricks and pigs	4,261
Coin	22
Sheets, nails, &c., (including mixed or yellow metal)	8,947
Copper wire	16
Wrought copper of other sorts	219
	13,465

The chief place of export is London, from which the quantity shipped abroad in 1849, was 6,502 tons. At Liverpool there were shipped 4,892 tons—at Swansea, 1,212 tons—in that year.

Of the total quantity of British copper exported in 1849, there were taken by—

	Tons.
United States of America	2,618
France	1,682
Holland	684
Hanseatic Towns	674
Belgium	650
Brazils	635
Foreign West Indies	264
British Territories in the East Indies ..	3,582

By this statement it will be seen how important a branch of this commerce is carried on with the British territories in the East Indies. I may add that our export of copper to the foreign West Indies was, in

1849, 264 tons; to the British West Indies, 130 tons; and to the Australian colonies it was 237 tons. In the last mentioned colonies they have erected smelting houses, chiefly, I am told, for the purpose of smelting the poorer ores, which will not pay for transport to England. Although we export at present manufactured copper to our Australian colonies, it may be doubted whether we shall long continue to do so—for I find it stated in the City Article of *The Morning Chronicle*, "that the smelting works at the Burra-Burra Mine, at Kooringa, were in full work, both smelting and refining being carried on with vigour."

Some idea of the astonishing advance made by South-Australia (only settled in 1836) in the copper trade during the past few years, may be obtained from this statement:—Value of copper ore exported in 1844, £4,009; in 1845, £17,179; in 1846, £54,168; in 1847, £171,883.

I may here add, that it appears by the speech of the Chancellor of the Exchequer upon the "Address," that our "exports of copper, in bricks and pigs, had increased from 85,224 cwts. in the year ending January 5, 1849, to 153,379 cwts. in the year ending January 5, 1850; and of wrought copper, from 5,156 cwts. in the year ending January 5, 1849, to 17,835 in the year ending January 5, 1850; and the exports of brass of all sorts from 13,094 cwts. in 1849, to 23,636 in the year ending January 5, 1850."

The foregoing particulars show the advance of this most important branch of British commerce. It should be borne in mind that the total yearly value of the copper manufactured in England is now something over one million and a half sterling! The capital embarked in the trade must be enormous; and the employment it gives to miners, sailors, colliers, and workmen in the smelting-houses, has become a valuable element in the market of labour.

LABOUR AND THE POOR.

———◆———

THE MINING AND MANUFACTURING DISTRICTS OF SOUTH WALES.

[FROM OUR SPECIAL CORRESPONDENT.]

SWANSEA—THE COPPER WORKS.

LETTER XIII.

Having given in my last Letter a succinct history and full statistics of the copper trade, down to the present time, I shall now speak of the "works" where the various and interesting processes of smelting and manufacture are performed, passing on to a description of the town and general trade of Swansea.

There are in England and Wales nineteen copper works. The following table shows the firms or companies to whom they belong, and the names and localities of the several works:—

Name of the Company or Firm.	Locality.
English Copper Company	Cwm Avon. Port Talbot.
Freeman and Company	White Rock, Swansea.
Pascoe, Grenfell, and Sons	Upper Bank, Middle Bank, } Swansea.
Crown Copper Company	Swansea.
Sims, Willyams, Nevill, Druce, and Company	Llanelly.
Vivian and Sons	Haford, Swansea. Taibach, Margam.
Williams, Foster, and Co.	Rose, Landore, Morva, } Swansea. Crown, near Neath.
Mines Royal	Neath.

J. Schneider and Co.	{	Spitty Loughar, near Swansea.
Mason and Elkington		Pembry, Llanelly.
Lowe's Patent Works		Penclawdd.
British and Foreign Copper Co.		Liverpool.
A small work (name unknown to me)	}	Anglesea.

All of the above works, with the exception of the two last-named, which are small works, are situated either in the Swansea Valley above the town, or within a distance of fourteen miles, so that in fact this neighbourhood is the seat of the British copper-works.

It is difficult to ascertain the exact number of hands employed in smelting and manufacturing copper, but I believe they are about 3,500; this is exclusive of colliers, who raise the fuel necessary for the works. The copper trade between Cornwall and Wales alone, according to Cliffe, gives employment to 1,200 seamen, and to shipping amounting to 20,000 tons. The number of "calciners" and "furnaces" used for smelting copper may be taken roughly at 550. The quantity of coal consumed in the whole of the works may be taken at 450,000 tons a year. The amount paid in wages by the smelting and manufacturing establishments may be estimated at £3,000 a week. I give these last particulars on the authority of Mr. H. Vivian; he declined giving the details of their own works—but I obtained without difficulty the information I required from the firm of Williams, Foster, and Co. (whose works I inspected after having gone over those of Vivian and Sons), and I shall give them when I come to speak of their establishment. But without exact returns from *all* the works, it is impossible to frame a general statement which is trustworthy: one refusal to contribute such information renders the particulars furnished in other quarters comparatively worthless, because a perfect and accurate summary obviously cannot be constructed where some of the details are conjectural.

The following tables of the purchases of copper-ores in Cornwall and Swansea, in the year 1848, will convey a tolerably just idea of the relative extent and importance of the several copper works. The purchases in Cornwall are, of course, of Cornish ore—whilst those made at the "ticketings" (as the sales are called) at Swansea comprise the South American, Australian, Cuban, Irish, and Welsh ores.

PURCHASES OF COPPER ORES IN CORNWALL FOR 1848.

Companies.	Tons.	Amount.		
Mines Royal	9,459 ...	£50,656	5	8
English Copper Company ..	19,880 ...	106,977	16	5
Vivian and Sons	32,701 ...	174,908	18	1
Freeman and Co.	18,006 ...	98,640	3	4
P. Grenfell and Sons	18,512 ...	103,276	19	5
Crown Copper Company ..	1,185 ...	7,091	10	0
Sims, Willyams, and Co. ...	19,213 ...	103,485	5	8
Williams, Foster, and Co. ..	34,064 ...	228,389	11	5
Total	153,120 ...	£873,436	10	6

PURCHASES AT SWANSEA TICKETINGS.

Companies.	Tons.	Amount.		
English Copper Company ..	5,592 ...	£71,458	18	1
Freeman and Co.	2,607 ...	35,691	16	0
P. Grenfell and Sons	5,432 ...	76,873	14	8
Crown Copper Company ..	16 ...	80	4	3
Sims, Willyams, and Co. ...	6,184 ...	97,934	11	6
Vivian and Sons	12,623 ...	147,070	10	6
Williams, Foster, and Co. ..	13,787 ...	185,168	4	0
Mines Royal	204 ...	2,334	0	0
Schneider and Co.	1,166 ...	24,444	11	0
Total	47,611 ...	£641,056	10	6

The respective purchases of ores, English and foreign (as shown by the above table), by the five largest works, in the year 1848, were as follows:—

	Tons.	Amount.		
Williams, Foster, and Co. ..	47,851 ...	£413,557	15	5
Vivian and Sons	45,324 ...	321,979	8	7
Sims, Willyams, and Co. ...	25,397 ...	201,419	17	2
P. Grenfell and Sons	23,944 ...	180,150	14	1
English Copper Company ..	25,392 ...	178,436	14	6

Introduced by a gentleman who represents a large firm in the copper-trade, I attended one of the "ticketings" which are held fortnightly, at the chief hotel in this place. The proceedings were characteristic, and were remarkable for the total absence of that kind of excitement which often accompanies business transactions on so extensive a scale; I shall therefore describe them. At a long table, arranged with blotting paper, pens and ink, as at a committee meeting, the proprietors or agents of the copper works take their seats. At twelve o'clock the chairman takes the chair, and opens the business by saying, "I'll take offers for the first four lots of Cobre, Burra Burra," or whatever may be the number of the lots and the kind of ore to be sold in the first group. Upon this the buyers before named, who have previously had each lot assayed and ascertained its worth, enter on a small billet of paper the amount they bid per ton for each lot, fold the paper, and hand it to the chairman. When all the biddings are received, the chairman opens them in a prescribed order, and calls out the bidding, which the parties present enter in a blank form supplied for the purpose; and when he has gone through the whole he names the buyer, and calls out the "excess"—that is to say, the sum per ton which the buyer's bidding exceeds that of the highest bidder below him. The chairman then offers the next group of "parcels," and the same routine is pursued as on the first occasion. Scarcely a word is spoken. In this manner, sales, in the course of an hour, are effected, amounting to between £20,000 and £50,000. At the "ticketing" held on 3d January inst., there were thus sold 1,447 tons of Cuba and South Australian ores, the proceeds amounting to £28,925 4s. 6d. The cargo of Burra Burra ore, brought by one ship, "the Ancient Briton," appears to have realized £14,666 4s. 6d. of the above total. What struck me as very remarkable was the nicety with which the calculations of the worth of the ores had been made by the buyers. The system of assaying must have been carried here to very high perfection; for the "excess" of the highest bidder over the bidder next below him, in the case of fifteen lots which I saw sold, was in two instances 2s. 6d. a ton, in five 1s. 6d. a ton, in two 1s., and in six only 6d. a ton. The price given per ton for Irish ores, sold at the "ticketing" I attended, varied from £8 10s. 6d. down to £3 15s. The following returns of the sales of copper ores at Swansea, for the quarter ended 31st December last, are extracted from the *Mining Journal*. "The sales show an increase of 1,649 tons—£52,779 19s., and £1 11s. 6d. per ton addition on the average price, as compared with the quarter ended 30th September; they stand respectively as follows:—

	Tons.	Amount.	Average Price.
Quarter ended Dec. 31. ...	11,212 ...	£157,694 0 6 ...	£13 11 10
Quarter ended Sept. 30. ...	9,563 ...	104,914 1 6 ...	12 0 4
	1,649	£52,779 19 0	£1 11 6

And with the corresponding quarter of 1848, as follows:—

	Tons.	Amount.	Average Price.
Quarter ended Dec. 31. 1849	11,212 ...	£157,694 0 6 ...	£13 11 10
Quarter ended Dec. 31. 1848	13,689 ...	167,877 15 0 ...	12 5 3
Decrease	2,477 ...	£10,183 14 6	Inc. £1 6 7

Being a decrease on the returns of 2,477 tons, and £10,183 14s. 6d., but an increase on the average price of £1 6s. 7d. per ton, arising, no doubt, from the higher dressing which the foreign ores receive before being shipped for England."

The vast extension of the copper trade within the past few years—as evidenced by the fact that, notwithstanding the admission of foreign ores, of which the imports are full 50,000 tons per annum (yielding a larger per centage of metal than our home-raised ores), and a considerable increase in the consumption of British ores, there have been few instances of an overstocked market—and the fact that the trade is now eminently prosperous, seem to show that we have by no means reached the limits of this branch of productive industry. Indeed, there is every reason to believe that this trade might be largely and profitably extended. The effect that the repeal of the navigation-laws must have upon the copper trade will be most beneficial. America, being admitted on a footing of equality into British ports, will greatly increase her mercantile navy; and, being a ship-building country, almost entirely dependent upon England for her copper, she will require annually a larger and still larger quantity of copper sheathing, nails, bolts, and other necessaries for ship-building. The relaxation, too, of foreign tariffs, will also, beyond question, extend the field for the consumption of copper and brass, so that many circumstances unite to render probable the further extension of the copper-trade.

The location here of the copper-works, though it has been the chief, is by no means the only benefit which a commodious and safe harbour, having a coal-field behind it, has secured to Swansea. There is here an extensive pottery in full work—formerly there were two; there are two thriving manufactories of "patent fuel" (Warlich's and Lyons's); some iron, tin-plate, and chemical works; a silver mill and zinc works, up the valley; and in the town there are two ship-building yards for vessels of wood, and one for building vessels of iron. In short, the town everywhere presents evidences of great and increasing prosperity. The port is crowded with ships, the quays swarm with men in active employment, and the warehouses, ore-yards, ship-building yards, &c., betoken in various ways the successful trade which is carried on in them. "Of all the ports in the Bristol Channel," remark the Admiralty hydrographers, "there is perhaps none more favourably situate than that of Swansea; for it is an important fact that Swansea harbour is accessible to any stranger that may arrive in the bay, when blowing too strong for pilots to get off." Swansea-bay has been frequently compared with that of Naples. Its width may be about ten miles from Sker-weather point to the rocky sentinel called the Mumbles. Within the sweep of this bay lie three points—Port Talbot (of recent construction), Neath, and Swansea—this place being near the centre of the curve. The view from a vessel on a fine day is very pleasing. In every direction there is a distance of lofty mountains rising behind each other, and presenting finely varied outlines by contrast of the bluff and round hills on the coast with the peaked summits of the furthest ranges. On the right hand, from Taibach and various works, there stream huge and enlarging clouds of smoke, which in part obscure, and at the same time beautify, the landscape. From the summit of a conical mountain 1,000 feet high, you see huge volumes of what appears like steam issuing from the crater of a volcano; it is the smoke from Cwm Avon Copper Works, which is carried through a large flue of upwards of a mile in length along the face of the mountain to its peak, in order that the poisonous vapour may not prejudice the health of the neighbourhood. Swansea—with its pier-head and light-house, its churches and chapels, its old Norman castle, its shipping, and its long lines of smart houses stretching westward above the yellow sandhills—next attracts attention. Following the line of coast to the left you see the picturesque village of Oystermouth, with its ruined castle perched on a hill; still further westward, nestling under a boldly rising slope of the mountain, is the fishing village of "the Mumbles." Again further, as the hill slopes down towards the sea, are cliffs of red-stone, quarried freely for lime and iron. Standing apart, and insulated from half to full tide, on a blackened and water-fretted rock, the "Mumbles Lighthouse" lifts its tall head—an object equally conspicuous by night and day. Pursuing their course outwards or homewards the sails of a hundred vessels glance white, or red, or brown in the sunlight against the deep blue sea, and impart animation and interest to this varied scene.

Over the narrow cleft through which flows the Swansea river, on whose banks are the sources of the town's prosperity, there hangs a lazy and dense cloud of white vapour—it is the smoke from the copper works. This is the greatest inconvenience the townspeople and the neighbouring farmers have to endure from the settling of the copper trade at Swansea. This smoke, which contains large quantities of sulphuric and arsenious acids, corrodes the glass in the windows, and is fatal for a long distance to vegetable life. Its direct effect upon animals is not so visible; but that it is injurious in some degree there can be no doubt. Not a tree can endure this vapour; they are scorched up and perish immediately. The face of the mountain against which the smoke drifts is literally denuded of its grasses, and, having no turf to support and cover it, the alluvial soil has been washed away by rains until nothing but the *skeleton-block* of the mountain, if I may so call it, remains. At a distance, where the smoke is so diluted that grasses can exist, it nevertheless affects them by altering their physical character, and by this means it produces a specific action upon cattle, horses, and sheep which are pastured upon them, causing luxations and enlargements of the joints and giving a metallic coating to the teeth. For these nuisances the proprietors have had true bills found against them at sessions, and they have been obliged to defend actions at law. But though cases of individual hardship from injuries to cattle have often occurred, it is a question of vital moment to the town whether it is not better to endure considerable inconvenience for so large a share of prosperity, than to compel the proprietors to seek another locality, and to take away the trade, which more than any other has benefited the neighbourhood. Often the town is enveloped in this sulphurous and pernicious smoke; yet the inhabitants feel the necessity of endurance, and the copper-masters have long ceased to be harassed with law proceedings on account of this nuisance. Endeavours were at one time made to deprive copper smoke of the sulphuric acid, arsenic, and other of its constituents which are injurious, but they have long been abandoned. That the science of chemistry is quite equal to the task of separating the noxious from the innoxious smoke, there can be no doubt; but it is said that this can only be done at an expense so great as to render it impossible, with such a tax, profitably to carry on the trade.

As a town, Swansea has no rival in the principality. Its streets are wide and airy, its public buildings handsome, and in good taste. A great many of the shops have showy elevations and stylish plate-glass fronts; these, however, are intermingled with the old Welsh houses, which are low, and have peaked gables. Two or three leading minds have given to its society a decided scientific and literary bias. In the Philosophical Institution here, there was held two years ago the great annual meeting of the "British Association for the Advancement of Science." Mr. Grove, the Vice-President of the British Institution, whose discoveries in electricity have given him a European reputation, is from this town, and often comes here. Mr. Jeffreys, of the Royal Society, whose contributions to the science of conchology are well known; Mr. L. Dillwyn, of the Linnean Society, whose works on phytology are justly valued; and Mr. Francis, of the Antiquarian Society, who has thrown much light upon antiquities in this neighbourhood, all reside here, and are active in their respective pursuits. Formerly, before the extension of the copper-works to their present magnitude, Swansea was visited as a watering-place, for which its fine sands and picturesque rides, drives, and walks eminently fitted it. But the copper smoke has changed this, and the town is at present little resorted to as a watering-place. Beau Nash was born here—a fact commemorated by an ornamental inscription of far greater pretension than that which announces in Frankfort the birth-house of Goëthe, or that of Rubens in Cologne. Here also lived and died one of the Kemble family, who, in various novels that she published under the name of "Anne of Swansea" (which had the charm of mystery to recommend it in preference to her real name, "Hatton"), lampooned the local gentry, and it is said scandalised them greatly. She died here in humble, if not embarrassed, circumstances, a few years ago.

In speaking of the sanitary condition of the town of Swansea, my labours are lightened by an admirable report on the town, made about four years ago by Sir Henry De la Beche, and a second report (just published) to the General Board of Health, by Mr. Clark, the Superintending Inspector, who visited the town on the petition of the rate-payers for the application of the provisions of the Public Health Act, in aid of the existing arrangements for sewerage, scavenging, and water supply. The drainage of the town of Swansea is very imperfect. Only 3,180 out of 15,000 yards of high and by ways have covered sewers. Of these, the longest and most important is the least efficient. The surrounding villages, whose population mainly consists of working people and the poor, are not drained at all. "They are," says Mr. Clark, "it is true, almost all built upon high and sloping ground; but although such situations offer great facilities for house drainage, if these be not taken advantage of, drainage does not take effect, and the condition of the houses, even in the best of such situations, when

neglected, is not unfrequently as bad as in those less favoured by nature. The brooks and watercourses which traverse these villages, as at
Morriston, Llandore, and Foxhole, are used extensively as sewers, and
in the summer are thus converted into nuisances."

The town is chiefly supplied with water by the Swansea Water-
works, from public wells and springs, and from wells and pumps.
"The public springs," observes Mr. Clark, "are numerous, though ill-
managed, and rendered foul by privies, and for want of being collected
in proper cisterns. Those from which the poor derive their supply are
the *Dyvatty pistyll*, the washing-lake, and about five others in different parts of the town. There are five 'public' pumps. Notwithstanding
all these sources, the inhabitants, even in their immediate vicinity, are
badly off for water. In dry weather the springs are crowded, and the
poor have a long time to wait to fill their pitchers." In the village of
Trevivian the people fetch their water from the canal, or from a pump
in the works. I also saw them at a walled spring, which had a depth
of about three feet of the most singularly pellucid water I ever saw;
this spring is in a hollow outside the Morfa Copper Works.

The scavenging and cleaning of the town I consider very defective. During a portion of the time I have been here the streets have
been deep in mud. Although there is a board of commissioners, to
whom is confided by local act the paving, lighting, cleansing, water-
ing, regulating, &c., the town and borough, they certainly cannot be
complimented upon the efficiency of their arrangements, or the success of their labours. To a person accustomed to the compact and even
pavements, the well kept roads, and the sufficiently lighted streets of
an equal-sized English town, Swansea appears a neglected and a filthy
place.

Many of the streets and courts I inspected, which are inhabited
by the working classes and the poor, were nearly in as abominable a
condition as I have described those I visited in Merthyr. Although
wages here, in the copper-works and the pottery, are on the whole
good, as I shall in due time show, one sees in Swansea a far greater
number of barefooted women and children than in Merthyr. This I
am assured (and I can well believe it, knowing the prejudices of the
people, and observing that in other respects they are well clothed)
arises more from habit than from want of means to procure shoes and
stockings. The custom of the lowest class of the Welsh women and
children is to go barefoot; and here the population is more decidedly
Welsh, and further from the influences of English example, than that

of Merthyr. I was told by Miss Marianne Jones, a lady who performs the charitable duty of a Church district-visitor, that the poor here suffered great distress during the cold weather last winter. "It is aged widows," said she, "and widows having families, who, taking out-door relief, endeavour to keep themselves from the union-house, that suffer most severely. The families of masons, plasterers, bricklayers, and the Irish labourers who tend on them, were very badly off last winter, because in the frost they could not work. The worst of it was, that the men, being idle, many of them spent their time in drinking, getting money, I suppose, by pawning their goods. I saw much misery and privation amongst their wives and children."

Anticipating the visit of the cholera, great exertions were made by the authorities to prepare against its coming. It came, but happily its ravages were not great; the judicious precautions that had been taken, beyond all question greatly mitigated the severity and limited the extent of the disease. The inspector under the General Board of Health has recommended that the provisions of the Public Health Act be applied to the town; and, as I know no place the inhabitants of which have more public spirit, or who are more strenuous in their endeavours to effect any object they have in view, when they are of one mind, it is to be hoped and expected that they will act promptly, liberally, and with unanimity in the application of the remedies provided by that Act for the removal of evils and the remedy of defects such as at present exist in the town of Swansea.

Below I give a table affording a general view of the mortality in the Swansea district during five years, up to 1843 inclusive, the whole being divided into three classes—gentry, tradespeople, and labourers. I extract it, with some very useful comments upon its particulars, from the Report made by Sir Henry De la Beche in 1845:—

DEATHS IN SWANSEA FOR FIVE YEARS, ENDING 1843, STATING THE RANK IN LIFE AND MEAN AGE AT DEATH; AND DISTINGUISHING DEATHS BY DECLINE, CONSUMPTION, AND EPIDEMIC DISEASES.

Population, 1841—18,278.	Total Deaths from all Causes during 5 Years.	Mean Age at Death.	Decline. No. of Deaths.	Decline. Mean Age.	Consumption. No. of Deaths.	Consumption. Mean Age.	Epidemics. No. of Deaths.	Epidemics. Mean Age.
MALES.								
Gentry { Under 5 years	3	:	:	:	:	:	:	:
Above 5 years	25	44	3	:	3	:	2	:
Of all ages	28	39	3	33	3	28	2	25
Tradespeople { Under 5 years	42	:	:	:	:	:	9	:
Above 5 years	94	43	27	:	4	:	13	:
Of all ages	136	30	27	41	4	24	22	12
Labourers and Artisans { Under 5 years	285	:	8	:	1	:	106	:
Above 5 years	367	37	117	:	25	:	60	:
Of all ages	652	22	125	34	26	31	166	9
FEMALES.								
Gentry { Under 5 years	:	:	:	:	:	:	:	:
Above 5 years	18	44	8	:	2	:	2	:
Of all ages	18	46	8	41	2	25	2	28
Tradespeople { Under 5 years	24	:	1	:	:	:	8	:
Above 5 years	80	43	21	:	6	:	9	:
Of all ages	104	34	22	36	6	25	17	12
Labourers and Artisans { Under 5 years	259	:	12	:	:	:	106	:
Above 5 years	397	45	102	:	9	:	74	:
Of all ages	656	28	114	34	9	30	180	11

"From this table it appears that, taking the population of the district at 18,278, according to the census of 1841, the middle of the five years noticed, the rate of mortality is 1.74 per cent.: that the average number of male deaths per annum is 163.2, and of female deaths 155.6, or 7.6 less than the male; and that this difference in the number of male and female deaths is due to the fewer females who die among the gentry and tradespeople relatively to the males, than among the artisans and labourers, the deaths among whom are nearly even, as regards the sexes, for the five years.

"It will be seen that the mean age of the gentry who died in the five years was, for the males 39, and for the females 46 years; the mean age of the tradespeople, for the males 30, for the females 34 years; the mean age of the labourers and artisans, for the males 22, for the females 28 years; in all the three classes, showing a higher age at death for the females than the males, in the first class, of seven years; in the second, of four years; and in the third, of six years; so that this difference is less observable among the tradespeople than among the gentry and artisans and labourers. The total mean age of the males who died was 23 years, and of the females 29 years.

"It will be observed that, as usual, the numbers who die under five years of age are considerable, being 1 in 2.6, the mean age for whom, both males and females, being one year. The mortality of this kind is, however, very different in the three different classes, being, for the gentry, only at the rate of 1 in 15.3 of the total deaths, while for the tradespeople, it is 1 in 3.6, and for the artisans and labourers 1 in 2.4, results strongly marking the difference of the sanitary conditions under which the children of the three classes must be placed."

The means of education provided for the rising generation of all classes in Swansea seem to be abundant, cheap, and good. According to Mr. Lingen's Report to the Committee of the Council for Education, there are in Swansea 54 day-schools and 20 Sunday-schools; the former accommodating 2,122 scholars, the latter 1,987—of whom 225 are in Church and 1,762 in Dissenting Sunday-schools. There are here, I may observe in passing, three churches and a great many dissenting meeting-houses. The Normal College for Wales, established on the voluntary principle, has been removed here from Brecon.

In connexion with the Church there is a fine range of schools, comprising national, infant, and Sunday schools. The scale of weekly payments in the boys' school is 2d., 3d., and 4d. a week, according to the character of the instruction given; in the girls' school it is 2d. and 3d., in like manner; in the infants' school it is 2d. a week. These schools accommodate about 500 scholars. There is a clothing fund attached to the girls' and also to the infants' school, payments to which are made once a week. The clothes are made up in the school. As Mr. Lingen was unable to get accurate returns of the school accommodation provided in this town by Dissenters, a circumstance of which he has complained, I applied to Mr. Evan Davies, of the Normal College, who promptly and obligingly furnished me with the following table and remarks:—

SWANSEA SUNDAY-SCHOOL UNION.
ENGLISH SCHOOLS.

	Denomina-tion.	No. of Teachers.	No. of Scholars.	No. of Books in Library.	No. in Infant Classes.	Above 14 years old.
Bethany	Cal. M.	18	156	125	37	11
Burrows	C. H.	17	129	140	20	14
Kilvey	Do. Branch	16	160	277	50	29
Castle-street	Independent	19	117	24	15	26
Mount-pleasant	Baptist	22	134	...	94	40
Tower-lane	P. M.	12	121	...	44	13
Wesley Chapel	W. M.	25	154	...	11	16
Green-hill Brook ...	W. M.	17	190	...	120	35
Wicliffe	C. H.	15	160	100	33	26
York-place	Baptist	27	210	120	...	54
Ten schools	...	188	1531	786	424	253

WELSH SCHOOLS.

	Denomina-tion.	No. of Teachers.	No. of Scholars.	No. of Books in Library.	No. in Infant Classes.	Above 14 years old.
Babell	C. M.	7	49	...	31	18
Bethesda	B.	27	118	...	...	61
Ditto English	B.	10	202	...	...	10
Green-hill	C. M.	26	160	...	...	70
Port Tennant	Do.	5	20	...	...	4
Trinity	C. M.	15	75	20	12	32
Ebenezer	Independent	61	236	303	60	50
Wannmen	Do.	19	100	...	8	50
Tabernacle	W. M.	8	46	...	18	15
Total of Welsh Schools		178	1006	327	129	317
Total English and Welsh ...		366	2537	1113	553	570

C. M.—Calvinistic, or Welsh Methodists.
W. M.—Wesleyan Methodists.
P. M.—Primitive Methodists.
C. H.—Countess of Huntingdon's Connexion.
B.—Baptists.
I.—Independents.

"The annexed list only contains those schools in connection with the union. All those mentioned are Dissenting Institutions. There are, not in connection with the union, but also Dissenting schools, two ragged schools having 80 children; Capel Zion (Independent Welsh) 100; Zoar (Welsh Independent), 120; Cana, Welsh Independent, Pontestill, ditto, ditto, Kilary Baptist Chapel, and Glandwer Welsh Independent, 500.

"The last is only an estimate; but if anything, it is below the mark. The total of the Dissenting Sunday schools will therefore be at least 3,337.

"I know nothing of the Church schools, and do not therefore pretend to give any information respecting them. Five of the schools in the table have day schools also. Three have clothing societies. One a sick relief fund."

Of the school accommodation provided by the proprietors of the works I shall speak in my next Letter, where I purpose describing the workman, his home, and his family, as I found them in this place.

I have next to invite attention to an exceedingly interesting table, showing the depositors in the Swansea Saving Banks, classified under their various callings, with the number of each class of depositors, the amount of balances due to each class, and the individual average of each class. For this useful table I am indebted to the treasurer of the bank, Mr. Thomas Edward Thomas, a gentleman who has watched over the interests of this institution with paternal care, and who in his capacity of magistrate, and as a benefactor in every form of this town and neighbourhood, has conciliated the esteem of those who most widely differ from him in opinion, and the warm regard of an extensive circle of friends. I may add, that I gave attention, at his request, to the system of checks on the passbooks—a system devised by himself, and observed at this bank; and I do not hesitate to say, that if the same precautions had been observed in every savings bank, we should not have heard of the painful instances of fraud on the one hand, and of loss on the other, which recent disclosures have made notorious.

SWANSEA SAVINGS BANK.

CLASSIFICATION OF DEPOSITORS ON 20TH NOVEMBER, 1848,
ACCORDING TO THEIR RESPECTIVE OCCUPATION.

	No. of each Class.	Amount of Balances due to each Class.	Individual average.
Small farmers and country butchers	250	£8,823 16 4	£35 5 8
Small shopkeepers, clerks, accountants, teachers, schoolmasters, Excise officers, &c.	149	8,730 11 9	58 11 10
Mechanics, viz., shoemakers, tailors, carpenters, masons, smiths, weavers, &c.	607	16,527 3 8	27 4 6
Coppermen, colliers, labourers, bargemen, &c.	338	13,040 9 5	38 11 7
Marines and pilots	129	3,734 11 6	28 19 0
Dressmakers and sempstresses	76	2,438 0 5	32 1 7
Female servants	266	8,046 12 2	30 14 1
Male servants	72	3,107 13 0	43 3 2
Victuallers	81	3,879 0 1	47 17 9
Children and apprentices	153	2,953 18 4	19 6 1
Widows and persons of small income	109	4,463 1 8	40 18 10
Nurses, charwomen, &c.	49	2,397 2 4	48 18 5
Trust accounts	99	3,187 15 3	32 3 11
Total	2,378	£81,329 15 11	

The number of our large deposits was lessened during 1849, several being paid off.

Accounts.

On Nov. 20, 1848, were 2431 Amt. of balances £97,355 0 9
"   1849, "   2505 Ditto 97,365 1 1

Increased during the year 1849 74   While amt. of balance incr. only £10 0 4

The principal increase in the number of accounts was among the small depositors.

By this it will be seen that the class of mechanics are the largest depositors, and next to that comes the class of coppermen, labourers, bargemen, &c. But without an accurate knowledge of the proportion in regard to numbers which the one class bears to another (and this it is impossible to obtain, for the "Occupation Abstract" of the general census of ten years ago is of no value now for this purpose), of course I cannot say which is the most provident of these classes.

I have spoken at some length of the benefit societies in the Iron-works; below I give a table of the friendly societies and the charitable and provident societies depositing at this bank, whereby the reader may learn which are the classes most attached to those institutions. I was pleased to see that one of these societies is composed of the *wives* of *workmen*—good wives they are, no doubt; and that not less than four societies of workmen are here in existence, whose purpose is to provide *against casualties*—an object much to be desired in a district where the life of the workman is exposed to so much risk as it is in this neighbourhood. Two of these I perceive are in connection with dissenting chapels:—

SWANSEA SAVINGS BANK.
FRIENDLY SOCIETIES ON NOVEMBER 20, 1848.

Description of Members.	Balances.			Description of Members.	Balances.		
Mechanics, coppermen, colliers	£379	2	8	Mechanics, mariners .	£546	7	8
Colliers, labourers . . .	721	9	11	(Iron) workmen	380	9	2
Coppermen, colliers .	206	0	0	Mechanics, labourers .	195	17	1
ditto ditto . . .	182	19	4	Coppermen	269	17	0
ditto ditto . . .	274	9	2	Potters and labourers .	46	16	2
Mariners, pilots, me-chanics	447	14	7	Female Society, wives of workmen	109	15	3
Mechanics, &c.	578	5	6	Mechanics	643	4	11
Coppermen, colliers .	294	12	6	Farmers, labourers . . .	111	6	3
Farmers, labourers . . .	307	13	3	Mechanics, labourers, coppermen	322	3	11
Mechanics, mariners .	451	15	9	Farmers, bargemen, labourers	614	5	9
Potters, coppermen, me-chanics	283	14	9	Colliers, labourers . . .	1,110	10	10
Artisans of the town .	363	11	10	Mariners, farmers, la-bourers	309	12	4
Farmers, &c.	681	13	7	ditto ditto ditto	161	11	9
ditto	265	7	1	ditto ditto ditto	416	3	5
ditto labourers . . .	559	6	4	Farmers, labourers . . .	64	1	2
ditto ditto . .	195	1	8	ditto ditto . . .	520	14	6
Various working men	349	13	11	Colliers, labourers . . .	124	12	8
Potters, coppermen, mechanics	164	16	0	ditto ditto . . .	233	7	7
Female Society, wives of colliers, &c.	332	3	5	Workmen on tin, copper, and iron	590	16	4
Farmers, labourers . . .	252	6	7	Colliers, bargemen, &c.	230	11	6
Potters and mechanics	112	6	9				
Coppermen and iron-workers	624	0	1	Total £14,989	9	11	

SWANSEA SAVINGS BANK.
CHARITABLE AND PROVIDENT SOCIETIES.

Description	Balances.	Description	Balances.
Infant Friend Society	£30 11 0	Girls School, Fisher-street	125 18 9
Provision against casualties, Methodist Chapel	144 10 5	Charitable institution, Bishopston Parish ..	30 18 3
Member's Fund Clothing Society, by Miss Lewis	181 3 3	Ditto, by Rev. R. Morgan, for poor of Baglan	41 4 7
Provision against casualties, Libanus Chapel	138 15 11	Provision against casualties, workmen, Vale of Neath	130 16 11
Swansea Infant School	51 10 10	Sick Fund for Poor, by Capt. E. Morgan ...	77 9 10
Provision against casualties, by workmen at Morriston	82 15 2	Total	£1,035 14 11

LABOUR AND THE POOR.

—◆—

THE MINING AND MANUFACTURING DISTRICTS OF SOUTH WALES.

[FROM OUR SPECIAL CORRESPONDENT.]

SWANSEA—THE COPPER WORKS.

LETTER XIV.

In this Letter I purpose giving an account of the several processes of smelting and manufacturing copper, as now performed at the largest establishments in this kingdom, describing the various classes of workmen as I found them in their labours; and making, as I advance, any remarks which it may appear to me that the existing relations of master and workman require.

The only foreign ores used in this country are imported from South America, the foreign West Indies, and Australia. The mines in those countries are worked chiefly by English adventurers, the head quarters of the several companies being in London. These companies charter vessels of large burden to convey the ores from Chili, Cuba, and Australia to Swansea, where they are stowed in yards, crushed, sampled, and sold to the respective copper-masters at the "ticketings," one of which I described in my last communication. The vessels engaged in this trade are almost entirely ships and barques of from 500 to 1,000 tons burden, manned by crews numbering from 16 to 25 hands, whose pay is the same as that of the seamen engaged in other branches of our maritime commerce. A ship trading round Cape Horn, with Chili, makes a voyage out and home in from eight to ten months; a vessel trading with Australia makes one voyage, and a vessel trading with Cuba two voyages, in a year.

I have said that the ores are stored in yards, and are there crushed and heaped for sale. I visited two of those yards. The first I inspected was Mr. Richardson's, where I found a number of men and women at work, crushing the ores on a wooden stage with large flat-headed iron hammers, and passing the fragments through sieves. The ores are in this manner reduced to the size of gravel. There were belonging to their yard two brigs, of 400 tons burthen and with crews of 14 hands, trading with *St. Jago de Cuba,* and making two voyages a year. Sometimes the ore is weighed as it is wheeled from the vessel—at others the weight is taken at the Custom-house returns, according as weather and time permit. Some of the ore comes from Cuba as "dust ore," highly comminuted; other portions come as "ragging ore," of the consistency of gravel; another kind is "stone ore," and this it is that is broken up. The labourers here work in the open air. They told me they were all paid alike, men, women, and boys. When the weather is bad and they cannot work full-time for rain, they earn, perhaps, 6d. a day—at others 1s. 6d. In the long days of summer they earn 2s. 6d. Suspecting they were mostly Irish, I asked if that was the case; a man replied, "Yes, it is Irish we are; there is nobody else would work for the price we do it. Last week I earned but 7s. 3d.; the gintlemen who deals in copper be too sharp for us, and the times are bad." When broken the ore is stored in square beds, some three to four feet deep, and perhaps twenty feet long. Samples are taken from this to the assay-master, Mr. Penrose, and each lot is ticketed with the name of the company (whether Copiapo, Cobre, St. Jago, Burra Burra, Kapunda, Cornish, Irish, or Welsh, as the case may be), and so remains till its sale, when it is removed in large barges up the river to the copper-works. The bargemen (as I was informed by an intelligent, old, weather-beaten mariner, working a ferry-boat on the river) earn £1 a week, taking the year throughout. "There used to be lumpers," said he, "who took the job of discharging vessels and loading barges, and employed others under them; but the owners of the yards and works thought they put too much on the men's backs, and put an end to that custom." This man gave me something of his own history. He said: "I was fifty-five years at sea. I have been all over the world. The last vessel I was in was of twenty tons; she was in the fruit trade. I was sailing-master of her for three years, and earned on an average 50s. a month. Through my life I never saved anything. I left most of it in public-houses. First and last a good deal of it went there (pointing to a public-house near the river). I am now seventy-three years old. I had a wife and two children; all are dead and I am left alone. I live by this boat on what I can catch."

I next visited the "Cuba Company's yard." There the ore is crushed by passing through rollers moved by steam-power. The ores—some of a brassy lustre, some dark green, and others of a rich grey—were stored in large beds under an extensive roof, supported on iron pillars.

Here I saw the ore weighed, and its value was made apparent by the caution with which the turn of the scale was watched, and the delicacy observed in giving not a fraction more than the just weight. I was here informed that this company employed eighteen vessels in trade with Cuba, of which fifteen were barques of not less than 500 tons burden, and the remainder brigs.

Until within these two years past, the arrangements in Cuba for carrying the ore from the mines to the sea shore, and for putting it on board the vessels, were very imperfect, and the trade was thereby proportionably obstructed. The ores were brought to the water's edge on the backs of camels, and carried out to the vessels in boats. But recently railroads have been constructed, and stages erected over the water, so that vessels are now loaded there as conveniently and expeditiously as in an English harbour; by this means the vessels are enabled to perform a greater number of voyages within a given time than they previously could, and of course the cost of the ores, now that there is no such demurrage, is in a corresponding degree reduced. In Swansea, owing to the want of a floating dock, the discharging of copper ore is performed, I should say, less conveniently and with less despatch than it otherwise might be. However, a company for constructing docks was formed, and an act was obtained in 1847; but unexpected difficulties have arisen, which render it at present doubtful whether this useful scheme will ever be completed. The proposed works include a basin 100 yards long, and a dock 480 yards in length by 100 in breadth.

I need not describe the other "ore-yards;" there is no difference in them, nor in the classes who work there, with the exception that some yards are devoted to Welsh and Irish ores, and some to the Chilian ores, according to the particular trade of the companies or individuals to whom they belong. When the ores have been sold they are removed to the works whose proprietors become the purchasers. We have next to follow them there.

The first copper works I visited were the "Hafod Works," belonging to Messrs. Vivian and Sons. They are situated about two miles above the town, on the left bank of the Tawey, which is at this place narrow, but deep, having a flow of tide sufficient to carry up Cornish and other vessels of about 110 tons burden to the quays alongside the works, where they unship and deliver their cargoes. On the opposite bank stand Mr. Grenfell's works.

Viewed as a field for the employment of labour, the copper trade sinks into insignificance by the side of the iron trade. There are more than double the number of hands in one of the great iron works than are employed at all the copper works in the kingdom. But the workmen engaged in the copper trade have this advantage over their fellows in the other business, that their wages are, on the whole, better and steadier. There does not appear to me any reason, based on the degree of skill required of workmen in the copper as compared with the iron works, why the one should be better paid than the other. There is no process in copper smelting requiring more judgment or experience, or higher manual skill, than is required of a puddler in the iron works. Yet the hands who in the copper works perform duties corresponding with those of the puddlers, earn from 38s. to 44s. a week, whilst the puddler, working his full number of "turns," gets only from 22s. to 25s. in that time. The only manner in which I can account for the difference is this: Copper being an expensive metal, and not so much in demand for the rough purposes of commerce as iron is, does not fluctuate in value according to the prosperity or depression of the times in a like degree with iron. Add to this that the copper trade is in a very few hands, and these, acting in concert, can better regulate prices and keep them at such a rate as to allow of good wages; and it always has been the endeavour of the copper masters, through every change of circumstances in their trade, to keep the wages as equal, year after year, as they possibly can, in which they have so far succeeded that the changes have been very few. Indeed, I believe there is scarcely any branch of our manufacturing industry, where the transactions are so large, in which there has been less variation in the price of labour during the past ten years than in the copper trade. The effects are visible in the content and comfort of the workmen—strikes are of very rare occurrence indeed. The son succeeds his father in the works, and lives his time out, without apprehension of change or discomforts arising from adverse times.

The outward appearance of copper works differs from that of iron works chiefly in the absence of huge smelting furnaces, with their waving lines of flame, and in the colour and quality of their smoke. Both have an infinity of chimneys of similar height and dimensions; and both have stacks, but those of the copper works are the loftiest. However, once within the circle of the works, the difference is more striking; the copper works are not open at the sides to a like extent, and they do not show ponderous machinery in rapid motion, such as

you see in iron works. Neither is there in the copper works that show
of bustle and activity which is everywhere visible in the iron works;
and they are throughout darker, less dirty, less noisy, and less thickly
peopled.

The first and most disagreeable sensation which the visitor experiences on entering copper works is an irritability of the lungs, occasioned by the white sulphurous smoke he necessarily breathes. This
smoke, in some, if not in all, states of the atmosphere, is heavier than
air, and descends to the ground. On the morning that I visited Hafod-
works, it hung low—magnifying the men and horses at the canal in
the same manner as a wet fog does, and concealing the works except
the chimney-tops and stacks. I have already described the deadly effect this smoke has upon vegetation, and the singular diseases it occasions in cattle, horses, and sheep. As it may be interesting to many
to learn the constituents of this pernicious vapour—and as the knowledge may be serviceable in directing the attention of some scientific
mind to the discovery of that great desideratum, a cheap method of
depriving it of its poisonous qualities—I quote, from a tract on the
subject by Mr. Vivian, the following particulars:—

> "*Copper smoke*, or what may be properly considered under that head,
> as being peculiar to the operations in a copper work, may be said to
> consist of the following substances or chemical compounds, formed
> during the calcining processes by the evolution of substances contained
> in the ore:—
>
> "1. Sulphurous acid; 2. Sulphuric acid; 3. Arsenic; 4. Arsenious
> acid; 5. Fluoric compounds; and mechanical impurities. Of the above
> substances, the two first are formed by the combustion of the sulphur.
>
> "The *sulphurous acid*, which is by far the most abundant, is evolved
> in the state of a pungent and penetrating gas.
>
> "The *sulphuric acid*, which is composed of sulphur combined with
> more oxygen than exists in the sulphurous acid, and water, appears as
> a dense white vapour.
>
> "The *arsenical* contents of the copper ores expelled by heat, appear
> partly as *arsenic*, in the metallic state, partly as combined with oxygen,
> forming *arsenious acid*, or *white oxide of arsenic;* in both cases it assumes
> the form of vapour.
>
> "The *fluoric compounds* are produced by the decomposition of the
> fluor spar, or fluate of lime, during the chemical changes occurring in
> the calcination of the ore. The property of the fluoric acid to act on
> silica is well known, and probably, if the contents of the flue from the

calciners were accurately examined, *silicated fluoric acid gas* and *hydro-fluoric acid* would be found. The *mechanical impurities* consist of the fine particles of the ore carried over by the draught of the furnaces. They may contain a portion of copper; but the quantity of this is unquestionably very small, as has been fully proved by the deposits obtained from the various chambers; although by the most absurd and exaggerated statements it has been otherwise represented."

Several years ago a fund, amounting to £1,065, was raised, "for the purpose of remunerating any person who might completely obviate the inconvenience arising from copper smoke." A committee was appointed to decide upon the relative merits of the different plans proposed for effecting this object. Three competitors contended for this prize—Mr. Vivian, Mr. Bevington Gibbins, and Mr. Young. The system preferred was Mr. Vivian's; but as the committee were specially appointed to adjudicate the premium "for the total and effectual destruction of all noxious matters produced in the operations of copper smelting," and for nothing less—that requirement not being fulfilled—the premium does not appear to have been awarded. Beyond doubt, at that time and since, Mr. Vivian incurred heavy charges (he estimates the cost of his experiments at £6,000) in his endeavours to find a method of making copper smoke innoxious. He procured the assistance of Sir Humphry Davy, of Professor Faraday, and Mr. Phillips—but all to no purpose, as has since been proved by the abandonment of every attempt to correct this evil, though there was not a little self-gratulation at one time on the success of the simplest of all contrivances—the passing of the smoke through showers of water. In some of the works the lofty *stacks*, erected to carry up the poisonous smoke so high that it should become freely diluted before it reached the ground, have been disused—the farmers and neighbours stating that their effect was only to increase the evil by diffusing the smoke over a wider area. This was the case with the great stone *stack* at the Morfa Works, which, though built at an immense expense, is now abandoned.

Before entering upon any description of the works, I should state that, having been foiled in my endeavours to obtain from books and parliamentary papers an account of the number of hands employed, and of the calcining, smelting, and refining furnaces used, in the different copper works, with the quantity of coal daily consumed in each—particulars which are obviously essential to enable a writer to give a clear and complete view of the extent and importance of the copper trade and of the productive value of the Welsh coal-field, I applied to Messrs. Vivian for this information, as regards their works; at the same time stating that I wanted it for a public purpose, which I explained to them, and I showed them similar statements that had been obligingly furnished to me at other works, in order to further, as far as propriety and convenience would allow, the purposes of my inquiry. They declined giving me this information as regards their own works; but Mr. H. Vivian furnished me with a rough estimate of the entire of the copper-works, which I used, on his authority, in my last letter. At the adjoining works of Messrs. Williams, Foster, and Co., my wishes in this regard were courteously and promptly responded to; and the reader will be enabled to form a tolerably accurate estimate of the hands employed, the number of furnaces used, and the quantity of coal consumed in Messrs. Vivian's works, by taking the statements of these particulars as I shall give them in describing the works of Messrs. Williams, Foster, and Co., and reducing the numbers by the excess of 1,000 over 850, which is the difference in magnitude between the works of the two firms in favour of the last mentioned.

The following are the rates of wages paid by Messrs. Vivian, to the different classes of workmen in the Hafod Works, as returned to me by Mr. H. Vivian:—

"Ore calciner-men, 13s. to 14s. per week; metal calciner-men, 16s. to 17s. per week, with the privilege of discharging vessels, which, when they are so employed, gives them 4s. per day extra.

Ore furnace-men	23s. to 24s. per week.
Metal furnace-men	27s. to 28s. "
Roaster-men	38s. "
Refiners	44s. "
Boys	5s. to 7s. "
Labourers	12s. "

The calciner-men work intermittently during twenty-four hours, and rest twenty-four hours, unless they are employed in discharging vessels. The whole of the other men are on duty twelve hours, but no furnace-man's work is constant throughout the day.

There are at these works the following funds, created by stoppages out of the wages:—Doctor's fund, 6d. per month; sick fund, 8d. per month; school fund, 4d. per month. Many, if not most of the workmen, reside in houses the property of Messrs. Vivian, which I shall hereafter allude to; the rents vary from 1s. 6d. to 2s. a week.

I now proceed to describe the processes of smelting and manufacturing copper as I witnessed them at the Hafod Works; and I take this opportunity of making my acknowledgments to Mr. H. Vivian for his kindness in accompanying me through the works, and explaining the nature and object of every process. We first visited the laboratory, which is fitted up with the requisite accommodation for making the assays of the ores before purchase and manufacture. A number of experiments on various ores were in progress, the powdered ores being placed in small crucibles of clay ready for the reverberatory furnace, which a man and boy were then heating. We next visited a room where I learnt from a person in charge of it, that the women employed in these works are not numerous, that their occupation is wheeling ore and loading trams with clay, for removal to the cinder heaps. They earn from 7s. to 9s. a week. As they marry off, or die, they are not replaced by females, but by boys. Formerly the "slag-tramming" was performed entirely by women. I was glad to find that the system of employing females in the laborious duties they have here to perform is gradually dying out. Instead of being educated amongst men, away from the domestic hearth, and without opportunity of learning domestic duties, and the obligations of a wife and mother, they will now be home educated, and the benefit of this will be apparent in the improved morality of the generation of labourers who will rise up to fill the place vacated in the course of nature by the present workmen. I was also informed that boys get from 4s. 6d. to 7s. a week, which agrees very well with the written statement furnished by Mr. H. Vivian; indeed, to avoid the necessity of repeating what each class of workmen informed me was the rate of wages, I may once for all remark that the particulars above given I found on the whole very accurate.

The next scene to which the visitor is led, in the copper works, is the discharging of the copper ore from the vessels. The hands who perform this duty are the ore and metal "calciner-men," who do this sort of work in the intermediate twenty-four hours between their turns at the furnaces, and earn about 4s. a day. Boys also get on the list of "ore stage-wheelers" when they arrive at the age of 16; they then earn about 9s. a week. The ore is wheeled along stages from the vessels, and stored in large beds and heaps under a spacious iron-tied roof to protect it and the workpeople from the weather. There were Burra Burra, Cornish, and Irish ores in large quantities. This appears to me the proper place to give some account of the comparative richness of the various foreign and British ores smelted in this country. Here I should caution the reader against supposing that because the yield of foreign ores per cent. is nearly thrice that of British ores, the foreign mines are more productive; it by no means follows that such is the case, for it is only the best and richest lumps of foreign ore that are exported—the poor ores will not pay freightage, and are therefore left behind. I have constructed the following table showing the average produce per cent., the average price per ton, and the value of ore to produce a ton of copper, of the Chilian, Cuban, and Australian foreign ores; and of the Cornish, Irish, and Welsh, of the home-raised ores:—

COMPARATIVE VIEW OF BRITISH AND FOREIGN ORES FOR
THE QUARTER ENDING 31ST DECEMBER, 1848.

Ores.	Average Produce per cent.	Average Price.			Value of Ore to produce one ton of Copper.		
BRITISH.							
Cornish ore	8.564	£4	18	4	£57	8	3
Irish and Welsh ores . .	9.472	6	2	1	64	9	2
FOREIGN.							
Cuba	15.862	10	0	5	63	3	8
Chili	36.325	23	11	4	64	17	6
Australia	28.710	19	15	11	69	5	4

The relative values of foreign and British mining produce during twelve months, extending up to June, 1847, is thus given in the *Mining Almanac:*—

RETURNS OF BRITISH AND FOREIGN MINES, WITH COMPARATIVE
PRODUCE AND PRICE PER TON.

"The returns made of the produce of British mines for the twelve months ending June, 1847, as compared with the returns of foreign mines, will give some idea of the richness of the latter in comparison with our own.

"The following table we believe to be perfect, giving the produce of British mines, while the remarks appended will show the difference in value of home and foreign ores, the former, say 4*l*. 10s. per ton, and the latter, 15*l*. 5s., or an excess as shown of 223 per cent.

No. of Mines.	Price per Ton.	No. of Tons.	Amount in value.
10	Under £3	1,713	£4,297
12	„ 4	9,123	32,025
29	„ 5	45,942	209,276
23	„ 6	30,558	165,748
15	„ 7	58,700	369,688
6	„ 8	15,477	115,642
1	„ 9	101	845
1	„ 10	84	774
2	Above 10	1,873	23,584
99		163,571	£921,879

"From the above statement it will be seen that of the quantity raised, about two-fifths of the mines produced 56,778 tons, or one-third the quantity, the value of which was 245,590*l.*, giving an average of 4*l.* 6s. 8d. per ton, while the remaining three-fifths produced 87,336 tons, being upwards of half the entire quantity raised, yielding 411,338*l.*, or an average of 4*l.* 14s. 2d., thus showing that of the quantities of ores raised by two-thirds of the mines, of which returns are given, the produce was little more than four-ninths in value.

"On comparing these results with the price of the foreign ores, for the like period, it will be found that the average of the latter was 15*l.* 4s. 9d. per ton, which, if compared with that of British mines, gives the excess in favour of foreign at 10*l.* 10s. 7d. per ton, or 223 per cent."

The subjoined table, which I also extract from the *Mining Almanac*, is interesting, as contrasting the quantities of copper produced from British ores, during five years, against that produced from foreign ores, with the total value, separate and united:—

QUANTITIES OF COPPER CONTAINED IN ORES PURCHASED BY SMELTERS IN FIVE YEARS ENDING 30TH JUNE, 1848; DISTINGUISHING THOSE OF BRITISH AND FOREIGN PRODUCTION, AND QUANTITIES PURCHASED AT TICKETINGS, THOSE IMPORTED BY SMELTERS, OR BOUGHT BY PRIVATE CONTRACT, WITH AGGREGATE VALUE, &C.

	Copper produced from British Ores.			Copper produced from Foreign Ores.			Total Purchases.	From British Ores.	From Foreign Ores.	Total Value.
	Purchased at Ticketings in Cornwall & Swansea.	Purchased by Private Contract.	Total British Ores.	Purchased at Ticketings at Swansea.	Imported and bought by Private Contract.	Total Foreign Ores.		Total Value of British Ores computed at Average Prices.	Total Value of Foreign Ores at Average Prices.	
	Copper. Tons.	Copper. Tons.	Copper. Tons.	Copper. Tons.	Copper. Tons.	Copper. Tons.	Copper. Tons.	£	£	£
1844	12,908	1,873	14,841	9,387	3,287	12,674	27,515	1,089,603	1,006,851	2,096,454
1845	13,818	1,121	14,939	8,770	2,106	10,876	25,815	1,028,535	798,528	1,827,063
1846	13,958	997	14,955	8,278	2,814	11,092	26,047	1,073,924	848,677	1,922,601
1847	13,160	625	13,785	7,663	1,377	9,040	22,825	965,661	690,038	1,655,699
1848	14,364	356	14,720	7,151	1,312	8,463	23,183	943,846	631,643	1,575,489
Total Amounts.	68,268	4,972	73,240	41,249	10,896	52,145	125,385	5,101,569	3,975,737	9,077,306
Average per an.	13,654	994	14,648	8,250	2,179	10,429	25,077	1,020,314	795,147	1,815,461

By this it will be seen that the quantity of copper made yearly from British ores exceeds that made from foreign ores by 4,219 tons; while the total value of the former annually exceeds that of the latter by £225,167.

I resume my description of the works at the ore-sheds amongst the heaps of ore from various countries, some glittering with a brassy brilliancy, some deep green, some of a blue cast, and others (which had been already treated for the extraction of tin and sulphuric acid) of a deep crimson. I there saw women, dressed in the linsey-wolsey garments of the country, loading and wheeling the ore in barrows to the bottom of an incline, worked by steam, up which the barrows were drawn to the platform over the calcining furnaces. I questioned one of these women. She wore a red and white Welsh plaid woollen gown, gathered up behind, black petticoats, sleeves of blue cotton, a white apron, a neat cap, and jaunty Welsh hat. She was thin, sallow, and smoke-dried; at one time she must have been handsome. She said— "I have been working here these fifteen years. We work nine hours a day, but not by night. We earn 9s. a week." Another of them told me the work agreed pretty well with their health. We now ascended the incline to the stages over the calcining furnaces; here we found men wheeling the ores to the "hoppers" above, and leading into the calcining furnaces. Each hopper receives about forty-five hundred weight of ore, and when twice filled and emptied, the "charge" is complete, and the process of calcining commences. The effect here is striking; you see men flitting about the dark and long stages in various directions; below you are vaults and arches stretching away until form is lost in the darkness, gleams of red fire peep out here and there from the furnaces, and the rattle of trains as they run along their iron rails on this or that line quickens your faculties to keep out of danger, for the gloom is such that you see but a short distance around you. The sulphur here is scarcely endurable. You next descend to the level of the "calciners." Here I should state that all furnaces employed in the copper-works are reverberatory; there are no open furnaces. The ore is placed in the body of the furnace, which is separated from the fireplace by a bridge of bricks, over which the flame passes, reverberating from the roof upon the charge of ore, and passing off through a flue, carrying with it any volatile matter given out by the ores. The calcining and other furnaces stand in rows, each having an open and deep trough in front, into which the charge, after calcination, is drawn. Each furnace has six openings, three on each side, for the purpose of stirring the ore. On looking through one of these, you see the flames curling thin and vapoury along the arch of the furnace; and the ore beneath looks of a dull deep red, with occasional spots of a brighter colour. You see the operation of a "rabbling," which is performed at regular intervals by means of an iron instrument called a "rabble;" this is moved to and fro in the ore by the "calciner man." The ore opens in deep red masses to the "rabble," and fresh surfaces are in this way presented to the action of the fire. The object of this process is to dis-engage the sulphur and such other impurities as are volatile from the ores, and the endeavour is to heat the mass for this purpose to the highest point it will bear short of fusion. When calcined and cooled, the ore has the appearance of small, black gravel. It is next wheeled to a narrow railway, where it is put into trams, which are hauled to a water balance, and by it lifted to the stages above. It is then put into bins or hoppers, and let down into the "ore furnaces" in the same manner as we have seen it admitted to the "calciners."

I saw two of the workmen at dinner at the fire-place of one of the calcining furnaces, and I questioned them. One was a robust and healthy-looking young man, who had been only a few months in the works; the other looked spare and sallow, was married, and his wife and daughter, clean and well dressed, were waiting whilst he made his dinner. They had savoury dinners of breast of mutton, turnips, and potatoes; and their drink, as they showed me, was water. They were dressed (as nearly all the labouring men dress here whilst in their work) in white canvas trowsers, a blue woollen shirt, and checked neckerchief. They had each a handkerchief bound round the head in lieu of cap or hat. The strongest and youngest of them said, "I am 19 years of age, and I earn, as a calciner-man, 13s. a week. I am on duty twenty-four hours together; but I sleep here before the fire, from twelve at night till two in the morning. I 'come on' at six in the morning; we then wheel ore from the bottom of the furnace to the receiving-house, 'turning by;' this takes us from six till eleven o'clock. Every two hours we are called by the watchman to *stir* the calciner, which takes a quarter of an hour. At ten at night we are called to 'pull out;' this takes one hour, and 'recharging' takes one hour; it is then twelve at night. The watchman then calls us to *stir* at two, at four, and at six o'clock, when the twenty-four hours are up. I then go home and am off duty twenty-four hours; but in the meanwhile I can work at un-loading vessels, by which I earn sometimes 4s. in the course of twelve hours. I get my 13s. a week for attending the furnace only."

At the ore-furnaces the second process is performed, which consists of melting the calcined ore. Here the metallic oxides and earthy matters, being lighter than the metal, float on the surface and are skimmed off as slags. I saw a man "skimming;" he stood before the open door of a furnace, exposed to a white heat, which made the perspiration start in big drops and run in streams from his face and neck. With a long *rabble* he drew out the liquid slag white-hot through the door into a trough in front. It had the frothy appearance of barm, seemed heavy, and broke off short as it fell from the furnace. A man with a ladle took part of it, and cast it into moulds for "coping" walls; the remainder, when cool, is taken to the slag-yard, broken, examined to see whether it contains any particle of copper; such as does, is sent back for re-melting, and the remainder put into trams for removal to the cinder-heap. I also saw here the process of *tapping.* Between every two furnaces there is a circular pit of water some 18 feet deep; to this a spout reaches from each furnace, and the fluid metal, red and grouty, is by this means run off into the water, where it becomes granulated in sinking, and collects in a pan at the bottom; this, in due course, is lifted by a crane, and the metal is wheeled to the place where the next process is performed. From five to eight charges are thus melted in the twenty-four hours, slags from former processes being thrown in with the calcined ore. Smart streams of water run through the works to cool the workmen's tools, and refrigerate the pits into which the melted copper is run, as we have seen. The metal thus granulated contains generally about one-third copper; its components are chiefly copper, iron, and sulphur. We next went into the slag yard, where we found a number of men and boys breaking the slag with hammers, and diligently searching it for traces of copper. Such as they found unclean— that is, containing specks of metal—were thrown back for re-melting; the remainder was placed, by women called "slag-trammers," in trams for lifting to the lofty cinder-heaps at the back of the works.

In the third process, the granulated metal is exposed to fire in calcining furnaces, precisely similar to the first. The sulphur is here given off in such quantities as to make respiration painful to a person unaccustomed to the fiery and suffocating atmosphere of these works. The metal in the furnace has now a bright crimson hue, and is sandy, with an uneven surface. A man here, on being asked how he endured the heat and sulphur, replied, "I stand the work as well as can be expected in so much smoke. There is not much sickness amongst us—we live like other people, as well as we can." The smoke from these calciners, and from that where the ore is first submitted to the action of fire, is conveyed along flues, supported on arches, to the main stack. It is the smoke from these furnaces that is most poisonous: that from the melting furnaces, being little more than coal-smoke, passes upwards through ordinary chimneys.

The fourth process is performed in furnaces similar to those in which the ore is first melted. The granulated copper is here thoroughly melted, the produce being copper and slag—the former containing 70 per cent. of the pure metal; the latter should be cleaner than that from the first melting furnace. The slag is here skimmed off with a "rabble" as before, leaving the copper in the bottom of the furnace. When cooled and broken the metal has a white, crystalline, and sparkling appearance, and is a combination of sulphur and copper; it is here run into pigs, about three feet long and eighteen inches wide.

In the fifth process the pigs are introduced entire to the *Roasting Furnaces,* which are the same in form and size as the melting furnaces. The heat is here gradually increased, and the pigs are slowly melted down during 24 hours. This is chiefly an oxidizing process; the whole, or nearly the whole, of the sulphur is here disengaged, and the metals still combined with the copper are oxidized. The produce is coarse copper, of about 95 per cent. The metal has now become tough, is porous, of a brilliant red, and rings to the hammer most musically. On looking through the plug-hole in the furnace door I saw the metal simmering and bubbling, with a frothy even surface. Atmospheric air is here freely admitted, and the sulphur passes rapidly off—in the shape of sulphuric acid vapour, thick and white—to the stack. Up to this point the intention has been to retain sufficient sulphur in combination with the copper to protect the latter from oxydation; here the object is to eliminate the sulphur as quickly and as completely as possible, which this process effects in the most economical manner. The metal is run into pigs as before.

We now come to the sixth and last process, which is *refining.* The furnace in which the metal is refined is similar to the melting furnace, except that its floor inclines to a pool, or well, near the door. The pigs from the "roasters" are here put in entire, and exposed at first to a moderate fire, so as to drive away any remaining sulphur or other impurities. The refining furnace is charged over-night, and at eight o'clock in the morning the first operation of refining is commenced, by the insertion of long poles of wood (they call them *branches*); these are permitted to burn in the fluid metal, by which means any oxygen which it may have absorbed is removed. When the operation of "*pol-ing*" is complete—which is not the case until the whole of the oxygen in the copper has been taken up—the metal is ready for "lading." It is then taken from the pool, or well, near the door of the furnace, by means of ladles, and poured into moulds of any form which the market requires—whether bricks, pigs, cakes, ingots, or other denominations. Often the metal is poured into a water-well to be "feathered" for brass-making. I saw this performed. The mouth of the well was closed with wood, all but the centre, from which arose a conical iron funnel, with the narrowest end uppermost. The men—having covered their hands and arms with canvas mittens, lined with clay, for protection from the fire—advanced to the furnace door, plunged their ladles in the pool of copper, and carried them to the well, into which they poured the copper; this is of a beautiful green colour, and indicates its weight by falling in a straight line from the lip of the ladle, through the funnel, to the water, which seeths and explodes noisily as the intensely hot metal sinks rapidly, downwards. The heaps of feathered copper, reflecting the light in a thousand points, have a richness of colour that must be seen to be appreciated. With this the process of smelting copper terminates. The metal, brilliant in colour, tough and malleable, is now ready for the market or for manufacture. Ingots for making brass are about 10½ inches long by 2½ thick, and weigh about 14 lbs. Copper cakes for rolling are 15 inches long by 11 in width, and weigh about 1 cwt. I reserve description of the manufacturing department of those works for a future letter.

―――――――――

LABOUR AND THE POOR.

THE MINING AND MANUFACTURING DISTRICTS OF SOUTH WALES.

[FROM OUR SPECIAL CORRESPONDENT.]

SWANSEA—THE COPPER WORKS AND POTTERIES.

LETTER XV.

Having described in a former Letter the several processes of calcining, roasting, and refining copper, I now come to the particulars of manufacture. The machinery here, moved by steam power, is ponderous and gigantic. In construction it is similar to that which I have described as used in the rolling mills at the iron works; and the method of working is nearly the same as that by which sheet-iron is produced. They were making sheet-copper when I entered the rolling-house. For this purpose the cake of copper is heated to a proper degree in an "annealing furnace," and it is then passed through successive pairs of rollers, until it is distended to the required size. When reduced in this manner to the prescribed thickness, the sheet is next presented to a large shears, by which the "shruff," or uneven edges, are cut off. The appearance of the copper at this time is of a glossy black, the sheet seeming to have been black-leaded. This is the result of oxidation of the metal. Men and boys perform all the work at the rolling-mills. The rollermen earn about £1 a week. Occasionally, by working "overtime," they make eight "stems" a week, which brings them 25s. Boys at the "rolls" earn on an average 6s. a week. They roll here copper plates for boilers, weighing, sometimes, as much as 17 cwt. the finished plate.

The next process of manufacture is called "pickling." The object here is to cleanse and brighten the copper by removing the coat of oxide which covers it. For this purpose the sheet of copper is dipped in uric acid, then placed in a wide-mouthed furnace, and heated red hot. It is then taken out, and the "pickler" plunges it, with a dexterous side-jerk of the arm, edgeways into a cistern of cold water, which it enters with a loud snarl. The effect is magical. The black scale of oxide disappears, and the sheet comes out of the trough of a clear, bright, and true copper colour. It is now ready for shearing and use. The sheets are next piled together, counted, weighed, and screwed down between boards, for market purposes.

In another department I saw the process of making pans and "bottoms," as they are called, for brewers' furnaces and other uses. The copper is beaten out and rounded by means of one of Nasmyth's steam-hammers. I was told that they once made under this hammer a circular "bottom" for a brewer's vat, which was not less than 10 feet three inches in diameter. Here ends what I saw of the interesting processes of smelting and manufacturing copper.

The general appearance of the workmen is not favourable, though they are undoubtedly well fed, well clothed, and well housed. Their countenances are sallow, and their persons desiccated, wiry, and thin. Breathing an air largely impregnated with arsenic and sulphur, it could scarcely be otherwise. Nevertheless, many of them live to a considerable age, proving the aptitude of the human body to accommodate itself to the circumstances which surround and affect it, even though these circumstances are in general prejudicial to life. Habit steels the constitution, and, like Mithridates,

"They feed on poisons and they live on such."

I am told that men coming from a distance and taking employment at the copper-works acclimatise, or die, within a very few months. They brought to me at these works some old men, whose statements, when they were called on to speak of their health, were as follows:—"I am 67 years of age," said the first, "and I have been 40 years engaged in the copper-works. In that time I have been through every stage of the business, from a calciner man upwards; my health has been always pretty good." Another workman said:—"I came here before I was 20, and am now 59. I work every day about ten hours. My health is now as good as ever it was. The general health of the men is pretty middling."

Upon the question of the health of the workmen here and their families, who reside near and within the range of the copper-smoke, Mr. Evans, the surgeon to the works, obligingly gave me the following information:—"The general health of the men engaged in the copper-works is pretty good. Sometimes they suffer from *pleuritis*, which is their prevailing disease. There are some men who have not lost a day from sickness these eight or ten years." Here the surgeon called a man from his work and asked him how long it was since he had given him a dose of physic? The man answered, "It is 12 years ago at least." Mr. Evans then resumed his remarks: "The general health in the works has been very much improved since the introduction of the 'water-balance' for raising the ores and metal to the furnaces. Formerly the men used to carry the ores in boxes on their heads to the hoppers. The 'firemen' will live ten years the longer for this change. There is a capacious warm bath erected here for the benefit of the workmen; but there exists a prejudice against the use of it among them: they fancy it will weaken their loins; but they are coming more to adopt it. Although the men, their wives and dependants, who are under my charge, number nearly 3,000, I have not at present a single serious case of illness to attend to. The cholera was bad here. On the other side of the river, at Lansamlet, scarlatina was and is very prevalent: it is remarkable that there was very little cholera there."

There is, within the same curtilage as the Hafod Works, a "silver-mill," also the property of the Messrs. Vivian. Great secrecy is observed with respect to this establishment for the manufacture of silver. I was not aware that any such existed when I visited these works; but I have since repeatedly heard it spoken of with allusions to the jealousy with which its precincts are guarded, and its proceedings shrouded in mystery. The copper ores frequently contain a large per centage of silver. I was informed that a German chemist is here employed for the extraction of the silver from the copper ores.

At the request of Mr. H. Vivian I here insert some remarks which he laid before me upon the several processes of copper smelting, as practised in South Wales:—

"A stranger, on leaving a copper smelting works, even though he may happen to be practically or scientifically qualified to judge of metallurgical operations, would in most cases have a vague feeling of confusion in his mind, arising from the number of processes which he has witnessed, and an impression that these processes might be materially shortened, and that with great economy. The former of these impressions would be correct, the latter incorrect, for probably no metallurgical processes exist better calculated to effect the end in view, viz., the obtaining the largest proportion of the copper contained in the ore; nor are there, perhaps, any processes based on more accurate practical and scientific results. In confirmation of this assertion, two rather singular facts may be cited:—1st. That the processes employed on the

Continent are in all essentials identically the same, although different furnaces, suited to the different fuel, are used, and it may be considered as almost certain, that no intercourse existed between the smelting establishments of this country and the Continent at the very remote period from which both date; and 2dly, although frequent attempts have been made to alter the process, still no material change has taken place in its principles, while great economy has been introduced in the practical working—so great that upwards of 20*l.* per ton more is given now for the copper in the ore, as compared to the value of copper, than at the commencement of the present century. The reason of this may be simply stated to be, that each part of the process has its particular end, and cannot be dispensed with without loss of produce. I will now proceed to describe shortly the process of copper smelting, which may be characterised rather as a separation of the extraneous matter from the copper than of the copper from the impurities present in the ore.

"The largest proportion, probably 9-10ths, of the copper ore found in the world, consists of the double sulphuret of copper and iron, mixed usually with a considerable quantity of iron pyrites. The produce of the English copper ores may be taken at rather more than 8 per cent., and that of those foreign ores which are sufficiently rich to bear the cost of transit, &c., from 15 to 25. In treating this subject, I shall exclude the Burra Burra ore, which, being a carbonate, requires a very simple process of reduction, while it forms an immaterial portion of the whole, and may be regarded rather as an exception. From the above data, and the relative quantities of British and foreign ores, we shall perhaps not be very wide of the truth if we state the average produce of ore smelted in the Swansea establishments at from 10 to 12 per cent. Its constituent parts may be assumed roughly to be as follows:—10 per cent. copper, 33 per cent. iron, 22 per cent. sulphur, and 35 per cent. earthy matter. The processes may be arranged in four classes, viz.—a calcination and melting, having for their object the getting rid of the earthy matter, together with such a portion of the iron freed from sulphur and oxidized by calcination as will combine with and fuse the earthy matters in such a manner as to produce a clean slag. The product of these two processes is almost one-third part regulus or sulphuret of copper, and of iron about 33 per cent. and two-thirds of slag, which, when examined, is thrown away. The next class is a calcination and melting similar to the first, their object being the getting rid of all metallic matter other than copper contained in the product of the first process, which is effected by calcining the regulus to such an extent as to drive off the whole sulphur combined with iron, and oxidize the latter, rendering it thereby readily fusible, while sufficient sulphur is left to combine with and protect the copper from oxidation and consequent slagging. The product of this process is a pure sulphuret of copper, of 70 per cent., and it will be seen that only one-third part of the original bulk of the ore comes to this process, while only one-seventh leaves it for the next, which—the 3d class—is termed a roasting process, whereby, in a short period, very large masses of sulphuret of copper are deprived of their sulphur, and coarse copper of 95 per cent. is obtained. So great is the simplicity of this process, that above one thousand tons of copper are deprived of their sulphur in one furnace each year. The fourth and last class is the refining process, in which the coarse copper of the former process is brought to a marketable state by a further roasting, to get rid of the last portions of sulphur, and subsequent de-oxidising, by inserting a pole to remove any oxygen which the copper may have absorbed by being melted in contact with air."

The houses of the workmen next had my attention. Within the past few years Mr. Vivian has erected a considerable number of dwellings for his workmen, upon a height above the works, bestowing upon the new village the name "Tre Vivian"—or Vivian town. I examined several of these houses. They are of two classes—one, having two rooms below and two above stairs, for which the rent is 1s. 6d. per week; the other having two good rooms, a parlour, kitchen, and passage on the ground floor, and three rooms up-stairs—one for the parents, another for the sons, a third for the daughters—a most judicious and praiseworthy arrangement. These let for 2s. a week. The kitchen floor is of brick; there is in the fire-place a good range and an oven; the parlour is boarded, and the rooms are lofty and sufficiently lighted. Behind the house is a strip of garden ground, at the end of which there are a privy and pigstye. A complete sewerage has lately been added to these most comfortable and convenient dwellings. I saw in the houses I entered the same wealth of furniture, the same love of display, and the same neatness and cleanliness which I spoke of as characterising the workmen's cottages in the iron works. I shall describe one or two presently. Not only at these, but at all the copper works, the men are allowed a certain quantity of coal for household use, cost free. This is a great boon to them.

Above these houses, and situated on a commanding eminence, are the new schools which Mr. Vivian has recently erected. They are built of blue limestone, and have a handsome elevation. The design, I am told, was Mr. Vivian's. There are here three school-rooms—one for boys, another for girls, and a third for infants. I first visited the boys' school. The master is from the training institution at Battersea. The room—which is lofty, well lighted and ventilated, and heated with warm water—has a sloping floor, with a dais at the lower end for the master. The walls are hung with maps and monitory precepts. The accommodation is for 200 boys, but the average attendance is about 100. The boys are taught reading, writing, arithmetic, grammar, and geography. They are to be taught singing. On the whole, the scholars were well clothed and clean. The master said that he insisted on these observances. Many of the copybooks showed very creditable writing. They admit boys whose parents do not belong to the works, on payment of 2d. a week—of these, however, there are not many. In the roof there is a square lanthorn, with moveable sashes, for ventilation, which gives an air of lightness and airiness to this fine school-room.

I next went to the girls' school. The room is similarly constructed, warmed, and ventilated. The governess is from the Borough Training Institution of the British and Foreign School Society. The number of scholars on the books was 150, but the average attendance in the summer season is 110. There are about from 40 to 50 "strangers' children" here educated; they pay 2d. a week. The girls learn sewing and knitting, reading, working, arithmetic, grammar, history, geography, and singing. Generally the girls were clean and neatly dressed; "they are improving," said the governess, "in that particular. We have conveniences here to wash them. They come here at seven years of age, and we have girls as old as sixteen. When the school was first opened, three years ago, the ignorance of the children was lamentable, but they are greatly better now." The system followed in this school is the "monitorial" plan of the British and Foreign School Society.

The infant school is held in an adjoining room. I here found the governess and a circle of infants kneeling at prayers. It was a touching and a beautiful sight. Afterwards I obtained the following particulars relative to this department of the schools. The governess, a very intelligent and, I should say, efficient teacher, is from the Home and Colonial Training Establishment. Infants from two to seven years of age are here educated. The average attendance is 110; the numbers have been as high as 180. Many infants attend whose parents do not belong to the works; when more than one of these come from the same family, the first pays 2d. and the others 1d. per week each. The system pursued is that of the Home and Colonial Society. The infants are taught reading, spelling, the rudiments of natural history, and singing. To these excellent schools there are attached convenient lavatories and spacious playgrounds, furnished with swings for girls, and gymnastic poles for boys. There are also commodious houses for the master and mistresses, and gardens attached.

From the above particulars, it will be seen that not only are the men in these works well paid, but their personal comforts and the wants of their families have been assiduously studied and liberally provided for. One only suggestion I will make—and that is, that the system of keeping men on continuous duty during twenty-four hours is bad, and ought to be abolished; it has been found to work ill in other copper works, as I shall presently show, and there, very properly, it was changed for the twelve-hour system. I must also remark upon the large deduction from the wages made for doctor, sick-fund, and school, which here amounts to 1s. 6d. a month on each man's wages. The same accommodations were provided at Dowlais, even in the time of the cholera (when the rates necessarily increased), for 6d. a month, and it is, I believe, now reduced to 4d. I could not learn that any account whatever is rendered to the men of the expenditure of the large fund which is in this manner raised from their labour.

A few days afterwards I visited the "Morva Works," the largest copper establishment in the world. They are the property of Messrs. Williams, Foster, and Co., and the resident manager is Mr. Pooley, a gentleman to whom I am indebted for the following interesting particulars relative to these works, and to the character and conduct of the men engaged in this branch of industry.

The works belonging to Messrs. Williams, Foster, and Co., with the number of furnaces employed in each, are as follows:—

Rose Works . . . . 50 calcining and other furnaces.
Landore . . . . 22 „ „
Morva . . . . 26 „ „
Crown (near Neath) .. 35 „ „
Ditto Spelter Works .. 9 furnaces and 6 calciners.

The number of hands employed in these works is 620. Only fourteen women are employed—four in the Morva and ten in the Rose works. They are on *task work*, wheeling coals to the furnaces, and earn about 7s. a week. The average number of boys employed is not more than 10 per cent. on the total of hands engaged in the works. The rates of wages here are as below stated:—

Foreman refiners (one in each works)	50s. a week.
Assistant refiners	40s. to 42s.
Roaster men	30s.
Furnace men	25s. to 27s.
Calciner men	16s. 6d. to 18s. 6d.
Roller men	25s. to 30s.
Cutters	30s.
Picklers	25s.

Engine men, 24s. (These men earn about 3s. a week more for manufacturing the gas used in the works.)

Boys (from 10 to 14 years), 6s.

Boatmen on the river, bringing up ores from vessels, 25s. a week (these pay their "hoblers"1s. 6d. a tide).

"Tradesmen"—that is, blacksmiths, carpenters, and masons, working from six till six—earn, according to their skill, 20s. to 30s.

Labourers unloading vessels, wheeling ore to the furnaces, and weighing copper, 20s. to 25s. a week.

There is here no "day-work"—all is done by "task;" and there is no working upon Sundays, a few calciners excepted, who keep the fires in. The men in these works are twelve hours on and twelve hours off duty. Formerly they used here, as at other works, to be 24 hours on continuous duty. "But there existed this evil," said Mr. Pooley, "from that arrangement, that the men, during the 24 hours they were off duty, used to go and discharge vessels, by which they earned a good deal of money, which they spent in drunkenness, and were, in consequence, often unfit for their regular work. They resisted the change, when we made it, and they 'struck;' but we compelled them to adopt our regulation of 12 hours' work. It was in the Crown works the men struck."

I was informed by Mr. Pooley that it was not only a frequent thing, but an object of ambition among the workmen to buy or build houses. Of the morals of the men engaged in the copper-works I cannot speak with so much confidence as a gentleman who has lived years among them. Preferring Mr. Pooley's statement to the opinions I gathered in other quarters, which I found conflicting and unsatisfactory, I give it as I noted it down from his lips. "I have now been," said he, "for thirty years an agent of mines and smelting-works, having from 250 to 1,000 men under my care during the whole of that time, with abundant facilities for observing and judging of their character and habits; and I can conscientiously say that there has been a great improvement in the morals and conduct of the men in that time, but more especially within the last two or three years. I had never had so little anxiety or trouble with the men as I have at present. We have made no reduction of wages here for the past six years. I never hear the slightest complaint as to their wages, or any expressions of discontent on other subjects. We have here no 'truck,' but pay the men every Friday afternoon between two and three o'clock, so that their wives may go with cash in their hands to market on the Saturday. A few of the men, and only a few, lose the Monday sometimes in drinking. They are mostly furnace-men who are thus intemperate; but we suffer no inconvenience by it, for there are always some 'hangers on' waiting an opening for steady employment, whom we put in the places of such as are absent until they return to their duty. As vacancies occur these 'hangers-on' are taken in as regular workmen. The health of the men upon the whole stands good. Drinking variously affects different classes of the workmen—for instance, refiners can bear almost any quantity of beer, they perspire so copiously at the furnaces. They drink beer chiefly—they very rarely touch spirits."

At the Rose works there is a manufactory of copper nails and bolts, where 80 tons of nails for sheathing ships, slating houses, and for the decks of vessels, are made yearly. The nailors are an exceedingly steady set of men. "We brought them up," said Mr. Pooley, "from boys to that work, and they never lose a day, unless it be from sickness. They are the most temperate class in the works."

The daily consumption of coal in the Morva and other works belonging to Messrs. Williams, Foster, and Co., is 430 tons. This firm, some years ago, united with Messrs. Vivian to work collieries for the supply of their works. Under the name of "The Swansea Coal Company" they also sell and export coal, but not in large quantities.

It were greatly to be wished that particular accounts of the quantities of coal yearly consumed in manufactures were kept in this country, and contributed to the "Mining Almanac," or some other central medium for collecting and publishing them. It is only by such means that an accurate idea can be formed of the productiveness of our coal fields, and the rate at which we are annually exhausting them. Of the coals sent coastwise and exported, and of those sent from the pits by rail and tram-roads for distribution and consumption in adjacent districts, proper returns *can* be obtained, though the last-mentioned have never been collected; but of the immense quantities raised by the iron and copper masters for use in their works, no estimate of practical value can at present be made. Yet nothing is more easy than for those parties to collect this desirable information. Their colliers are paid so much a ton for cutting and raising coal—consequently the books containing the colliers' accounts will show with the greatest precision the number of tons actually raised; from this the quantities supplied to the workmen for private use may easily be discriminated by means of the same books, which show the stoppages from the workmen's wages on account of coal for family consumption. In this manner every ton of coal used in the works and locally by the workmen may with sufficient accuracy be ascertained. I have done all in my power throughout this inquiry to furnish information on this interesting but neglected subject, always inquiring, at the works I inspected, the daily consumption of coal, which I have given in all cases where it was furnished me. I hope attention will be directed hereafter to this desideratum, which is necessary to enable us to form an accurate account of the value of our coal fields, and of the cost of producing a given quantity of our manufactures.

A few particulars of my house-visitation and of the examinations of individuals will carry greater weight than the general statements I have given as to the condition of the workmen and their families. The first house I entered had three rooms down stairs—a parlour, a kitchen, and a back kitchen. The parlour was boarded; it had mahogany tables and chairs, a handsome eight-day clock, a showy mahogany chest of drawers, a dressing-glass, a beaufet, and a profusion of articles in china and glass. The kitchen had a brick floor; the fireplace, kept neatly blacked, was furnished with a good kitchen range and an oven. The owner of the house, his wife, and three children, all clean and happy-looking, were at their tea, having a plentiful supply of good white wheaten bread and butter. The house was a model of cleanliness and order. The following is the man's statement:—

J—— E——: "I am a 'pickler' in the squire's works. This is my house. I built this house and another, partly by money I had with my wife, and partly by our savings. I have a small garden, a pigstye, and a privy attached to the house. I earn 15s. a week. We are allowed 14 cwt. of coals every six weeks cost free. (I should here say this allowance is made in all the copper works.) I am paid by task-work, so my earnings vary. I have made as much as 19s. and sometimes as little as 12s. a week. Promotion is slow in the works; but as those who are above me die off or leave I shall go forward to better work and better pay. I live in that hope. When I came here from the Iron-works six years ago, the change disagreed with me. I suffered much from my stomach; the sulphur affected me. I spat blood then for some time; but now I am become used to it, and my health is pretty good."

Turning in to a very large house which, to my surprise, I was told was tenanted by a workman, I found parlours to the right and left, with hair-bottomed sofas and good mahogany furniture. Behind these was a roomy kitchen, supplied with every convenience for comfort. The man told me he was a refiner, employed at the Morva works; he had a wife and four children. He had bought the house in which he lived, and three others, out of his own savings.

A little further on I came upon some houses inhabited by the Irish. I found them here just as I have described them in the Iron-works, living in filth, rags, and squalor. On inquiring of their neighbours on both sides as to their general behaviour and mode of life, I was told that often the wife, whilst the husband is in the works, betakes herself with her children to the road, or goes down to Swansea begging. I was also told that they save money and migrate to other places, that they have frequent street-brawls, and fight and quarrel continually. They drink a good deal; but, owing to the manner in which they are shunned and disliked by the Welsh, they carouse amongst themselves at home, more than in the public houses. I entered one of their cottages. That peculiar close and fetid stench which I observed in the houses of the Irish in Merthyr I found also here. The house was inhabited by two families. They had lived there three years last Easter. The husbands were not at home, but a vagrant ragged Irishman (looking, as he said, for work) was seated on a block of wood, rocking a cradle made out of an orange crate, in which, wrapped in dirty blankets, was a jolly-looking infant. A round three-legged table, two low benches, a stool, a tea-kettle on the fire, a pitcher of water, a teapot, a few plates and cups and saucers—crowded on the mantel-piece without any pretensions to neatness or order—formed the entire contents of the room. Upstairs were two beds on the floor, with filthy coverings. One of the women, in reply to my questions said, "My husband's name is C—— D——. He works at the 'squire's,' and earns 11s. a week. We pay 1s. 3d. a week for rent. We get meat, to tell the truth, *twice in the week and once on Sundays.*"

Next door to the Irish house I saw a woman engaged in cooking. I entered the house, and found it a model of neatness and comfort. The poor old Welsh woman said:—"My name is S—— J——. I have been a widow fifteen years, and am now dependent upon my sons, who live at home and support me. They are hard-working boys, and good to their mother. They have never given me any trouble. One is nearly twenty, in June, the other seventeen. The oldest of them earns 10s. and the other 6s. a week in the copper-works. Before they were able to work I laboured hard, late and early, to support six children, left dependent on me when their father died. Three of my children are dead. I used to work in the copper-works. I pay 5s. a month rent, and we get on very comfortably. We have a little meat every day." This good old woman was preparing the tea for her sons on their return from work. She had spread a clean cloth on the table, laid out the tea things with milk and butter, and even set chairs ready for them. When I entered she was engaged in preparing over the fire, on what is called a "bakestone," a thick hot cake to be used at the coming meal with butter.

In the last house I entered I found evidences of the sufferings occasioned by sickness. The husband, it appeared, had bad health, and in consequence was unequal to regular work. The wife, who had an infant at the breast, also bore unmistakeable signs of illness. She looked consumptive, and was greatly emaciated. The children were badly clothed, barefoot, and dirty. The following is her statement:—

E—— T——:—"My husband is a furnaceman. He has bad health, and cannot work full time. I also for a long while have been very unwell. We have nine children, of whom only one, a boy, is earning anything. Sometimes he gets a shilling or so in the works. We are, you see, very poor, having so many mouths to fill, and not strength to work. If my husband could but work like others, we should do very well. Last week he brought home only 5s., and 8s. the week before. One of his arms is weak. I am, as you see, barefooted. I have been down to the beach to-day gathering mussels. I got as many as I could carry on my head, which I sold for 8d. I carried them about from house to house, selling a pennyworth here, and another there. I send my daughter out to sell oranges, and we make a penny or two a day by that. We contrive to have a little meat for dinner on Sunday. My children are too ragged to send to school, and we cannot find money to clothe them."

It remains for me to give some account of the Potteries in this town; and, in doing so, I must either limit myself to a general summary of the works and trade, or enter into details as minute as those I have given of the copper-works. The necessary limits of this communication compel me to adopt the former alternative. There are two extensive potteries in Swansea—the Cambrian Pottery and the Glamorgan

Mussel Gatherers

Pottery. The trade having been for a considerable time in a depressed state, it was found necessary to close the Glamorgan Pottery. Both are the property of Mr. Lewis Llewellyn Dillwyn, a gentleman of distinguished scientific attainments, who, I believe, represented this county in Parliament for several years. Almost every variety of earthenwares are manufactured in the "Cambrian Pottery." The produce in printed, painted, dipt, and cream-coloured wares, is chiefly disposed of at home, but the foreign trade is extending. The average quantity of raw material here annually manufactured may be taken when at full work—

Poole clay	560 tons.
Flint	240 „
China clay and stone	300 „
Total	1,100 „

The annual consumption of coal is ordinarily 4,000 tons, but at present it stands at 3,300 tons.

The number of persons employed, when at full work, is—Men, 84; women, 66; children, 50; total, 200. The whole of the work is piece-work; the hours are from six till six. When trade is good the average of weekly payments in wages is £140. Men earn, when they have full work, from 27s. to 30s. a week. In the present state of the trade they get from 20s. to 22s. a week. Most of the women and children are employed by the men.

LABOUR AND THE POOR.

---◆---

THE MINING AND MANUFACTURING DISTRICTS OF WALES.

[FROM OUR SPECIAL CORRESPONDENT.]

THE WELSH LEAD MINES.

LETTER XVI.

Taken broadly, there is perhaps no district of equal area in the United Kingdom so prolific in minerals as the Principality of Wales. Having already shown the vast extent and resources of the South Wales coalfield, and described the collieries and smelting works for iron and copper located upon it, with the physical and moral condition of the swarms of population clustered around them, I have now to perform a like duty for another branch of mining enterprise extensively and successfully prosecuted in both divisions of the Principality.

Next after coal and iron, lead is the mineral most abundant in Wales. Indeed, it is more generally dispersed through the country than any other, coal being found in five of the twelve counties, whilst lead is worked, more or less, in eight. But in geologic position and relative quantity there exists as great a difference between these minerals as there is in their nature and in the method of working them—coal and iron lying, for the most part, in vast beds having a horizontal and continuous extension of several miles from the centre, whereas lead occupies but a narrow and ribbon-like breadth, running in thin veins, which dip vertically, and intersect the parent rock, like walls of metal. All through the country, from the sea-fretted cliffs of Gower, on the south, to the Great Orme's Head, on the north, I found at various points in my long journey the mining of lead in progress, and that it formed in many districts an important field for the employment of capital and labour. The counties in which lead is worked are Glamorgan, Carmarthen, Cardigan, Montgomery, Merioneth, Carnarvon, Denbigh, and Flint. In the first-named of these there is little done, operations being confined to the re-opening a few months ago of some old workings in Gower. The most productive counties are Flintshire and Cardiganshire, in which the mineral is very abundant, and extremely rich—the yield of the former, though the smallest county in Wales, doubling that of the latter, and considerably exceeding that of Cornwall, whose superficial area is five times larger.* I shall, however, give a table of the returns in the proper place.

The history of lead mining and of the advance of the lead trade, in which Wales must take a prominent place, remains to be written. It is surprising that, in a country which owes a large share of her opulence and prosperity to her mining industry, so little regard should have been paid to the statistics of its yearly condition. Without an accurate register of the produce of our mines, and the imports and exports of ores and metals, it is obviously impossible to ascertain, with the exactness necessary for practical purposes, whether a given branch of the metal trade is advancing or declining. The importance of having such information at command must be admitted by every one, and adds another consideration in favour of the establishment of a Government "school of mines," such as exists in Belgium, France, and Germany—to one department of which might be confided the duty of collecting and recording all the statistics relative to mining and the metal trades. We have, in the Museum of Practical Geology, the nucleus of such an institution; but it needs greatly extended powers to be efficacious in this particular. Such is the dearth of material for estimating the extension of the lead trade, that Mr. Porter, in the last edition of his "Progress of the Nation," gives *all* he has to say on the subject in a paragraph of a dozen lines, which I insert entire:—

> "There are no means," he says, "by which to ascertain the progress made at any time in the productiveness of the lead mines of this kingdom. To answer private purposes, the individuals by whom some of the most productive of those mines are worked, studiously conceal the amount of metal which they raise. Various conjectural estimates have been made as to that amount, but little dependence can be placed on their accuracy; and even if we could determine which is nearest to the truth, this would afford no help towards forming a comparison between different periods. Neither is any light thrown upon the subject by our Custom-house records, since the amount of our exports of lead is in a great degree governed by the comparative productiveness of the mines of other countries, and particularly by those of Adra, in Spain. The extent to which these are wrought appears to fluctuate considerably from one year to another."

---

* Produce of Lead Ore and Lead in the United Kingdom for 1848. By Robert Hunt, Esq., Keeper of the Mining Records, Museum of Practical Geology.

The lead mines of Wales were worked at a very early period of our history. Cwmsynlog, in Cardiganshire, was worked first by the Romans, then by the Saxons, next by the "patentees of royal mines," and after them by "the Company of Mine Adventurers." It is still worked successfully, the vein being larger than ever, and yielding above sixty ounces of silver in a ton of lead (Thiers' "Second Discourse"). The best possible proof that the Romans worked lead mines in this island was afforded by the discovery of a pig of lead on Cromford Moor in the year 1777, bearing the following inscription, "The sixth Legion inscribes this in memory of the Emperor Adrian." Similar discoveries of pigs of lead, bearing Latin inscriptions of the time of the Romans, have been since made in Derbyshire and in other counties. Certain old workings at Grogofau, in Carmarthenshire, are ascribed by tradition (and the Welsh are scrupulously careful of traditions) to the Romans. Speaking of these in a lecture on mining, Mr. Robert Hunt, of the Museum of Economic Geology, recently observed, "The old workings at Grogofau were rather quarrying than mining, the material being obtained in open caverns with levels run a short distance into the lodes, which consisted of lead mixed with a small portion of gold." The same may be said of the mining for copper by the Romans in Pary's Mountain, Anglesea. They worked from the surface, in the manner of a quarry. At Castleton, in Derbyshire, is the Odin Mine, named after the Danish deity, and probably worked by the Danes; it was certainly used by the Saxons about the close of the sixth century. The Beacon Rake lead vein, in the same county, is said to have been worked by the Romans. According to Holinshed (Chronicles II., p. 316), 1,600 pounds weight of silver were raised in three years from a lead mine in Devonshire. Until comparatively recent times Cornwall produced little or no lead.

In the reign of Queen Elizabeth the Welsh lead mines were worked under royal patent and stood in high repute. The most important were the Goginan mines in Cardiganshire, which were so productive of lead and silver as to cause the district to be called the Welsh Potosi. These mines are worked with great success at the present time. It was from them that Sir Hugh Middleton drew the wealth which enabled him to confer on the metropolis the benefit of a copious supply of water at a period when the greatest obstacles were opposed to cleanliness and healthfulness, and when the greatest inconvenience was occasioned by an insufficient service of that necessary element. As he was a Welshman, and employed, first and last, many thousands of the natives in his mines and in the preparation and transport of the ores, I make no apology for giving in this place a brief memoir of this enterprising man, whose personal history is too little known. I extract it from "Nicholson's Cambrian Travellers' Guide," where it appears in the description of the town of Denbigh:—

"In the parish Church of Denbigh, on brass, are the effigies of Richard Middleton, of Gwaenynog, and Jane, his wife, in a kneeling posture. He was Governor of Denbigh Castle, in the reigns of Edward VI., Mary, and Elizabeth. In relievo are nine sons, and behind the wife seven daughters. Several of these were men of distinguished characters, particularly the third, named William, a sea captain and poet, who received his education at Oxford. Thomas, the fourth son, became Lord Mayor of London, and founder of the family of Chirk Castle. The speculative genius of Hugh, the sixth son, appeared at an early age in attempts to find coal in the neighbourhood of his native place; but, not succeeding, he removed to London, where he became a citizen and goldsmith. His success in trade enabled him to farm the principal lead and silver mines in Cardiganshire, which he did at £400 a year; yet so profitable were these works that, from one mine, yielding nearly 100 ounces of silver from a ton of lead, he derived a clear profit of £2,000 a month. This immense revenue he expended in carrying into execution a plan he had formed of supplying the city of London with water. The proposal was made in 1608, and the work was completed in five years. The first issue of the waters from the head at Islington was honoured by the presence of King James I., with his Court, and the Corporation of London. He received the honour of knighthood, and afterwards of baronetage; but his property was exhausted by the undertaking, and the ingratitude of the public allowed him to be reduced to the profession of a surveyor. Mortifying as was the result of finishing the New River, his ardent spirit for public undertakings caused him to engage in reclaiming 2,000 acres from the sea, in the Isle of Wight, by embanking. He died in 1631, and his family declined into narrow circumstances, while the property which he had created rose to unexampled value. He left a number of New River shares to the poor of the Goldsmith's Company; yet, in after times, his descendant and representative, when a widow, was debarred from benefiting by the charity of her ancestor, because her husband had omitted to take out his freedom as a goldsmith."

Sir Hugh Middleton was succeeded in the tenancy of the Cardiganshire mines by Mr. Bushel, a servant of Lord Bacon, who worked them with the best effect. He clothed the army of Charles I., and lent that Sovereign £40,000—an enormous sum in those days—out of the profits he derived from them. In return for these services the King granted him the privilege of coining the silver he raised. Accordingly he established a mint at Aberystwith, where he struck half-crowns, shillings, and sixpences, all of which bore the national cognizance— the ostrich feather, on both sides. The mint was eventually removed to Shrewsbury. Prior to this, in the year 1604, some 3,000 ounces of Welsh silver were minted at the Tower. It is on record that in the time of the Civil wars the Cardiganshire mines yielded 80 ounces of silver to the ton of lead.* The richest mines give a larger per centage of silver at the present day; the limits in each direction are 14 ounces for the poorest, and 100 for the richest, in the ton of lead.

Lanvair Mine, between Landewi-Brefi, and Lampeter, yields the latter quantity, but is not rich in lead. Notwithstanding the productiveness of the Cardiganshire mines, they appear to have been almost abandoned for a long series of years. But they are now very extensively worked, and with the happiest effects, as will be presently shown. I have searched in vain for records of the early history of the Flintshire mines which are at present the richest in the Principality.

I have found no materials available for showing the extent of the lead trade prior to the year 1835. At that time Cornwall only yielded 140 tons of ore, whilst Cumberland, Northumberland, and Durham returned 16,626 tons; Yorkshire, 4,700; Derbyshire, 4,000 tons; Shropshire, 3,539 tons; Flintshire, 9,380 tons; Cardiganshire, 1,200; and Denbighshire, 177 tons. A just idea of the immense extension of lead mining in Cornwall during the past fifteen years may be formed from comparing the above returns for 1835 with the produce of the year 1848, which I find stated as 10,494 tons of ore, yielding 6,714 tons of lead, of which 5,333 tons of ore were raised from a single mine—the East Huel Rose.

Our foreign trade in lead is not inconsiderable. The countries importing lead and lead ore into England are Australia, Germany, Spain, Portugal, Belgium, Prussia, and Sardinia. Our chief export is to America. I find that between the 28th February and 28th December, 1849, there were exported to the United States 89,962 pigs of lead—a far larger quantity than the States received from any other country. Our export to India comes next in importance, amounting last year to some 3,230 tons. For the purpose of contrasting our im-

---

* Essay on Metals, by Sir J. Pettus.

ports and exports during the years 1847 and 1848, I subjoin the following table:—

LEAD ORE AND LEAD IMPORTED AND
EXPORTED DURING THE YEARS 1847 AND 1848.

IMPORTS.

	1847. Tons.	1848. Tons.
Lead ore	507	1,298
Pig, sheet lead, and shot ..	394	3,788
Total tons	901	5,086

EXPORTS.

Lead ore	86	135
Pig, sheet lead, and shot ..	3,435	6,128
Total tons	3,521	6,263

This table shows an increase of imports in the year 1848, as compared with those of 1847, of 791 tons of ore and 3,394 tons of manufactured metal, making a gross total of 4,185 tons increase in 1848; while the exports exhibit an increase of 49 tons of ore, and 2,693 tons of lead, making a gross total of 2,742 tons increase of exports in 1848 over those in 1847. The increase of exports over imports in 1847 being 2,620 tons, and in 1848 only 1,177 tons, it is clear we had not maintained the favourable difference in our foreign trade which existed in the former year. On the other hand, it is evident that both imports and exports were largely extended in 1848. The declared value of English and Irish lead exported during the past five years has been returned as follows:—Year ending 5th January, 1846, £210,974; 1847, £147,170; 1848, £181,771; 1849, £115,547; 1850, £287,337. It is encouraging to find so large an increase in the value of the exports during the past year.

Next, with regard to the home trade, I will give, in the first place, a complete set of returns from the principal lead mines for the year 1848, showing the counties in which each is situated:—

Mines.	Lead Ore Retns.	Lead Retns.	Mines.	Lead Ore Retns.	Lead Retns.
CARDIGANSHIRE.			Pary's Mine	21 ..	15
Lisburne Mines ..	2,454 ..	1,624	Trelogan	15 ..	10
Cwm-ystwyth ...	120 ..	71	Westminster Mines	659 ..	451
Esgair-hir	116 ..	70	Halkin Hall	39 ..	26
Cwm-sebon	31 ..	17	Garreg-y-boeth ..	6 ..	4
Llanfair	80 ..	53	Bodelwyddan	106 ..	69
Goginan	1,238 ..	816	Belgrave	375 ..	261
Gogerddan Mines	243 ..	162	Bryng-gwyrog ...	11 ..	7
Nant-y-creiau ...	17 ..	10	Jamaica	835 ..	590
Pen-y-bont-pren .	38 ..	22	Bwlch-y-ddaufryn	20 ..	16
Cefn-cwm-brwyno	36 ..	24	Gwern-y-mynydd	18 ..	13
Llwyn-malys	51 ..	33	Mostyn	13 ..	8
Bwlch-cwm-erfin	40 ..	26	Bagilt (ore sold at)	46 ..	20
Bwlch Consols ..	289 ..	192	Billings	45 ..	20
Nanteos	50 ..	30	Caelanycraig	14 ..	7
Aberystwith, small			Mostyn	12 ..	5
mines	20 ..	10	Clwtmilitia	16 ..	11
Llanymaron	11 ..	5	**MONTGOMERYSHIRE.**		
Llanbadarn	33 ..	18	Llangynnog	51 ..	31
Bron-berllan	15 ..	7	Cae-conroy	33 ..	20
CARNARVONSHIRE.			Rhos-wydol	26 ..	15
Penrhyn-du	21 ..	14	Dwn-gwn, or Dy-		
CARMARTHENSHIRE.			fagwm	13 ..	9
Nant-y-Mwyn ...	307 ..	204	Craig-Rhiwarth ..	27 ..	16
FLINTSHIRE.			Clyn	155 ..	100
Talargoch	1,500 ..	980	Bryndail and Pen-y-		
Fronfownog	1,695 ..	1,168	Gorn	43 ..	30
Hendre	1,040 ..	838	Machynlleth,		
Maes-y-safn	1,138 ..	824	including Delife	545 ..	300
Pen-y-rhenblas ..	1,160 ..	819	Nantmelyn	19 ..	13
Mold Mines	219 ..	153	Frontballan	15 ..	7
Long Rake	39 ..	21	**MERIONETHSHIRE.**		
Dingle and Deep			Cowarch	74 ..	42
Level	887 ..	643	Tyddynglwadus ..	18 ..	12
Milwr	117 ..	81			

I add a summary of the above Welsh counties, and also a statement of the total quantity of ores raised, and lead smelted, in the United Kingdom, for the year ending January 5, 1849, with the proportions contributed by the several counties of England as well as Wales.

TABLE SHOWING THE TOTAL QUANTITY OF LEAD ORE RAISED,
AND LEAD SMELTED, IN THE UNITED KINGDOM IN 1848.
ENGLAND.

	Lead Ore.		Lead.
Cornwall ..... Tons	10,494	Tons	6,614
Devonshire	1,334	...	844
Cumberland	8,272	...	5,684
Durham and Northumberland	18,815	...	14,658
Westmoreland	519	...	388
Derbyshire	5,185	...	3,370
Shropshire	4,130	...	2,762
Somersetshire	41	...	29
Yorkshire	6,848	...	4,793
	55,638	...	39,142

WALES.

Cardiganshire	4,902	...	3,180
Carnarvonshire ...	21	...	14
Carmarthenshire ..	307	...	204
Flintshire	10,056	...	7,069
Montgomeryshire .	927	...	601
Merionethshire ...	92	...	54
	16,305	...	11,122
IRELAND	1,912	... ...	1,188
SCOTLAND	2,588	... ...	1,736
ISLE OF MAN	2,521	... ...	1,665

Making a total of 78,964 Tons. 54,853

About one-fifth of the lead smelted in the United Kingdom is raised and manufactured in Wales, and the proportion borne by the Welsh lead to that smelted in England is something less than a third.

We have seen, by the above table, that the quantity of lead ore raised and sold in the United Kingdom in 1848 was 78,964 tons, and that of metallic lead sold was 54,853 tons. Contrasted with the produce of 1847—which was, of ores raised and sold, 79,311 tons, and of lead manufactured and sold, 53,410 tons—we have a decrease, in 1848, of 347 tons in the former, and an increase of 1,443 tons in the latter; a difference indicating an advance in the home trade.

Between the years 1842 and 1849 the price of English lead fluctuated considerably. It stood highest in 1845, when English pig lead brought £19 10s. a ton; and lowest in 1848, when it sold for £16 per ton. These variations in price show, with sufficient accuracy, the vicissitudes in the condition of the labouring classes dependent on the mines for subsistence. When the value of lead is depreciated, wages proportionately decline, because the means are not at command by which an increased quantity of ore can be raised to compensate in this way for the reduction in the price of labour—the same number of blows of the miner's pick are required to obtain a ton of ore, whether its price be £8 or £15. Royalty, tools, gunpowder, and other fixed charges remaining as before, it follows that whatever obstructs the trade, and thus lowers the value of the metal, is, in a corresponding degree, prejudicial to the workman.

The lead miners of Wales, as shown by the Occupation Abstract of the census of 1841, number more than one-fifth of the total employed in England and Wales, the proportions being 2,292 and 10,941. The following is a statement of the number of hands so engaged when the Census Returns were taken:—

LEAD MINERS IN WALES, IN 1841.

Cardiganshire	545 persons.
Carmarthenshire	74 „
Carnarvonshire	11 „
Denbighshire	84 „
Flintshire	1,439 „
Glamorganshire	4 „
Montgomeryshire	83 „
Merionethshire	52 „
Total	2,292 „

At the present time there is, no doubt, a far larger number of lead miners employed in Wales. They may safely be taken at 3,000, and the number of hands—men, women, and children—working the jiggers, picking and breaking ore, feeding the crushers, and washing, at as many; this will give 6,000 persons actively employed in the raising and preparing of ores in Wales, a computation certainly not beyond the number actually so engaged.

I passed through the district in which the largest of the Cardiganshire mines are situated, and made some inquiries into the state of the miners and their families. The Lisburne mine (the property of the Earl of that name) struck me as very complete in its outward appointments; the machinery was exceedingly good, and the arrangements appeared well studied for securing the convenience of the hands employed in cleaning and crushing the ores. But as I proposed visiting a less extensive mine, where I might see the miners in their average condition when at work, I did not enter this mine. In this district they earn from 11s. to 18s. a week, according as the rock proves favourable for their labour, or otherwise. I heard that the wages paid at the Lisburne mine amount to some £1,200 a month. The place of export for most of the ore raised in this district is Aberystwith, and it is said about £60,000 a year is spent in Aberystwith by the miners and workmen engaged in this branch of industry. The condition of the miner's home, his wife and family, is something better than that of the agricultural labourer and his dependents in Cardiganshire. House accommodation is almost everywhere insufficient and bad, and the provision for education is too much neglected. As this district is now under the care of one of the ablest and most diligent of the Government Inspectors of Education (Mr. Jelinger Symons), we may hope that the evil of deficient school accommodation will be yearly lessened.

Before I quit the subject of the Cardiganshire mines, it may be well to observe that, if one may judge of their prosperity by the amount of dividends declared, they appear to be flourishing. The following particulars of the dividends paid by the Lisburne and Goginan Mining Companies for the six months ending Midsummer, 1850, with the estimated per centage returned on the paid-up capital, were lately published:—

WELSH LEAD MINES.	Estimated Amount of paid-up Capital.	Amount of Dividends paid.	Amount of Dividend per Share.	Per Centage of Dividend on the paid-up Capital.
Lisburne Mine, £100 Shares, £75 paid up.	£7,500	£4,500	£45	£60
Goginan Mine, £100 Shares, £5 paid up.	500	1,500	15	300

The increase of dividends on the Welsh mines in the half-year ending June, 1850, over the corresponding six months of 1849, is stated at £1,000, and the same over that for the half-year ending Christmas, 1849.

At a distance of some eighteen miles from the Lisburne Mine lies the town of Llanidloes, in Montgomeryshire. In the neighbourhood are several lead mines and one copper mine, and I therefore determined on going there. It is a small town standing on the banks of the Severn, and surrounded with lofty hills agreeably diversified with woods and enclosures. A dilapidated market place, badly paved streets, and a total disregard of regularity in the line of the houses, indicate a want of municipal authority, and of funds to improve the town. The occupations of the inhabitants are suggested by long lines of flannel, stretched out for bleaching along the adjacent hill-slopes; by the pale and greasy weavers, in their blue shirt sleeves, taking rest at their doors; and by the round-hatted miners, who, in their clay-bedaubed yellow jackets, with their dinner-tins under their arms, are returning from their work in the mines. In short, Llanidloes is a town whose population is made up of flannel weavers and miners. Before I entered the houses I was struck with the appearance of the numerous children whom I saw playing in the streets. They were well clothed, clean, and looked healthy. At present I purpose confining myself to a description of the condition of the mining population, reserving what I have to say on the flannel workers till I treat of the woollen manufactures of Wales. In several houses I found that the inmates enjoyed a double source of income—the husband working in the mines, and the wife on a flannel-loom at the back of the house. Generally the houses were comfortably furnished, the floors being constructed of small pebble stones, fancifully arranged like the tesseræ in ornamental pavements. The families, as I learnt from numerous inquiries, mostly had meat once or twice a week, and the children went to school. On the whole, I found little discontent with their means and circumstances among the wives; the husbands in due place shall speak for themselves.

The mines now worked in the immediate neighbourhood of Llanidloes are, Byrn Dail, the property of a gentleman named March, which is worked by a company, of which I could obtain no further particulars than that the members were strangers; Pen y Clyn, belonging to Sir Watkyn Williams Wynn, and worked by Messrs. Le Faux and Company (I was told 150 hands were employed in the mine); the Gaer, belonging to a gentleman named Parry, of Liverpool, and worked by Mr. David Morris, a draper in the town; and the Gorn mine, the property of Lord Mostyn, worked by Messrs. Lloyd and Davies, of Newtown. Nearly 100 tons of lead ore are monthly raised from these mines, which give employment to about 300 men and women. The ores in this immediate neighbourhood are not rich in silver, but contain a very large per centage of lead, a ton yielding 16 cwt. of the pure metal, and from 7 to 10 ounces of silver.

On referring to the mine returns I found that the Gorn mine, being one of about average size—having indeed a greater number below than above it in extent—would afford me the fairest opportunity of acquiring a just opinion of the lead miner when actually in his labour, and I therefore determined to inspect it. In such a mine I thought I should find an average state of things, and from what I have since seen I was not disappointed. The captain of the mine, Mr. Owen, obligingly offered to further my wishes as far as might be in his power, and we started together for the place.

Before I describe what I there saw and heard, it may be well to make a few remarks upon the nature of the mineral deposits, and the conditions under which they are found. By this means the reader will more clearly understand my subsequent description of what I noted in the dark, damp, and sultry vaults, where I found the miners at work.

A comprehensive survey of the localities of mining will show us that it is in mountainous countries—or at all events in districts where there have been extensive disturbances and displacements of the granite floor of the globe—that minerals are found in most abundance. The theory of the formation of metals, adopted by Humboldt, and verified by analogous processes at present going forward, may be briefly and popularly stated as follows. Subsequently to the deposition of sedimentary rocks, the solid but thin crust of our planet, strained and shaken by earthquakes, and rent and fissured by the change of volume to which it was subjected in cooling, presented, wherever these forces acted with most effect—that is to say, in the direction of the weakest lines of resistance—many communications with the interior, and many passages for the escape of vapours impregnated with earthy and metallic substances. In these "dykes," or fissures of the rock, the minerals, according to the nature of the vapours, whether fitted for the production of copper, tin, lead or gold, have been deposited. Certain chemical affinities of the parent rock, and local circumstances, have no doubt been active in determining the nature of the deposits. Gradually these cracks and fissures have been filled up by matter thus deposited by sublimation. "The arrangement," says Humboldt, "of the particles in layers parallel with the margin of the veins, the regular recurrence of analogous layers on the opposite sides of the veins (on their different walls), and finally the elongated cellular cavities in the middle, frequently afford direct evidence of the Plutonic process of sublimation in metalliferous veins." This theory beautifully explains the formation of ores, but, carried no further, in my opinion it only goes to the deposition of metals combined with other substances, such as Silica, sulphur, and the like; whereas metals are sometimes found

in masses in a pure or native state. Here Crosse's theory of electric action set up by percolated water and the moisture of earths and rocks
comes in, and makes the explanation complete. Galvanic currents are
said to have been detected in the Cornish mines. Bearing this statement in mind, and anxious to verify it, I made inquiries at various
mines in South and North Wales, whether these currents had ever
been perceived in them. But though I asked the best educated, most
intelligent, and most experienced persons connected with the mines,
I could not find that an electrometer, or any device whatsoever for
the detection of electric currents, had ever been employed in them,
nor, indeed, that attention had previously been directed to the subject. Humboldt's theory is no doubt the correct one, so far as it goes,
but it has not been perfected; for, carried no further, it is insufficient
to account for the agglomeration of metals, as we find them in nodules
and in a "native" state. The truth of this theory of sublimation, as indicating the *source* of metalliferous deposits, has been happily reduced
to certainty by observations on volcanoes—mountains which present,
in our own times, just the same communication with the depths of
the interior of our planet as once existed wheresoever metallic veins
are now found. Stromeyer discovered five metals among the present
products of Vesuvius; in its crater are copper, iron, lead, arsenic, and
selenium. "The vapours that rise from the *fumarolles* cause the sublimation of the chlorides of iron, copper, lead, and ammonium. Iron
glance and chloride of sodium fill the cavities of recent lava streams
and the fissures of the margin of the crater."

We have now seen how minerals are formed—let us next note
where they are found, and the condition under which the miner re-
claims them. "It has been observed," says Johnson, "and as a general
principle correctly, that rocks of the older formation are more productive of certain metals than others; tin, for instance, being found
in granite or rocks contiguous to it; copper in the clay-slate, although
when this alternates with granite the ore is found more productive
than the latter; lead is found most productive in the limestone, but
in this rock seldom contains any silver worth extracting, while lead
in clay-slate, if in north and south courses, usually is very productive in silver, and when it exists in east and west courses in the same
rock is not so productive of silver, being then frequently merely the
rider or back of copper lodes." Excepting in Flintshire, where the
lead is found in lime-stone, the ores are found throughout Wales in
the clay-slate (argillaceous schist). This rock, forming the lower of

Silurian deposits, contains "all the constituents of granite, potash not excepted" (Humboldt). It extends from the southern border of Carmarthenshire, almost reaching the Bristol Channel, continuously to Pen-Maenmawr, where the Irish sea forms the northern boundary of the principality. At various points it changes into pure slate, and is in those places extensively quarried. Disposed at various and irregular intervals, occur veins of lead and copper, interspersed with zinc, arsenic, and other metals. The Cardiganshire mines occupy three "dykes" or fissures, running from ten to fifteen degrees east of south and west of north, and are distant from each other about three miles. The Montgomeryshire lodes have a greater inclination east and west; they vary in thickness from one to four or five feet, and are filled with what is called "vein-stuff," which consists of quartz, fluor spar, sulphate of barytes, and, in crevices, a little clay. The ore is scattered through this matrix in lumps or "bunces;" it is found in most abundance, in what the miners call "pipes"—which, as I understood them, are local enlargements of the vein, and where two lodes intersect each other, as they sometimes do. The vein stuff is exceedingly hard, and gives up its treasures to the miner's poll-pick and lever reluctantly, and not without heavy labour. On the other hand, the parent rock of clay-slate is not difficult to cut, and, having a perfect cleavage, is removed conveniently. The lead is found in various forms, as sulphurets, carbonates, and sulphates. The lumps vary in size exceedingly, from that of a walnut to that of the largest turnip; they are generally amorphous, but sometimes crystallised, in the form of the cube and octohedron. The sulphuret of lead (Galena) is very beautiful; externally, after exposure to the air, it becomes iridescent, like peacock copper ore; it is very brittle, and when fractured has a smooth surface with a most brilliant metallic lustre. It yields from 78 to 85 per cent. of pure lead, the remainder being sulphur.

The veins extend over the country for miles together. Beyond all doubt there are numerous lodes between the two seas, intersecting the rock, which have not yet been discovered. The lodes in many places reach the surface, and are there sometimes worked in open daylight. Accident, in a few cases, has discovered veins. I heard of a rich lode being found in North Wales, through the action of a waterfall, which, in the course of ages, wore away the rock till at length it reached and displayed the vein over which it tumbled. The usual method of working a lode of copper or lead is, first to ascertain its direction, and then to drive an adit level through the rock till the vein is struck, when it is worked up and down, right and left, as interest and circumstances dictate. With this preparatory information I shall proceed to describe the Gorn Lead-mine.

The Gorn lead-mine is situated in the mountain of that name, and is distant about two miles from the town of Llanidloes. Our road, after passing a watery lane leading from the town, lay for a distance through arable and pasture lands up the face of the mountain. Pausing to rest on the steep ascent, and looking back, the prospect was magnificent. The lofty mountain Plinlimmon, led up to by a wavy-lined horizon of lesser hills, formed the centre of a near back ground. On the left were the picturesque lines of the Cardiganshire mountains; on the right, far off, the triple peak of Cader Idris. Below the Plinlimmon, and stretching away to the right and left, were broad swelling banks, in some places darkened with pine and oak woods, which in turn were relieved by ruddy fallows and pastures of delicate green, and dotted with churches and village homesteads. Through the narrow valley beneath, the infant Severn pursued its devious course, fertilising the luxuriant meadows through which it passed. The party-coloured town, with its gabled market-house, its ancient church and bridge, with the before-mentioned lines of bleaching flannel, completed a picture which ever-varying effects of light and shadow (for the sun was near the meridian) beautified and enhanced in value exceedingly.

Resuming our course we passed a wood, and crossed, upon stepping-stones, a considerable mountain torrent, which formed, as it tumbled from ledge to ledge of rock, a very pleasing series of cascades. We now had passed the enclosures, and after ascending some distance along the breast of the mountain, through fern, gorse, and heather, swarming with snipes and rabbits, we came to a swamp. Here my guide told me I was standing over part of the mine. A little further on, having recovered the sound land, we came to some depressions in the soil. From these I was told large quantities of valuable lead ore had been extracted. I remarked they were all situated in a straight line, which was, in fact, the direction of the lode. Yet further, and we came to a square hole, railed off, from which there ascended thin curls of steam or smoke. This was a shaft of 72 yards depth, reaching to the bottom of the mine, and serving no other purpose than that of ventilation. Descending a cleft of the mountain, through woods and enclosures, we at length reached the mouth of the mine. I found it of much the same character as other lead mines which in various localities I had passed. They are generally situated on a steep declivity, and have shallow platforms cut away, stage above stage, for washing and dressing the ore, with a lofty but narrow water-wheel (sometimes more than one), to which a clear, rushing, and noisy stream descends, led round the face of the mountain to the wheels, the jiggers, and the washing pools. At the Gorn Mine, the large water-wheel is under cover. At this and most other lead mines there is little of the noise and bustle which abound at the coal and iron mines of South Wales. The ores here, when prepared, occupy relatively but a small space, and being removed in carts and waggons, the clanking of numerous trains on a railway, with the shrieking and puffing of locomotives, is entirely unknown. The work goes quietly forward; the only sounds are the rolling of ore over the ore stages, the musical beats of the great wheel as the water tumbles over each successive bucket, and the short rattle of the jiggers for screening the ore, the reverberations of which do not disturb the hare that squats in the oak wood over the mine, or the red squirrel that gambols in the trees.

In the first place, we went to the counting house, where I changed my clothes, putting on a round crowned waterproof hat, a white woollen jacket, fustian trousers, and heavy nailed quarter boots. Here Mr. Owen gave me the following information respecting it:—

"This mine was opened forty years ago by a Mr. Hilditch, who expended upon it above £12,000 unsuccessfully. He drove the lowest adit level, about half a mile into the mountain. The workmen hit and passed the lode; being much harder than the clay-slate rock, they could not mistake it, but it was their interest to deceive their employer, who knew nothing of mining, and they did so. The mine was not worked profitably till eight years ago. When I came here, I opened the old adit level. At that time, and for two years afterwards, we were bound to work with a boat—the water was so abundant. You saw the boat near the mouth of the mine. We now raise from 15 to 20 tons of ore in the month. We send it by carts to Newtown—about 17 miles—paying 5s. 6d. a ton for carriage. There it is placed in barges on the Montgomeryshire Canal, which convey it to Chester at a freight of 10s. a ton. At Chester and Bagillt we find a market for the ores. There are several smelting establishments on the Chester river. The miners in this neighbourhood are tolerably steady; some few drink; ours are remarkably regular and well conducted; they have never given us any trouble by strikes. We have 18 miners, two wheelers, and a waggoner working underground at present, but we have had many more. We employ 14 men, 6 women, and several children washing and preparing the ores in the open air. No women are permitted, here or at other neighbouring mines, to work underground. The men enter the mine at seven in the morning. They work eight hours underground, coming out at three o'clock, when they go home. They take one meal underground, but dine at home. Another set goes in at three, and comes out at eleven at night. They mostly live in the town, and go backwards and forwards by day and night, along the awkward road which brought us here. The women and boys who work at the ore stage, the jiggers, and the washing pools, come on duty at seven in the morning, and leave at six in the evening; they have one hour allowed them in the middle of the day. They are paid by the day. Boys earn from 4d. to 1s. 1d., and girls and women the same. The men employed in washing ore earn 1s. 6d. a day, working from seven to six o'clock. I consider the lead trade to be in a flourishing condition just now. All that is wanting in this neighbourhood is a free importation of capital to work the mines more vigorously. We are cramped in our operations for want of money. These mountains abound in lead, and would be extremely productive if properly worked. The veins here run nearly east and west. Occasionally we meet with lumps of copper ore. Zinc, which we miners call 'black jack,' abounds in them."

On our way to the mouth of the mine, we entered the "smithy," where we found several of the men and boys seated on the anvils and on benches at their dinner. Some had brown bread, but most of them had good white wheaten bread and butter. Some were toasting rashers of bacon, stuck on files and turn-screws, at the forge fire, which (rude as was the cookery) gave forth a most hunger-provoking and tantalizing odour. Here we were furnished with candles surrounded with the usual ball of clay—and thus accommodated, we proceeded to the mine. The mouth of the mine has the appearance of an open doorway in the face of the rock. On the right of it lay the boat formerly used for reaching the lode. We had scarcely entered before the captain of the mine said we must go back, as he heard the rumbling of a train of ore trucks, so we returned, and presently some donkeys, dragging a set of iron trams along the narrow railroad which runs through the lower adit, made their appearance. The trams were filled with ore, and were under the superintendence of a waggoner. We now re-entered the mine. The adit was about five feet high, and from three feet and a half to four feet wide. Over its rocky floor a stream of white whey-like water ran swiftly. Through this we had to walk. The roof was rough and uneven, and, being low, we had continually to preserve a stooping posture. In places where the rock was friable, it had been supported by rude props and cross bars of wood. Through fissures here and there the water streamed down literally in torrents, with a loud noise. There was no escaping them, so I was soon wet through. Having advanced about half a mile in a straight direction, we arrived at the juncture of the upper lode. Here there was a considerable water fall. On the left was an apparatus something like a large winnowing machine, having fans turned by water power, which drives the air through a wooden tube, like an organ pipe, along the roof of the upper adit, for the purpose of ventilation. It was not at work on that day. Quitting this spot, we proceeded a considerable distance further, to the end of the lower adit, passing a shaft of some seven fathoms and a half deep, and, at one or two points, cavernous openings to the adit and workings above, through which descended the loud noise of falling rock and masses of ore, as they were disengaged by the miners above. Some heavy pieces came through, and fell within a few yards of us; but our care was always to pass these chasms quickly, and not to stand at any point which had not a solid roof overhead. In a stranger there is awakened, when in a mine far within the bowels of the earth, a class of sensations wholly new to him. He hears the loud rushing of water which comes he knows not whence, the blows of hammers and picks, the falling of heavy fragments of rock, sometimes occasioning the vibration of the floor on which he stands, yet he sees none of the agents which produce these sounds. At first I was astonished at the loudness of every sound in this mine; but when I considered why this should be, all wonder ceased. In coal pits and iron mines, the large openings admit of a wide dispersion of the waves of sound; but here they are confined within, and reflected from, two walls of rock, only a yard asunder; hence their force and intensity. Where we passed the lode, my guide pointed out to me the nodules of metal imbedded in the "vein-stuff" of quartzose rock. He also showed me some thin veins of sulphate of barytes, which have a dip nearly vertical. "It is," said he "a deadly poison. The miners and others powder it, and make it into pills, with oatmeal, for poisoning rats."

Returning to the juncture of the two adits, we had to ascend some fifteen feet by climbing and swinging from one wooden rail to another. This accomplished, we entered the upper adit, which was very low, tortuous, and in places steep, with a rugged roof, side-walls, and floor. At 300 yards distance we reached the end or "breast" of the adit. Here was at work a fine muscular young man driving a blast-hole. He wore a flannel shirt, tucked up at the sleeves, and fustian trowsers. He carried his candle in a ball of clay, stuck on the broad brim of his round crowned hat. The water fell in streams, and he told me that to keep his head and face dry, he was bound to waterproof his hat, as I saw it, with wax and rosin. The following is his statement:—

Robert Jones: "I am thirty-seven years' old, unmarried, and have been a miner ever since I was big enough to work. I am here eight hours a day, and am paid £3 a fathom of 36 square feet for driving this adit. By this I earn about 12s. a week, sometimes a little more, and at others less, as the lode proves hard or otherwise. We blast the rock with gunpowder, and then work the 'loose' with poll-picks, iron bars and hammers. We find the ore in 'bunces,' these lie in what we call 'pipes' by various points of the lode. These 'pipes' are sometimes 20 fathoms or more in extent, containing perhaps a ton and a half per fathom. My health has always been good; I never suffered in my hands or arms." Here I should say that Mr. Owen informed me that in no instance within his experience had lead miners suffered in health from handling the mineral. Though so pernicious when reduced to the pure metallic state (in which it gives rise to painters' cholic, and occasions paralysis of the arms and hands), it seems quite innocuous in the form of ore. I subsequently verified this information by repeated inquiries of miners in Flintshire. But all lead miners suffer from asthma when they become old. There being no danger from explosions of fire-damp in lead mines, there does not exist the same urgent inducement to give a thorough ventilation to the mine. The atmosphere is always close and warm, and is still further injurious from being contaminated by the sulphurous smoke of the gunpowder used in blasting. I found the air extremely exhausting, and though wetted to the skin from time to time with droppings of water I was in a bath of perspiration from heat during the three hours and a half I passed in the mine. Returning from this man we sat a few minutes on a rail placed across a hollow in the rock, where some of the men take their meals. One of the "wheelers" who removed the rubbish and ores from the miner I had just examined here came to us. His candle was stuck in front of his barrow. He told me he and his fellow "wheeler" earned each 1s. 8d. a day, and that they were paid by the last-mentioned miner out of his £3 a fathom allowed for cutting the adit.

We now turned aside to what is called "a stowp" in the lode, in which were several miners at work. It was a kind of irregular shaft, of about 15 fathoms (or 90 feet) high. Some were at work on the sides, and some at the top of the stowp. The men follow the ore as they best can, working on stages, and leaving here and there a ledge of rock on which to place their ladders for ascent and descent. How to describe the course I took in order to reach a point where I might see the extent of the present workings, I scarcely know. We had to ascend a great distance through narrow openings quarried in the rock, dragging up after us a crazy ladder of birch-wood, and placing it on slimy and sloping shelves of the rock (with an abyss on both sides), to enable us to reach ledge after ledge till we attained the desired elevation. Sometimes the ladder was too short to reach further than the edge of a sloping stage, in which case we had to climb by means of our hands and feet to the place of safety. Descending again it was worse at these points; for we had to hit with great nicety the first round of the ladder or fall a distance of some twenty feet to the nearest ledge below. In more than one place I had to squeeze through tortuous apertures, barely admitting passage for the body, and to pick my way on all fours for a long distance over declivities of loose ore and rock, fragments of which rattled down from ledge to ledge with a noisy crash, as I displaced them on my way up and down. Hanging by both arms from a stick let into the rock, and feeling with my feet for the ladder, which was too short to reach the ledge I was descending from—or at least some resting place till the miners below could raise, support, and steady the ladder—I found my position a somewhat critical one. However, I was well repaid for the risk and exertion by what I witnessed. Standing at a point where two miners were at work, I had an opportunity of seeing the wonders of the mine. Men with candles were directed to go to various points above and below me, and display their lights. Allowing a few minutes for their ascent and descent, the candles were uncovered in several directions, and at vast heights, and depths, above, below, and on all sides. The masses of ore hanging in the rock reflected the light upon their smooth fractured surfaces, at a hundred points, shimmering with a glorious lustre! It was a scene I shall never forget. One of the men overhead, whose voice reverberated strongly through these caverns, informed me that he was a weaver by trade, but a miner by choice. He came to work here five years ago, had a wife and four children. This he said in reply to questions I put to him on learning from his companions that he was a weaver. I examined the men who were working by my side:—

Edward Powell: "I have been twenty-five years a miner; have a wife and three children. I earn from 11s. to 14s. a week. My health, on the whole, has been pretty good. Once I was badly hurt with blasting. In the old time, fifteen years ago, I have earned as much as £9 a month. We work by the bargain at 43s. a fathom. My wages are dependent upon my bargain. If I take what turns out a hard piece of rock, I get perhaps not more than £1 a month. At those times I am bound to run in debt to support my family, and so are all miners. When the ground turns out very hard we are allowed from £3 to £8 a fathom. Things are middling cheap now, and therefore I get meat every day, and so do my family. When I make a bad 'taking,' we only get bread and coffee. I have seen the time, only three years ago, when we could not get that. I pay £3 10s. a year house rent, and 10s. a year poor-rate. I feel the poor-rate a hardship, because I am myself poor."

At another place I questioned two other miners, who were driving blast holes in the rock. The first said, "I pay the company for powder, helves, candles and tools, once a month. They stop it from our wages; we have a weekly draw. I am 33 years of age, and have always been a miner. I, my old woman, and children, go to the Sunday school at the Baptist Chapel, where we read the Bible. One of my children attends a day charity school belonging to the Church." The other said, "I am 40 years old, am married, and have a family of six children. I earn the same as the other men. Two of us work together, one making the bargain. I can read, but cannot write."

Full of thankfulness to the poor miners, who seemed most anxious to give me every information in their power, working with great vigour to show me their method of cutting out the lead, I now retraced my steps to the mouth of the mine. On reaching it, I was entertained with a curious optical illusion, arising, no doubt, from the length of time my eyes had been accustomed to the darkness of the mine. The vegetation, and, in short, every object, seemed covered with snow; but my eyes soon recovered their usual condition. I reserve a description of the processes of crushing and preparing the ores for a future communication.

LABOUR AND THE POOR.

———◆———

THE MINING AND MANUFACTURING DISTRICTS OF WALES.

[FROM OUR SPECIAL CORRESPONDENT.]

THE WELSH LEAD MINES AND WORKS.

LETTER XVII.

I have now to describe the several operations of crushing, washing, and dressing the lead ores, as performed at the Gorn lead mine, and generally throughout the Principality. Although these ores, when cleaned and prepared for the smelting furnace, are purer than any others obtained in this country—containing a larger per centage of metal than the ores of copper, iron, or tin—they come from the mine in a very crude form, and require considerable labour to fit them for manufacture. As cut from the parent lode, they are found intermixed with quartz, spar, and other constituents of the "vein-stuff," all of which must be carefully eliminated before the ores are available for market. This separation is effected by crushing, sifting, and washing—processes carried on by men, women, and children, as we shall presently see.

When cut by the miners, the ores are wheeled or carried to points convenient for loading and removal. They are next placed in narrow iron trams containing each about 25 cwt., and hauled by donkeys out of the mine to the first stage or terrace of the dressing-floors. Here the trams are canted over, and the work commences. At the Gorn mine, now under notice, there are several dressing-floors, cut in the left bank of the ravine, and descending by successive steps downwards. Through these, a stream of water is conveyed for the purpose of washing the ores.

Commencing with the first process, the following is a description of the operations. Standing upon a wooden platform, a lad of sixteen, fenced about with sacking to protect himself from splashings, draws the lumps of ore by means of a rake, from the heap deposited by the trams, under and through a smart stream of running water falling from a spout, down to the stage on which he stands. The effect of the water upon these masses is, by washing off the clay and impurities, to display the dark blue veins of lead interspersed through the stone. A number of boys, by means of short iron hooks, then drag these lumps over an iron grating, through which any fragments of the lead ore which, by this process, may be disintegrated fall, and are carried into a trough overflowing with water. The large pieces of rock which contain no particles of the mineral are thrown into barrows and wheeled away. The lumps of ore considered too large for passing through the "crushers" are next picked out, set aside, and broken with hammers—in the ordinary way of breaking stone—by girls and boys. When reduced to a convenient size, the broken ores, and the fragments deposited in the trough, are from time to time carried to the crushers. The lad on the platform raking down the ore, informed me that he earned 6d. a day, and that, though continually wet, he very seldom took cold; the others said they earned 4d. a day. The biggest of them said he could read a little, the others could neither read nor write. All had been to the Sunday-school, but could give no reason why they had learnt nothing there. They were comfortably clothed, looked healthy, and pursued their occupation diligently and in silence. A girl breaking ore, neatly dressed in a blue frock, spotted pinafore, yellow cape, and a blue cloth bonnet, who might be perhaps fifteen years old, said, "I do not know how old I am. I have been to New Chapel school, and can read but not write. I earn 5d. a day, and live at home with my father and mother. My health is very good."

We next come to the operation of crushing the ores. For this purpose an apparatus, consisting of a pair of large iron cylinders, put in motion by an overshot waterwheel of some twenty feet diameter, is employed. This operation is carried on in a building of two stories, the upper floor being on a level with the stage where the ore is broken. When I entered the "crushing-house" a girl was feeding the machine. She placed the broken ore, as brought to her by the boys, in a hopper leading to the cylinders, through which it passed to the lower room, where, for convenience sake, we will follow it. After going through the cylinders, which are weighted so as to accommodate the strain of any unusually large or hard fragment, the ore falls into a revolving wire sieve leading diagonally from the cylinders to a bucketed wheel of some twelve feet diameter, revolving at a short distance off. The effect of this is, that the ore, reduced to the size of coarse sand, passes through the upper part of the sieve into a stream of rushing water, and is carried into a small pool or trough, while the unbroken lumps and "gravel ore" fall from the lower end of the sieve into the bucketed wheel, which carries them back to the upper floor, and deposits them near the hopper. The girl then passes them a second time through the cylinders, and this process goes forward simultaneously with the feeding of the machine with new ores, so that very little passes into the water larger than is convenient for the purpose of washing. The following is the statement of the girl supplying the "crushers":—"I am sixteen years of age, and have been engaged at this work about nine months. My wages are 6d. a day. I live with my father and mother—we have meat very often for dinner. I can read, but cannot write. I never was at any other than a Chapel Sunday School." This girl was fresh-coloured, and seemed to enjoy good health. The ore, which we have seen pass through the sieve to the water-trough, is stirred freely about by a boy using a shovel, so as to wash away as much as possible of the comminuted quartz, spar, and other impurities, with which it is intermixed. This boy now and then throws aside a few shovels-full of the ore for the women, who carry it to the "jiggers." The latter are cradles of wood (suspended from uprights) having sieve-bottoms of iron wire. They are worked by means of lever handles in a square deep trough of water. Women are employed for this duty. They take a quantity of the crushed ore, and place it in the "jigger," which at that time stands above the surface of the water in the trough. Seizing the lever-handle, they raise it, and the jigger cradle descends into the water. This done, the women press the lever handle against their knees, and move oddly on tiptoe up and down, making a monotonous and peculiar rattling sound with the frame-work. By this motion—the water flowing meanwhile rapidly through the sieve cradles—the finest particles of the ores are carried through the wires, and by their gravity sink rapidly and accumulate in the bottom of the trough; while the rubbish and coarse matter accumulate on the surface of the mass in the jigger sieve, whence it is dexterously skimmed off, and returned to the "crushers," or put through the washing pools, as circumstances require. The jigger troughs are emptied of the pulverised ore twice a week: each contains several hundredweight of ore. All were single women whom I saw working the jiggers. They were dressed, some in linsey-wolsey garments, of a cut peculiar to the country, with straw hats—others in cotton gowns and bonnets. They were all of large stature and of masculine frame—height and strength being necessary for this work. Their features were weather-tanned, and their bare arms had a muscular development like that of a working man. They all wore wooden shoes. I examined the nearest of them, M. E——: "I have worked nine years, in one duty or another, at lead mines. My health, though I am exposed to all weathers, is good, and so is that of my companions. We work from seven in the morning till six in the evening, and earn 1s. 1d. a day." Not one of these women could read or write. Mr. Owen (captain of the mine) informed me that most of the single women lived at a kind of barrack about half a mile down the ravine, and that they were extremely well conducted, rarely giving occasion for scandal or censure of any kind.

We now come to the washing pools. These, as I have said, are situated one below the other—a spout of some twelve to eighteen inches diameter conveying a stream of water successively through them. The ores, reduced to the size of sand by the process of crushing, are here exposed to the current of water, being continually stirred by a man with a kind of hoe, called a "corluck." This operation requires much judgment and experience;—the workman, by a dexterous turn of the wrist, throwing the ores from the corluck in a semicircular line like the opening of a fan, so that every particle is fully exposed to the action of the water. The specific gravity of the lead causes it to sink rapidly, while the crushed stone and spar, being lighter, are washed away. The lead is next raked on one side, to be taken to the storehouse. But a portion of the finest-grained ore escapes by force of the current of water; hence it is necessary that the operation should be repeated in the pool below. This is done in the very same manner at three successive stages, till all the lead is removed, and the water flows off turbid and milky, carrying away nothing but the impurities. The process is much the same as is pursued in other countries for the preparation of lead ore. Though extremely simple, it is not the less efficacious; and if the metal were gold instead of lead, it could hardly be more completely separated from the matrix, cleansed, and collected, than it is by this method. The only "washer" I examined was a hale-looking man, of some thirty years old. He said:—"I am married, and have three children. I earn 2s. a day. We have a comfortable house, and have animal food most days. I have been engaged in this duty sixteen weeks. It agrees with me very well. I work always in the open air, except during hard frosts in winter, when we are employed in the house."

The ore, thus washed and dressed, is now taken to the storehouse, where it is deposited for removal. Its appearance is that of a coarse metallic sand, having a ground tint of indigo blue, and a greyish "shot"

over the whole, with a few brilliant shining points, when the light is
casually reflected on the *laminæ* of metal. Mr. Owen here informed
me that those ores contain most silver which break with steel-like
uneven surface and texture. Vast quantities of zinc, called "black jack,"
are found in this and the neighbouring mines, interlaid with the lead,
but they are either altogether neglected in the vein or cast aside, when
accidentally cut amongst the more valuable substance. The lead ore is
conveyed in waggons from the mine to Newtown (as before stated)
at a charge of 5s. 6d. a ton, where it is shipped on the Montgomery
Canal, and carried, at a freight of 10s. a ton, to Chester or Bagillt for
smelting. The Cardiganshire and Montgomeryshire ores have thus a
disadvantage to contend with, as compared with the Flintshire ores,
owing to the latter having a coal field near the mines to supply fuel to
the smelting-houses, whereby a difference of from 12s. to 15s. a ton in
the cost of the ores arises in favour of those raised in the latter county.
This being so—assuming royalty and "galeage" on the ores in these
counties to be nearly equal, and the trouble of cutting and raising no
greater—the Flintshire miner ought to be better paid and in a more
enviable condition than the miners of Cardigan, Montgomery, and
Merioneth; yet, owing to circumstances hereafter to be stated, such
is not the case.

Not sorry to change the garments I had worn in the mine (which
were still dripping wet), for my usual clothes, I returned to Llanidloes. We visited several of the miners' houses on our way back. We
found them comfortably furnished, and I heard no complaint from
the inmates—unless the expression of a wish that wages were weekly
paid in money, instead of by weekly written orders and monthly set-
tlements, as at present, could be so construed. At one of the houses
the miner's wife informed me that she earned from 5s. to 7s. a week
herself, by working at a flannel-loom which I saw in the back kitchen.
The children very generally went to school. Many of the older children in the town of Llanidloes earn their subsistence by weaving; so
that, upon the whole, the market being well supplied and the necessaries of life cheap, the condition of the working classes in and around
the town (I stated in my last Letter that they are chiefly miners and
weavers) is very comfortable. Here I close my remarks on the lead-
miners of Montgomeryshire and Cardiganshire.

It may be desirable, both for convenience sake and for the completeness of this account of the state of the labourer in the Welsh
lead-mines and works, that I give in a continuous form the whole

of the information gathered on this subject in the course of my journey through the Principality—instead of distributing it, as collected in my note-book, under the various counties where these branches of industry particularly invited and received my attention.

The remaining counties of North Wales in which lead is mined are Merioneth, Denbigh, and Flint. In the first-named county the lead trade is perhaps not so prosperous just now as it was a few years ago. The lead-mines of Merionethshire at present worked are not numerous; but I am informed that a company, in connection with Mr. Harvey, of Dolgelly, is about largely to extend the mining of lead and copper at various points of the county. The number of hands actually engaged in mining lead at the census of 1841, as returned for Merionethshire, was 52; but 111 were described simply as miners—and as lead and copper were then pretty equally worked in that county, the number of lead miners may be set down as having been at that time about 110. As few mines are now worked in Merionethshire, if the number has not really diminished, I do not think there has since been any increase. The condition of the lead-miners of Merionethshire is, I think, below that of their fellows in Cardiganshire and Montgomeryshire. They complain of the "long-pay" system, which occasions general inconvenience, and in many instances works positive hardship. I give the following statements of a miner and a washer whom I examined at Dolgelly. They were father and son (the former a man of thirty years' experience as a lead-miner), and lived in what may be better described as a "stone hut" than a house. Descending a few steps from the road, and entering at a low doorway, I found the family at home. It consisted of the miner, a middle-aged man, a lad of 17, the miner's wife, and a daughter of about eleven years of age. The two females were seated knitting in the opposite angles of a capacious chimney, beside a handful of fire which was burning in a grate of the smallest dimensions. The man and his son, having not long returned from the mine, had changed their working for their holiday clothes, their wet garments hanging suspended to dry on a line before the fire. The light, admitted through a very narrow deep-seated window, was barely sufficient to show the contents of the room, and the order, neatness, and cleanliness which characterised them. The furniture, though blackened with smoke, similar to the naked rafters overhead, shone like polished ebony, and, with a few prints hanging on the walls, gave evidence of the industry and even taste of the owners. The little window, decorated with a flower pot, and skirted by white calico curtains, was kept scrupulously clean, and the uneven clay floor and hearth were swept carefully. A small settle, a dresser, with a small nest of shelves and crockery, a round table, a chair and a few stools, formed the contents of this room. The man, his wife, and son, received me with that cordial but respectful politeness which, I am not singular in saying, forms a marked feature in the character of the labouring classes among the Welsh. They answered my questions with equal earnestness, readiness, and apparent sincerity. H. P.: "I am a miner, working in the Hafod Morfa lead-mine, three miles distant from this place (Dolgelly). I am forty-five years old; am married, as you see, and have five children, the youngest being eleven years old. I have worked in the lead mines ever since I was fifteen years of age. The most I ever earned was about twenty-five years ago, when I got as much as 30s. a week. In these times I think myself well off if I earn from 12s. to 15s. a week. Work is not steady hereabouts. I have not been employed of late half my time. For the last three months I have not earned by mining 5s. a week. I account for this by my having 'taken' a hard unproductive piece of the mine. This, however, is not general, but it is my case. I am just about leaving that mine, because I cannot earn there enough to live. I have had many severe accidents in my time. Once I fell down a shaft twenty-six yards deep, when I broke my thigh (in two places), my ancle, and three of my ribs. I have been twice burnt with fire-damp, in a copper mine, but was not much injured either time. I pay £2 a year for this poor house. With the exception of that boy (his son, present), I did not give my children schooling. We were so many, and wages so low, that I could not afford it. I have not seen meat for dinner these two months; neither has any one of my family had meat during that time to my knowledge. (The wife corroborated this.) Generally, if we get half-a-pound of bacon between us on Sunday, we think ourselves well off. My work affects my health very much; the air of the mine is close, so that I breathe very hard when in my work. My breath is at all times short, and I suffer with my chest. The manner in which we miners are kept down is this—We get one month a 'taking,' on which we earn perhaps £3; that is thought a good 'taking.' The masters of the mine, knowing that we did well on that, beat us down in price, and next time we have a 'taking' on which we earn only 30s. to £2; the consequence is, that during that month we must go on credit; and the month after, when we may perhaps have another good 'taking,' the benefit goes to clear the debt incurred in the preceding month. Another and a very great hardship the miners suffer, is the irregularity which prevails in the settlement of their accounts and payment of their money. The agreement is for a payment at the end of the month; but we always work two months before the first month's wages are paid us. Generally our payments are three months in arrear of our earnings. Sometimes the 'pays' are four months distant from one another. The workmen meanwhile get their goods on credit, and are charged by the tradesmen a higher rate as a matter of course. In this way the miner's condition is much worse than it otherwise would be. My son assists by his earnings in the support of the family; if it was not for his aid we should not have been able to get along during the past few weeks."

I next questioned the son, E. P——: "I am a 'washer' of ores at the mine, and earn about 8s. a week. We are not paid by piece-work, but by the day. Though the work is cold and wet, it agrees with my health very well. I can both read and write." Turning to the miner's wife, I received from her the following particulars of their daily life:—"We usually get bread and salt for breakfast, with a little tea. Sometimes we have butter. We very seldom have sugar, only when we can spare a penny to buy it. If my husband's work was regular, we could have a little meat, and some sugar; but we live very poor because we are unwilling to get into debt. For supper we have 'yeud' (oatmeal stir-about), with a top dressing of treacle." There was an iron three-legged pot by the fire. I asked her what was in it. She took off the lid, and showed me therein a black dye for stockings. She said that the scarcity and dearness of potatoes added to the sufferings of the poor very much.

The lead ores raised in Denbighshire are insignificant in quantity, and consequently give employment to few hands. But the adjoining county of Flint, though small, forms the great field of the lead trade in the Principality. It abounds with mines of lead and coal, the presence of the latter mineral securing for Flintshire the location of extensive works for the smelting and manufacture of the former. Hence the working population are here largely dependent upon this branch of commercial enterprise. By the census returns of 1841 it appears that there were 3,941 persons engaged in mining in this county, and 308 in the smelting and manufacture of the metals; giving a total of 4,249. At the same time there were only 3,559 agricultural labourers in the county; so that, viewed in every light—whether as a field for the occupation of capital or employment of labour—the lead trade forms the most important branch of industry in this county.

In the neighbourhood of Holywell there are several very large lead mines. I therefore visited this district for the purpose of examining into the condition of the miners and others engaged in the lead trade. At that place I chanced to meet Sir Edward Walker, a gentleman thoroughly conversant with the entire economy of the lead mines and manufactures of Flintshire. Being a large shareholder in the most extensive lead smelting works in the kingdom, the "Dee Bank Works," situated at Bagillt, distant two miles from Holywell, he obligingly offered me an opportunity of inspecting them, of which I availed myself, and he introduced me to the manager, Mr. Henry, who was charged with conducting me over them. The result of my visit to these smelting works will appear in my next letter; at present I confine myself to particulars relating to the lead trade, giving especial regard to the condition in which I found the miners of Flintshire.

The lead ores are sold at bi-monthly "ticketings," held at the White Horse Hotel, Holywell. I was there on the occasion of one of these sales, but was not present in the room. They are conducted, as I was informed, in precisely the same manner as the "ticketings" of copper ore at Swansea, one of which I attended, and have already described. English, Irish, Scotch, and Welsh ores are here sold. Very little Australian or other foreign ore comes to this market. After the "ticketing," a table of the sales was placed in my hand, from which I learned that the total number of tons of ore then sold was 691; of this 45 tons were Irish, 35 tons Scotch (from Taindrum, Dumbarton), 6 tons were from Montgomeryshire, and the remainder was the produce of the Flintshire mines. The highest price realised per ton was for Shalley (Irish) ores, £18 6s., and the lowest for Dumbarton (Scotch), "Odd Fellows," £10 14s. 6d. a ton. The average price is about £13 a ton. The competitors were J. P. Eyton, Llanerchymor; Mather and Co., Bagillt; Newton, Keates, and Co., Bagillt; and Walker, Parker, and Co., Dee Bank, Bagillt. Of the 691 tons of ore then sold, the last-named firm purchased at that sale exactly 454 tons. Sir Edward Walker informed me that not less than 1,500 tons of lead ore are at present raised every month in Flintshire alone. "The trade," said he, "experiences some inconvenience just now, in consequence of the miners adventuring on their own account. When solely employed by the proprietors of mines they used to work in relays, making three 'stems' a day of eight hours each; but they now only work six hours for their employers, and two, or perhaps more, for themselves. In consequence of many small proprietors having sprung up, nearly all the money earned by workmen and others in mining in Flintshire is spent in Holywell, which has thus become a very thriving place. Formerly there were large cotton works here, but they failed."

The reader will presently see, from the statement of a miner whom I examined, and whose evidence I shall give, that the proprietors of the mines have themselves to blame alone for giving occasion for this daily extending practice among the miners of working upon their own account. The workmen were so much beaten down in wages that they were compelled to resort to the system in self-defence. The "long-pay" system also exists in Flintshire, and occasions, in some instances, even greater hardship than any which have appeared in the course of my investigations up to this place. I give the statements of some miners whom I examined, and who work in different mines.

J. W——, Brognallt, Flintshire: "I am a lead-miner, working at the Holway Mine, the property of the Holway Mining Company. I am now fifty years old, and have worked in the mines just twenty-six years. I am married, and have nine children, all of whom live at home with me. Two of them are earning their living. My eldest boy works in the mine when he can get employment, but the mines are now so full, and there are so many applying, that he has been out of work for the last twenty weeks. My second son carries the post-bag for Sir Pierce Mostyn, of Tal-Acre, and earns 5s. a week. I have sometimes met with accidents, but had only one severe one. I was then twenty-six weeks obliged to keep my bed. I am on my own 'adventure' in the mine, paying a royalty of 50s. a ton to the company. We have paid as much as £3 royalty; but it was reduced. I am partner with another man in the adventure. There are seven others besides us who work in this way in the same 'level.' We wash our own ores and sell them as we can, having to pay for powder, tools, and candles, which come heavy. There are in the Holway mine, in the employ of the company, fifteen men at work in the shaft, and six men 'huffing a chump' (sump). They are paid so much a fathom, and earn about 10s. a week each— sometimes a little more, and sometimes less. It is now fifteen years since I worked in that way, by the fathom. The rock is very hard here at the Holway mine, and I have done badly for three years past. I am sure I have not earned all this time more than 6s. a week. The lode runs east and west. We go half a mile into the mine in boats, and about 180 yards in the cross before we reach the workings. I have worked six years in this mine. There is plenty of air here; but in some mines where I have worked it is very bad. The men there suffer from pain in the chest and shortness of breath. Most miners when they get old suffer in that way; it is common to hear them complain of their stomach and breath. I account for my earning so little and being badly off in this way—Say I raise a ton of ore, and can sell it for £11; out of that I have to pay £2 10s. royalty, and for gunpowder, candles, tools, blacksmith's work and crushing, as much as a full quarter of the sale price of the ore, if not more—so that we get but £5 16s. 6d. in repayment for labour in raising a ton of ore. I and my partner were ten weeks raising 1 ton 17 cwt. of ore which we last sold; for this we worked always ten, and sometimes twelve hours a day. If the air in the mine was not good, we could not work there so many hours continuously. We divide the profits equally. We have been as much as two months raising a single ton of ore." I walked with this man to his house, which I found decently furnished, clean, and orderly. The kitchen was small, and pretty well filled with children. A girl aged eight years, seeing her father approaching, ran out to kiss him. On my remarking that he was fond of her, he replied, "Yes, I like well to have them round me. I work in the mine all day, and at night have the comfort of them. This one is now sick; she has the hooping-cough." The wife had an infant at the breast; she had been sickly for the past three years. In reply to my questions, she said, "We have given schooling to all our children. Two of them are now in the British and Foreign School, about a mile and a half distant; they get on very well. We pay 2d. a week for one, and 3d. for the other. Time ago we paid more. We have strived very hard to keep them in school, eating dry bread many times to be able to do this for them." The miner's tea was awaiting him, spread on a deal table scoured as white as a linen table-cloth. He sat down to it, taking a child betwixt his knees; he had weak tea, without sugar, good wheaten bread, and lard or dripping (I can't say which it was), in lieu of butter. He seemed, nevertheless, to enjoy this frugal meal exceedingly. Touching the "long-pay" system, this man said—"There is a company working a mine on the other side of Holywell, at which the men have now run 26 weeks without receiving any wages at all. I heard a shopkeeper last week complaining that the time during which he had to give the workmen credit was now so long that he must refuse to supply goods without the money. I continually hear the men grumbling and complaining of this system as a very bad one. In fact, if the men did not take a 'venture' of their own in the mine, by which they earn a few shillings to get along, they never could endure it. They are bound to live without fresh meat, because they have not ready money to buy it, for the butchers will not give credit. But there are among my neighbours many families who cannot get meat of any kind; they don't see even a bit of bacon for months together. Bread and buttermilk form their chief support." This man's statement fully accounted for the indisposition shown by the miners to work all their time for "masters," of which Sir Edward Walker had complained, and for the preference they reasonably give to "adventuring" for themselves.

I next examined a man working in another mine. G. W——: "I am a lead-miner, aged thirty years, am married, and have three children. I work in the Grainge mine, the property of Sir Pierce Mostyn, Bart. A small company, consisting of eight persons, work the mine. We divide the mine into what we call 'ounces,' and of the sixteen I hold two 'ounces,' or shares. I am paid for working so much a fathom when I work for the company, but I also work on my own private account. I can earn from 7s. to 10s. a week. The average in the long run may be 9s. I have met with several accidents in my time; the worst was from a fall of rock, which crushed me and broke my leg. The air is at present pretty good where I work, but the summer time is coming, when it is always a great deal worse. I suffer like other miners from shortness of breath and pain in my chest. The reason why the men resort to 'ventures' and work so much on their own account is this— wages sometime ago were so much reduced by the masters, when the men were working by the fathom, that they could not live, and were therefore bound to adventure for themselves." This man lived in a small cottage consisting of two rooms, unceiled and having a mortar floor. It was decently furnished, clean, and everything kept in good order. His wife, a neatly-dressed young woman, said, "We pay £3 a year rent for this cottage. They called on us for rates and taxes, but we had not the means to pay them. We get meat once a week, on Sundays, and not oftener. My husband takes bread and butter with him into the mine. We live entirely on bread and butter, coffee, tea, and buttermilk. We get good wheaten bread; we find it better for the children and ourselves than barley-bread, which we have tried. My eldest child is only five years old; she does not yet go to school." Observing a quantity of prints hung round the walls, with an abundance of substantial furniture; I said, "Your house is very comfortable, and you have even some elegances here." "Yes," replied the miner, stepping briskly up to, and laying his finger on a large print of her Majesty, mounted on a prancing charger, and wearing a green turban with a fine flowing scarlet head-plume, and a most copious, sweeping riding habit, "Here is Queen Victoria. We miners are very loyal. You will see in every house a good picture of the Queen."

About half a mile distant from this man's residence, I found another row of miners' cottages. I entered one of these at random, and there gathered the following particulars. I should first observe that it was a four-roomed cottage, unceiled, with a brick floor, and a good kitchen-range. It was well furnished, a pattern of neatness and cleanliness, and had a small garden in front and behind. The miner had not returned from his work, therefore I examined the wife, a very intelligent woman, who was ironing linen:—

J. H.: "My husband is a miner. We have been married seventeen years and had eight children, of whom six are living. We pay £4 10s. a year rent for this cottage, and 12s. taxes. I assist my husband by taking in washing from the town; that accounts for our house being so well furnished. My husband is paid so much a fathom; his wages vary from 9s. to 11s. a week; he never earns more. They profess to pay him every month, but his last 'pay' extended to eight weeks. He does not get one sixpence advanced him, but goes from one pay to another without money, no matter how long it may be. We are, therefore, bound to go on trust. The shops give us credit, we carrying a book backwards and forwards for the entry of our debt. It would be a world better for poor labouring people if they could get paid every week. We should find the benefit of it in a hundred ways. It has been hard with us often through this bad arrangement. We have felt it very often, particularly in wet weather, when our children wanted shoes, or at seasons when we needed coal, for these things we cannot get readily on trust. At those times we are bound to borrow of each other. There is no compulsion on us to deal at any particular shop; we take whatever shop we like of those tradesmen who will give us credit. We are certainly served with much worse goods for our money than we should have if we could pay ready cash. The miners and their families are continually speaking of the shifts and hardships they are bound to make and undergo. A woman whom I met when in the town last week told me that at ——, where her husband worked, they had been *nine months* without a 'pay,' and that, during all that time, they had not received one shilling of wages. It has also been very bad at the —— mine, but the men there have been promised a monthly pay for the future. My eldest boy is fifteen years old. He has begun to work as a miner, and earns 4s. a week. But it is difficult to obtain for a boy constant employment hereabouts. He has had no work this week. We have sent all our children to school; one is now at Lady Fielding's school at Pent Issa, and I shall send another there next week: they have their education free of charge. Her ladyship is very good to poor children about this country, and we have every reason to be grateful to her; she has a clothing club, to which every child pays 1d. a week; her ladyship adds 2s. 6d. at Christmas, and the amount is laid out in clothes. She also gives clothing and coals to the poor every winter. We have meat on Sundays, but on no other day. We all live on bread and butter, tea, coffee, and buttermilk; we never get cheese. My husband takes with him good wheaten bread and butter when he goes to his labour in the mine."

Such is the present condition of the lead miners in the Principality; and such are their grievances as related by themselves. The principal hardship under which they labour is the system of "long-pay." This evil, we have seen, presses cruelly upon them. Their wages are low, and the little they earn is lessened materially by the additional charge which tradesmen are compelled to impose upon their goods in order to compensate for the lengthened credit they are constrained to give. It is to be hoped the masters will as soon as possible make arrangements for obviating this evil, for it is a most unjust and pernicious system.

The Morning Chronicle, Thursday, December 26, 1850.

COLLIERY ACCIDENTS.

The occurrence, during the past two months, of several colliery explosions—attended with loss of human life, the disablement of survivors, and the entailment of present and lasting distress upon families who have been suddenly bereft of a husband, a father, or a brother—recalls our attention to a subject on which we have more than once dwelt, and to which we revert with pain. On the present occasion we forbear from alluding to the fatal explosions which recently happened in certain collieries of the North of England, further than to say that the frequency of those calamities in that great coal field (where it is generally understood that the economy of the pits is as perfect as it is anywhere), sufficiently demonstrates the inefficiency of the precautionary measures now in use, and shows that nothing short of a Parliamentary revision of the regulations for colliery management will secure that protection for human life which the perilous occupation of the miner demands, and which it is the duty of society to provide.

It is but a few days ago that two explosions, both resulting in loss of life, occurred in Glamorganshire. One of these happened in the Morfa pit, belonging to Messrs. Vivian, the copper-smelters at Swansea; and on that occasion two men were killed, and thirty more were severely injured. The other took place, on the same day, at the New Dyffryn Colliery, Aberdare; and there, as our informant states, "three were actually killed, thirteen were severely burnt, and several of the wounded were so much injured that they are not expected to survive." The collieries in the valley of Aberdare have, of late years, acquired a painful notoriety for the wholesale sacrifice of the lives of the hardy men who, a hundred fathoms deep, in hot, dark, and sulphurous chambers, excavate the minerals, and raise them to the surface. Scarcely a season passes without the occurrence of at least one extensive explosion within this limited area of four miles. It is just eleven months since our Special Correspondent for Wales, in the course of his inquiries into the then existing strike of the colliers, paid a visit to the locality of the late accident. Not many weeks previously, an awful explosion in a neighbouring coal-pit had swept away fifty-two human beings, appalling the hearts of the bravest of their fellow-workmen, and carrying permanent desolation to many a hearth. Some idea of the destitution and suffering occasioned by that accident may be formed from the statistical details which our Correspondent gathered with reference to that calamity. We transcribe his statements:—

> "In this small valley, within five years past, there have been killed not fewer than 100 persons by explosions of fire-damp, not to mention the numerous deaths from the falling-in of the roof and the walls of the pits. Unless one of these catastrophes includes a score or two of human beings it passes unnoticed by the public. Many fatal explosions are never reported in the papers. In the year 1845 an explosion happened in which twenty-five lives were lost; and again, at the close of last summer, a second tremendous explosion occurred here, at the Lletty Shenkin colliery, by which fifty-two human beings were hurried into eternity. It is right the public should know that, within five weeks after the last-mentioned accident, two more explosions occurred in the same pit, by which some miners were burnt. This was kept as private as possible. I made some inquiries into the distress occasioned by the Lletty Shenkin explosion, and I found that there were remaining in the parish, of the families belonging to the miners killed, nineteen widows—of whom four were left with five children each, others with four, and three widows with two young orphan children. All these were left wholly unprovided for; and I was informed that nothing whatever was done by the proprietor of the pit for the assistance of the widows or the children."

Such are the fruits of a system where all is left to the superintendence of the owners of collieries, and to the precautions of the workmen. With regard to the latter, it is well known that a long familiarity with danger is a habit which, if it does not actually beget a careless confidence, extinguishes fear; indeed, men cannot for ever be vigilant and on their guard—yet a moment's forgetfulness, or the mere lifting of a candle to the head, may occasion death to hundreds. In South Wales, the use of the Davy lamp is not common, except for examining the workings before the men enter in the morning; and the temptation to set it aside—so miserable is the light it gives—and to employ the naked candle in the worse than Egyptian darkness wherein the men work, is so great, when they wish to make the most of their time, as to be often irresistible. If, on the other hand, we scrutinise the conduct of the colliery proprietors, we find, no doubt, that some are more conscientious in providing for the safety of the workmen than others; but, speaking of them as a class, it cannot be denied that a jealous regard for their pecuniary interests too frequently takes the precedence of a just and benevolent solicitude for the security of human life. We find explosion after explosion taking place in the same pits, year after year; and these accidents do not diminish—if, indeed, they do not increase—in number.

The value of a practical proposal, suggested by a common-sense view of what is needed at a colliery when an explosion has occurred, or when an injury has happened to the lifting machinery, was never more strongly exemplified than in the case of a deficiency which was pointed out in the communication of our Special Correspondent, written from the scene of the calamity in the Lletty Shenkin pit. He suggested that there "should always be at command a horse-gin or a capstan for manual power, which may be resorted to in the event of injury to the machinery, or of the temporary stoppage of a ventilator (where such is employed) from accident or for repair." He showed that, if such a provision had been made, an explosion which had then just taken place in the Eskern Colliery (owing to a want of means to work a ventilator where the usual motive power was accidentally deranged) would have been prevented. It now clearly appears that, had this suggestion—simple and inexpensive as the instrument is—been adopted at the Gelly-Gair Pit, where the late accident occurred, assistance would have been rendered to those below much earlier than was found practicable under the existing arrangements. The published account of the recent explosion contains the following statement:—"The only person at the mouth of the pit at the time of the accident was the engineer. Thinking, most rashly, that he could lift the carriage at the bottom with all the superincumbent weight of the shattered and fallen bratticing upon it, in a pit 167 yards deep, he set the engine at work, and the natural consequence was that the engine was broken and totally disabled—thus cutting off from the poor men below the best hope they had of being extricated. The only remedy now was to send a bucket down the pumping well. *This bucket took nearly one hour to go down;* such was the character of the only machinery at hand after the reckless folly of the engineer. It was after midnight before the last man (a cooper) was brought up. Two more are missing, but they will probably be found to-day; they are supposed to be lying under a portion of the roof which has fallen in." We need hardly say that, had an auxiliary motive power, such as our correspondent suggested, been at hand, a delay of five minutes would have been the most that could have intervened between the breaking down of the engine and the placing of the capstan in gear; and, under such circumstances, men might have descended into the very pit where their companions lay buried, and perhaps have saved their lives; whereas, as the case stood, they were compelled to descend another, and probably a distant pit, after an interval of at least an hour and a half, during which the sufferers remained unassisted. This, however, is but one of many instances in which insufficient means are provided by the masters for the protection of human life. The employment of unsteady and careless superintendents—too often arising from parsimonious considerations—is another evil to be complained of. The superintendent is not unfrequently himself a workman, who receives a small extra pay for his peculiar office.

Experience has afforded appalling proofs that both of the parties engaged in coal-mining—the masters and the men—are to blame; the one for not providing an efficient ventilation, together with the best means of escape when an accident occurs—and the other for using naked candles where the Davy lamp alone should be employed. The question arises, therefore, how is this state of things to be remedied? We believe that the end can only be attained by Parliamentary inter- ference. We fully appreciate the objection commonly urged against State interposition in matters of trade and commerce, and there can- not be a doubt that the latter should be encouraged in self-reliance rather than encumbered by Legislative regulations. But the utter in- sufficiency of the existing provisions and safeguards for the security of life must strike every observer; and, indeed, the necessity for State in- terference has been publicly admitted by the appointment of Govern- ment officers for the inspection of mines. But what has been hitherto done for the correction of the evil has proved altogether inadequate to the exigencies of the case. A terrible accident occurs; a Government Commission hurries down to the spot; an inquiry is instituted, and ev- idence is taken—but it all results in nothing, for when do we hear of a prosecution being ordered, or a conviction obtained? Matters resume their old course, and, perhaps within six months, a second explosion takes place in the same pit—of which, as it injures or destroys only a few, the public are uninformed.

In the present advanced state of science (we say it advisedly, and without forgetting the difficulties that are to be overcome), there is no excuse for the insufficient ventilation of our coal-pits—which oc- casions nine-tenths of the casualties that prove so destructive of hu- man life, besides producing a deplorable amount of destitution and suffering. All that is necessary for the purification of a coal mine is the free movement, at a given velocity, of a current of air along a contin- uous passage, with an outlet. This, with the admirable inventions of

Brunton, Struve, or Gurney, is always attainable; and the force of the current can be increased at pleasure, when the pressure of the super-incumbent air is lessened (indicated by a fall in the barometer), and when the tenuity of the inflammable gas is thereby augmented so as to occasion danger of an explosion—or whenever there is, from the opening of new inlets for it, a greater flow of gas than usual into the pit. Another class of accidents—namely, the breaking of the rope or chain, and the drawing of the cage over the pulley (and the annual total of deaths from these causes is not inconsiderable)—may always be rendered harmless by the use of Foudrinier's ingenious apparatus. It has often been tested, and, we believe, has never failed; yet there are extremely few collieries where it has been adopted.

We earnestly hope that due consideration will be given to the facts which we have now set forth. We will only add, in conclusion, that it is the bounden duty of the State to take every possible care of the gallant men through whose nerve and sinew, skill and courage, that mineral is raised upon which reposes the substantial prosperity of this kingdom—and who are content, not merely to face a momentary danger, but to work for many hours daily in continual peril, for a pittance of twelve shillings a week, and with an average duration of life extending only to the age of forty.

Titles Available In This Series

{div class="fig first"}

{div class="row"} {bimg}lpv1-200x300.jpg|Vol I{bimg} {div class="cell"} {p class="ni"}Volume I{br /}The Metropolitan Districts{br /}by *Henry Mayhew*{/p} {/div} {/div}

{div class="row"} {bimg}lpv2-200x300.jpg|Vol II{bimg} {div class="cell"} {p class="ni"}Volume II{br /}The Metropolitan Districts{br /}by *Henry Mayhew*{/p} {/div} {/div}

{div class="row"} {bimg}lpv3-200x300.jpg|Vol III{bimg} {div class="cell"} {p class="ni"}Volume III{br /}The Metropolitan Districts{br /}by *Henry Mayhew*{/p} {/div} {/div}

{div class="row"} {bimg}lpv4-200x300.jpg|Vol IV{bimg} {div class="cell"} {p class="ni"}Volume IV{br /}The Metropolitan Districts{br /}by *Henry Mayhew*{/p} {/div} {/div}

{div class="row"} {bimg}lpv5-200x300.jpg|Vol V{bimg} {div class="cell"} {p class="ni"}Volume V{br /}The Manufacturing Districts{br /}by *Angus B. Reach*{/p} {/div} {/div}

{div class="row"} {bimg}lpv6-200x300.jpg|Vol VI{bimg} {div class="cell"} {p class="ni"}Volume VI{br /}The Rural Districts{br /}by *Alexander Mackay & Shirley Brooks*{/p} {/div} {/div}

{div class="row"} {bimg}lpv7-200x300.jpg|Vol VII{bimg} {div class="cell"} {p class="ni"}Volume VII{br /}The Rural Districts{br /}by *Alexander Mackay & Shirley Brooks*{/p} {/div} {/div}

{div class="row"} {bimg}lpv8-200x300.jpg|Vol VIII{bimg} {div class="cell"} {p class="ni"}Volume VIII{br /}Wales{/p} {/div} {/div}

{div class="row"} {bimg}lpv9-200x300.jpg|Vol IX{bimg} {div class="cell"} {p class="ni"}Volume IX{br /}Birmingham{br /}by *Charles Mackay*{/p} {/div} {/div}

{div class="row"} {bimg}lpv10-200x300.jpg|Vol X{bimg} {div class="cell"} {p class="ni"}Volume X{br /}Liverpool{br /}by *Charles Mackay*{/p} {/div} {/div}

{/div}

{div class="fig7 first"}

{div class="row"} {boimg}lpv1-200x300.jpg|Vol I{boimg} {div class="cell"} {p class="ni"}Volume I{br /}The Metropolitan Districts{br /}by *Henry Mayhew*{/p} {/div} {/div}

{div class="row"} {boimg}lpv2-200x300.jpg|Vol II{boimg} {div class="cell"} {p class="ni"}Volume II{br /}The Metropolitan Districts{br /}by *Henry Mayhew*{/p} {/div} {/div}

{div class="row"} {boimg}lpv3-200x300.jpg|Vol III{boimg} {div class="cell"} {p class="ni"}Volume III{br /}The Metropolitan Districts{br /}by *Henry Mayhew*{/p} {/div} {/div}

{div class="row"} {boimg}lpv4-200x300.jpg|Vol IV{boimg} {div class="cell"} {p class="ni"}Volume IV{br /}The Metropolitan Districts{br /}by *Henry Mayhew*{/p} {/div} {/div}

{div class="row"} {boimg}lpv5-200x300.jpg|Vol V{boimg} {div class="cell"} {p class="ni"}Volume V{br /}The Manufacturing Districts{br /}by *Angus B. Reach*{/p} {/div} {/div}

{div class="row"} {boimg}lpv6-200x300.jpg|Vol VI{boimg} {div class="cell"} {p class="ni"}Volume VI{br /}The Rural Districts{br /}by *Alexander Mackay & Shirley Brooks*{/p} {/div} {/div}

{div class="row"} {boimg}lpv7-200x300.jpg|Vol VII{boimg} {div class="cell"} {p class="ni"}Volume VII{br /}The Rural Districts{br /}by *Alexander Mackay & Shirley Brooks*{/p} {/div} {/div}

{div class="row"} {boimg}lpv8-200x300.jpg|Vol VIII{boimg} {div class="cell"} {p class="ni"}Volume VIII{br /}Wales{/p} {/div} {/div}

{div class="row"} {boimg}lpv9-200x300.jpg|Vol IX{boimg} {div class="cell"} {p class="ni"}Volume IX{br /}Birmingham{br /}by *Charles Mackay*{/p} {/div} {/div}

{div class="row"} {boimg}lpv10-200x300.jpg|Vol X{boimg} {div class="cell"} {p class="ni"}Volume X{br /}Liverpool{br /}by *Charles Mackay*{/p} {/div} {/div}

{/div}
{p class="c"}For more details on these and other titles available please visit:{/p} {p class="c"}www.dittobooks.co.uk{/p}

Index

Titles Available in the Series

LABOUR AND THE POOR

For information on these and other titles available please visit:

DittoBooks.co.uk

www.ingramcontent.com/pod-product-compliance
Lightning Source LLC
Chambersburg PA
CBHW060309030426

42336CB00011B/976